Regarding Yura's Kansai accent:

Originally, in order to be more feminine, Yura spoke with a Kyoto accent. But after her true colors hit the page, well, her accent sort of migrated south to Osaka. (LOL)

Still, it's not exactly an Osakan brogue either! (Some readers have commented on that.) Even within the Kansai region, accents vary from area to area. I'm from the northern part, and when I hear that southern Osaka Prefecture accent on TV, it still sounds foreign to me. So if Yura's Osakan drawl sounds funny to you... it's just one of those richly diverse Kansai region inflections.

—HIROSHI SHIIBASHI,
2011

HIROSHI SHIIBASHI debuted in BUSINESS JUMP magazine with *Aratama*. NURA: RISE OF THE YOKAI CLAN is his breakout hit. He was an assistant to manga artist Hirohiko Araki, the creator of *Jojo's Bizarre Adventure*. *Steel Ball Run* by Araki is one of his favorite manga.

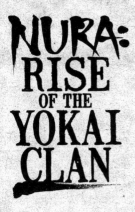

NURA: RISE OF THE YOKAI CLAN
VOLUME 18
SHONEN JUMP Manga Edition

Story and Art by HIROSHI SHIIBASHI

Translation — Yumi Okamoto
English Adaptation — Ross Anthony
Touch-up Art and Lettering — Annaliese Christman
Graphics and Cover Design — Fawn Lau
Editors — Joel Enos, Megan Bates

NURARIHYON NO MAGO © 2008 by Hiroshi
Shiibashi. All rights reserved. First published in
Japan in 2008 by SHUEISHA Inc., Tokyo. English
translation rights arranged by SHUEISHA Inc.

Printed in the U.S.A.

Published by VIZ Media, LLC
P.O. Box 77010
San Francisco, CA 94107

10 9 8 7 6 5 4 3 2 1
First printing, December 2013

www.viz.com   www.shonenjump.com

NURA: RISE OF THE YOKAI CLAN

18

THE GOLDEN AGE OF EDO

STORY AND ART BY
HIROSHI SHIIBASHI

CHARACTERS

NURARIHYON

Rikuo's grandfather and the Lord of Pandemonium. He has appointed Rikuo the Third Heir of the Nura clan, a powerful yokai consortium. He's a mischievous sort who enjoys slipping out of diners without paying his bill.

RIKUO NURA

Though he appears to be a human boy, he's actually the grandson of Nurarihyon, a yokai. His grandfather's blood makes him one-quarter yokai, and he transforms into a yokai at times.

YAMABUKI-OTOME

Rihan's ex-wife. She's a warmhearted and beautiful yokai, but being unable to give a child to Rihan, she decides to leave the Nura clan and, sadly, the world of the living. Nue's spell revives her as a surrogate body for Hagoromo-Gitsune.

RIHAN NURA

Rikuo's father. Under his leadership as Second Heir, the Nura clan flourished. He was killed by his ex-wife Yamabuki-Otome, who was under Nue's control. Rikuo was just a young child at the time.

SETSURA

Nura clan yokai and mother of Tsurara, Rikuo's attendant. She has helped the Nura clan since Nurarihyon's leadership. In fact, Tsurara is now in charge of the territory that she used to look after.

KUBINASHI

A Nura clan yokai. He joined the ranks of Rikuo's guards ever since the boy became the official successor to the Supreme Commander. Handsome, but has a low tolerance for alcohol.

KUROTABO

A Nura clan yokai, also known as the Father of Destruction. One of the clan's best warriors, he hides a healthy arsenal of lethal weapons under his priest's robe. He teaches Rikuo an Equip technique called Meld.

AOTABO

Another Nura clan yokai who, along with Yuki-Onna, looks after and protects Rikuo when he attends school. He uses the name Kurata when disguised as a human. He feels a strong urge protect children.

YANAGIDA

A yokai of the Hundred Stories clan who collects strange experiences from various places to include as part of the Hundred Stories. He kidnaps Torii and attempts to incorporate her into a story, but Kurotabo stops it.

GOROZAEMON SANMOTO

Has a history with Rihan and holds a grudge against the Nura clan. In order to take revenge against Rihan, he manipulates Nue into using Yamabuki-Otome. He leads the Hundred Stories clan.

STORY SO FAR

Rikuo Nura is a seventh-grader at Ukiyoe Middle School. At a glance, he appears to be just another average, normal boy. But he's actually the grandson of the yokai Overlord Nurarihyon and is now the Third Heir of the Nura clan, leaders of the yokai in the region. He is expected to become a great Overlord like his grandfather, but in the meantime he lives his days as a human being.

Ryuji and Yura investigate a reputed village of vanishing people. Soon the resident yokai show their true form and attack, but they prove to be no match against Ryuji and Yura. When Ryuji stumbles across an ayakashi bystander, he wonders if he's out collecting for the Hundred Stories clan.

One day on her way home from school, Rikuo's classmate Torii sees Kurotabo in the distance. Wanting nothing more than to express her gratitude for a favor he did for her in the past, Torii follows him, but is nabbed by Yanagida of the Hundred Stories clan. Rikuo sets out to find Torii, suspecting that her disappearance is connected to a popular urban legend. He utilizes all of the Nura clan's resources to rescue her. Fittingly, Kurotabo gets to her first, but Yanagida, with whom he has a complicated history, reveals that Kurotabo was once an executive member of the Hundred Stories clan!!

Going back in time to the Golden Age of Edo, the Nura clan's Second Heir, Rihan, takes a break from the festivities when he notices some of the strange phenomena rumored about among the people of Edo...

TABLE OF CONTENTS

NURA: RISE OF THE YOKAI CLAN

18

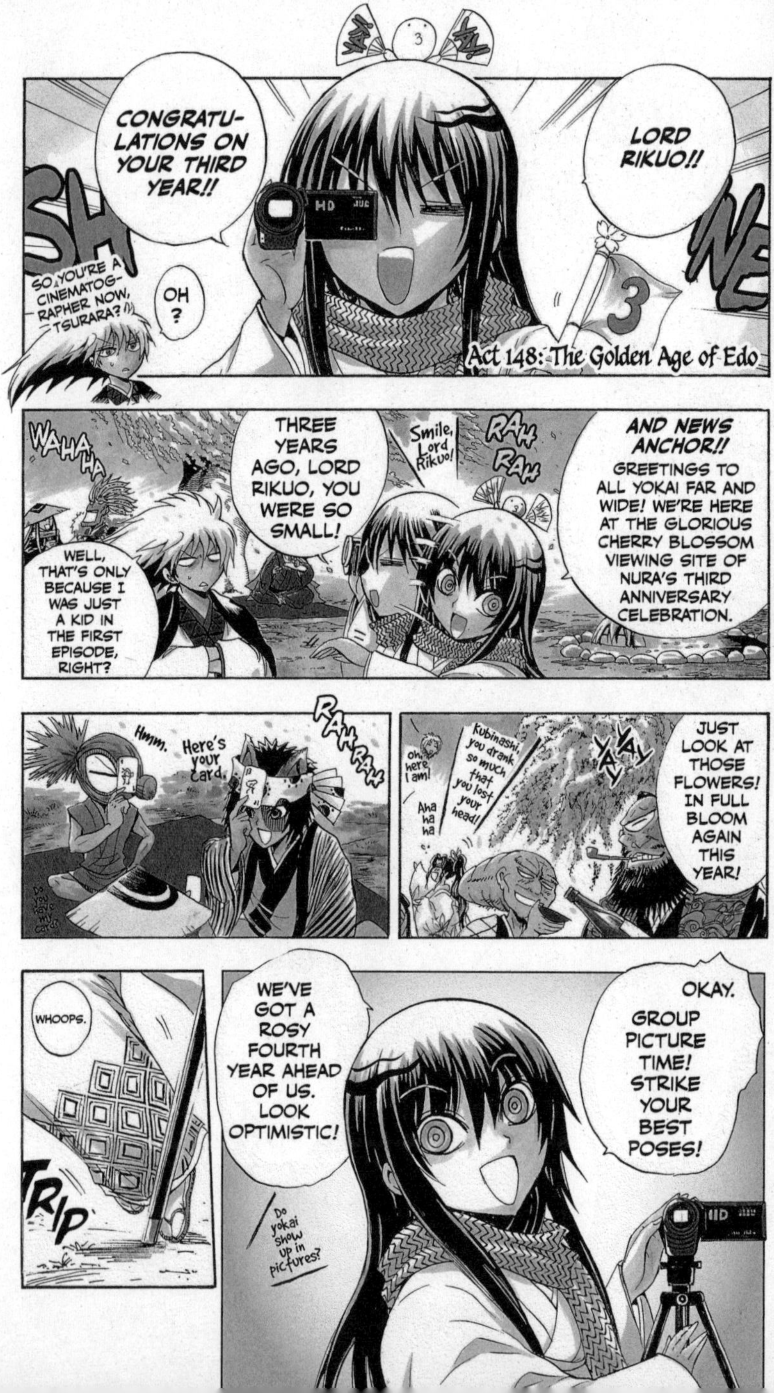
LORD RIKUO!!
NE
CONGRATULATIONS ON YOUR THIRD YEAR!!
SH
Act 148: The Golden Age of Edo
OH?
SO YOU'RE A CINEMATOGRAPHER NOW, TSURARA?!
AND NEWS ANCHOR!! GREETINGS TO ALL YOKAI FAR AND WIDE! WE'RE HERE AT THE GLORIOUS CHERRY BLOSSOM VIEWING SITE OF NURA'S THIRD ANNIVERSARY CELEBRATION.
RAH RAH
Smile, Lord Rikuo!
THREE YEARS AGO, LORD RIKUO, YOU WERE SO SMALL!
WAHAHAHA
WELL, THAT'S ONLY BECAUSE I WAS JUST A KID IN THE FIRST EPISODE, RIGHT?
JUST LOOK AT THOSE FLOWERS! IN FULL BLOOM AGAIN THIS YEAR!
YAY YAY
Kubinashi, you drank so much that you lost your head!
Oh, here I am!
Aha ha ha
RAH RAH
Here's your card.
Hmm.
Do you have my cards?
OKAY. GROUP PICTURE TIME! STRIKE YOUR BEST POSES!
WE'VE GOT A ROSY FOURTH YEAR AHEAD OF US. LOOK OPTIMISTIC!
Do yokai show up in pictures?
WHOOPS.
TRIP

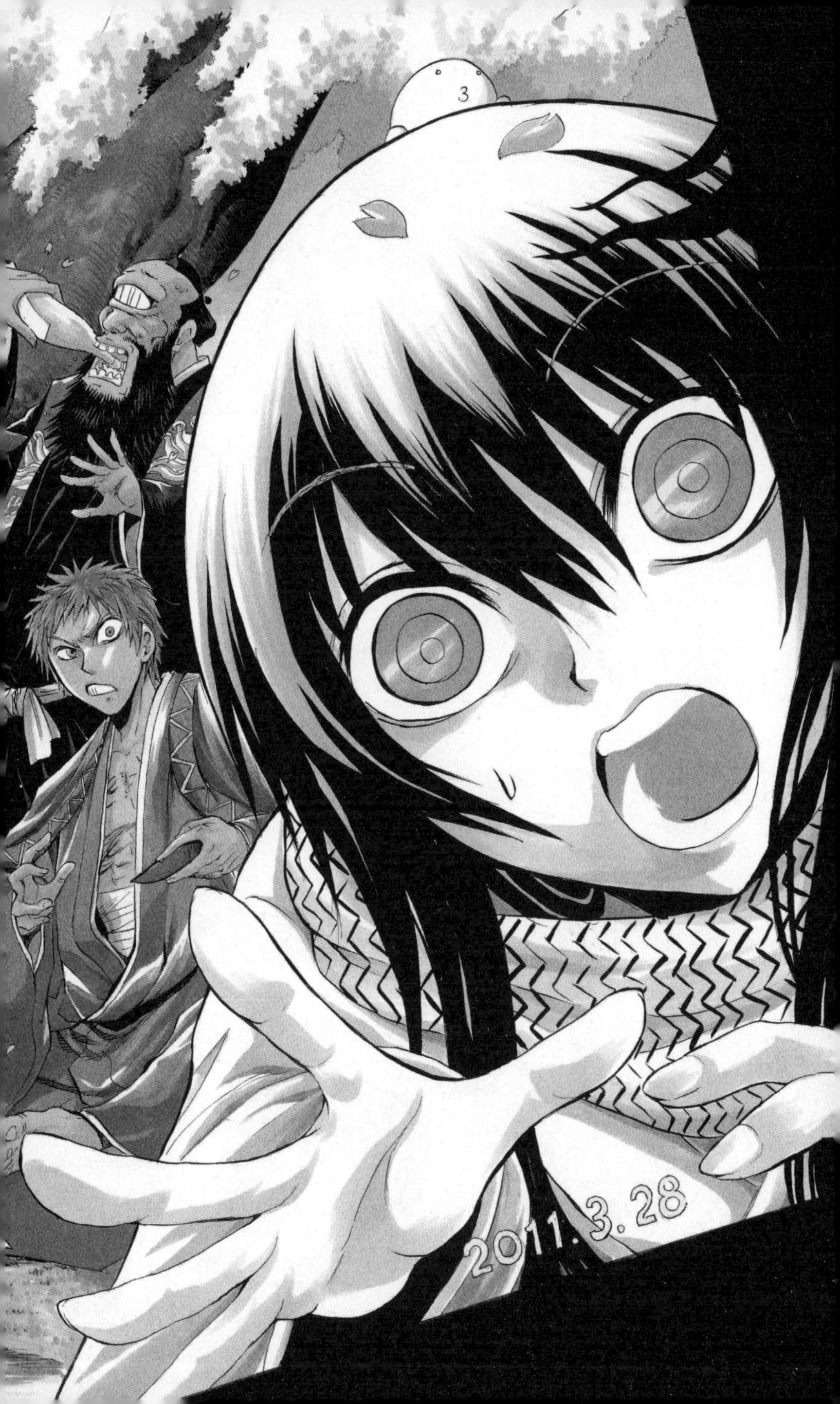
2011. 3. 28

Act 148: The Golden Age of Edo

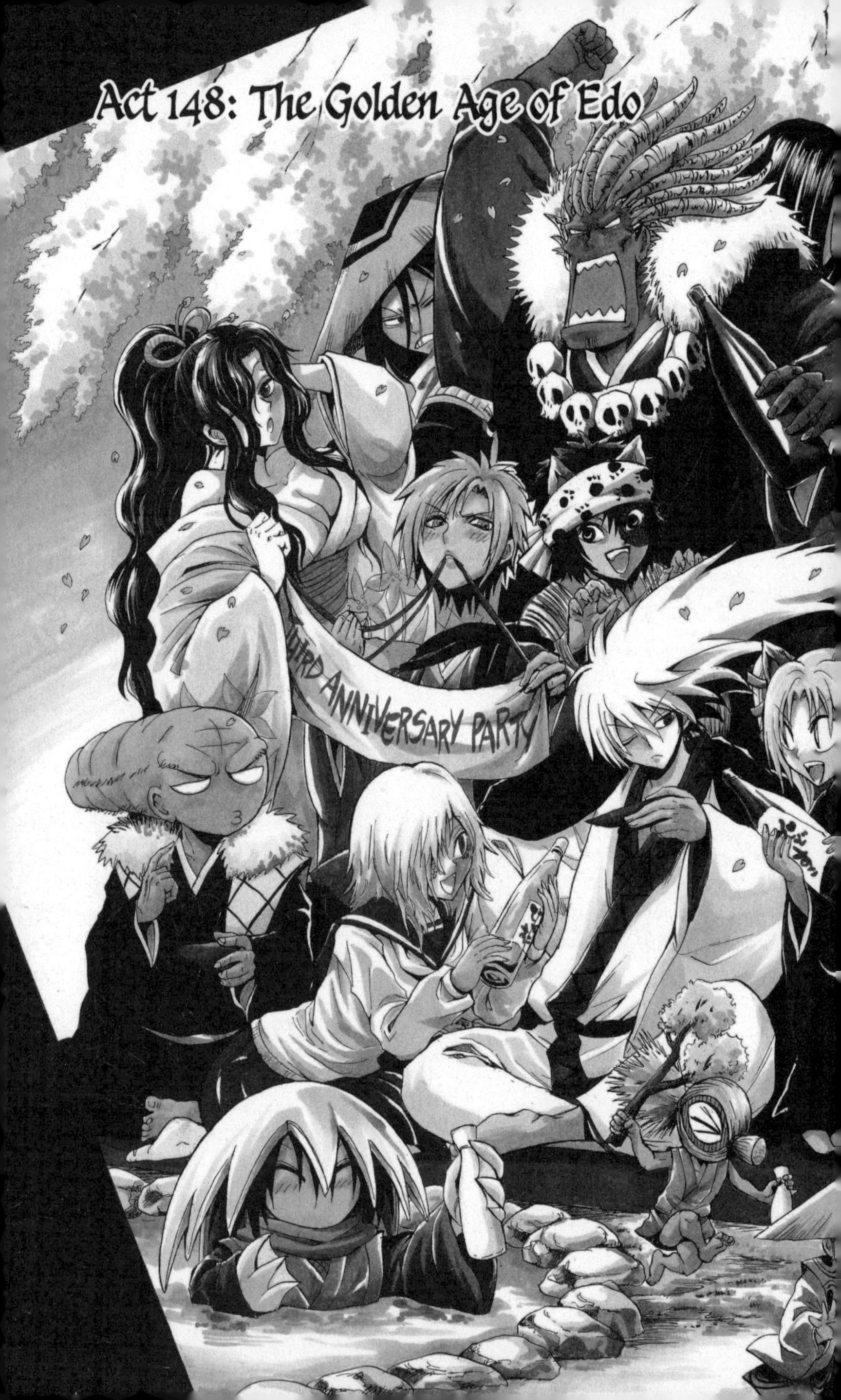
HIRD ANNIVERSARY PARTY

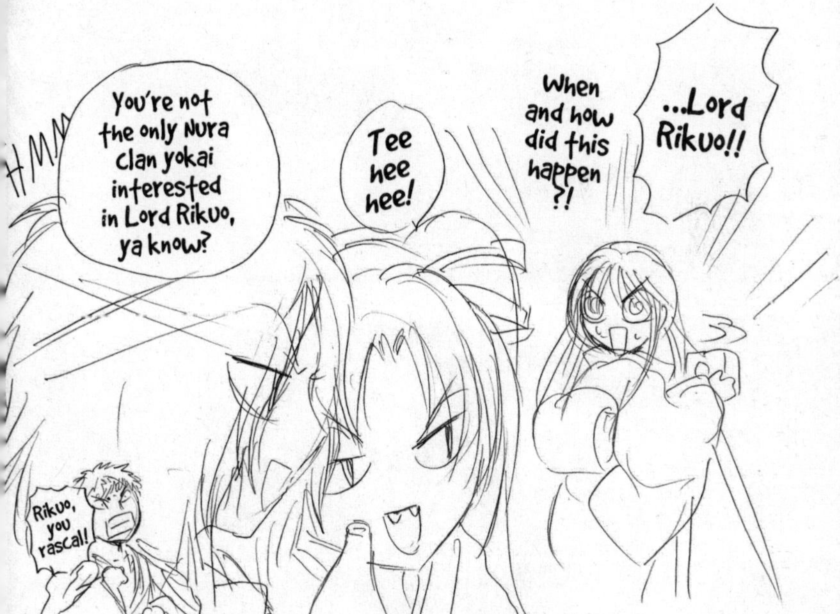
...Lord Rikuo!!
When and how did this happen?!
Tee hee hee!
You're not the only Nura clan yokai interested in Lord Rikuo, ya know?
HMM
Rikuo, you rascal!

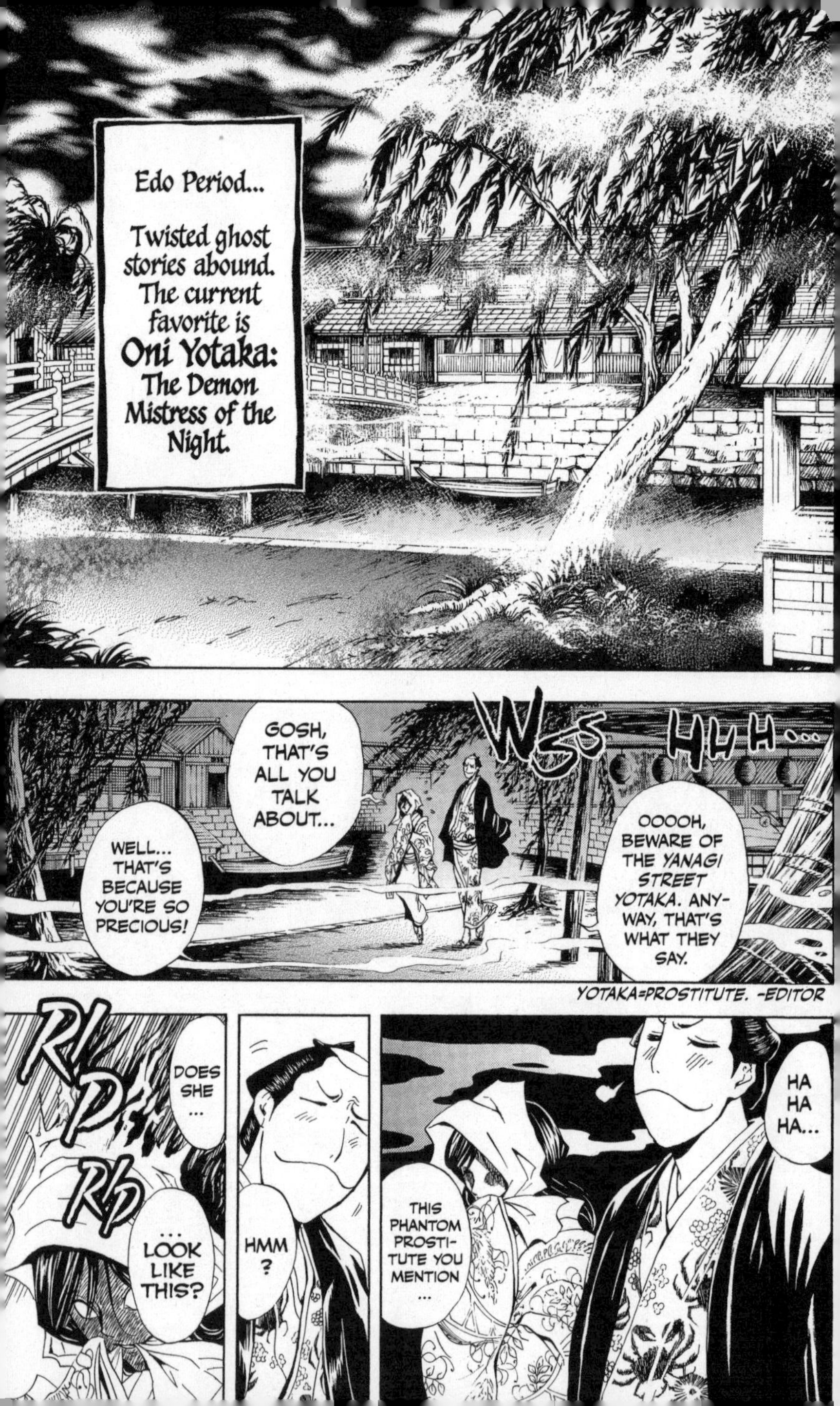
Edo Period...
Twisted ghost stories abound. The current favorite is **Oni Yotaka:** The Demon Mistress of the Night.
WSS HHH...
OOOOH, BEWARE OF THE *YANAGI* STREET YOTAKA. ANY-WAY, THAT'S WHAT THEY SAY.
GOSH, THAT'S ALL YOU TALK ABOUT...
WELL... THAT'S BECAUSE YOU'RE SO PRECIOUS!
YOTAKA=PROSTITUTE. -EDITOR
HA HA HA...
THIS PHANTOM PROSTI-TUTE YOU MENTION ...
HMM ?
DOES SHE ...
... LOOK LIKE THIS?
RIP
RIP

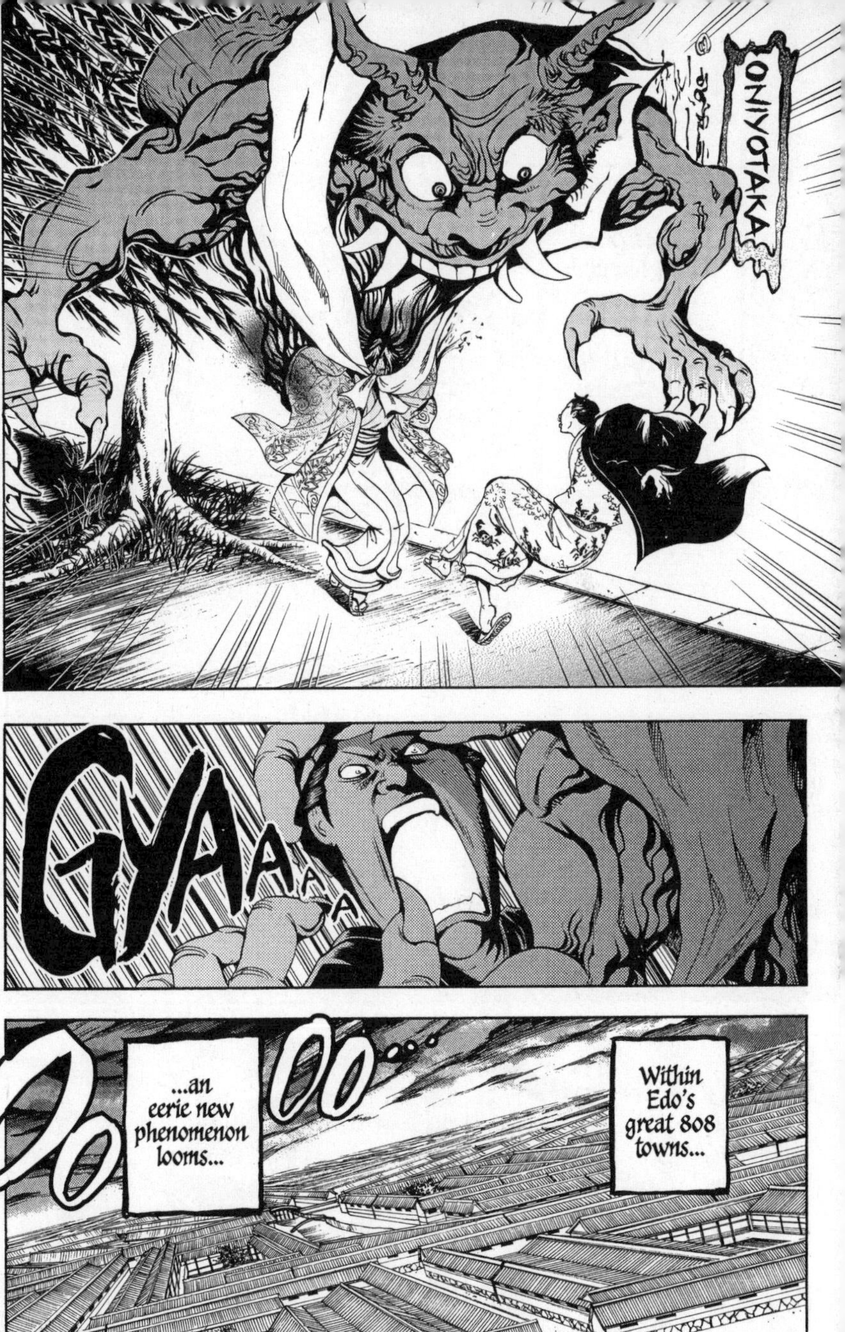
ONIYOTAKA
GYAAAA
Within Edo's great 808 towns...
...an eerie new phenomenon looms...
OOOO...

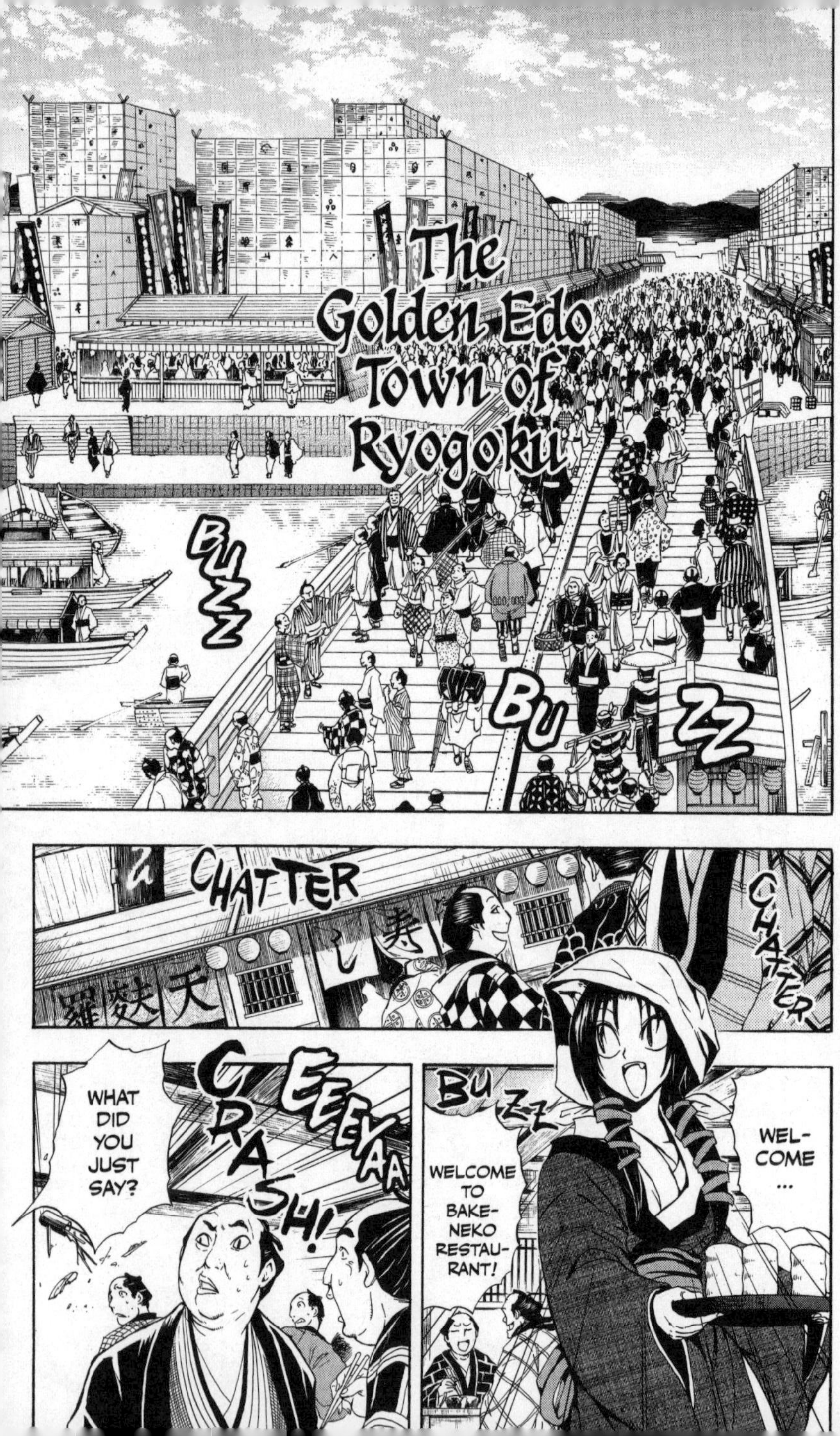
The Golden Edo Town of Ryogoku
BUZZ
BUZZ
CHATTER
寿し
天麩羅
CHATTER
WELCOME ...
BUZZ
WELCOME TO BAKENEKO RESTAURANT!
EEEEYAA
CRASH!
WHAT DID YOU JUST SAY?

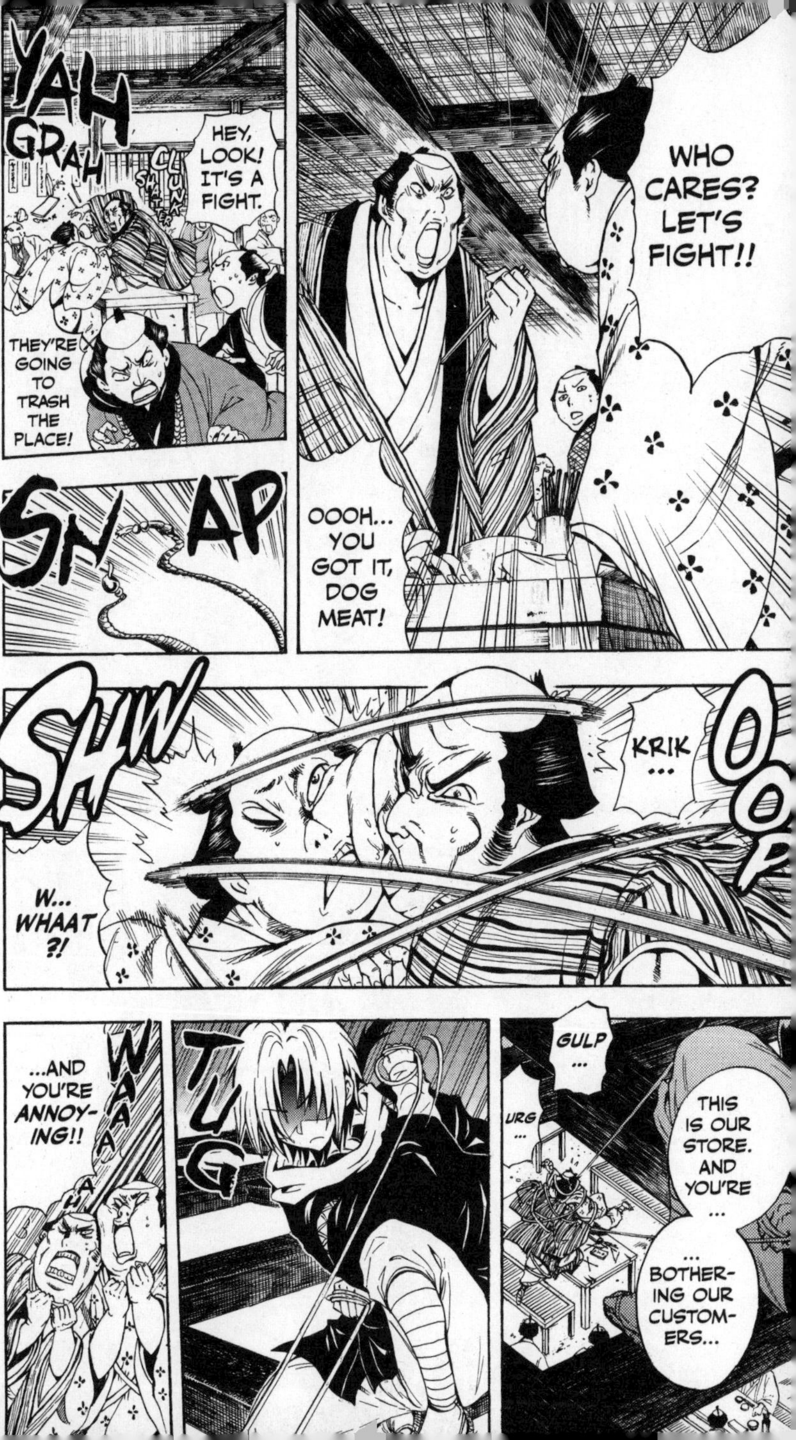
WHO CARES? LET'S FIGHT!!
OOOH... YOU GOT IT, DOG MEAT!
YAH GRAH
HEY, LOOK! IT'S A FIGHT.
CLUNK
SHATTER
THEY'RE GOING TO TRASH THE PLACE!
SH AP
OOOP
KRIK ...
SHW
W... WHAAT?!
GULP ...
THIS IS OUR STORE. AND YOU'RE ...
URG ...
... BOTHER-ING OUR CUSTOM-ERS...
TUG
...AND YOU'RE ANNOY-ING!!
WAAAAH

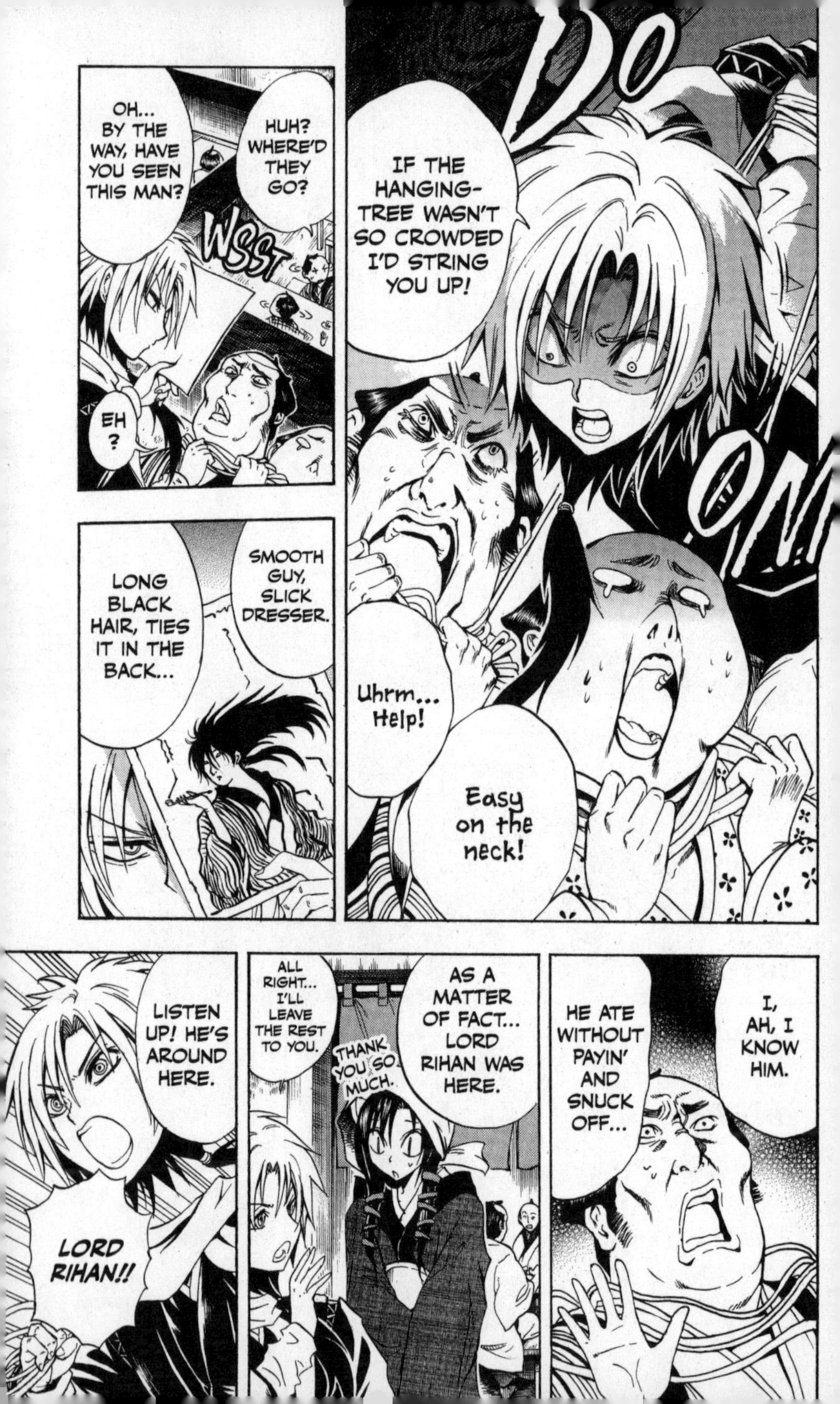
DO
OM
IF THE HANGING-TREE WASN'T SO CROWDED I'D STRING YOU UP!
Uhrm... Help!
Easy on the neck!
HUH? WHERE'D THEY GO?
OH... BY THE WAY, HAVE YOU SEEN THIS MAN?
WSST
EH ?
SMOOTH GUY, SLICK DRESSER.
LONG BLACK HAIR, TIES IT IN THE BACK...
I, AH, I KNOW HIM.
HE ATE WITHOUT PAYIN' AND SNUCK OFF...
AS A MATTER OF FACT... LORD RIHAN WAS HERE.
ALL RIGHT... I'LL LEAVE THE REST TO YOU.
THANK YOU SO MUCH.
LISTEN UP! HE'S AROUND HERE.
LORD RIHAN!!

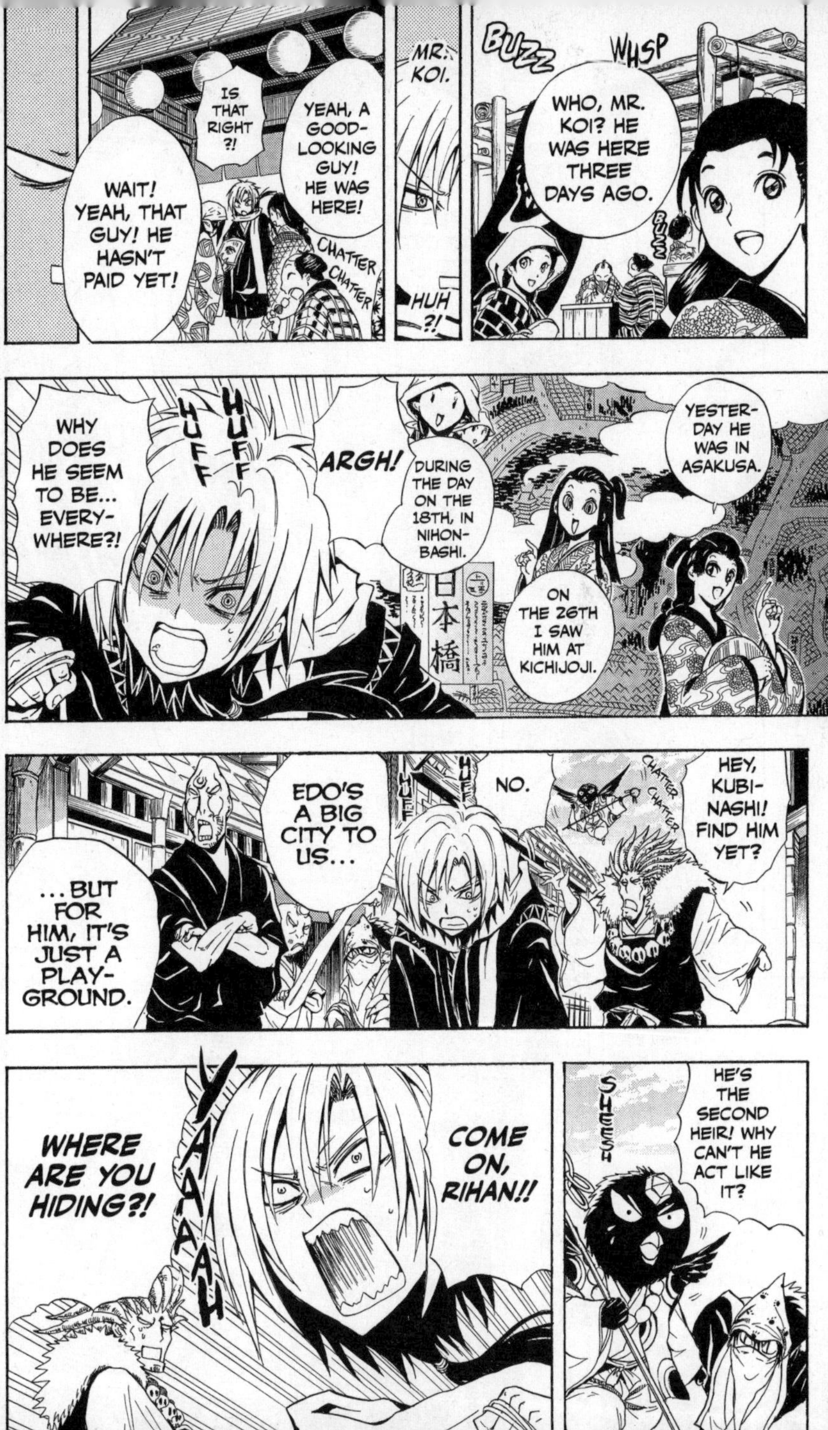
BUZZ
WHSP
WHO, MR. KOI? HE WAS HERE THREE DAYS AGO.
BUZZ
MR. KOI.
HUH ?!
YEAH, A GOOD-LOOKING GUY! HE WAS HERE!
IS THAT RIGHT ?!
CHATTER CHATTER
WAIT! YEAH, THAT GUY! HE HASN'T PAID YET!
YESTERDAY HE WAS IN ASAKUSA.
DURING THE DAY ON THE 18TH, IN NIHONBASHI.
日本橋
ON THE 26TH I SAW HIM AT KICHIJOJI.
ARGH!
HUFF HUFF
WHY DOES HE SEEM TO BE... EVERYWHERE?!
HEY, KUBINASHI! FIND HIM YET?
CHATTER CHATTER
NO.
HUFF
EDO'S A BIG CITY TO US...
...BUT FOR HIM, IT'S JUST A PLAYGROUND.
HE'S THE SECOND HEIR! WHY CAN'T HE ACT LIKE IT?
SHEESH
COME ON, RIHAN!!
YAAAAAH
WHERE ARE YOU HIDING?!

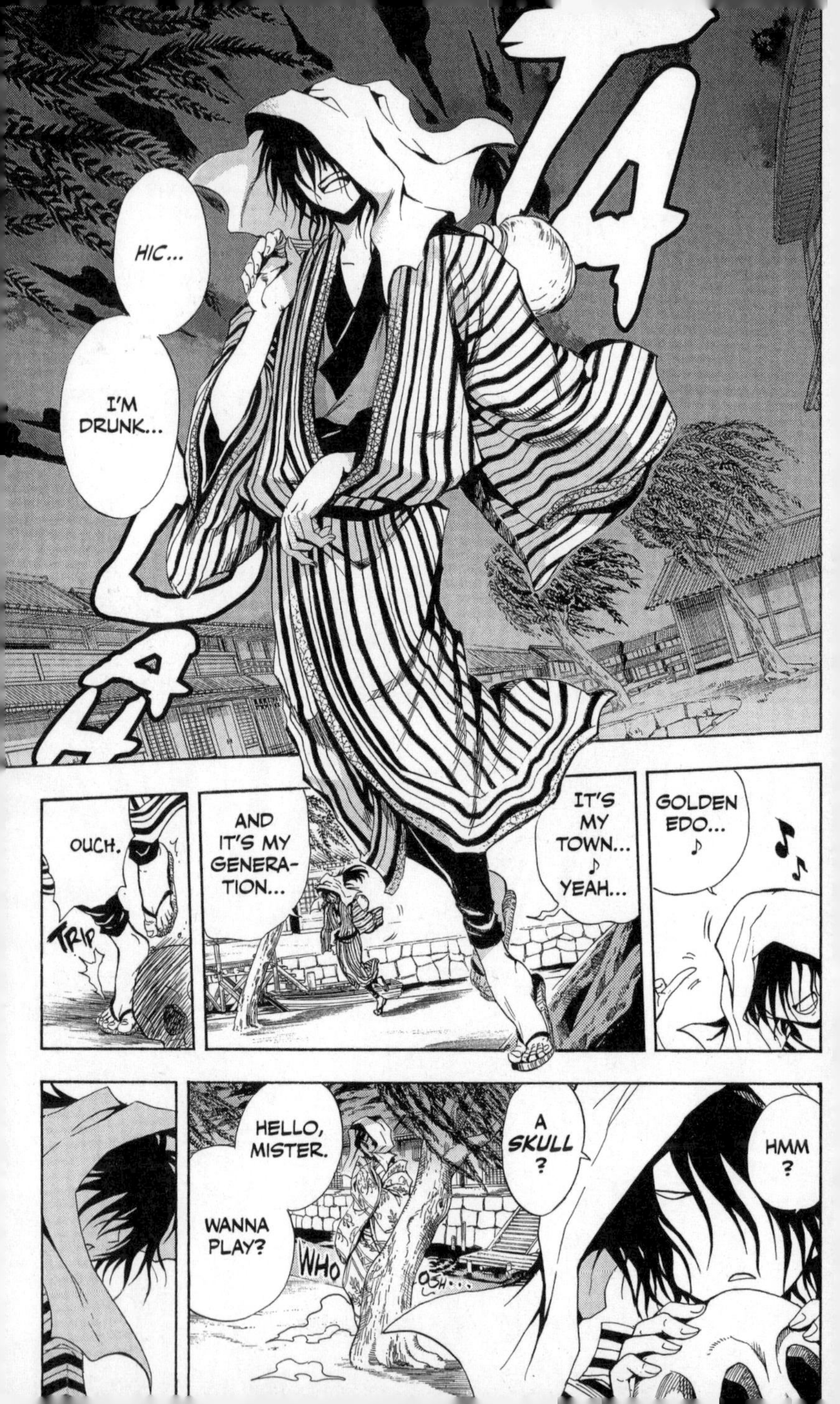

HA
HIC...
I'M DRUNK...
HA
GOLDEN EDO... ♪
IT'S MY TOWN... ♪ YEAH...
AND IT'S MY GENERATION...
OUCH.
TRIP
HMM?
A SKULL?
HELLO, MISTER.
WANNA PLAY?
WHOOSH...

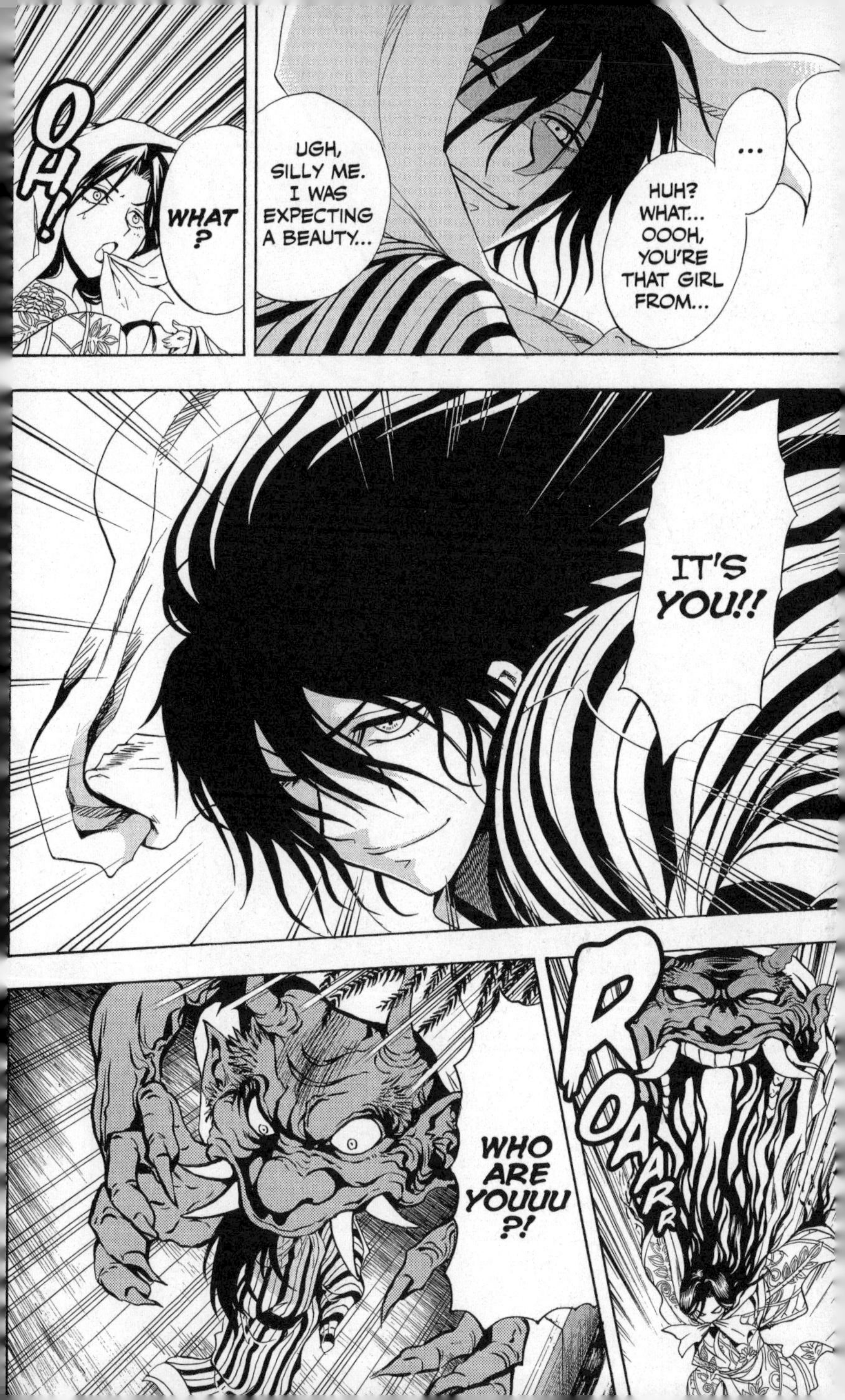
...
HUH? WHAT... OOOH, YOU'RE THAT GIRL FROM...
UGH, SILLY ME. I WAS EXPECTING A BEAUTY...
WHAT?
OH!
IT'S YOU!!
ROAARR
WHO ARE YOUUU?!

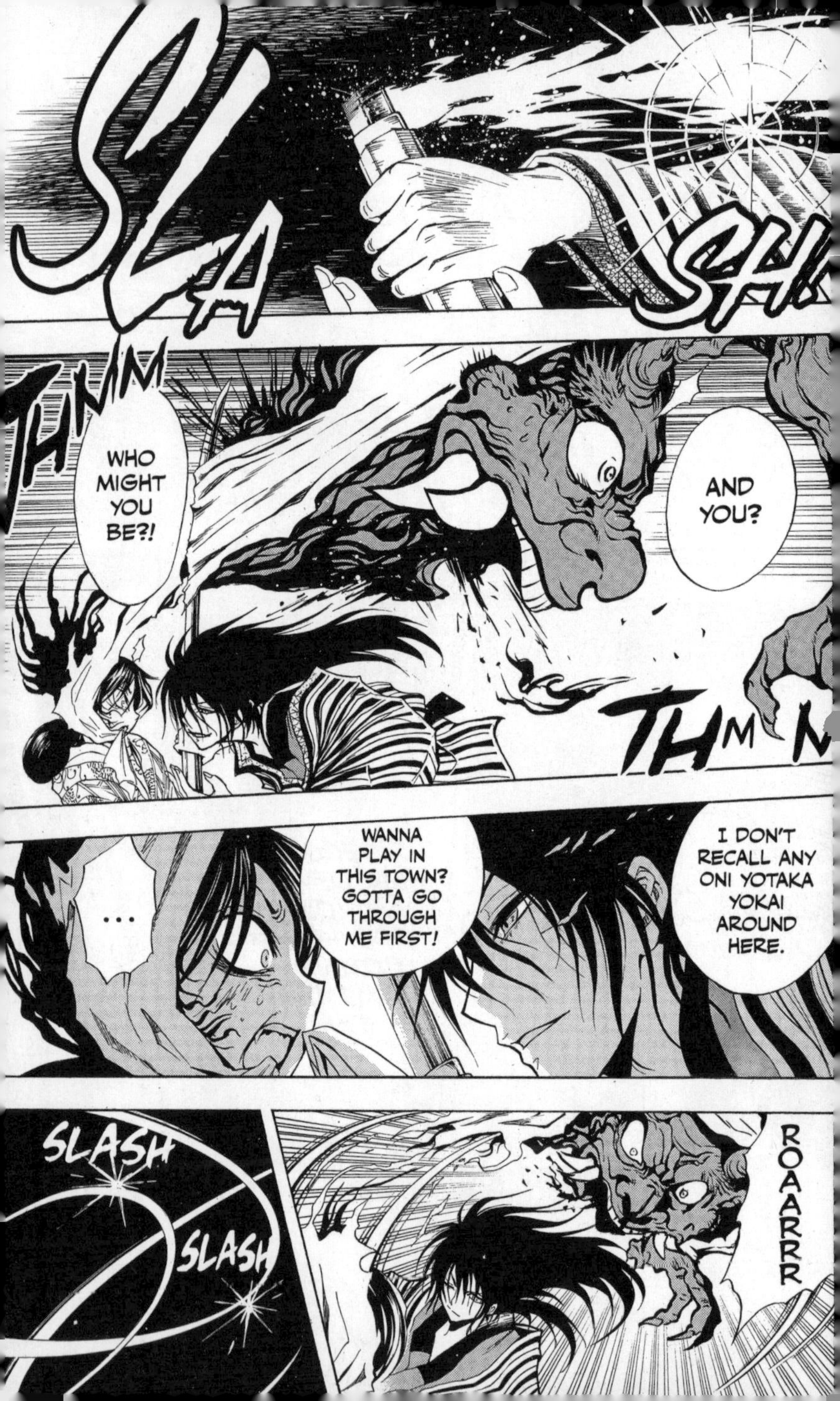
SLA
SH
AND YOU?
THM M
WHO MIGHT YOU BE?!
THM
I DON'T RECALL ANY ONI YOTAKA YOKAI AROUND HERE.
WANNA PLAY IN THIS TOWN? GOTTA GO THROUGH ME FIRST!
...
ROAARRR
SLASH
SLASH

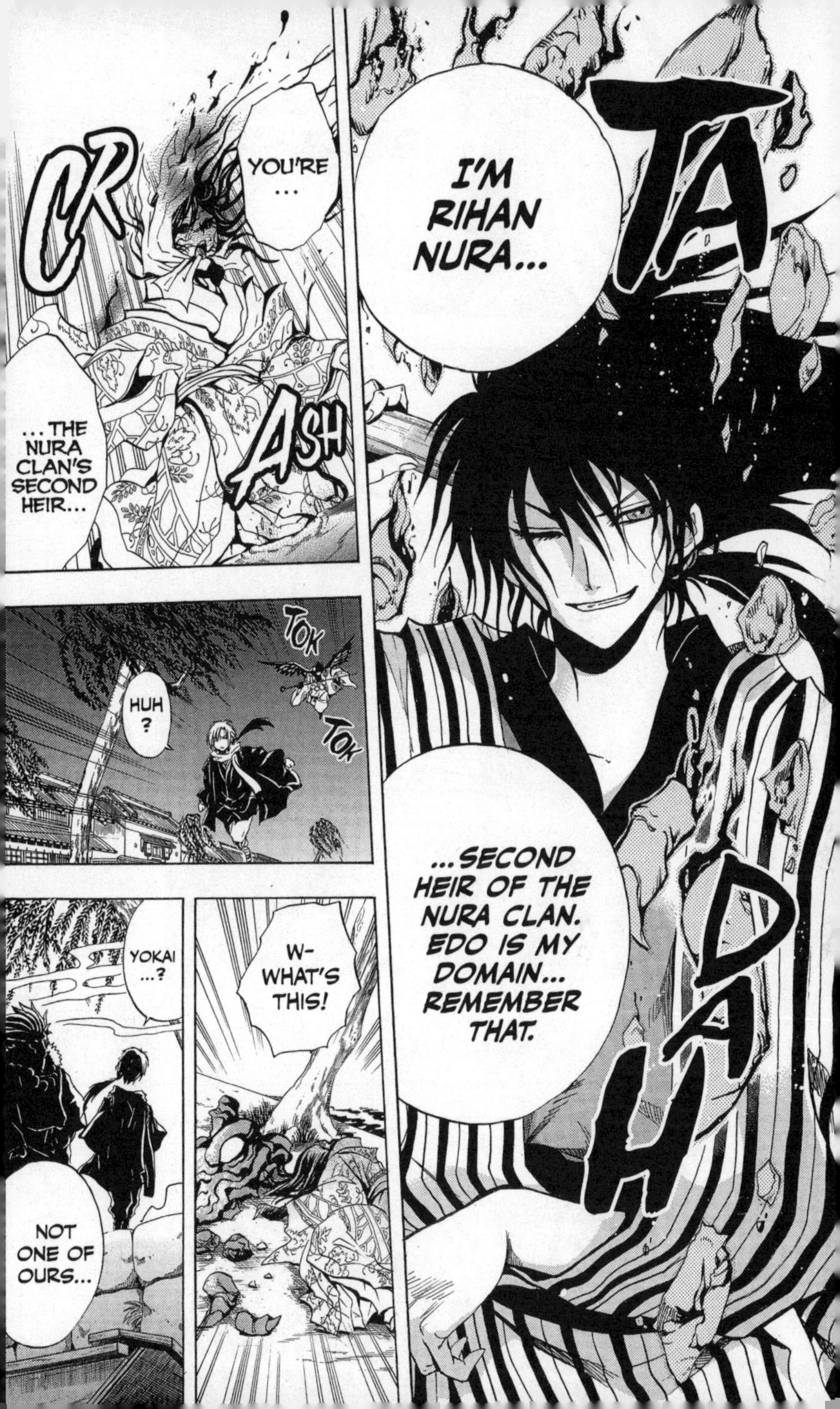
TA
I'M RIHAN NURA...
...SECOND HEIR OF THE NURA CLAN. EDO IS MY DOMAIN... REMEMBER THAT.
DAH
YOU'RE ...
CR
ASH
... THE NURA CLAN'S SECOND HEIR...
TOK
TOK
HUH ?
W- WHAT'S THIS!
YOKAI ...?
NOT ONE OF OURS...

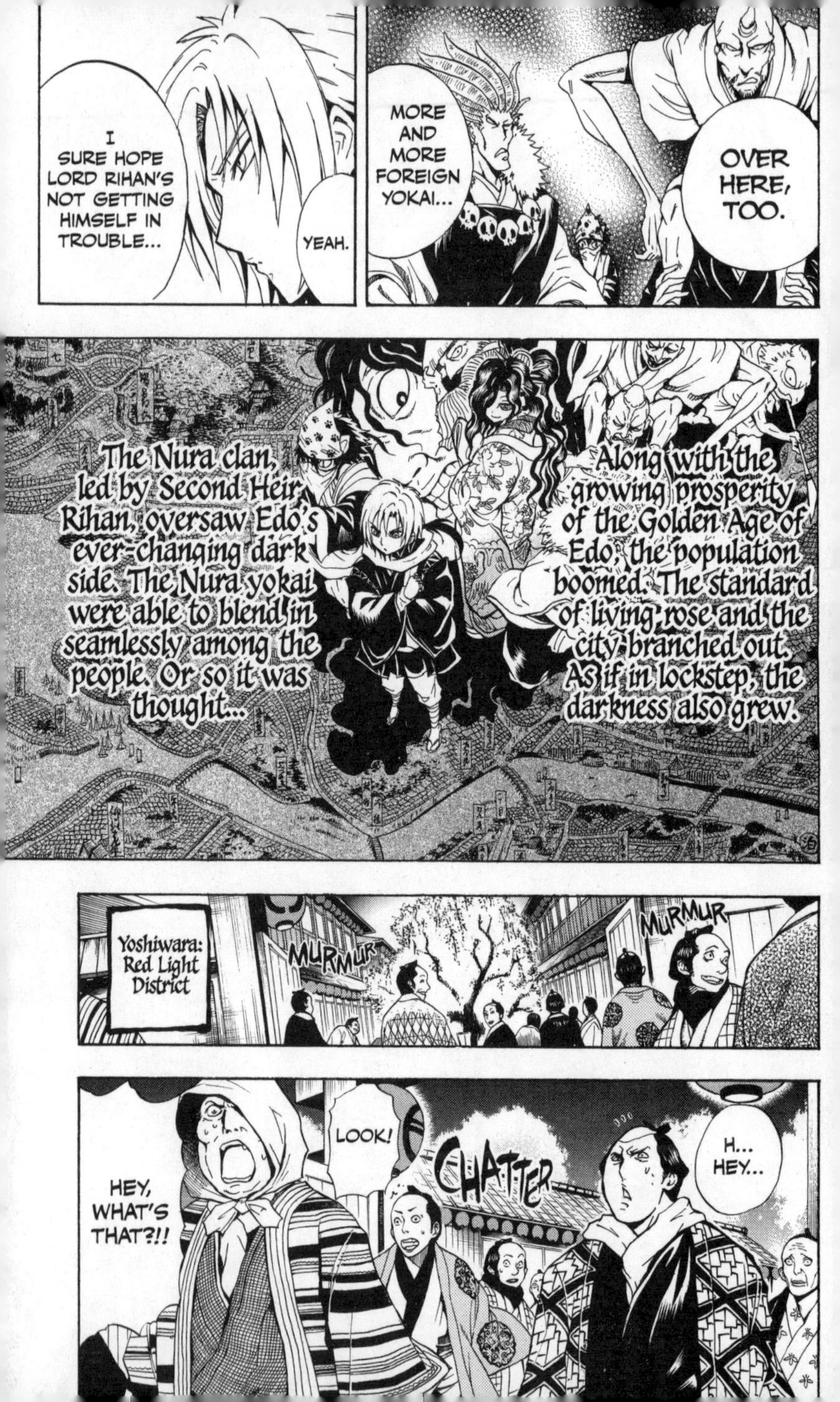

MORE AND MORE FOREIGN YOKAI...
OVER HERE, TOO.
I SURE HOPE LORD RIHAN'S NOT GETTING HIMSELF IN TROUBLE...
YEAH.
Along with the growing prosperity of the Golden Age of Edo, the population boomed. The standard of living rose and the city branched out. As if in lockstep, the darkness also grew.
The Nura clan, led by Second Heir Rihan, oversaw Edo's ever-changing dark side. The Nura yokai were able to blend in seamlessly among the people. Or so it was thought...
MURMUR
MURMUR
Yoshiwara: Red Light District
H... HEY...
CHATTER
LOOK!
HEY, WHAT'S THAT?!!

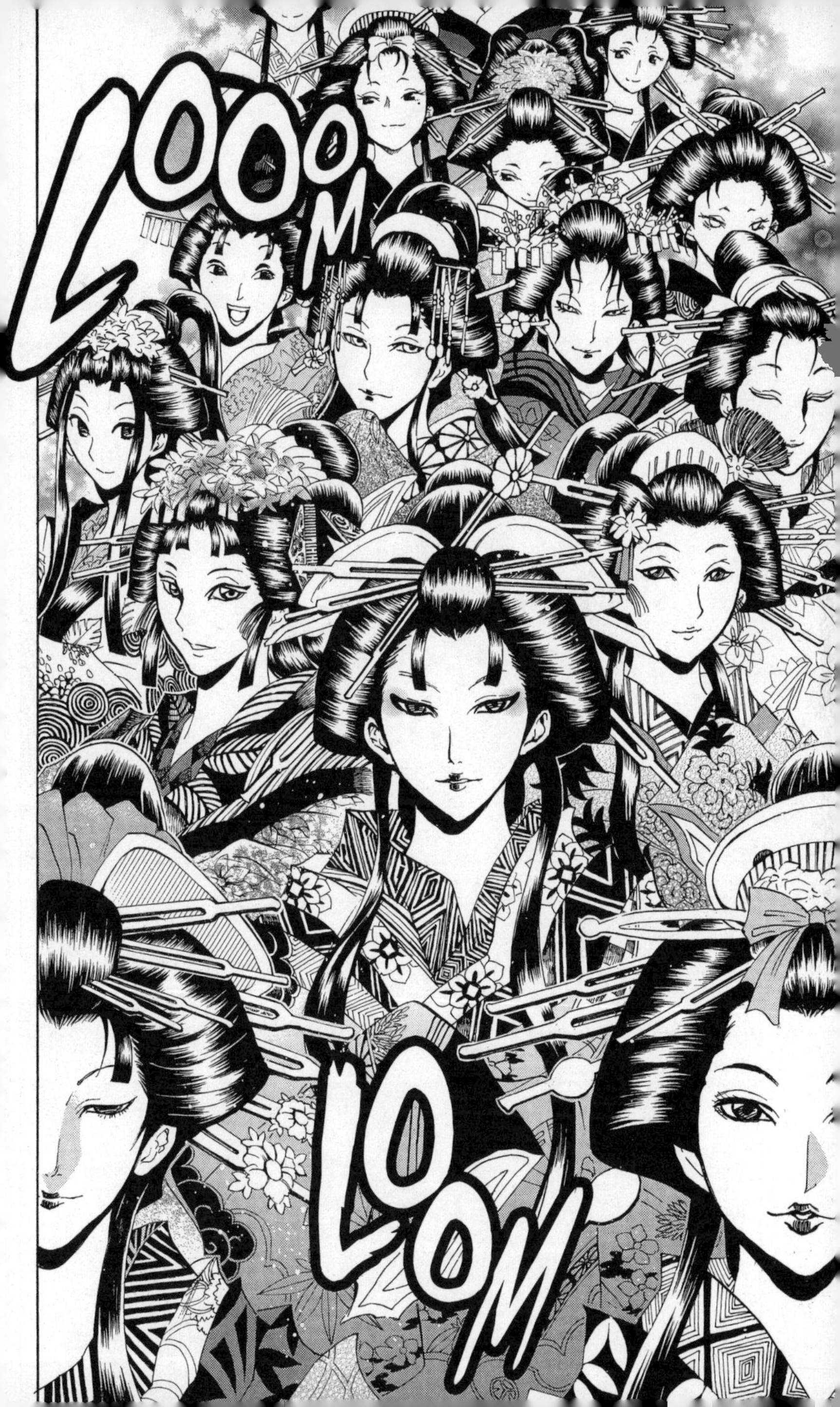
LOOOM
LOOM

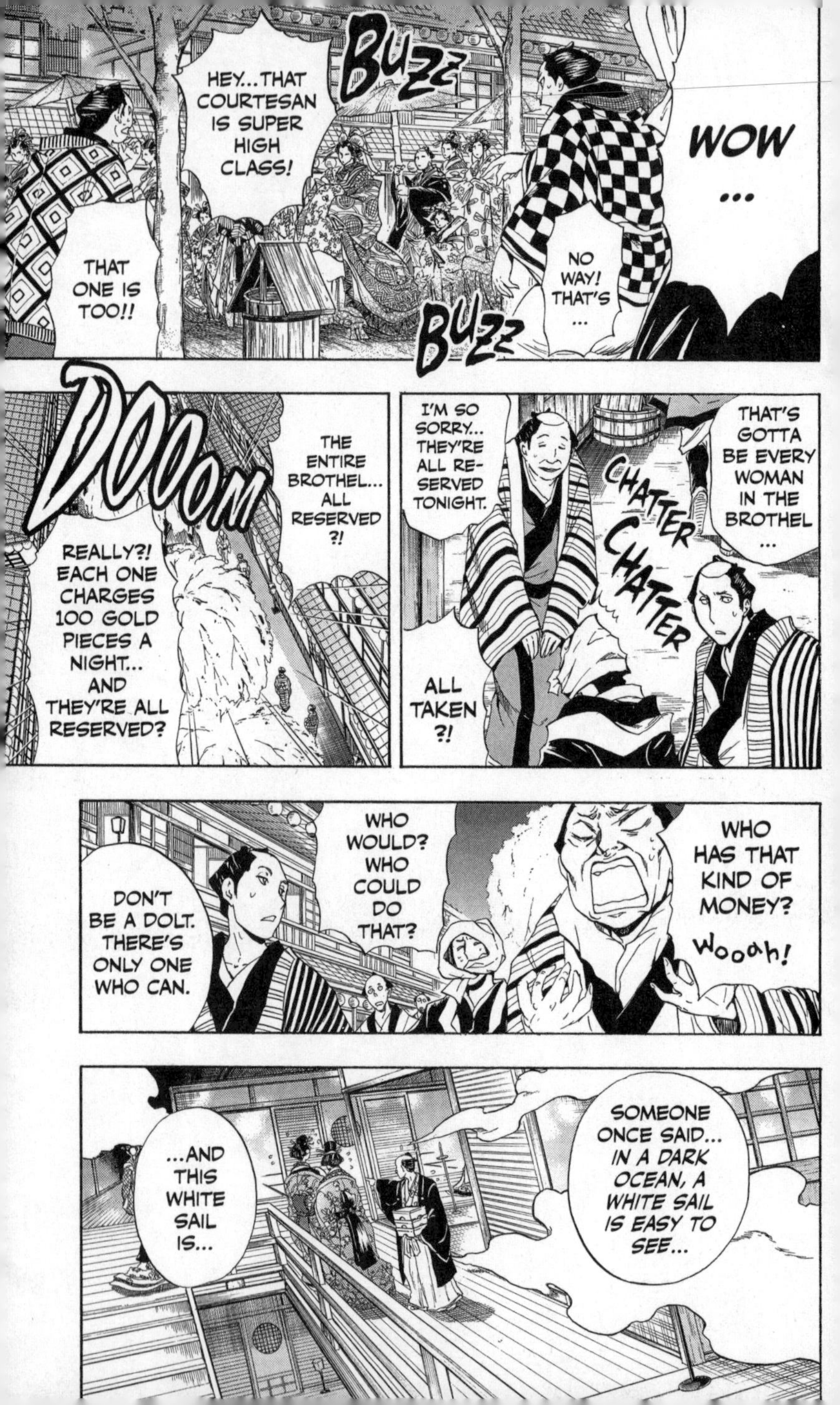
WOW ...
BUZZ
HEY...THAT COURTESAN IS SUPER HIGH CLASS!
NO WAY! THAT'S ...
BUZZ
THAT ONE IS TOO!!
THAT'S GOTTA BE EVERY WOMAN IN THE BROTHEL ...
I'M SO SORRY... THEY'RE ALL RE-SERVED TONIGHT.
CHATTER CHATTER
ALL TAKEN ?!
THE ENTIRE BROTHEL... ALL RESERVED ?!
DOOOM
REALLY?! EACH ONE CHARGES 100 GOLD PIECES A NIGHT... AND THEY'RE ALL RESERVED?
WHO HAS THAT KIND OF MONEY?
Wooah!
WHO WOULD? WHO COULD DO THAT?
DON'T BE A DOLT. THERE'S ONLY ONE WHO CAN.
SOMEONE ONCE SAID... IN A DARK OCEAN, A WHITE SAIL IS EASY TO SEE...
...AND THIS WHITE SAIL IS...

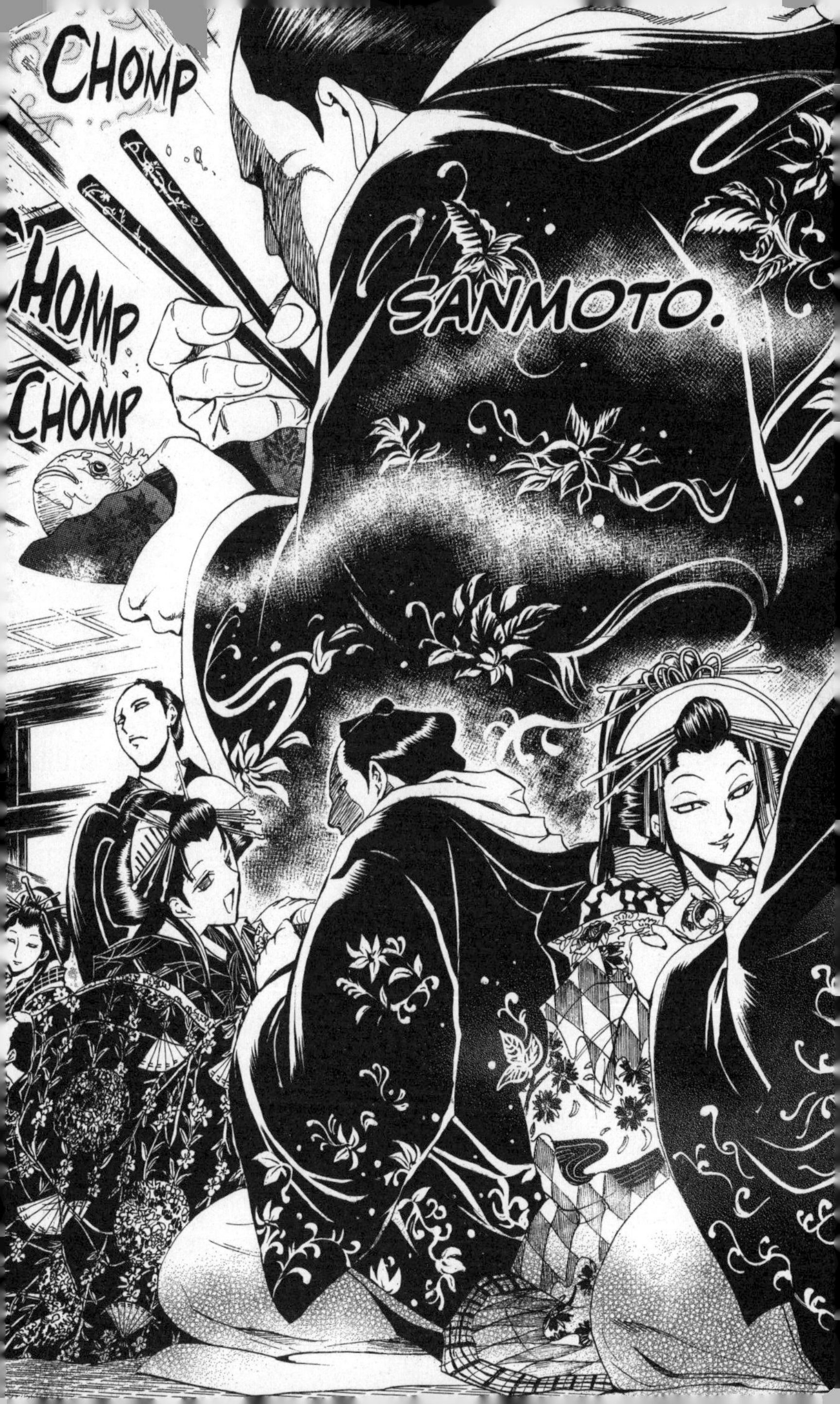
CHOMP
CHOMP
CHOMP
SANMOTO.

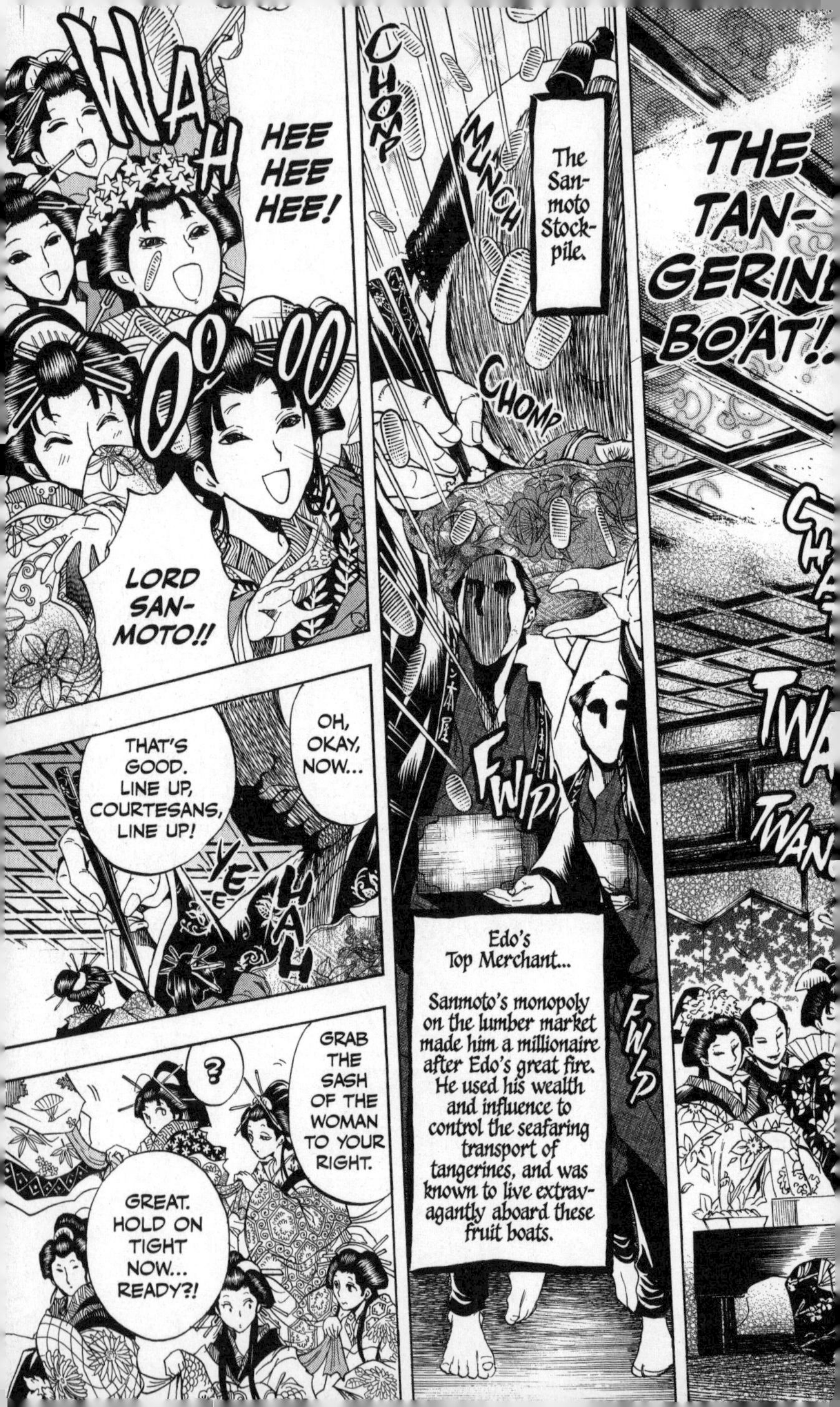

THE TAN-GERINE BOAT!!
The San-moto Stock-pile.
CHOMP
MUNCH
CHOMP
FWIP
Edo's Top Merchant...
Sanmoto's monopoly on the lumber market made him a millionaire after Edo's great fire. He used his wealth and influence to control the seafaring transport of tangerines, and was known to live extravagantly aboard these fruit boats.
FWIP
WAH
HEE HEE HEE!
OOOO
LORD SAN-MOTO!!
OH, OKAY, NOW...
THAT'S GOOD. LINE UP, COURTESANS, LINE UP!
YEE
HAH
GRAB THE SASH OF THE WOMAN TO YOUR RIGHT.
?
GREAT. HOLD ON TIGHT NOW... READY?!

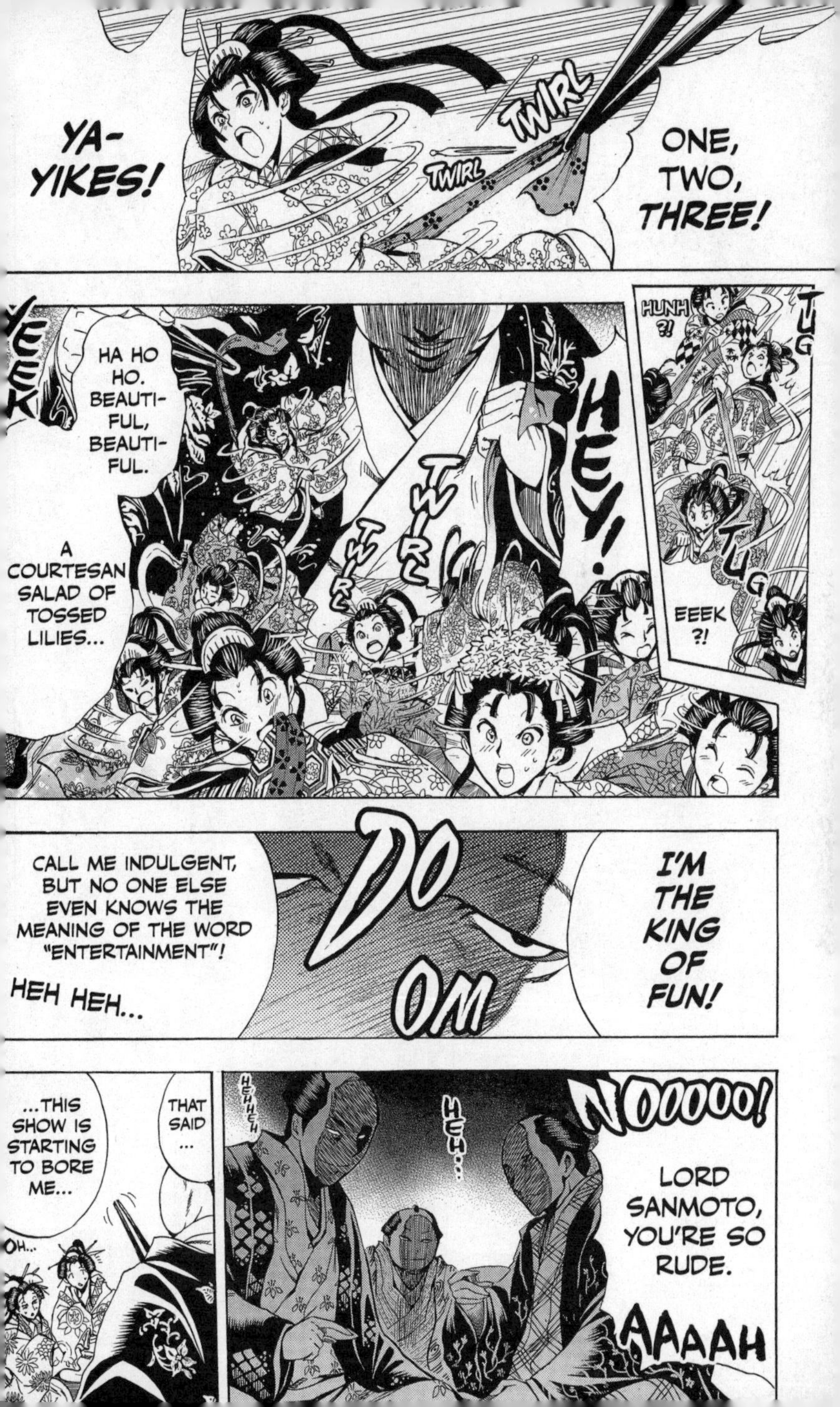
ONE, TWO, THREE!
TWIRL
TWIRL
YA-YIKES!
TUG
HUNH ?!
TUG
EEEK ?!
HEY!
TWIRL
TWIRL
HA HO HO. BEAUTIFUL, BEAUTIFUL.
A COURTESAN SALAD OF TOSSED LILIES...
YEEEK
I'M THE KING OF FUN!
DOOM
CALL ME INDULGENT, BUT NO ONE ELSE EVEN KNOWS THE MEANING OF THE WORD "ENTERTAINMENT"!
HEH HEH...
NOOOOO!
LORD SANMOTO, YOU'RE SO RUDE.
HEH HEH...
HEHHEH
AAAAH
THAT SAID ...
...THIS SHOW IS STARTING TO BORE ME...
OH...

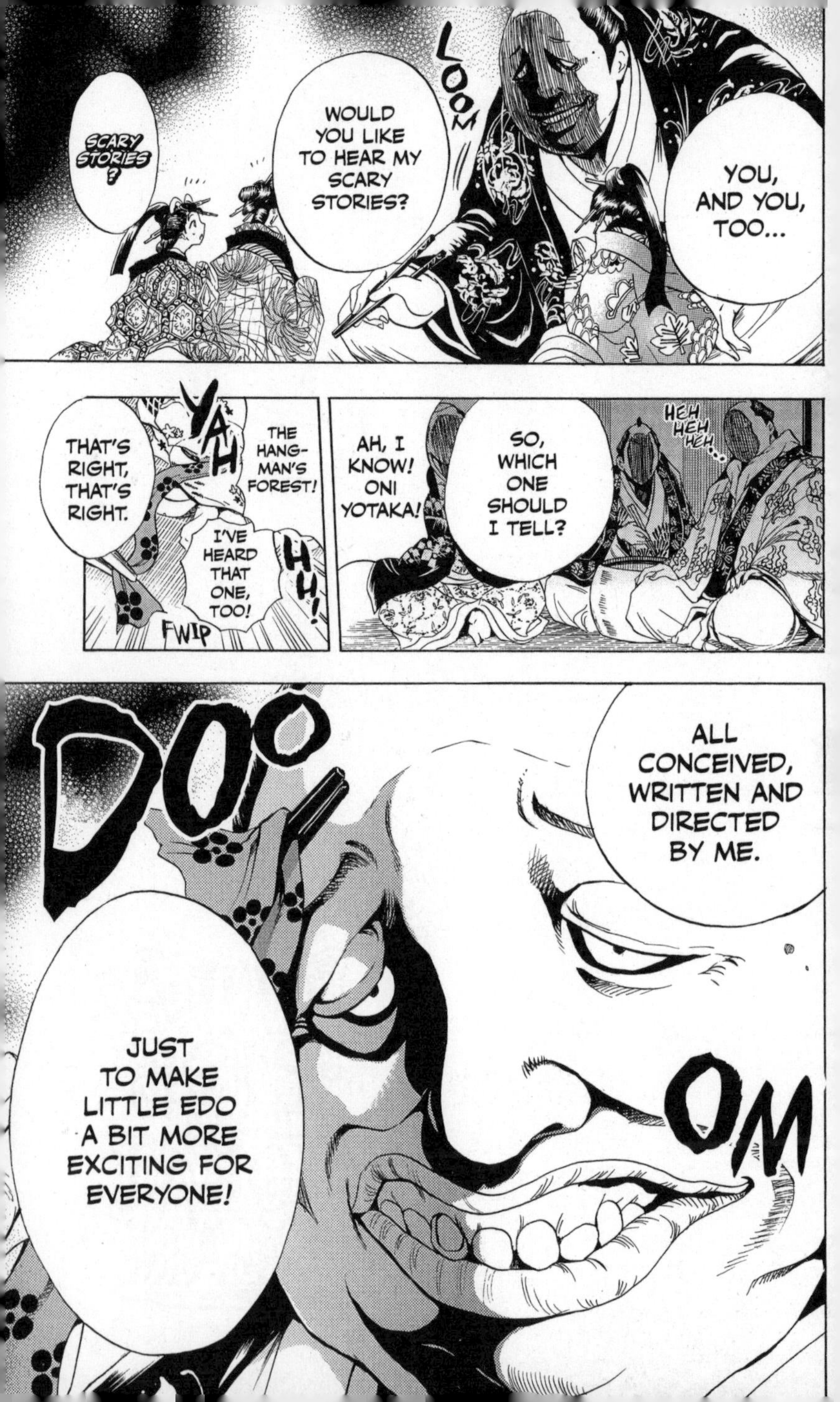
YOU, AND YOU, TOO...
LOOM
WOULD YOU LIKE TO HEAR MY SCARY STORIES?
SCARY STORIES?
HEH HEH HEH...
SO, WHICH ONE SHOULD I TELL?
AH, I KNOW! ONI YOTAKA!
THE HANG-MAN'S FOREST!
YAH
THAT'S RIGHT, THAT'S RIGHT.
I'VE HEARD THAT ONE, TOO!
HH!
FWIP
ALL CONCEIVED, WRITTEN AND DIRECTED BY ME.
DOO
OM
JUST TO MAKE LITTLE EDO A BIT MORE EXCITING FOR EVERYONE!

NURA: RISE OF THE YOKAI CLAN

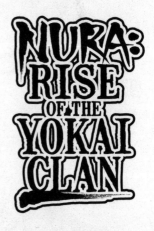

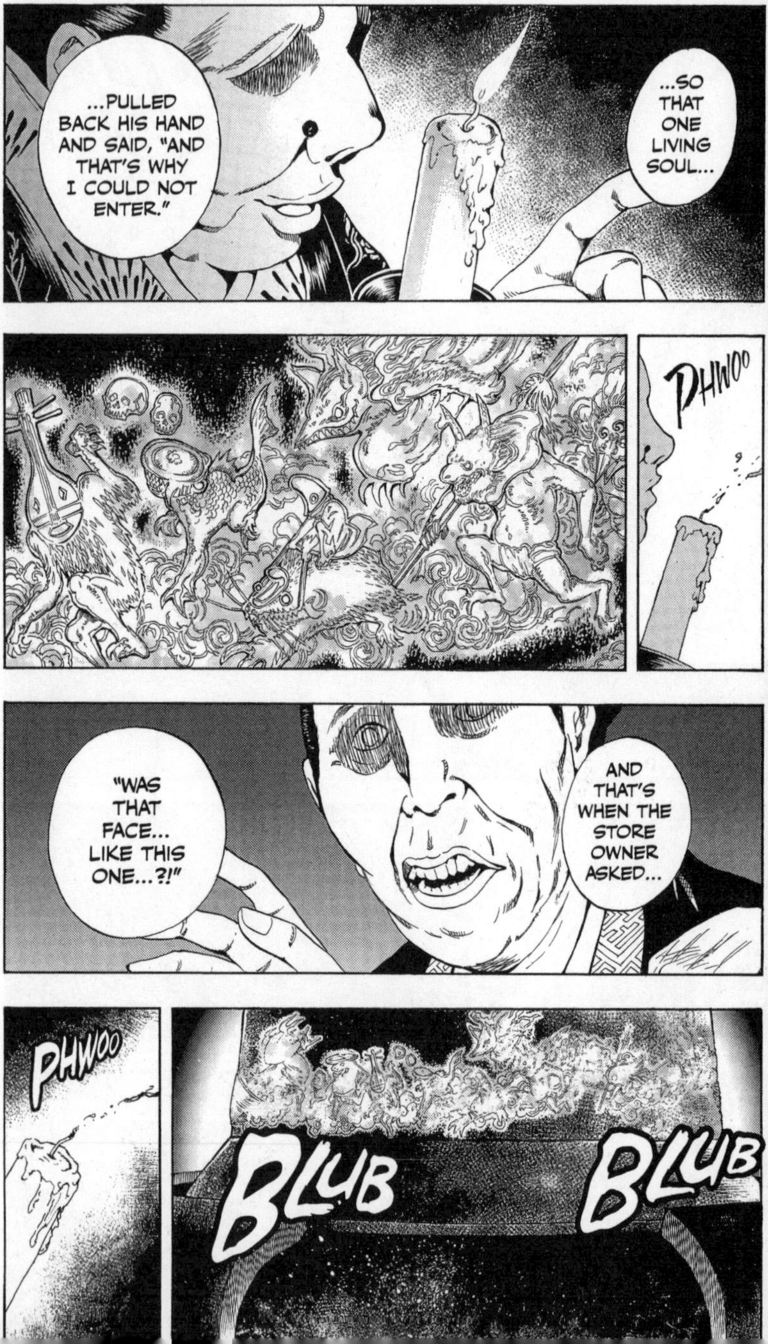
...SO THAT ONE LIVING SOUL...
...PULLED BACK HIS HAND AND SAID, "AND THAT'S WHY I COULD NOT ENTER."
PHWOO
AND THAT'S WHEN THE STORE OWNER ASKED...
"WAS THAT FACE... LIKE THIS ONE...?!"
BLUB
BLUB
PHWOO

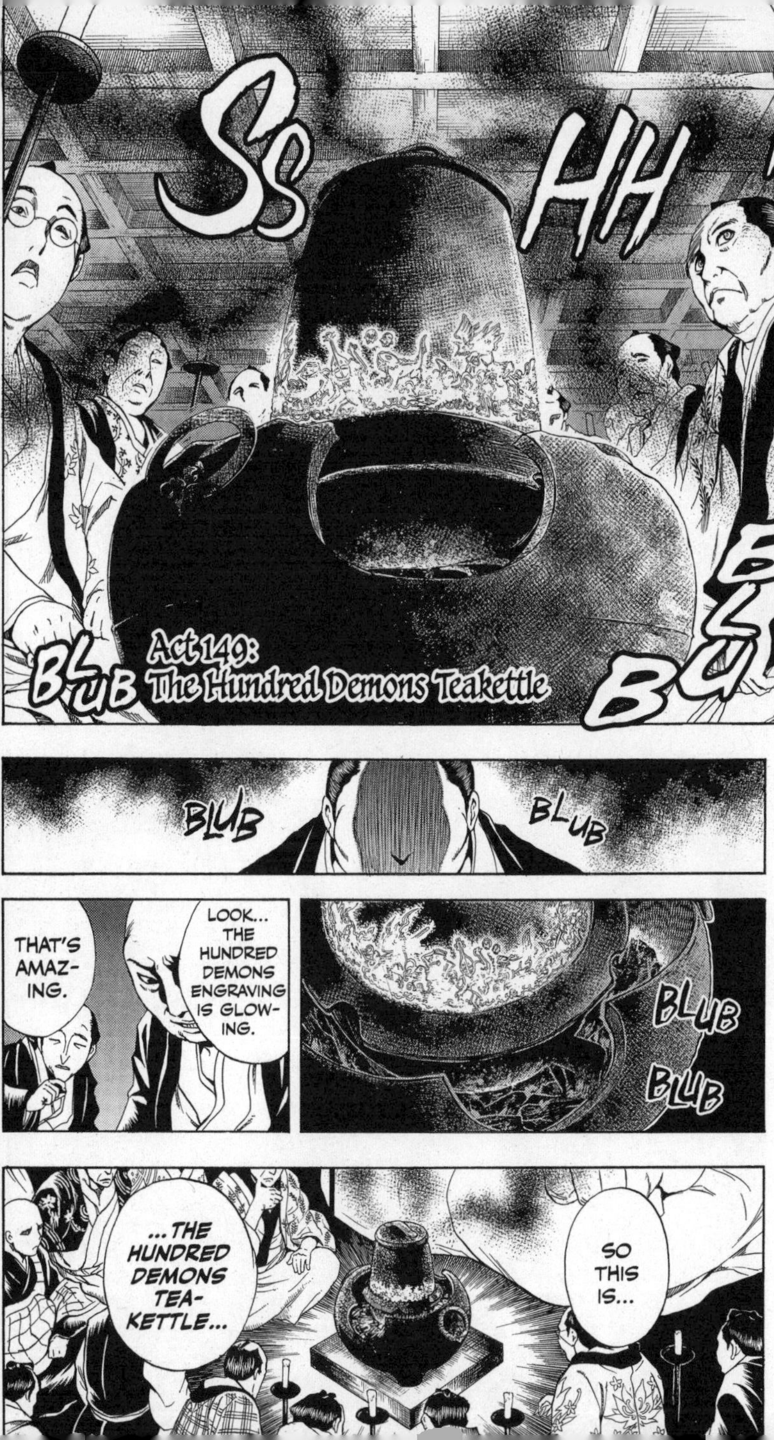
SSHHFF
BLUB
Act 149: The Hundred Demons Teakettle
BLUB
BLUB
BLUB
BLUB
BLUB
LOOK... THE HUNDRED DEMONS ENGRAVING IS GLOWING.
THAT'S AMAZING.
SO THIS IS...
...THE HUNDRED DEMONS TEAKETTLE...

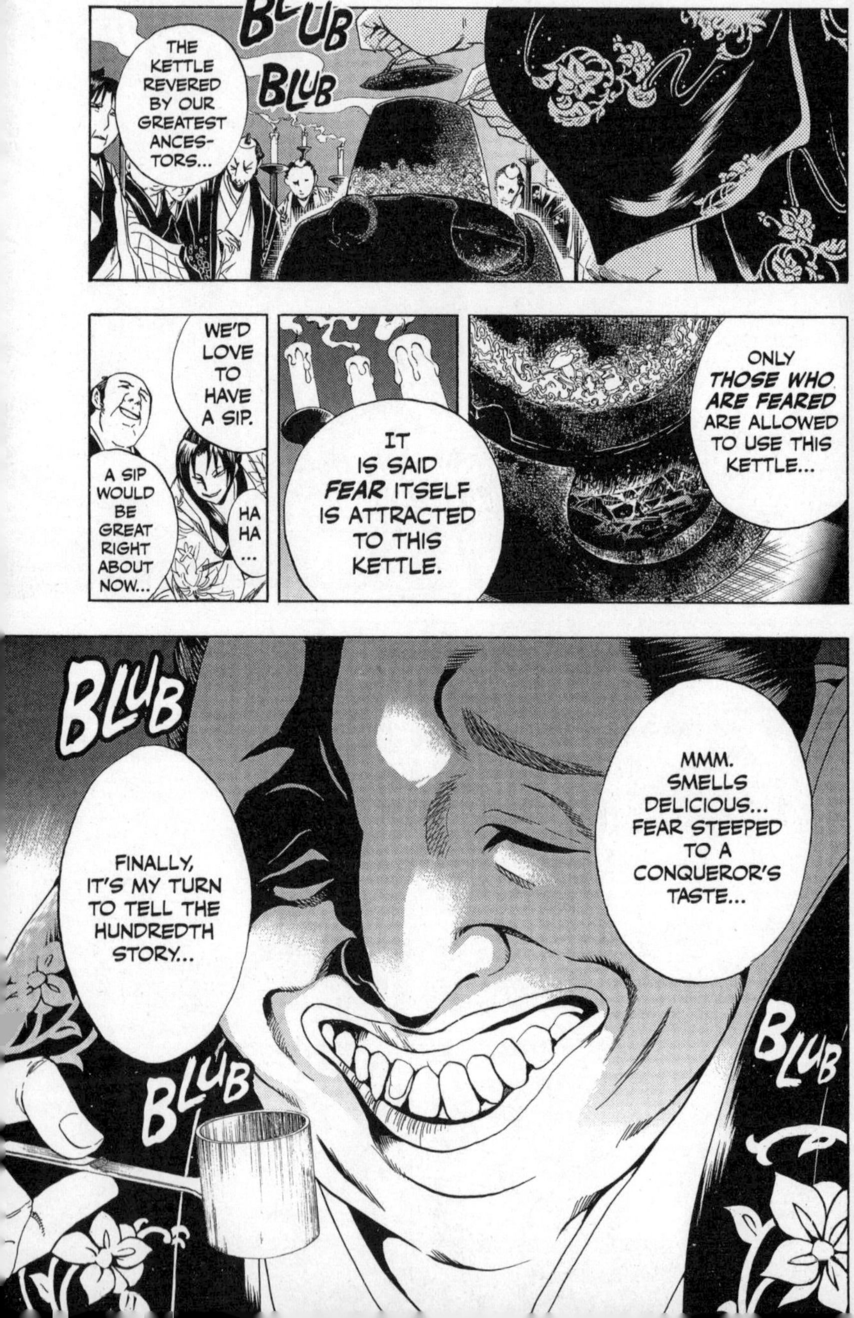
BLUB
BLUB
THE KETTLE REVERED BY OUR GREATEST ANCES-TORS...
ONLY *THOSE WHO ARE FEARED* ARE ALLOWED TO USE THIS KETTLE...
IT IS SAID *FEAR* ITSELF IS ATTRACTED TO THIS KETTLE.
WE'D LOVE TO HAVE A SIP.
HA HA ...
A SIP WOULD BE GREAT RIGHT ABOUT NOW...
MMM. SMELLS DELICIOUS... FEAR STEEPED TO A CONQUEROR'S TASTE...
BLUB
FINALLY, IT'S MY TURN TO TELL THE HUNDREDTH STORY...
BLUB
BLUB

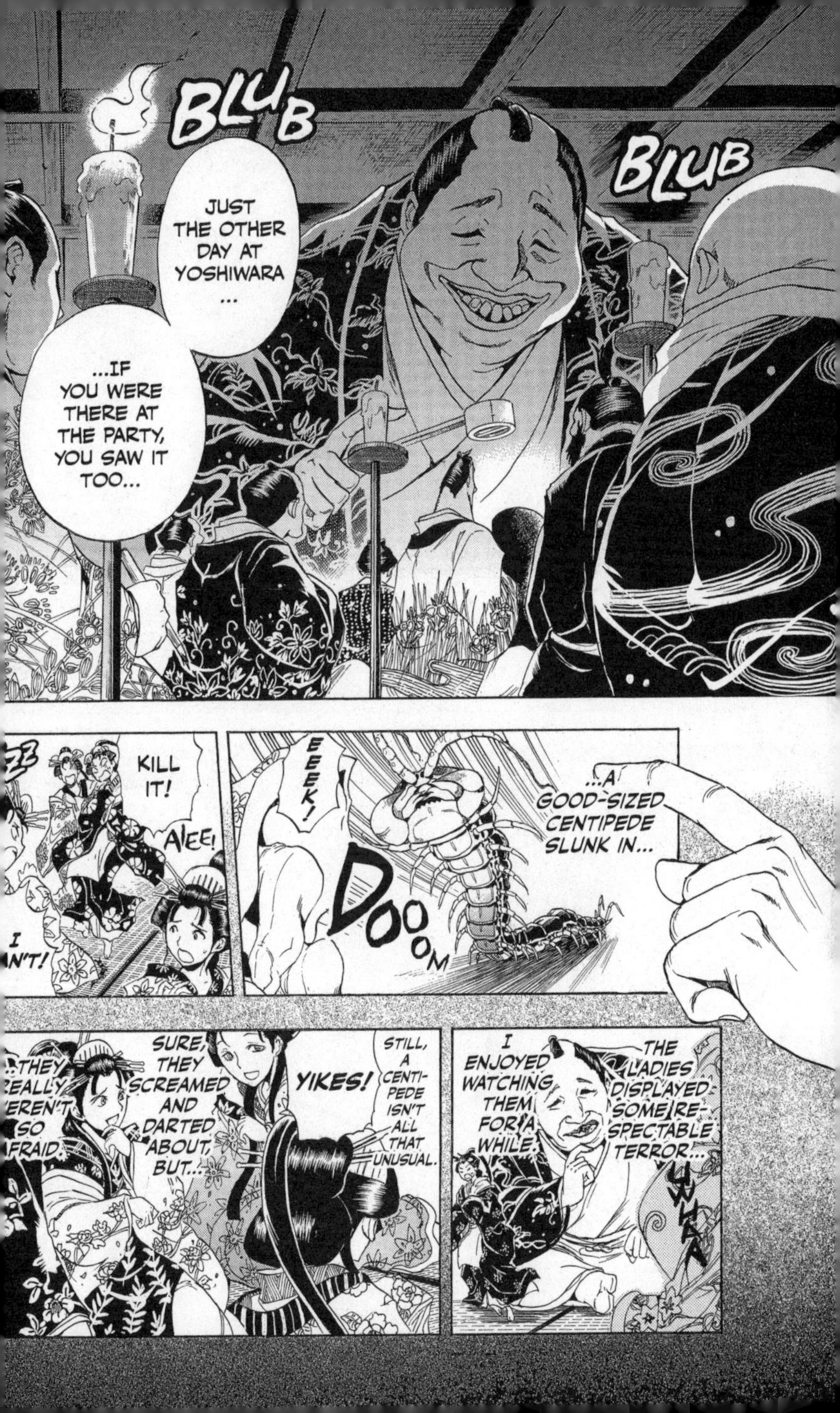
BLUB
JUST THE OTHER DAY AT YOSHIWARA ...
BLUB
...IF YOU WERE THERE AT THE PARTY, YOU SAW IT TOO...
...A GOOD-SIZED CENTIPEDE SLUNK IN...
EEEEK!
DOOOM
KILL IT!
AIEE!
I
AN'T!
THE LADIES DISPLAYED SOME RE-SPECTABLE TERROR...
I ENJOYED WATCHING THEM FOR A WHILE.
STILL, A CENTI-PEDE ISN'T ALL THAT UNUSUAL.
YIKES!
SURE, THEY SCREAMED AND DARTED ABOUT, BUT...
..THEY EALLY EREN'T SO FRAID.

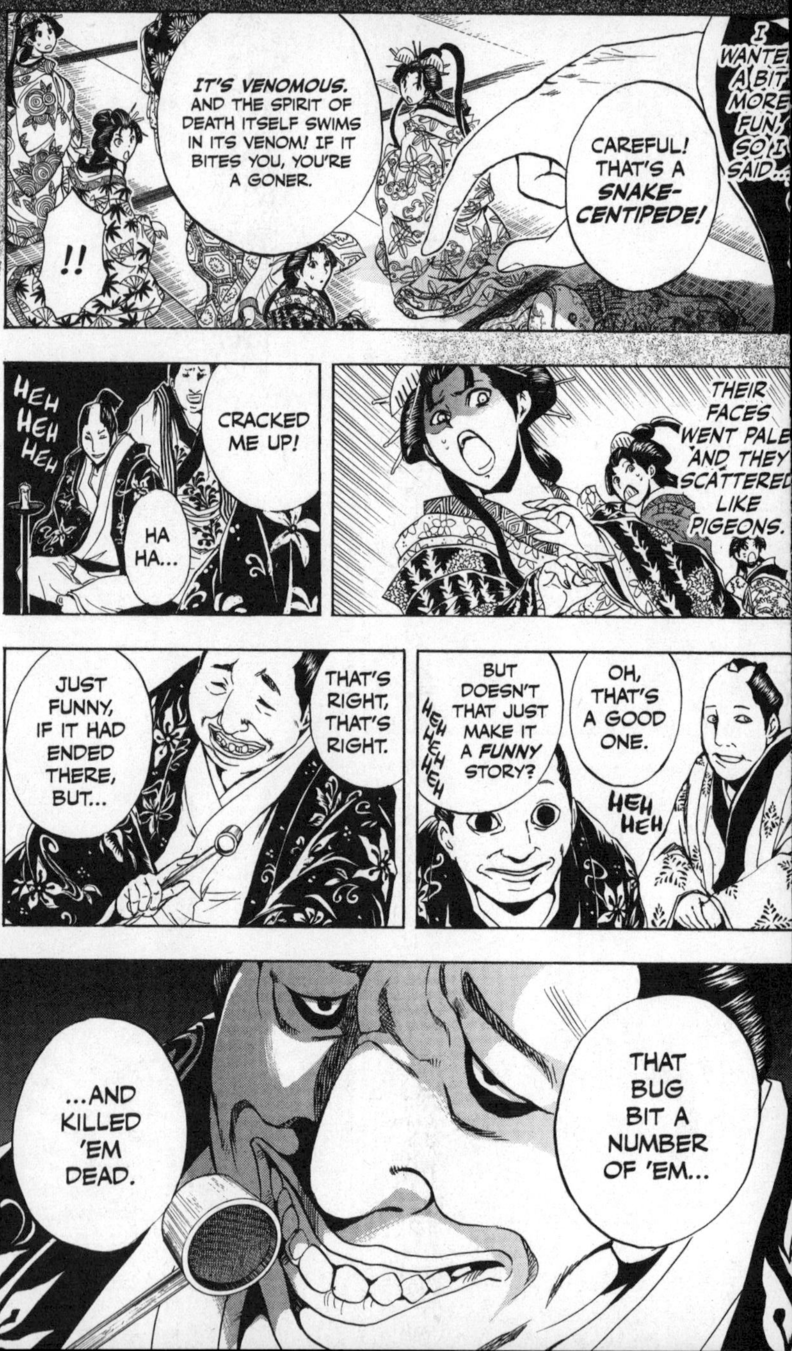
I WANTE A BIT MORE FUN, SO I SAID...
CAREFUL! THAT'S A SNAKE-CENTIPEDE!
IT'S VENOMOUS. AND THE SPIRIT OF DEATH ITSELF SWIMS IN ITS VENOM! IF IT BITES YOU, YOU'RE A GONER.
!!
THEIR FACES WENT PALE AND THEY SCATTERED LIKE PIGEONS.
CRACKED ME UP!
HEH HEH HEH
HA HA...
OH, THAT'S A GOOD ONE.
HEH HEH
BUT DOESN'T THAT JUST MAKE IT A FUNNY STORY?
HEH HEH HEH HEH
THAT'S RIGHT, THAT'S RIGHT.
JUST FUNNY, IF IT HAD ENDED THERE, BUT...
THAT BUG BIT A NUMBER OF 'EM...
...AND KILLED 'EM DEAD.

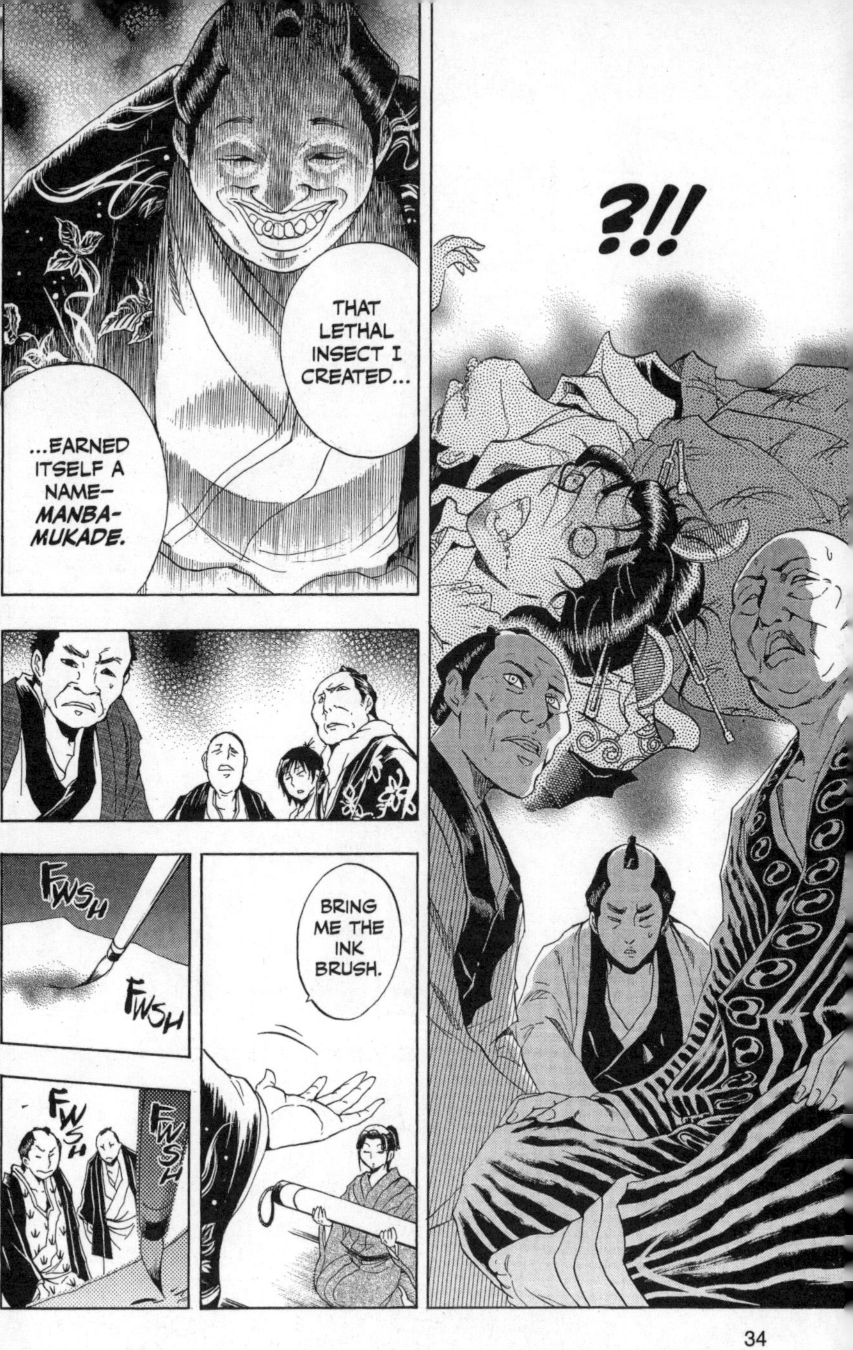
?!!
THAT LETHAL INSECT I CREATED...
...EARNED ITSELF A NAME— MANBA-MUKADE.
BRING ME THE INK BRUSH.
FWSH
FWSH
FWSH
FWSH

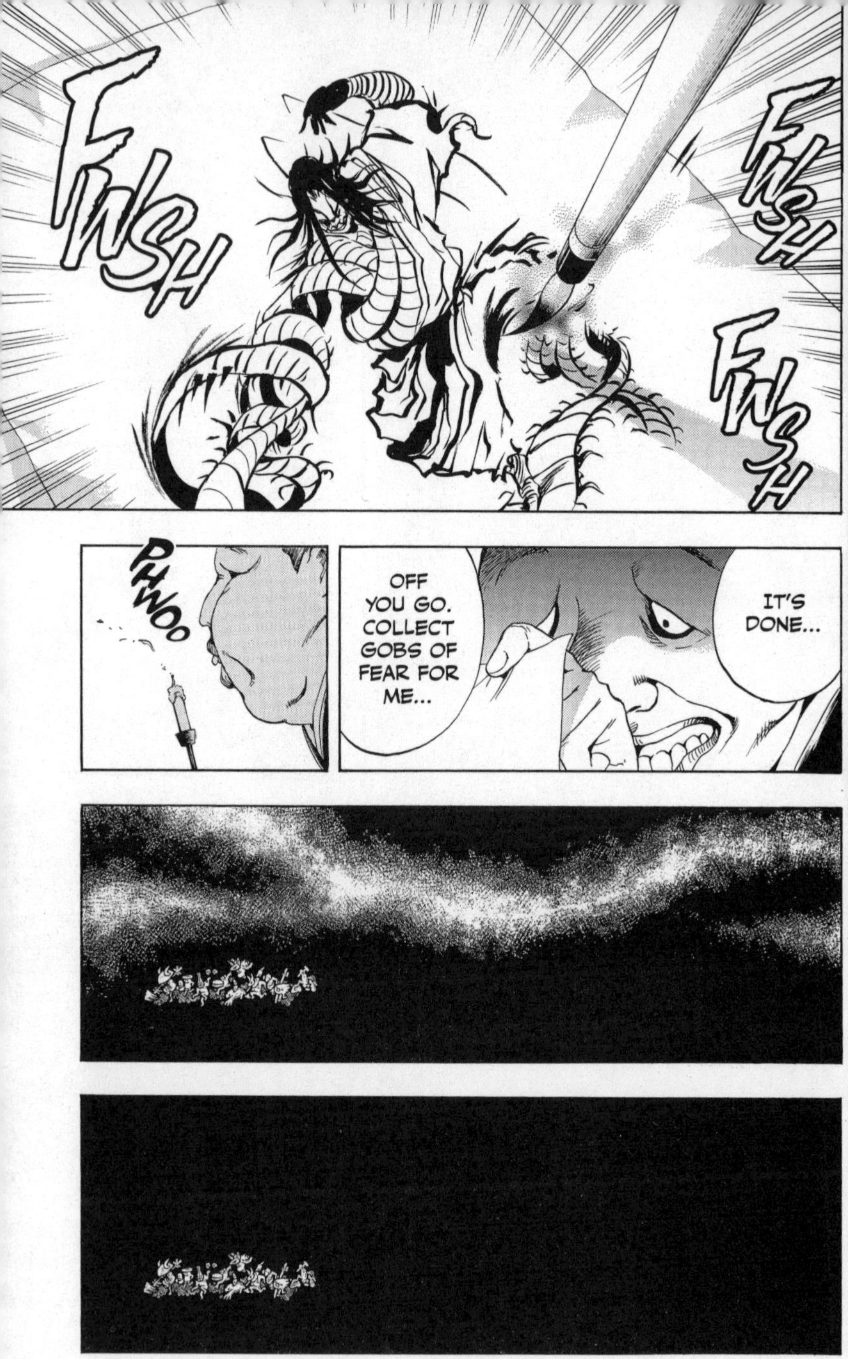
FWSH
FWSH
FWSH
IT'S DONE...
OFF YOU GO. COLLECT GOBS OF FEAR FOR ME...
PHWOO

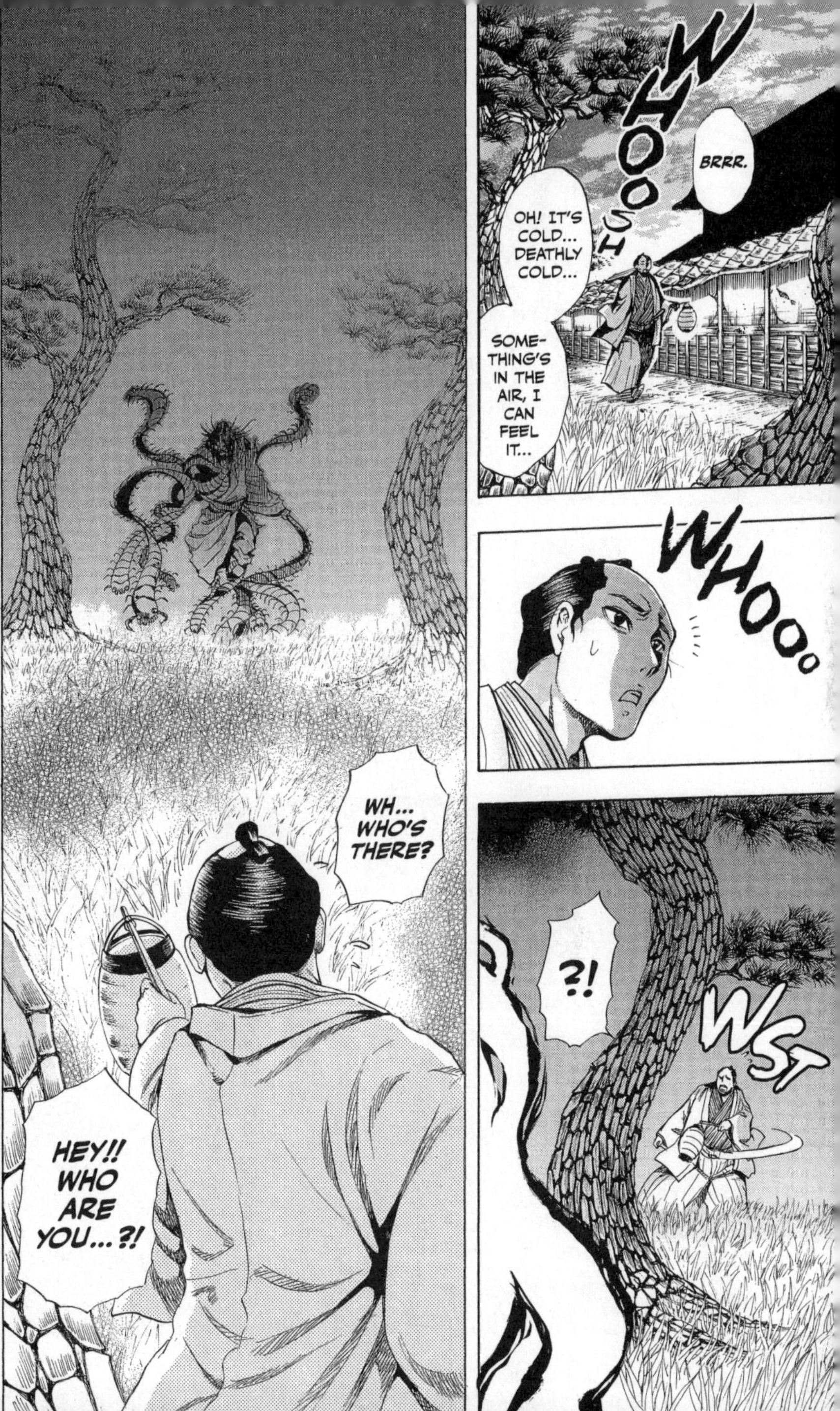
WHOOOSH
BRRR.
OH! IT'S COLD... DEATHLY COLD...
SOME-THING'S IN THE AIR, I CAN FEEL IT...
WHOOOO
?!
WST
WH... WHO'S THERE?
HEY!! WHO ARE YOU...?!

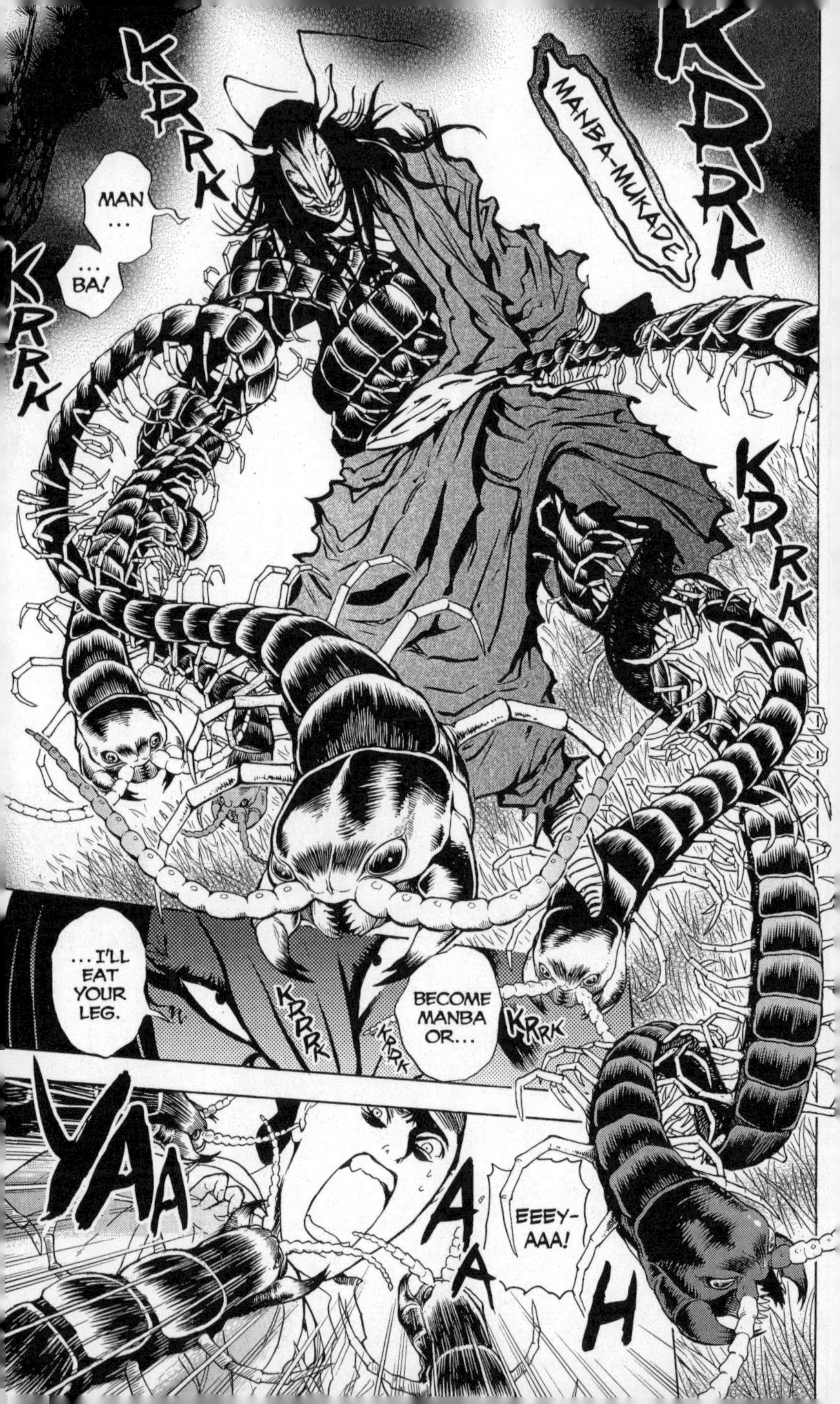
KDRRK
MANBA-MUKADE
KDRRK
MAN... ...BA!
KRRRK
KDRRK
BECOME MANBA OR...
KRRK
KRRK
KDRRRK
...I'LL EAT YOUR LEG.
EEEY-AAA!
YAAAAH

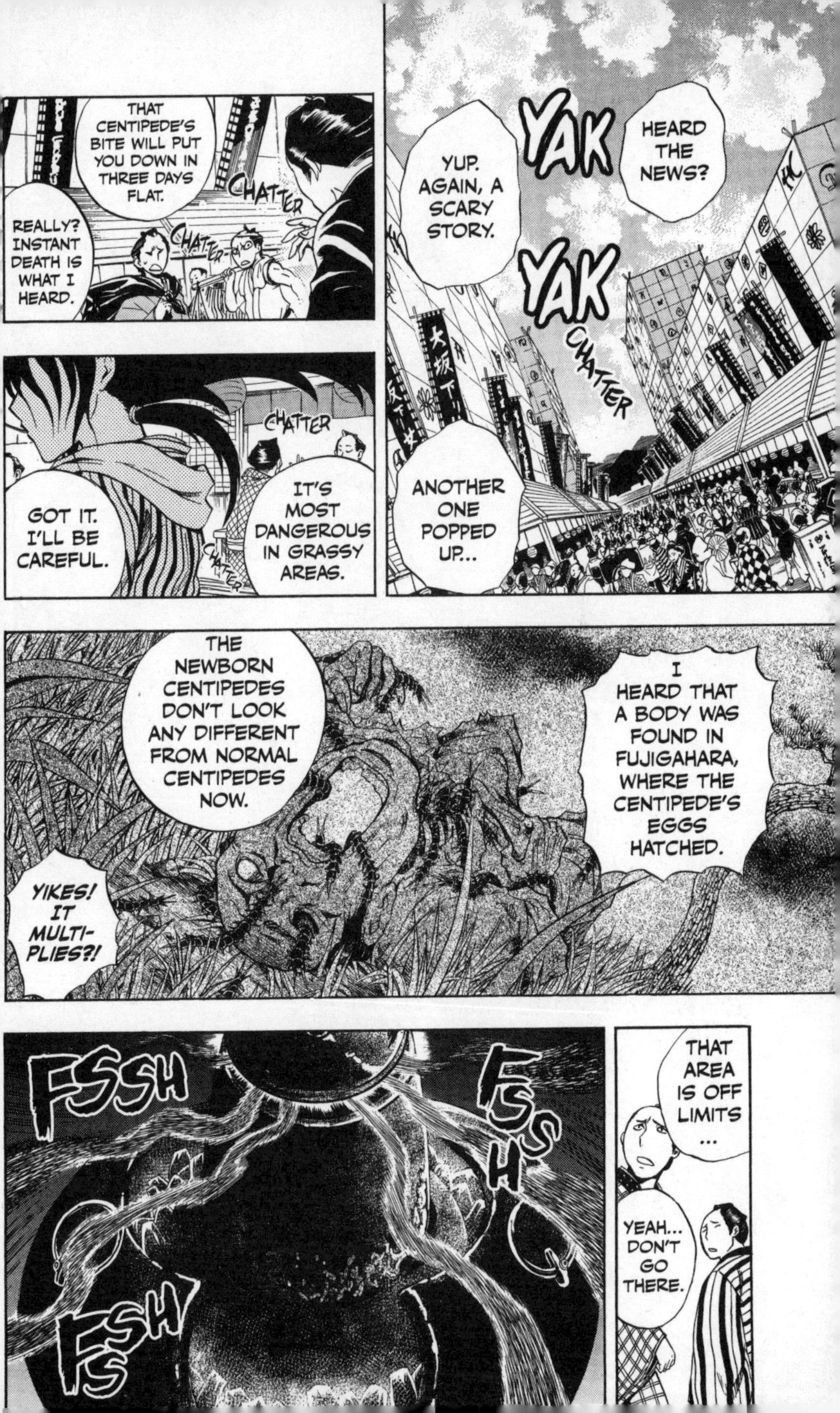
HEARD THE NEWS?
YAK
YUP. AGAIN, A SCARY STORY.
YAK
CHATTER
ANOTHER ONE POPPED UP...
THAT CENTIPEDE'S BITE WILL PUT YOU DOWN IN THREE DAYS FLAT.
CHATTER
CHATTER
REALLY? INSTANT DEATH IS WHAT I HEARD.
CHATTER
IT'S MOST DANGEROUS IN GRASSY AREAS.
GOT IT. I'LL BE CAREFUL.
CHATTER
I HEARD THAT A BODY WAS FOUND IN FUJIGAHARA, WHERE THE CENTIPEDE'S EGGS HATCHED.
THE NEWBORN CENTIPEDES DON'T LOOK ANY DIFFERENT FROM NORMAL CENTIPEDES NOW.
YIKES! IT MULTIPLIES?!
THAT AREA IS OFF LIMITS ...
YEAH... DON'T GO THERE.
FSSH
FSSH
FSSH

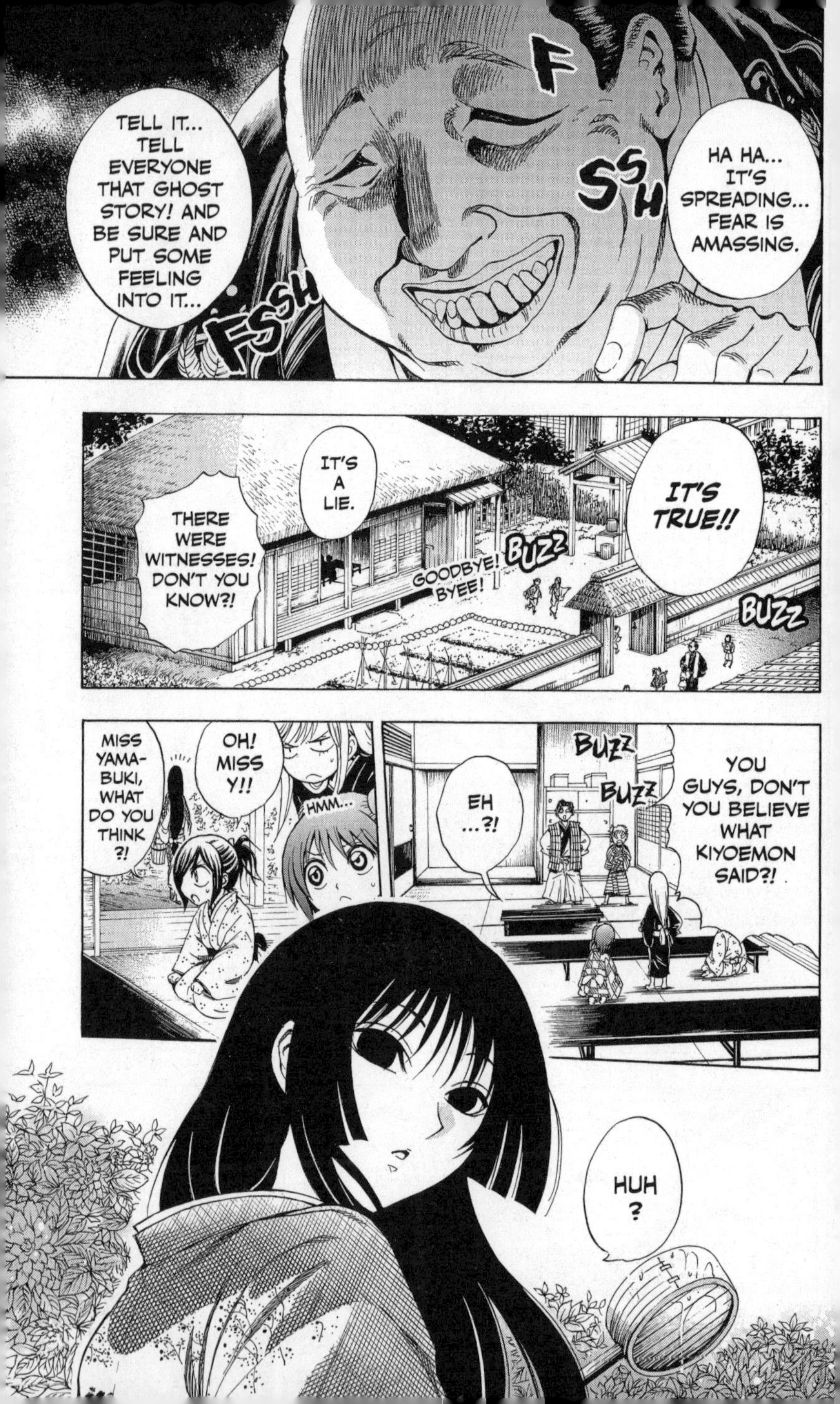
F
SSH
HA HA... IT'S SPREADING... FEAR IS AMASSING.
TELL IT... TELL EVERYONE THAT GHOST STORY! AND BE SURE AND PUT SOME FEELING INTO IT...
FSSH
IT'S TRUE!!
BUZZ
IT'S A LIE.
BUZZ
GOODBYE! BYEE!
THERE WERE WITNESSES! DON'T YOU KNOW?!
YOU GUYS, DON'T YOU BELIEVE WHAT KIYOEMON SAID?!
BUZZ
BUZZ
EH ...?!
OH! MISS Y!!
HMM...
MISS YAMA-BUKI, WHAT DO YOU THINK ?!
HUH ?

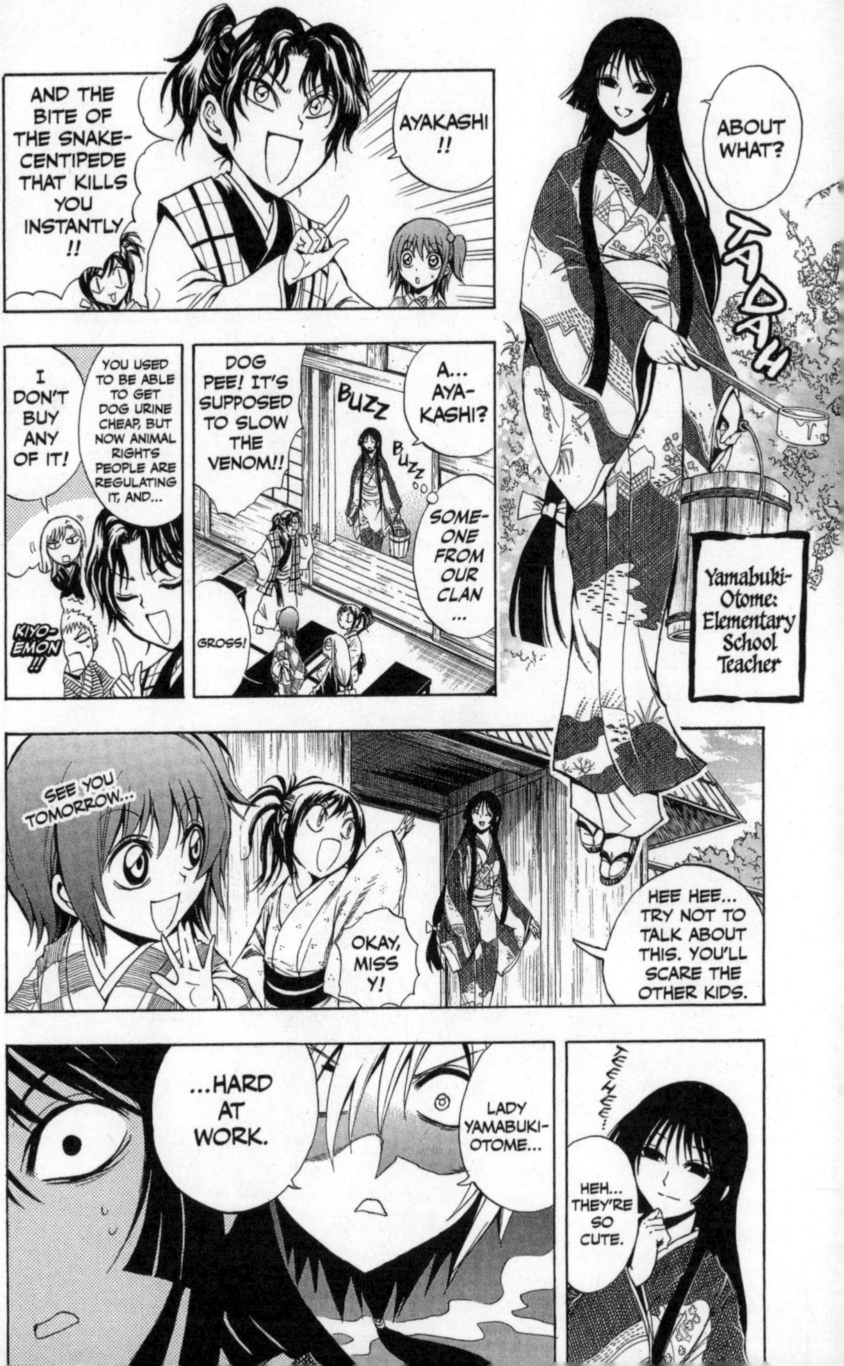
ABOUT WHAT?
TADAH
Yamabuki-Otome: Elementary School Teacher
AYAKASHI !!
AND THE BITE OF THE SNAKE-CENTIPEDE THAT KILLS YOU INSTANTLY !!
A... AYA-KASHI?
BUZZ
BUZZ
SOME-ONE FROM OUR CLAN ...
DOG PEE! IT'S SUPPOSED TO SLOW THE VENOM!!
GROSS!
YOU USED TO BE ABLE TO GET DOG URINE CHEAP, BUT NOW ANIMAL RIGHTS PEOPLE ARE REGULATING IT, AND...
I DON'T BUY ANY OF IT!
KIYO-EMON !!
HEE HEE... TRY NOT TO TALK ABOUT THIS. YOU'LL SCARE THE OTHER KIDS.
OKAY, MISS Y!
SEE YOU TOMORROW...
TEEHEE...
HEH... THEY'RE SO CUTE.
LADY YAMABUKI-OTOME...
...HARD AT WORK.

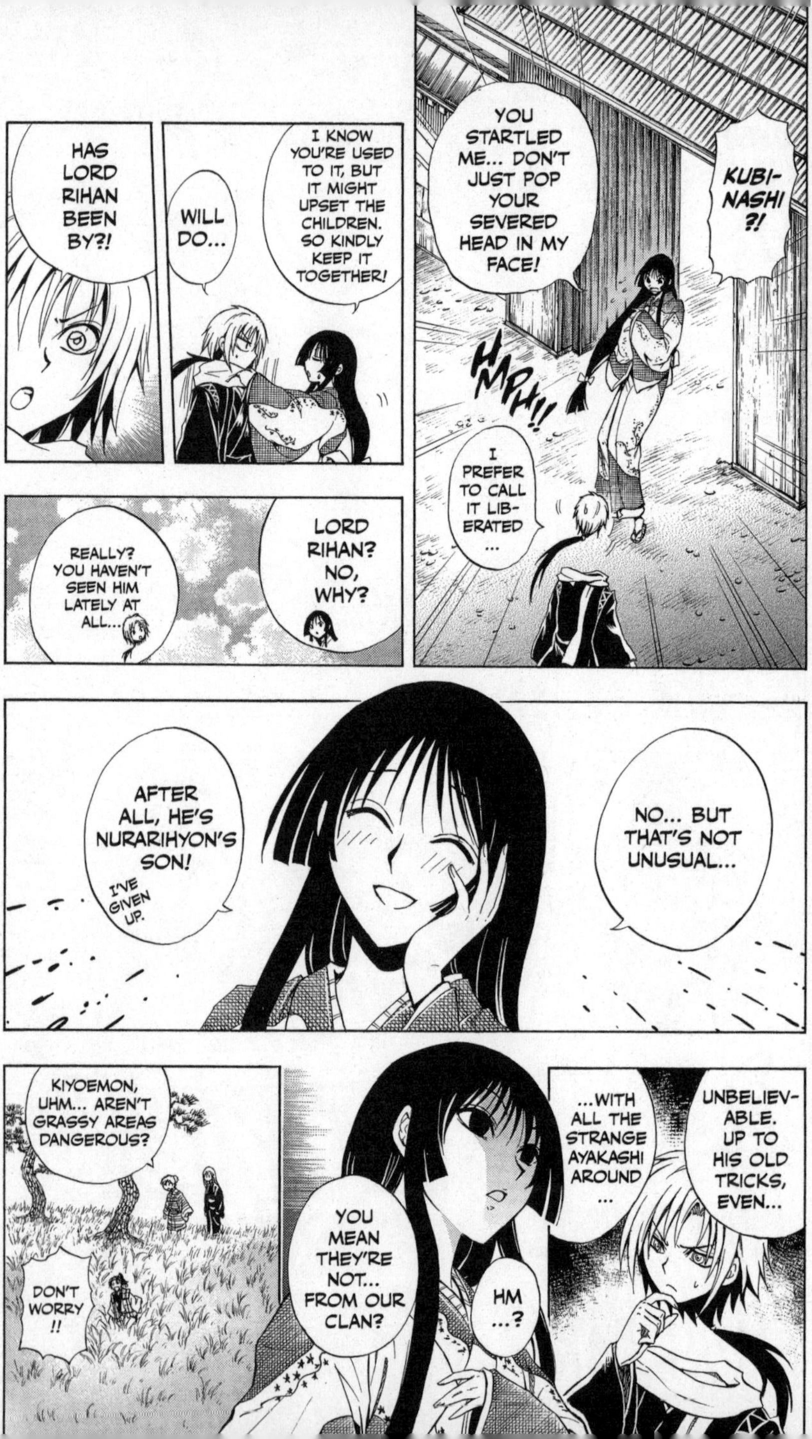
KUBI-NASHI?!
YOU STARTLED ME... DON'T JUST POP YOUR SEVERED HEAD IN MY FACE!
HMPH!!
I PREFER TO CALL IT LIB-ERATED...
I KNOW YOU'RE USED TO IT, BUT IT MIGHT UPSET THE CHILDREN. SO KINDLY KEEP IT TOGETHER!
WILL DO...
HAS LORD RIHAN BEEN BY?!
LORD RIHAN? NO, WHY?
REALLY? YOU HAVEN'T SEEN HIM LATELY AT ALL...
NO... BUT THAT'S NOT UNUSUAL...
AFTER ALL, HE'S NURARIHYON'S SON!
I'VE GIVEN UP.
UNBELIEV-ABLE. UP TO HIS OLD TRICKS, EVEN...
...WITH ALL THE STRANGE AYAKASHI AROUND...
HM...?
YOU MEAN THEY'RE NOT... FROM OUR CLAN?
KIYOEMON, UHM... AREN'T GRASSY AREAS DANGEROUS?
DON'T WORRY!!

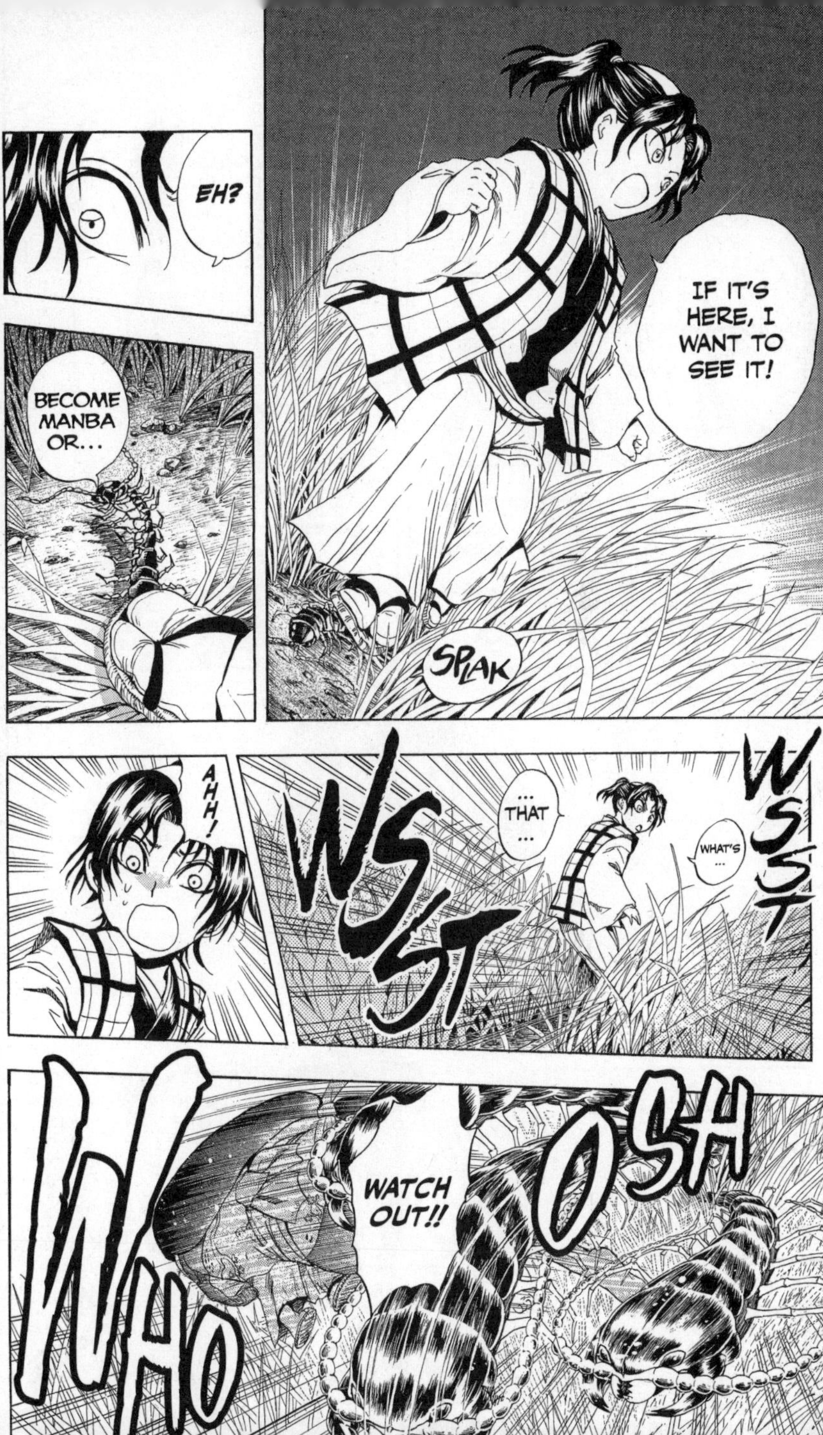
IF IT'S HERE, I WANT TO SEE IT!
SPLAK
EH?
BECOME MANBA OR...
WSST
WHAT'S ...
... THAT ...
WSST
AHH!
WHOOSH
WATCH OUT!!

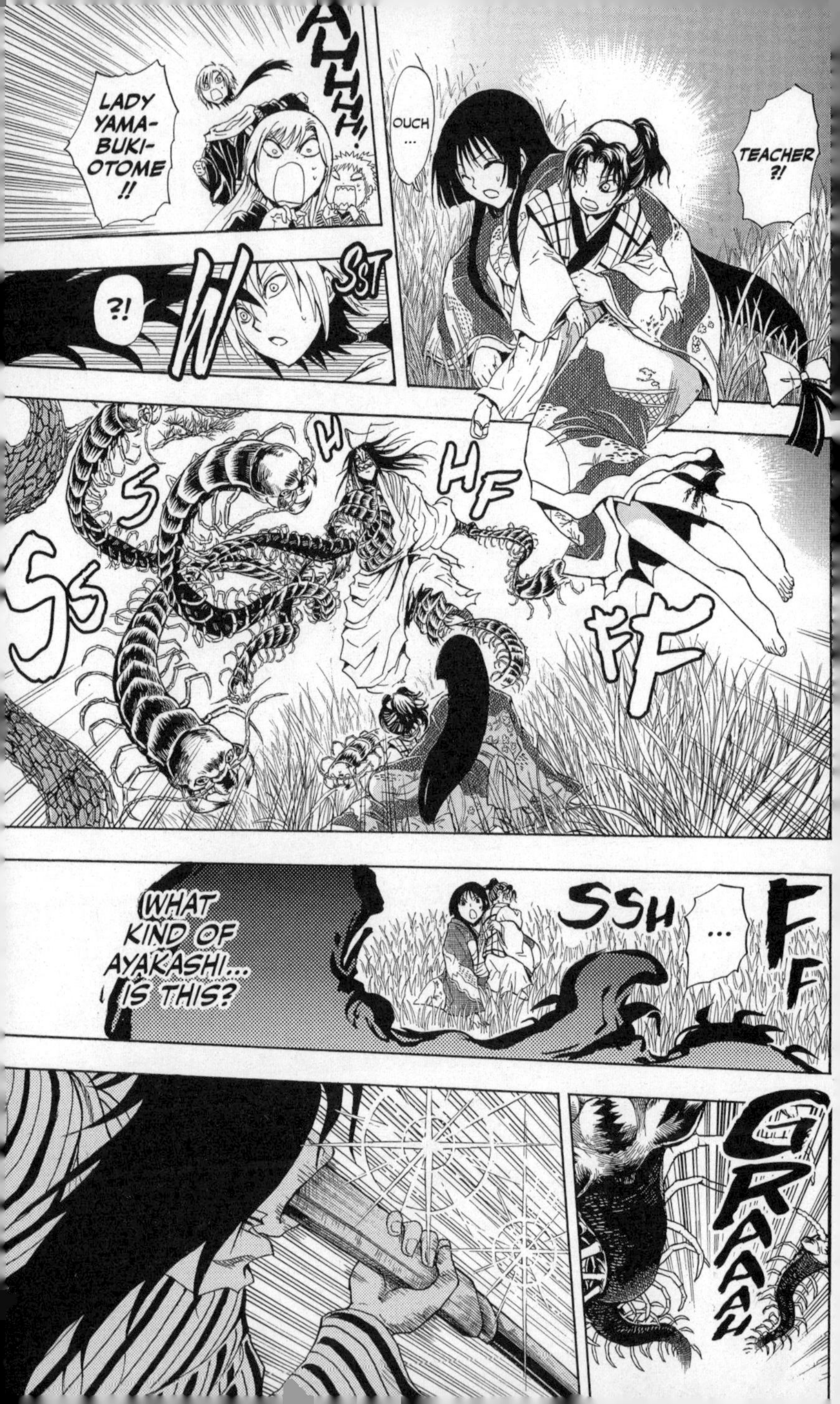
TEACHER?!
OUCH...
AHHHH!
LADY YAMA-BUKI-OTOME!!
SST
?!
FF
HF
H
S
SS
F
F
...
SSH
WHAT KIND OF AYAKASHI... IS THIS?
GRAAAH

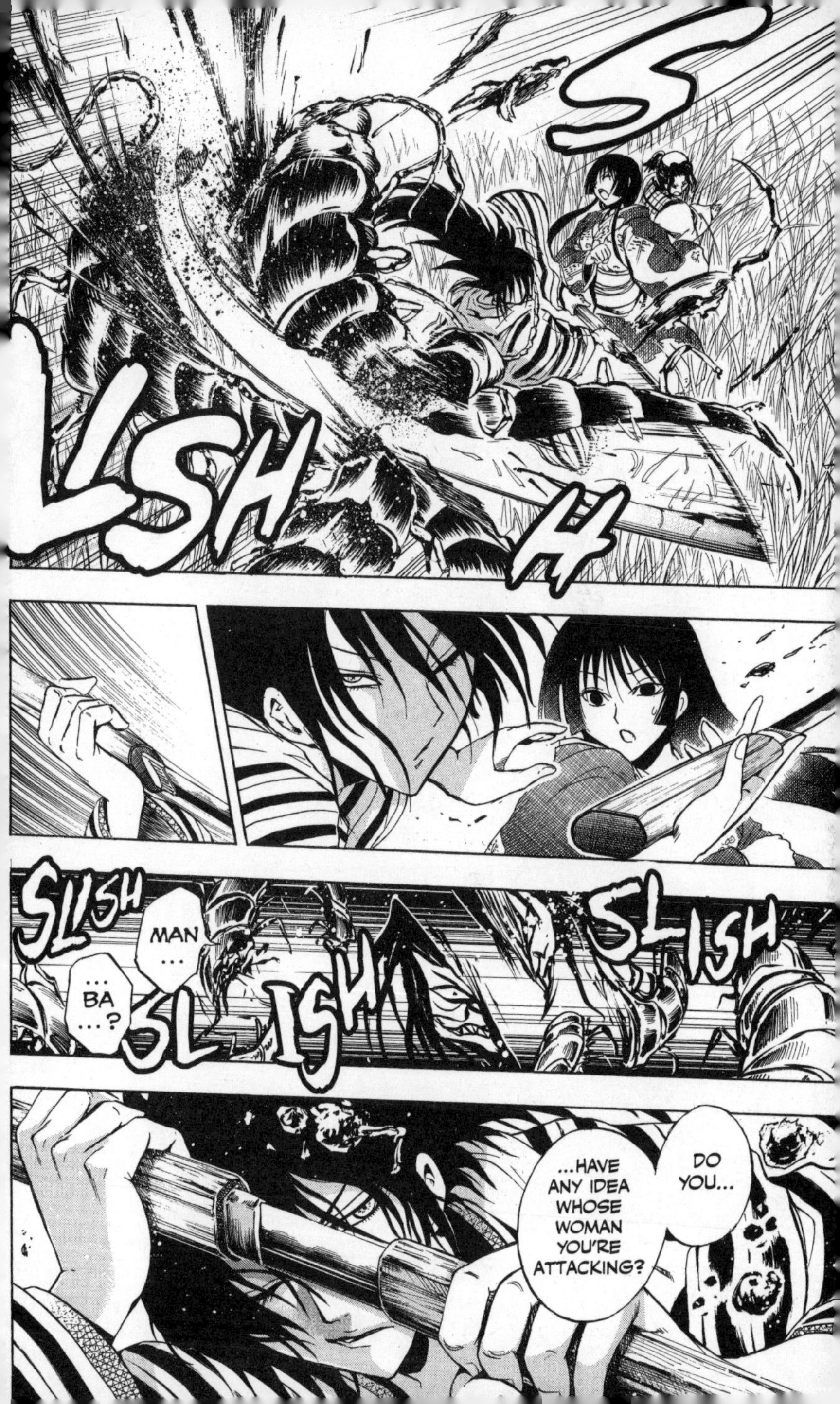
S
LSH
H
SLISH
SLISH
MAN...
...BA...?
SLISH
DO YOU...
...HAVE ANY IDEA WHOSE WOMAN YOU'RE ATTACKING?

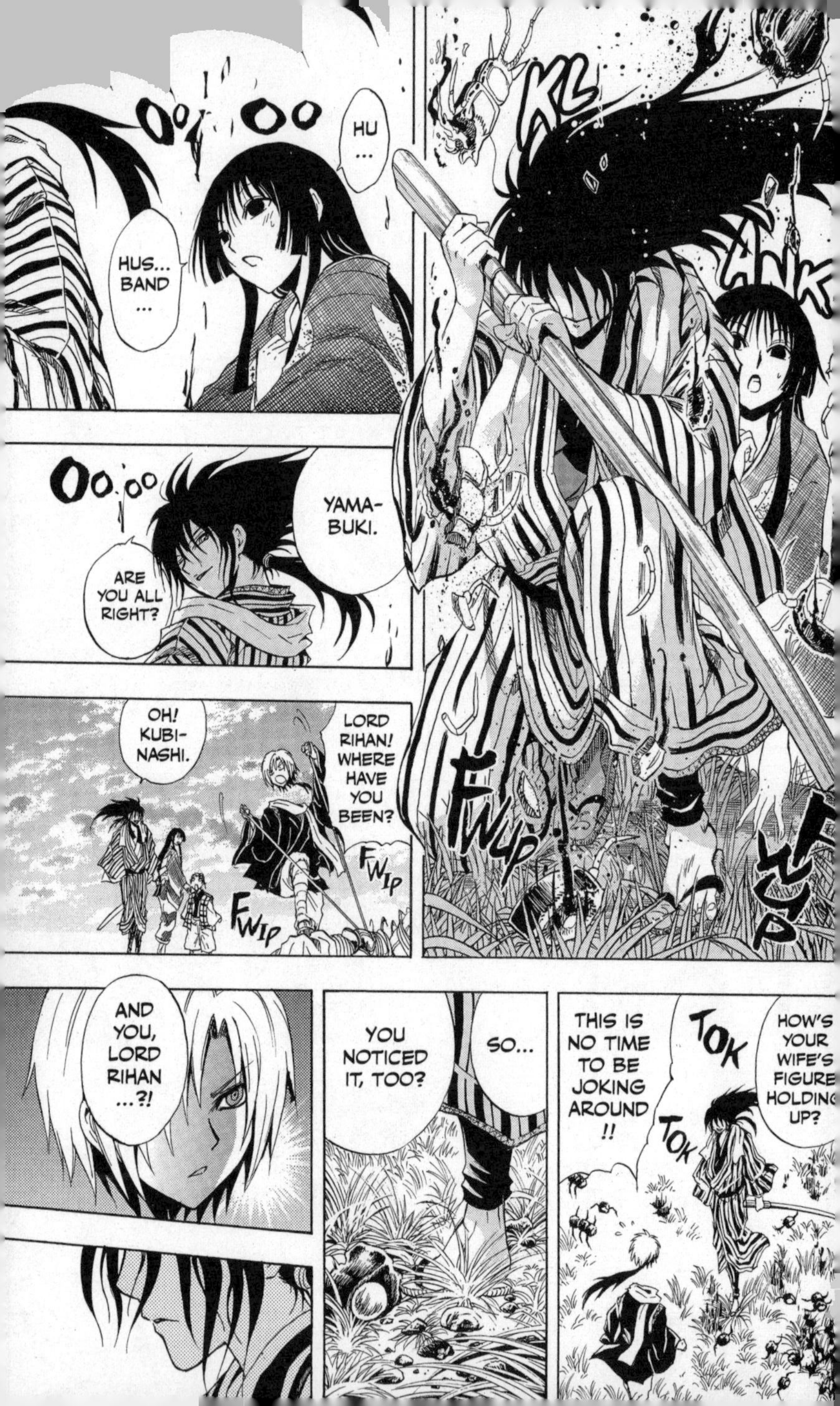
KLANK
FWUP
FWUP
HU...
OO OO
HUS... BAND...
YAMA-BUKI.
OO OO
ARE YOU ALL RIGHT?
LORD RIHAN! WHERE HAVE YOU BEEN?
OH! KUBI-NASHI.
FWIP
FWIP
HOW'S YOUR WIFE'S FIGURE HOLDING UP?
TOK
TOK
THIS IS NO TIME TO BE JOKING AROUND !!
SO...
YOU NOTICED IT, TOO?
AND YOU, LORD RIHAN ...?!

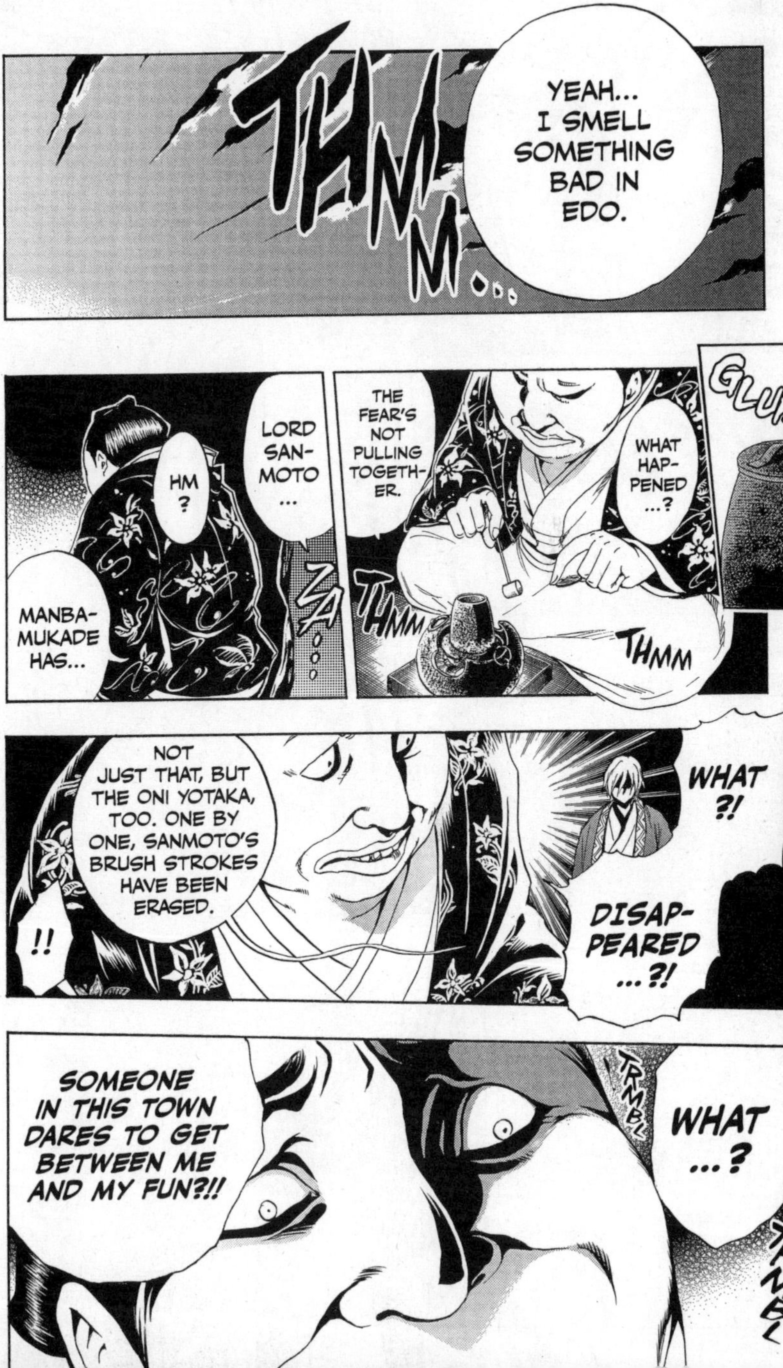
YEAH... I SMELL SOMETHING BAD IN EDO.
THMM...
GLUP...
WHAT HAP-PENED ...?
THE FEAR'S NOT PULLING TOGETH-ER.
THMM
THMM
LORD SAN-MOTO ...
HM ?
ZA...
MANBA-MUKADE HAS...
WHAT ?!
DISAP-PEARED ...?!
NOT JUST THAT, BUT THE ONI YOTAKA, TOO. ONE BY ONE, SANMOTO'S BRUSH STROKES HAVE BEEN ERASED.
!!
TRMBL
WHAT ...?
TRMBL
SOMEONE IN THIS TOWN DARES TO GET BETWEEN ME AND MY FUN?!!

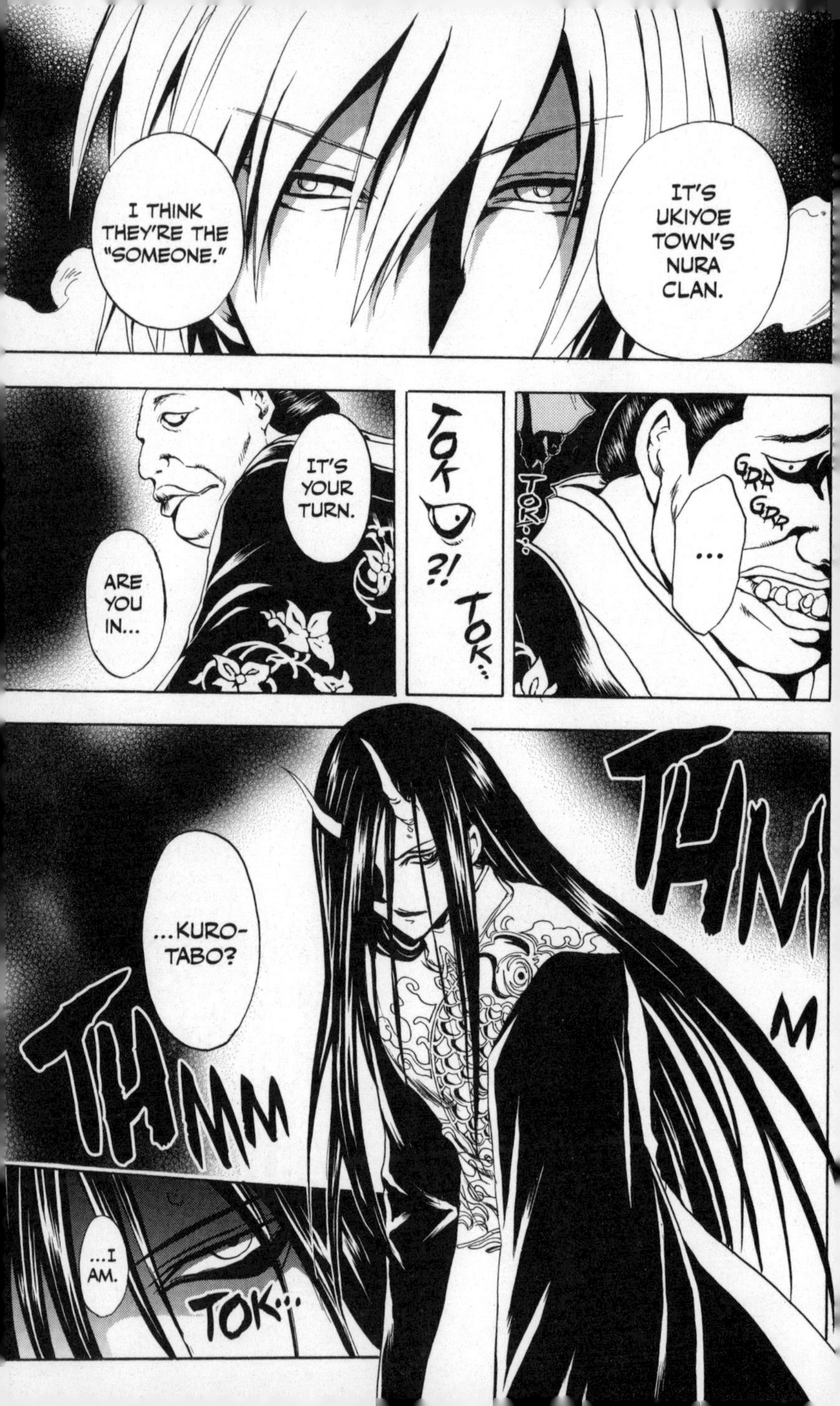

IT'S UKIYOE TOWN'S NURA CLAN.
I THINK THEY'RE THE "SOMEONE."
GRR GRR GRR
...
TOK TOK
TOK
?!
TOK...
IT'S YOUR TURN.
ARE YOU IN...
THMM
...KURO-TABO?
THMM
...I AM.
TOK...

NURA: RISE OF THE YOKAI CLAN

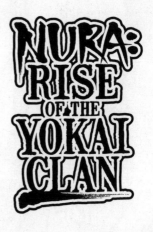

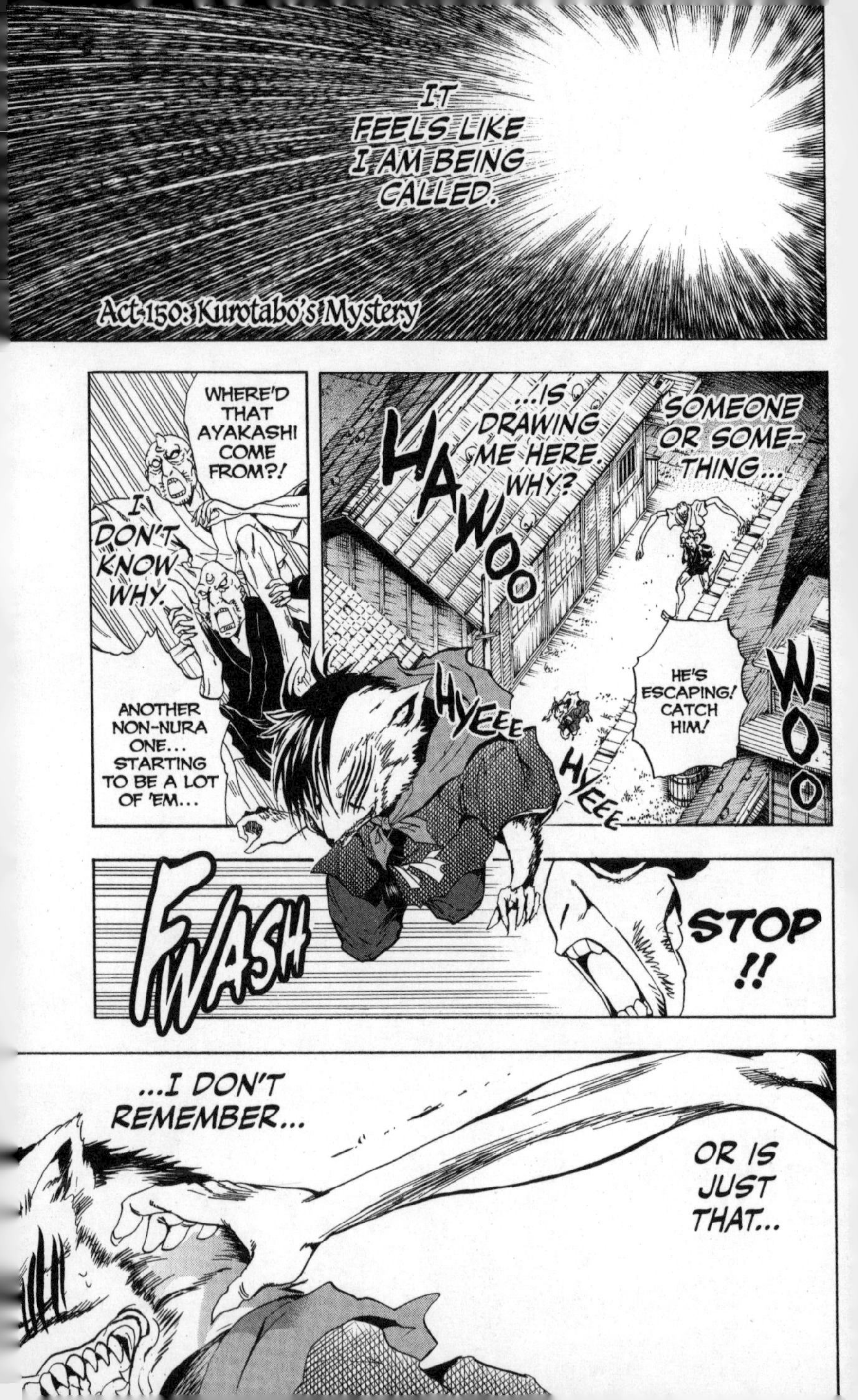
IT FEELS LIKE I AM BEING CALLED.
Act 150: Kurotabo's Mystery
SOMEONE OR SOME-THING...
...IS DRAWING ME HERE. WHY?
HAWOO
WOO
HE'S ESCAPING! CATCH HIM!
HYEEE
HYEEE
WHERE'D THAT AYAKASHI COME FROM?!
I DON'T KNOW WHY.
ANOTHER NON-NURA ONE... STARTING TO BE A LOT OF 'EM...
STOP !!
FWASH
OR IS JUST THAT...
...I DON'T REMEMBER...

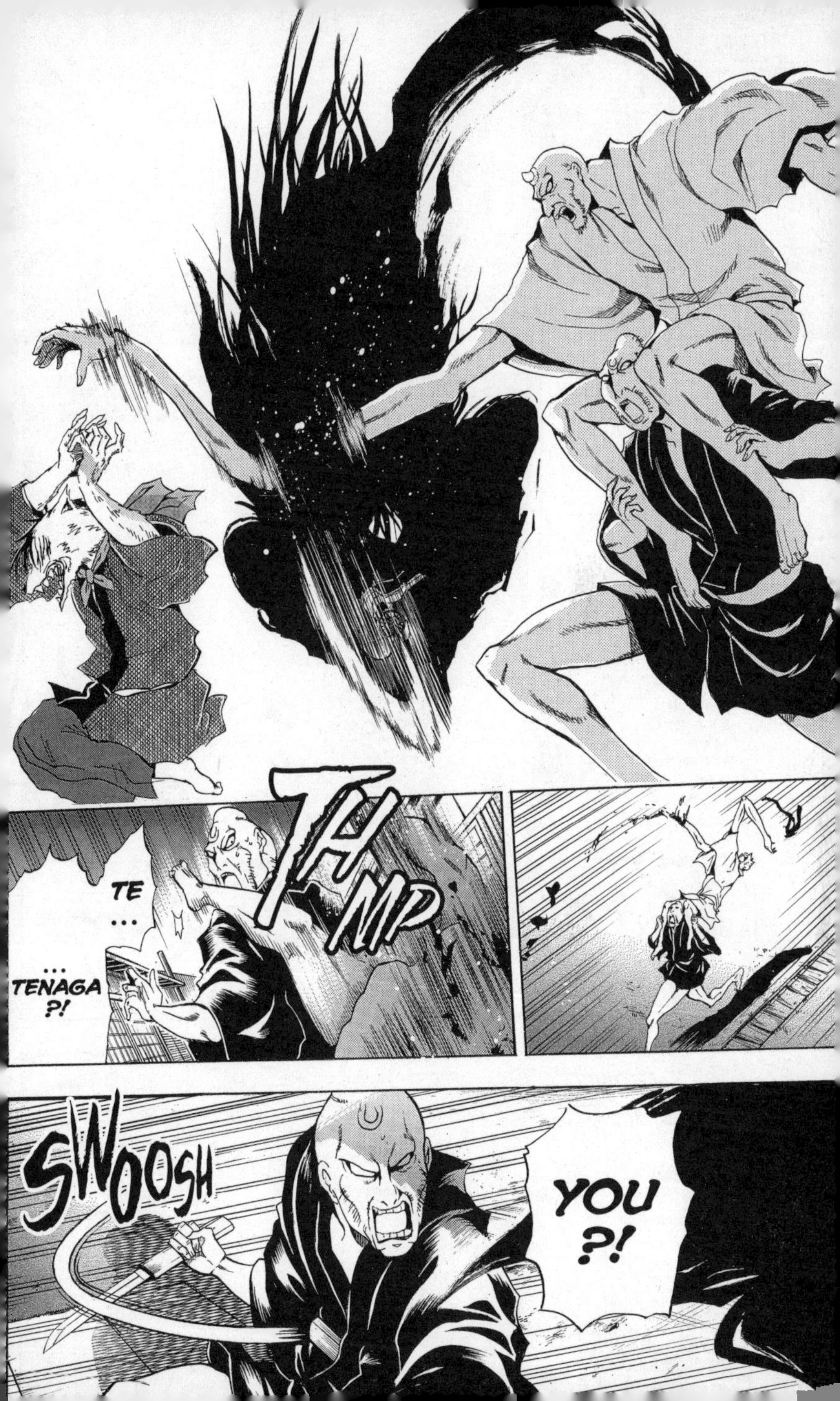
THMP
TE...
...TENAGA?!
YOU?!
SWOOSH

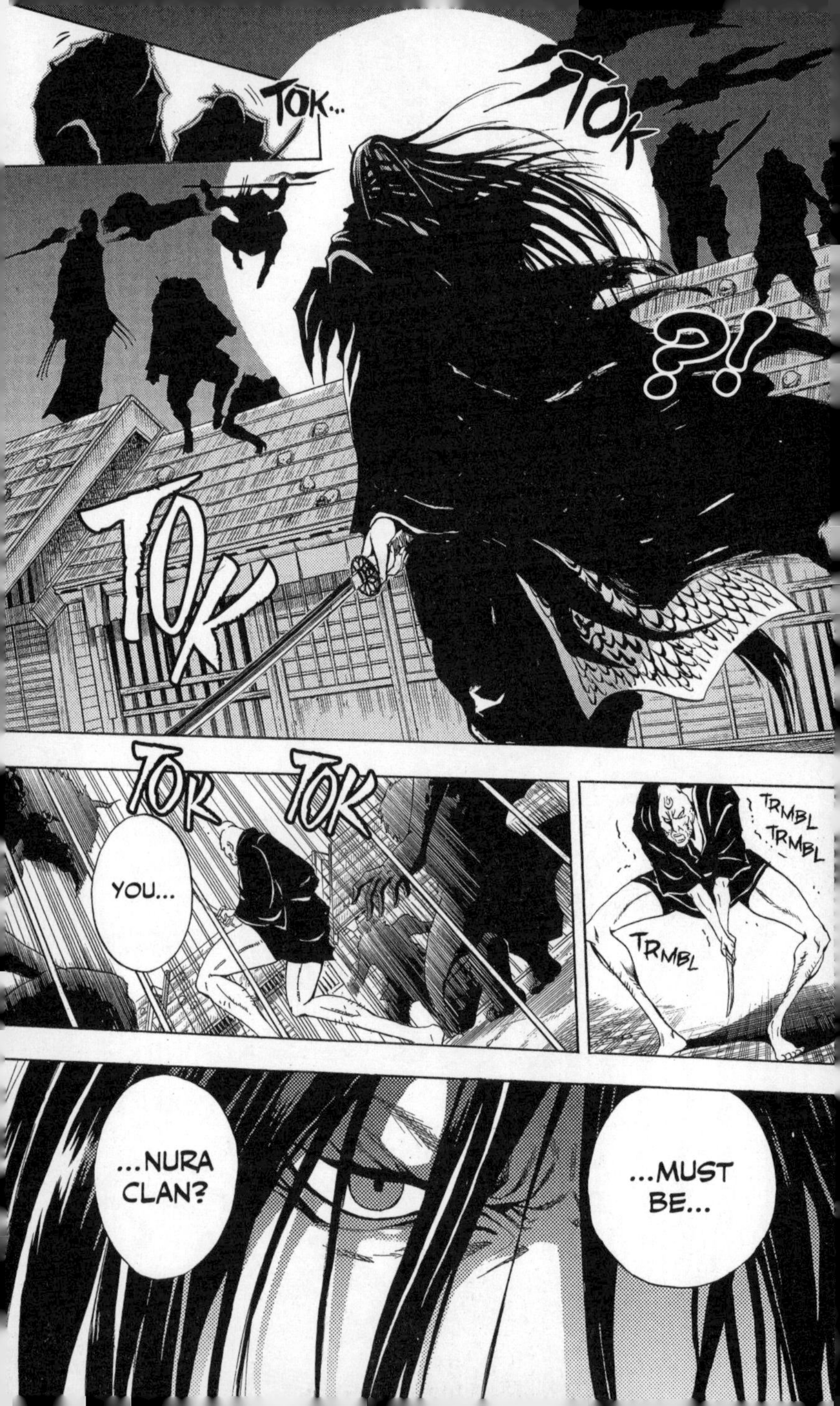
TOK
TŌK...
?!
TOK
TRMBL
TRMBL
TRMBL
TOK TOK
YOU...
...MUST BE...
...NURA CLAN?

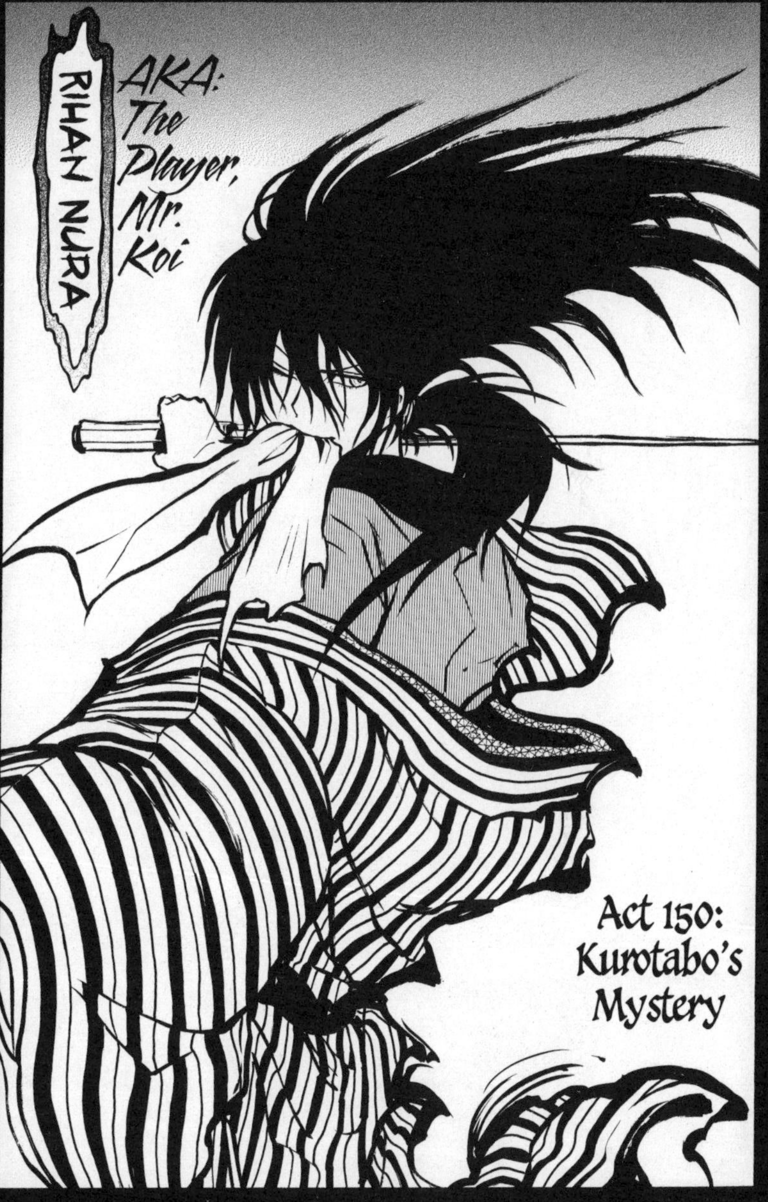
RIHAN NURA
AKA: The Player, Mr. Koi
Act 150: Kurotabo's Mystery

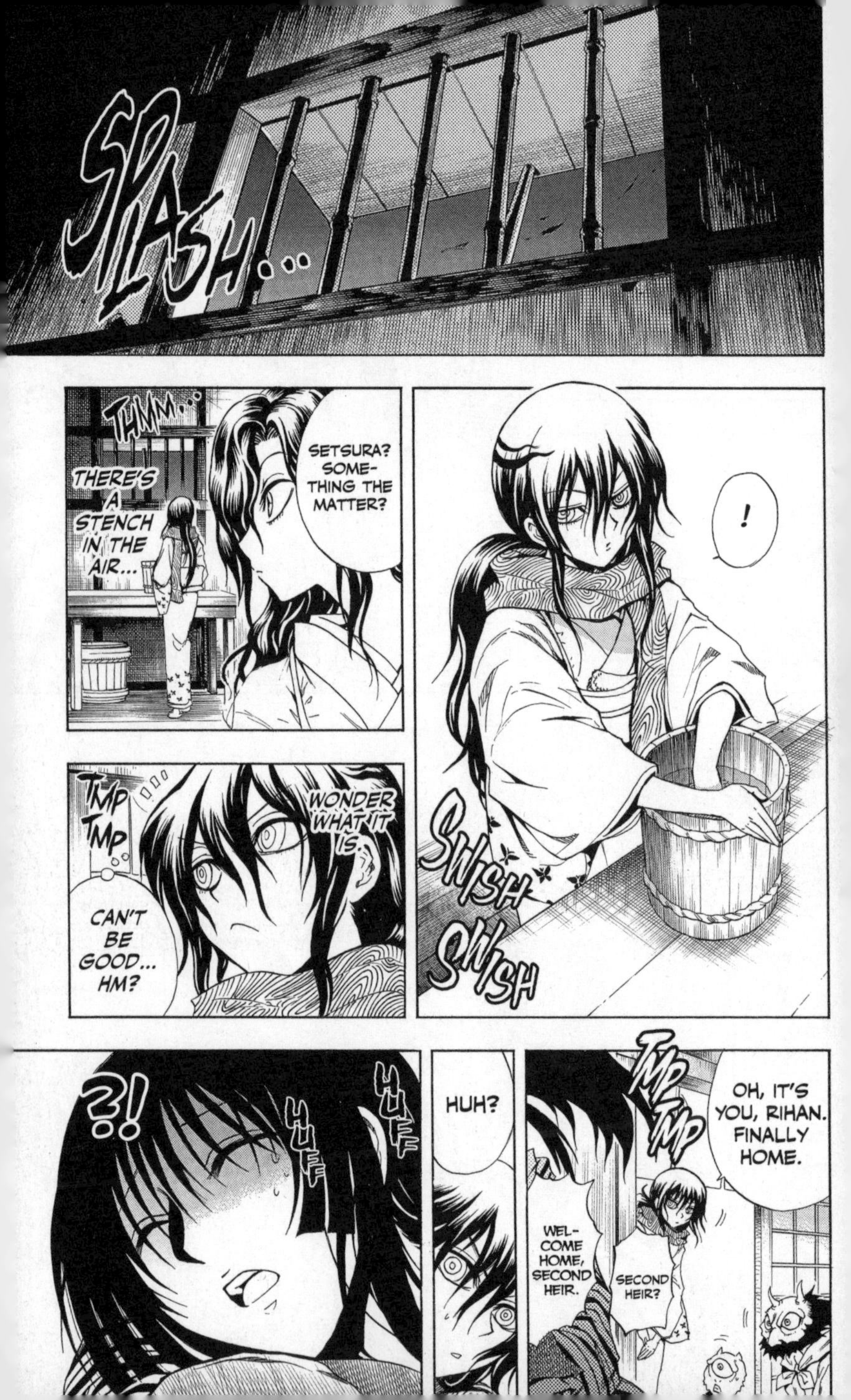
SPLASH...
!
SWISH
SWISH
SETSURA? SOMETHING THE MATTER?
THMM...
THERE'S A STENCH IN THE AIR...
WONDER WHAT IT IS.
TMP TMP
CAN'T BE GOOD... HM?
OH, IT'S YOU, RIHAN. FINALLY HOME.
TMP TMP
SECOND HEIR?
WELCOME HOME, SECOND HEIR.
HUH?
HUFF
HUFF
?!

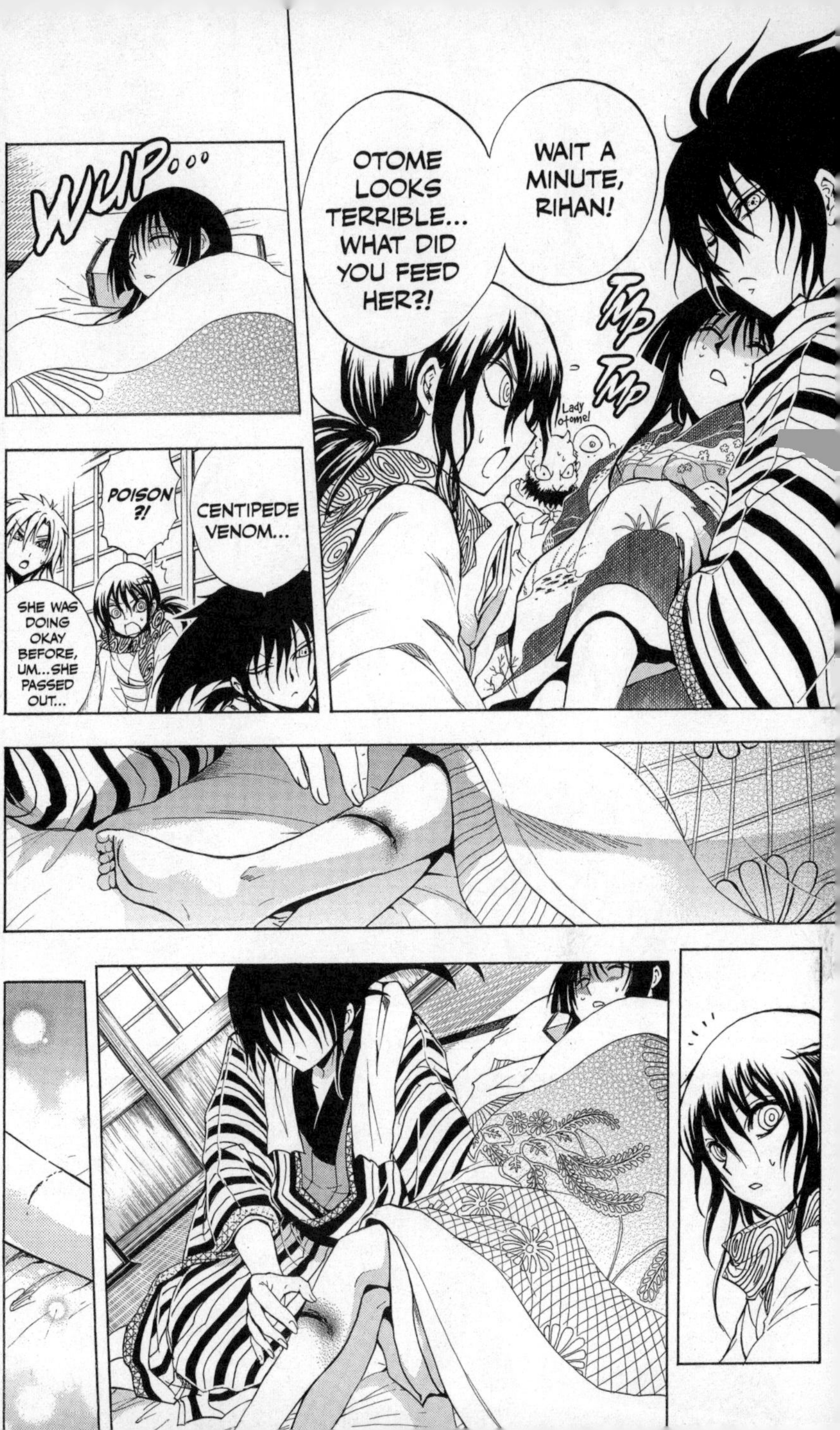
WAIT A MINUTE, RIHAN!
OTOME LOOKS TERRIBLE... WHAT DID YOU FEED HER?!
TMP TMP
Lady otome!
WUP
CENTIPEDE VENOM...
POISON?!
SHE WAS DOING OKAY BEFORE, UM...SHE PASSED OUT...

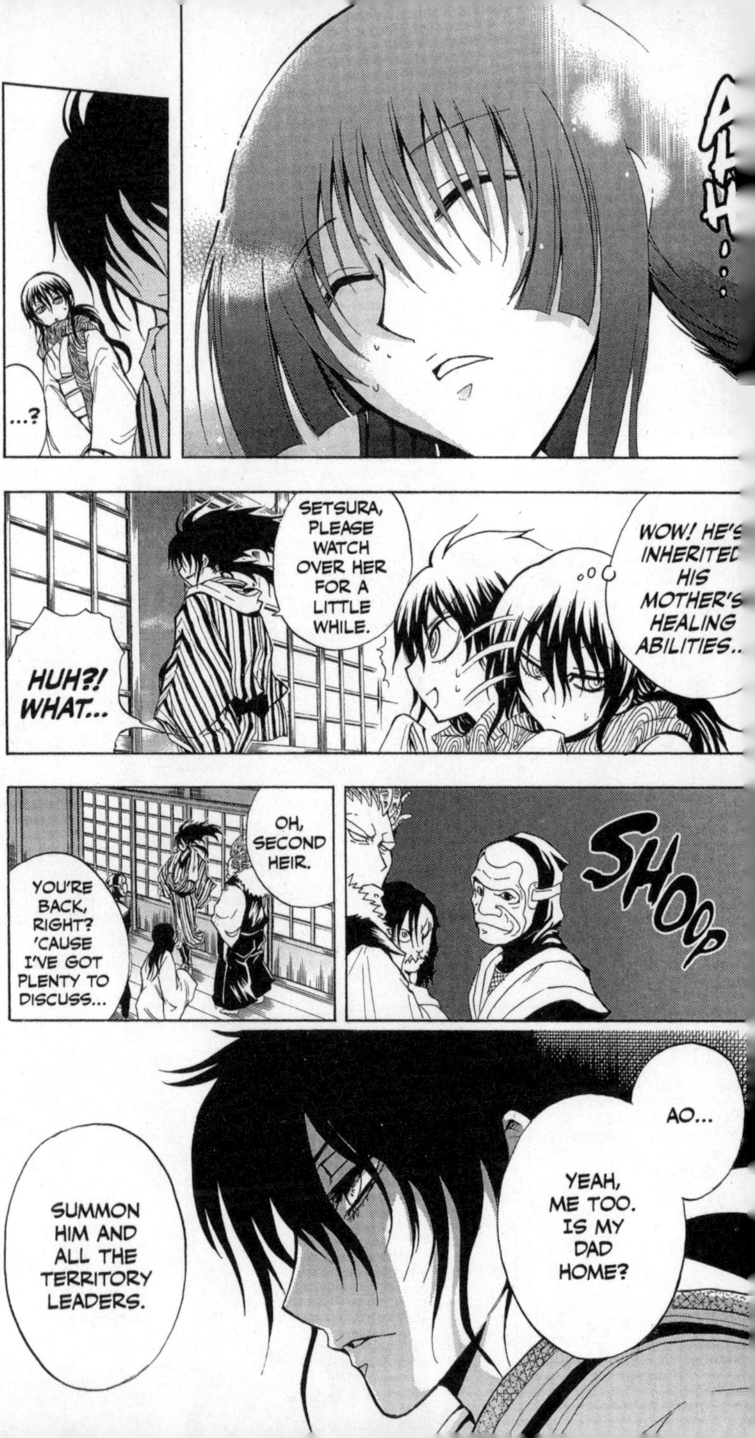
AHH...
...?
WOW! HE'S INHERITED HIS MOTHER'S HEALING ABILITIES...
SETSURA, PLEASE WATCH OVER HER FOR A LITTLE WHILE.
HUH?! WHAT...
SHOOP
OH, SECOND HEIR.
YOU'RE BACK, RIGHT? 'CAUSE I'VE GOT PLENTY TO DISCUSS...
AO...
YEAH, ME TOO. IS MY DAD HOME?
SUMMON HIM AND ALL THE TERRITORY LEADERS.

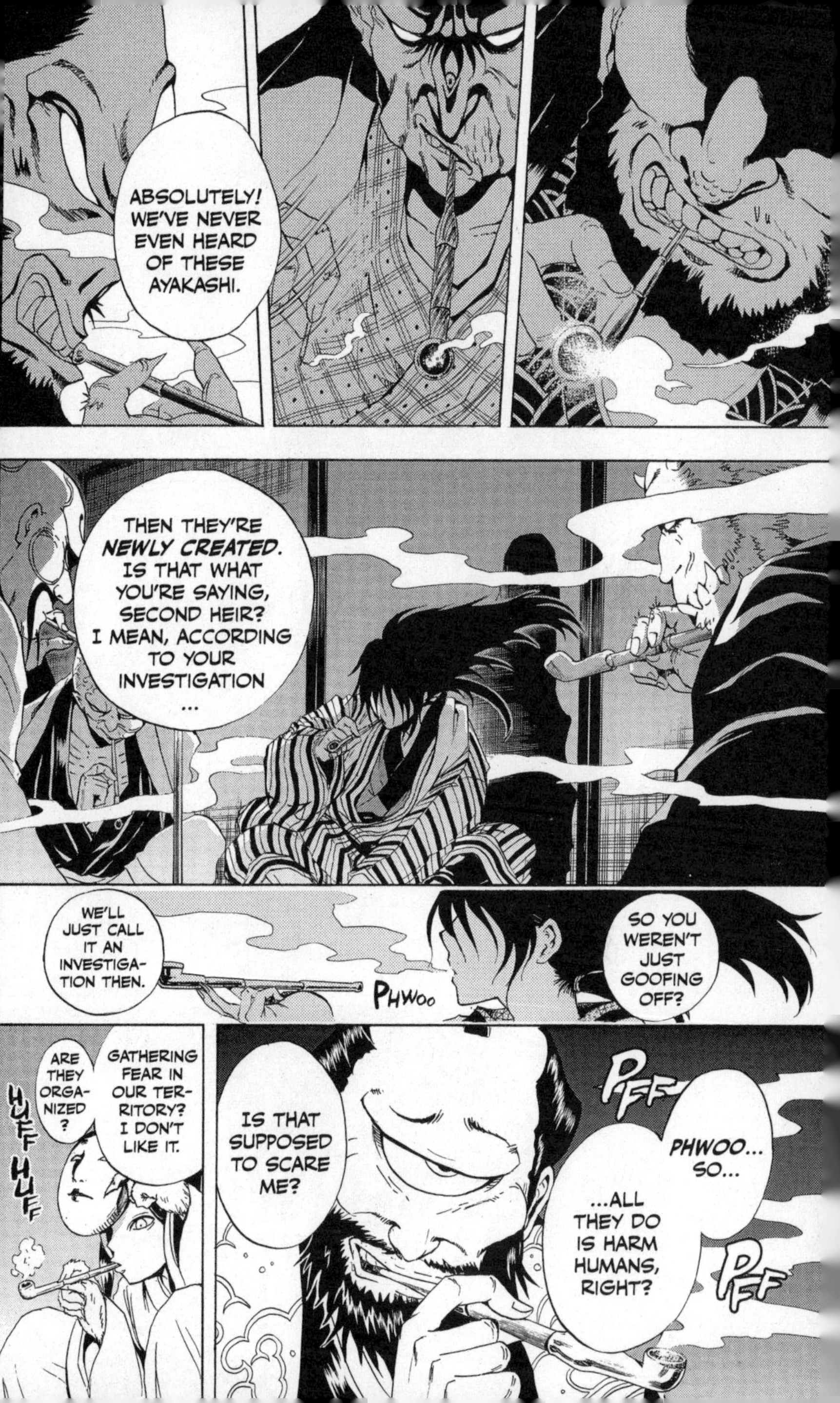
ABSOLUTELY! WE'VE NEVER EVEN HEARD OF THESE AYAKASHI.
THEN THEY'RE *NEWLY CREATED*. IS THAT WHAT YOU'RE SAYING, SECOND HEIR? I MEAN, ACCORDING TO YOUR INVESTIGATION ...
SO YOU WEREN'T JUST GOOFING OFF?
PHWOO
WE'LL JUST CALL IT AN INVESTIGA-TION THEN.
PFF
PHWOO... SO...
...ALL THEY DO IS HARM HUMANS, RIGHT?
PFF
IS THAT SUPPOSED TO SCARE ME?
GATHERING FEAR IN OUR TER-RITORY? I DON'T LIKE IT.
ARE THEY ORGA-NIZED?
HUFF HUFF

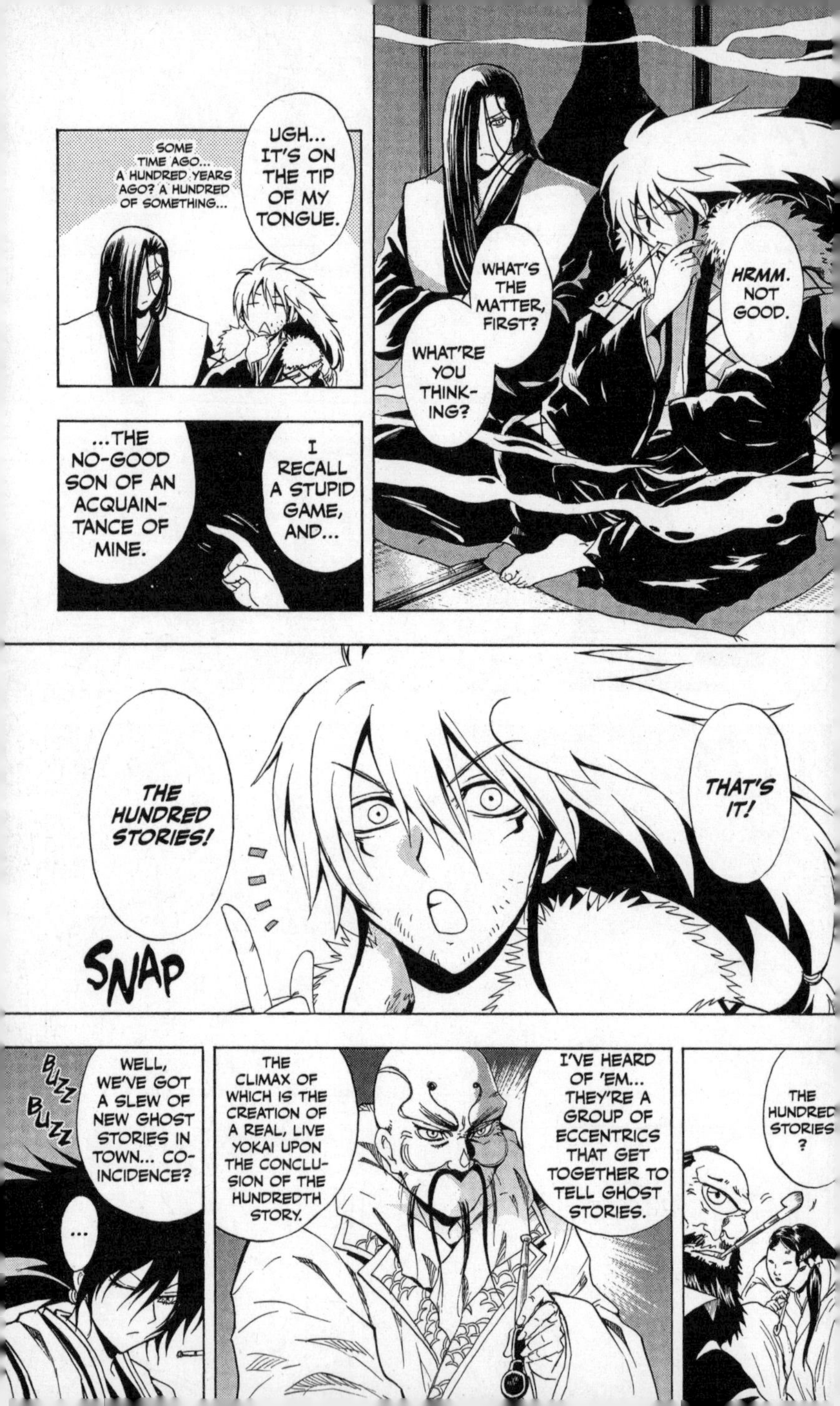
HRMM. NOT GOOD.
WHAT'S THE MATTER, FIRST?
WHAT'RE YOU THINKING?
UGH... IT'S ON THE TIP OF MY TONGUE.
SOME TIME AGO... A HUNDRED YEARS AGO? A HUNDRED OF SOMETHING...
I RECALL A STUPID GAME, AND...
...THE NO-GOOD SON OF AN ACQUAINTANCE OF MINE.
THAT'S IT!
THE HUNDRED STORIES!
SNAP
THE HUNDRED STORIES?
I'VE HEARD OF 'EM... THEY'RE A GROUP OF ECCENTRICS THAT GET TOGETHER TO TELL GHOST STORIES.
THE CLIMAX OF WHICH IS THE CREATION OF A REAL, LIVE YOKAI UPON THE CONCLUSION OF THE HUNDREDTH STORY.
WELL, WE'VE GOT A SLEW OF NEW GHOST STORIES IN TOWN... CO-INCIDENCE?
BUZZ
BUZZ
...

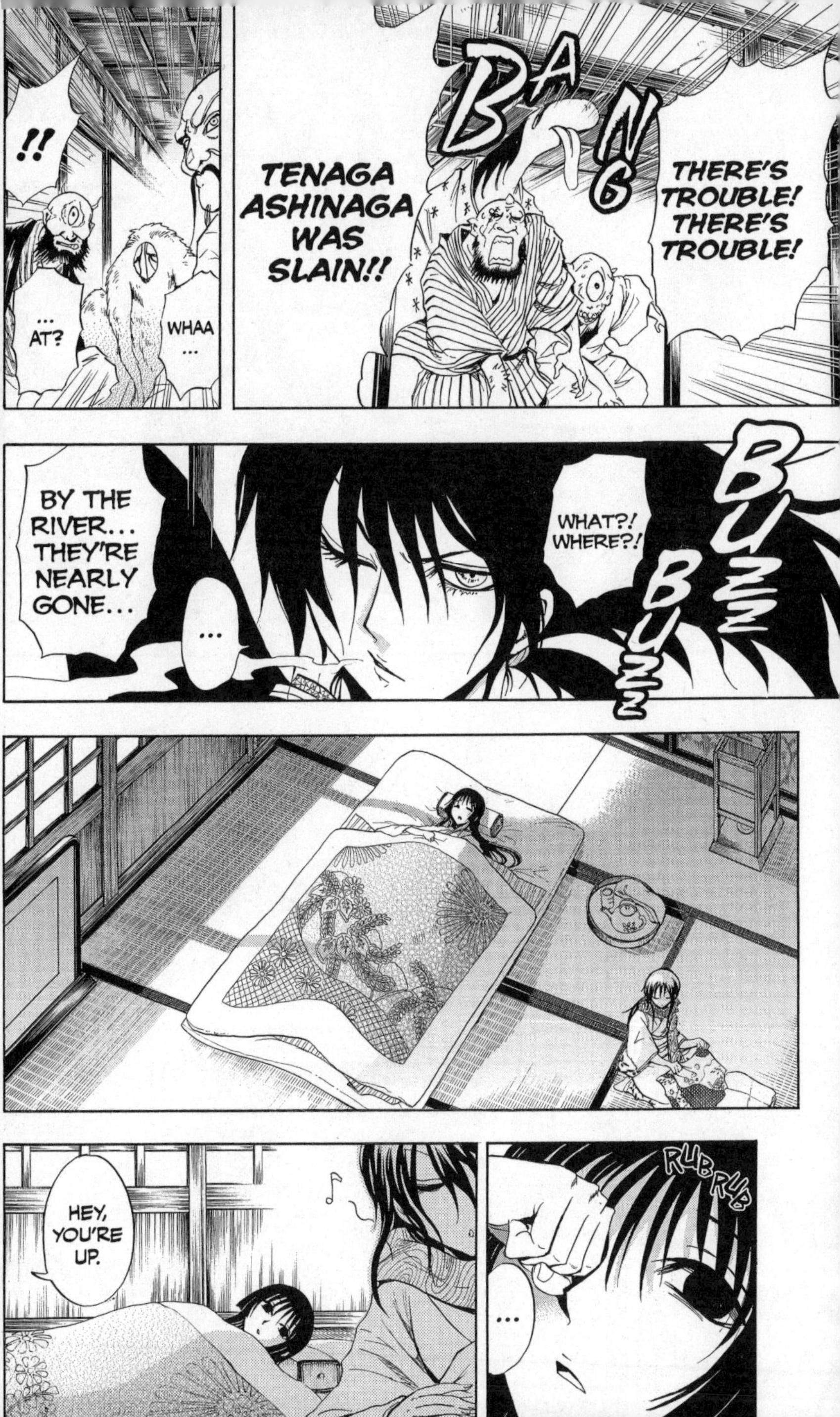
BANG
THERE'S TROUBLE! THERE'S TROUBLE!
TENAGA ASHINAGA WAS SLAIN!!
!!
WHAA...
...AT?
BUZZ
BUZZ
WHAT?! WHERE?!
...
BY THE RIVER... THEY'RE NEARLY GONE...
RUB RUB
...
♪
HEY, YOU'RE UP.

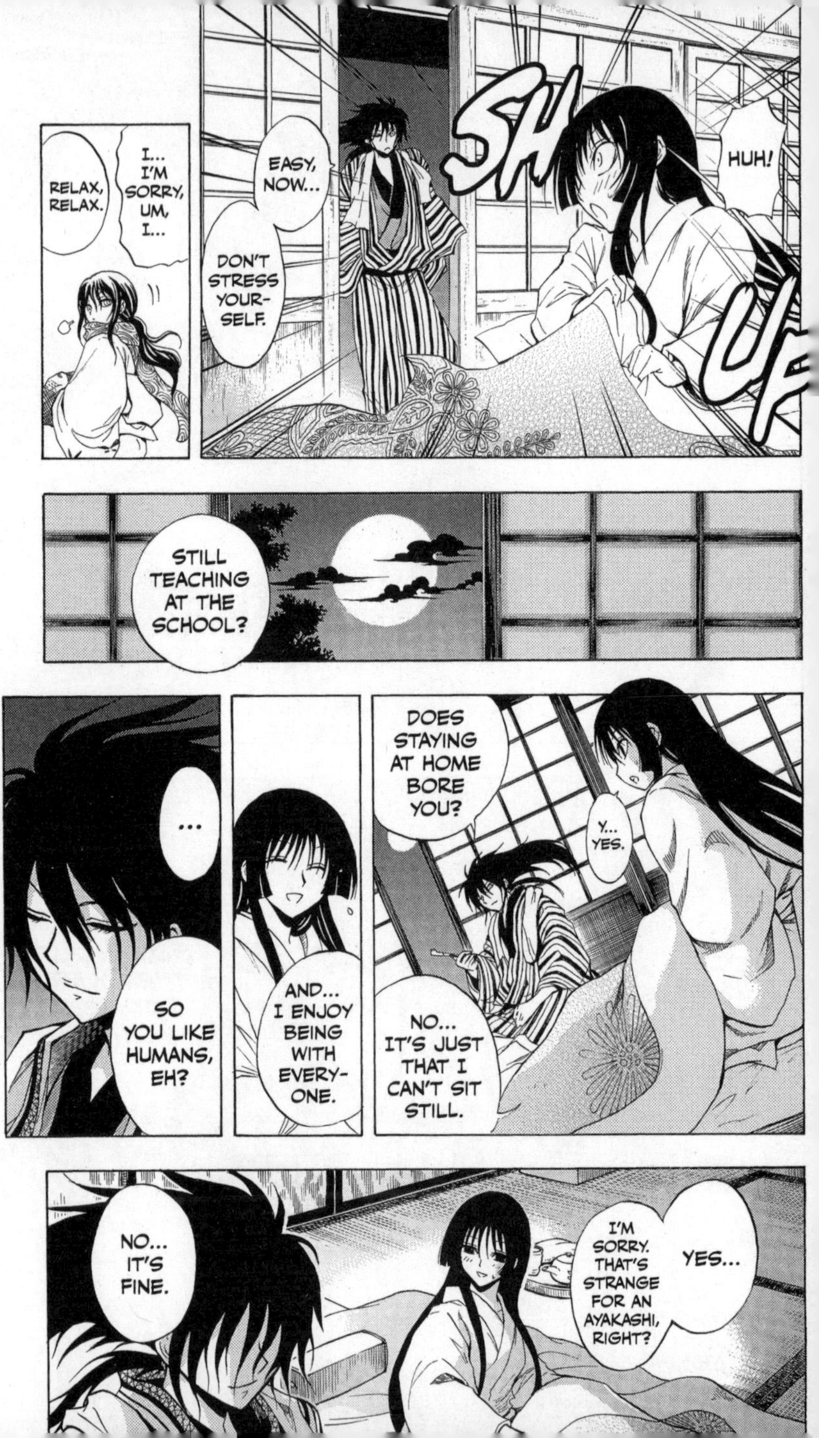

SH
HUH!
EASY, NOW...
DON'T STRESS YOUR-SELF.
I... I'M SORRY, UM, I...
RELAX, RELAX.
STILL TEACHING AT THE SCHOOL?
DOES STAYING AT HOME BORE YOU?
Y... YES.
NO... IT'S JUST THAT I CAN'T SIT STILL.
AND... I ENJOY BEING WITH EVERY-ONE.
...
SO YOU LIKE HUMANS, EH?
YES...
I'M SORRY. THAT'S STRANGE FOR AN AYAKASHI, RIGHT?
NO... IT'S FINE.

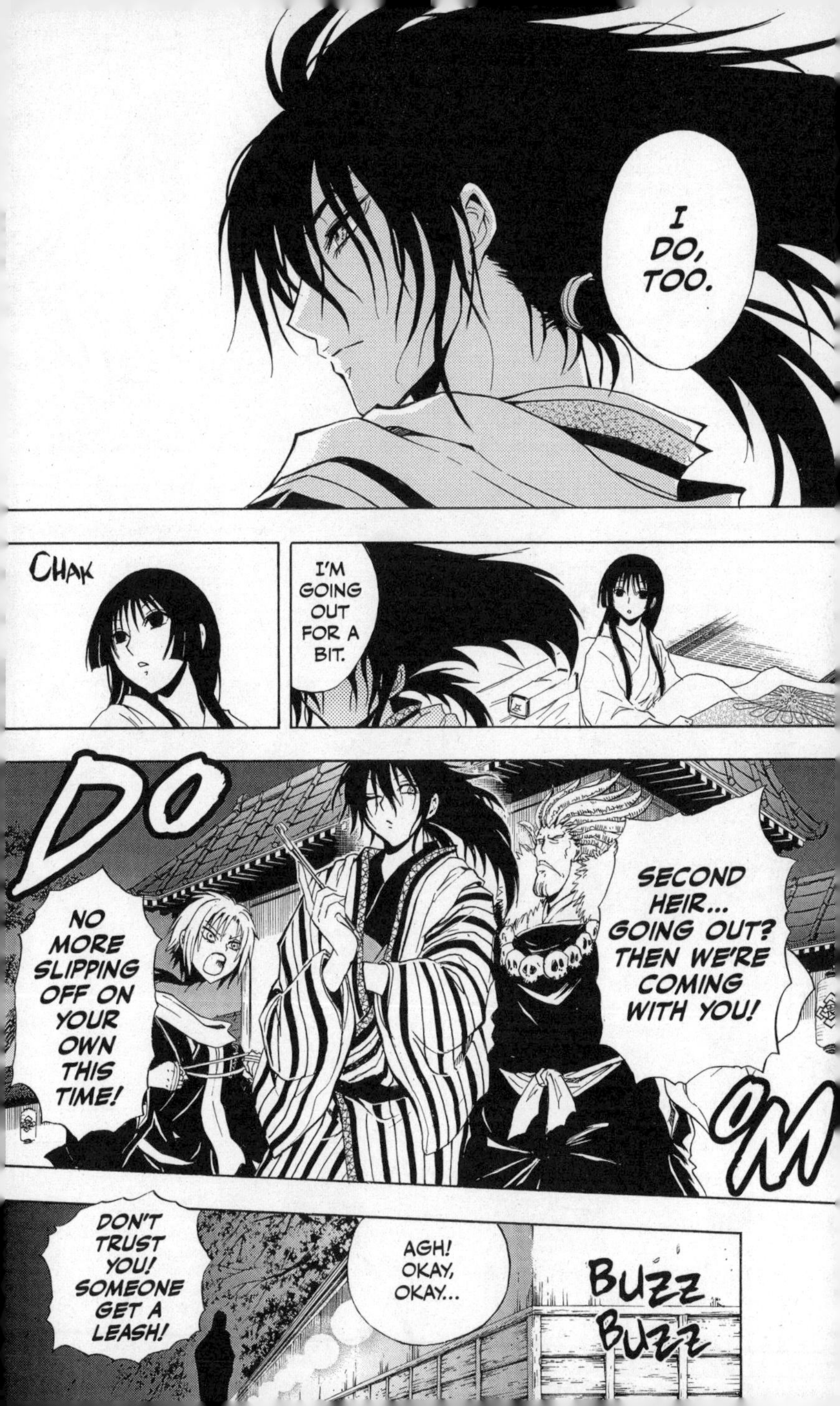
I DO, TOO.
I'M GOING OUT FOR A BIT.
CHAK
DO
SECOND HEIR... GOING OUT? THEN WE'RE COMING WITH YOU!
NO MORE SLIPPING OFF ON YOUR OWN THIS TIME!
OM
BUZZ BUZZ
AGH! OKAY, OKAY...
DON'T TRUST YOU! SOMEONE GET A LEASH!

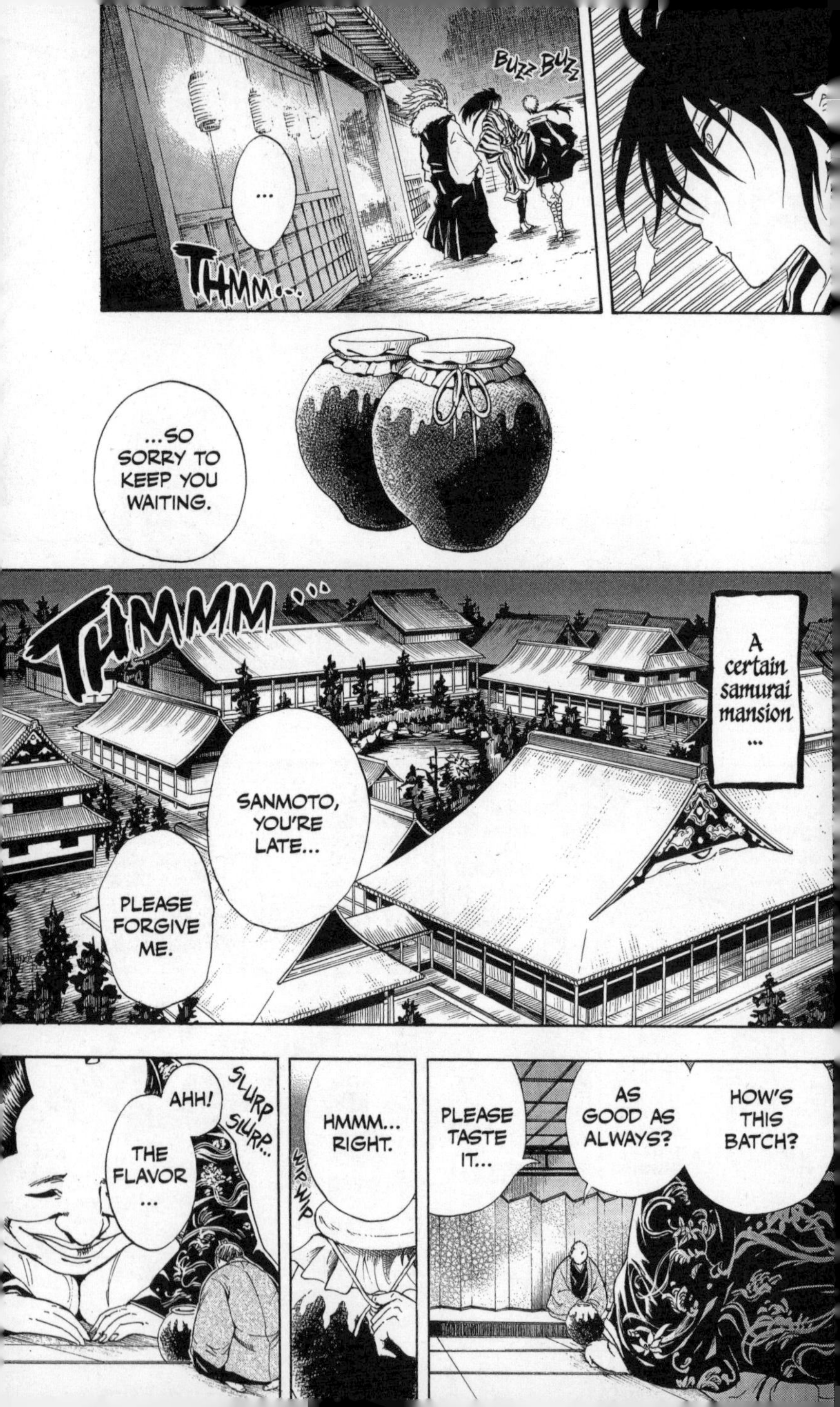
BUZZ BUZZ
...
THMM...
...SO SORRY TO KEEP YOU WAITING.
A certain samurai mansion...
THMMM...
SANMOTO, YOU'RE LATE...
PLEASE FORGIVE ME.
HOW'S THIS BATCH?
AS GOOD AS ALWAYS?
PLEASE TASTE IT...
HMMM... RIGHT.
WIP WIP
SLURP SLURP...
AHH!
THE FLAVOR...

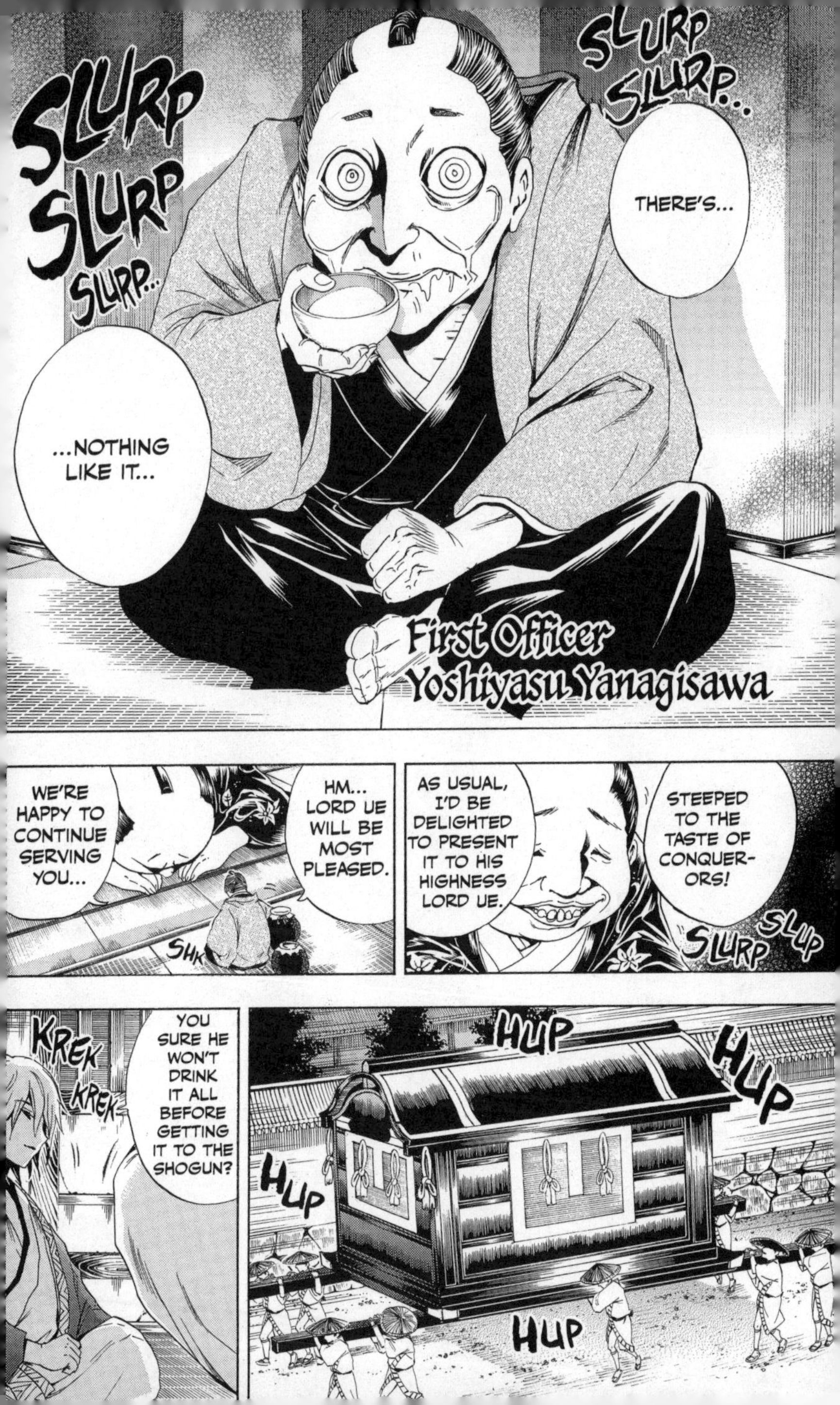
SLURP SLURP...
THERE'S...
SLURP SLURP SLURP...
...NOTHING LIKE IT...
First Officer Yoshiyasu Yanagisawa
STEEPED TO THE TASTE OF CONQUER-ORS!
AS USUAL, I'D BE DELIGHTED TO PRESENT IT TO HIS HIGHNESS LORD UE.
SLURP SLUP
HM... LORD UE WILL BE MOST PLEASED.
WE'RE HAPPY TO CONTINUE SERVING YOU...
SHK
HUP HUP
HUP
HUP
KREK KREK
YOU SURE HE WON'T DRINK IT ALL BEFORE GETTING IT TO THE SHOGUN?

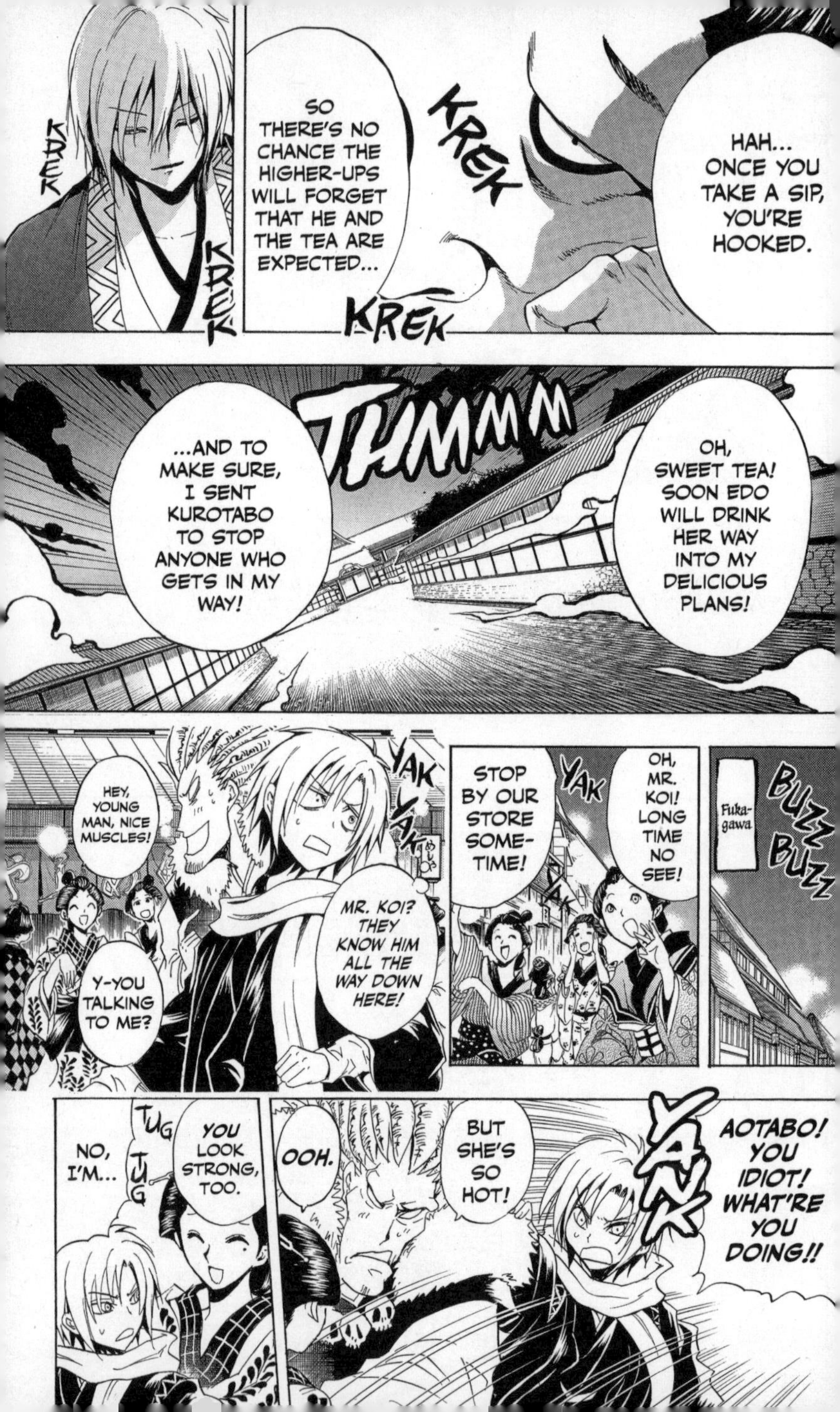

HAH... ONCE YOU TAKE A SIP, YOU'RE HOOKED.
KREK
SO THERE'S NO CHANCE THE HIGHER-UPS WILL FORGET THAT HE AND THE TEA ARE EXPECTED...
KREK
KREK
KREK
OH, SWEET TEA! SOON EDO WILL DRINK HER WAY INTO MY DELICIOUS PLANS!
THMMM
...AND TO MAKE SURE, I SENT KUROTABO TO STOP ANYONE WHO GETS IN MY WAY!
Fukagawa
BUZZ BUZZ
OH, MR. KOI! LONG TIME NO SEE!
YAK
STOP BY OUR STORE SOMETIME!
YAK
YAK YAK
HEY, YOUNG MAN, NICE MUSCLES!
MR. KOI? THEY KNOW HIM ALL THE WAY DOWN HERE!
Y-YOU TALKING TO ME?
AOTABO! YOU IDIOT! WHAT'RE YOU DOING!!
YANK
BUT SHE'S SO HOT!
OOH.
YOU LOOK STRONG, TOO.
TUG TUG
NO, I'M...

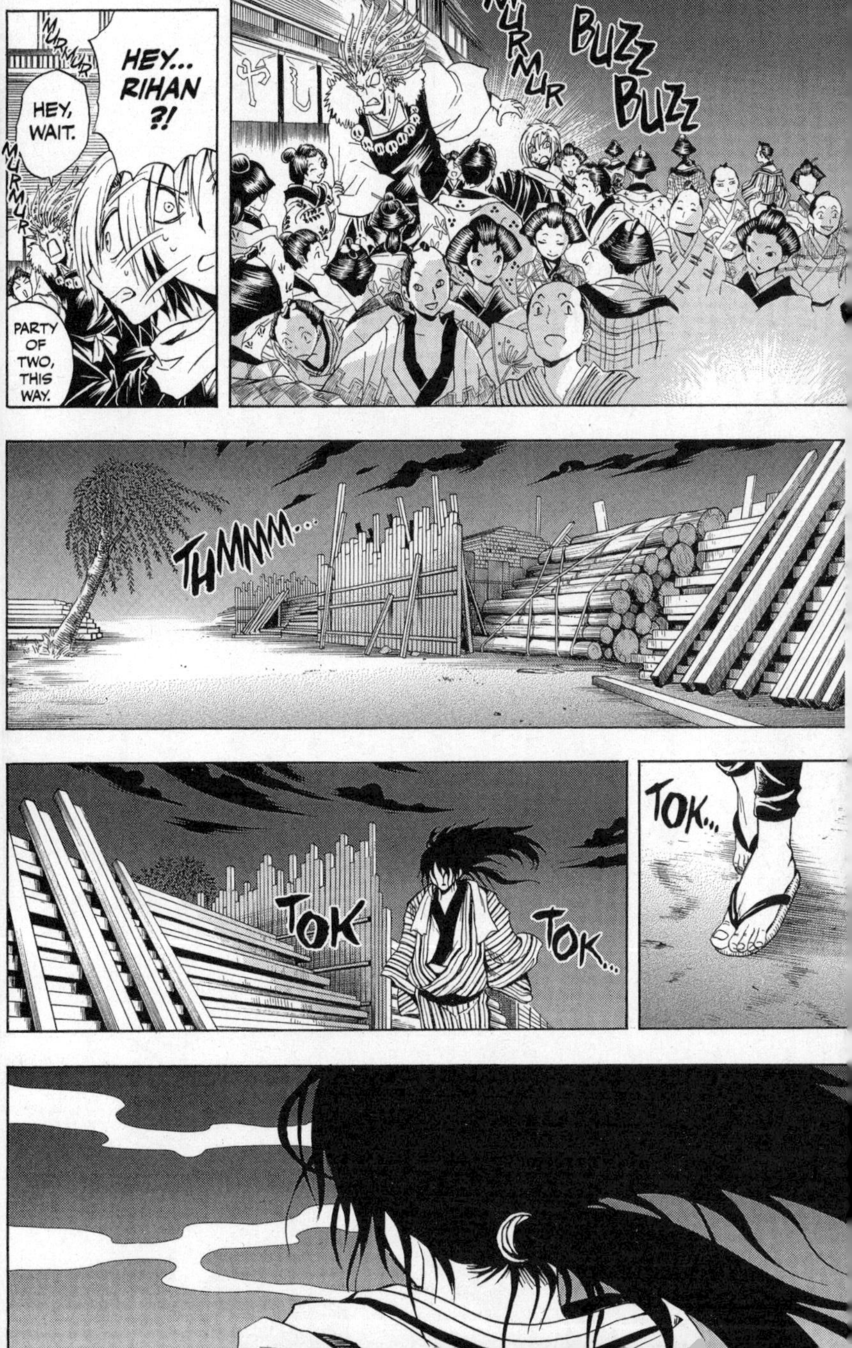
MURMUR
BUZZ BUZZ
MURMUR
HEY... RIHAN ?!
HEY, WAIT.
MURMUR
PARTY OF TWO, THIS WAY.
THMMM...
TOK...
TOK
TOK...

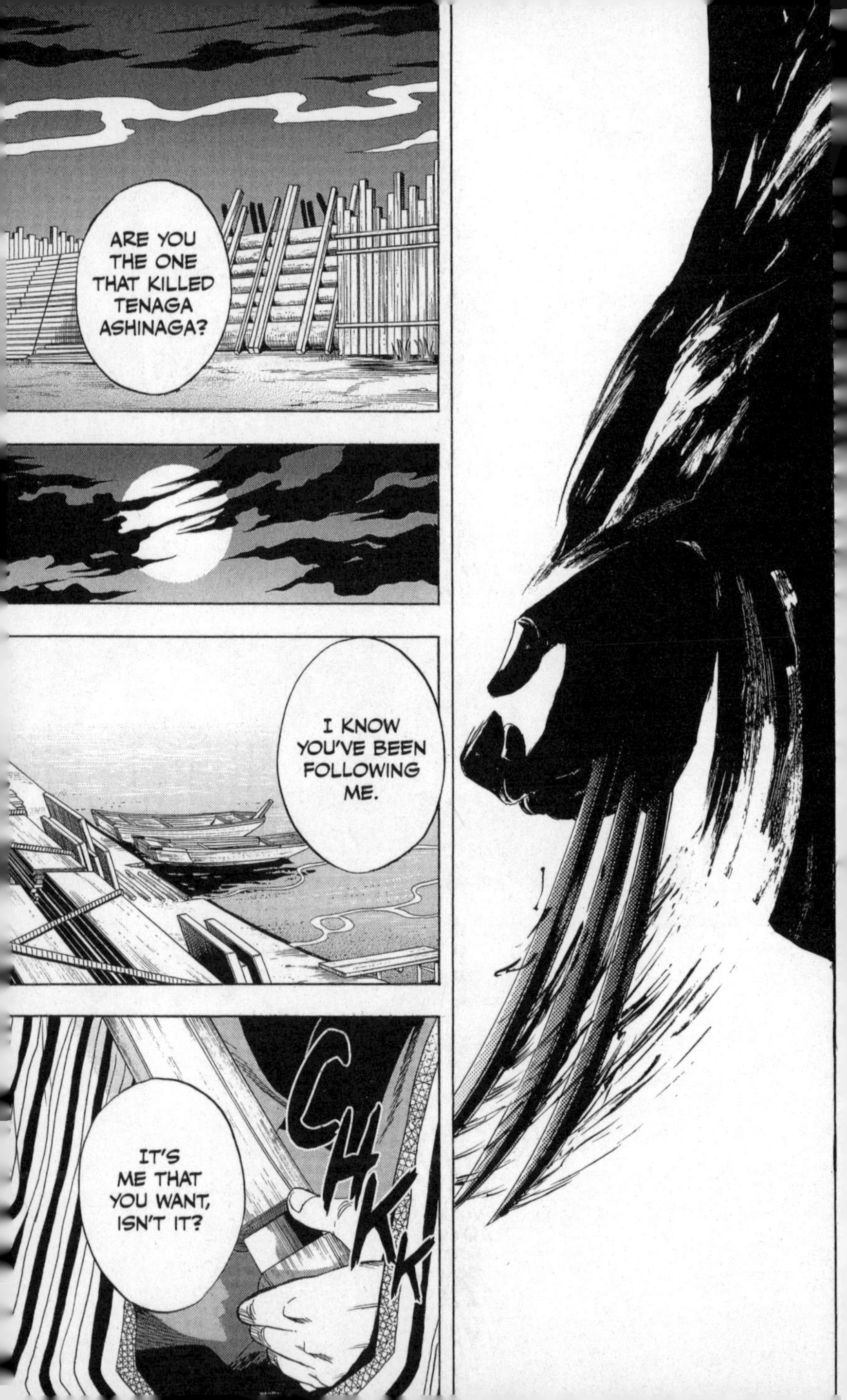
ARE YOU THE ONE THAT KILLED TENAGA ASHINAGA?
I KNOW YOU'VE BEEN FOLLOWING ME.
CHKK
IT'S ME THAT YOU WANT, ISN'T IT?

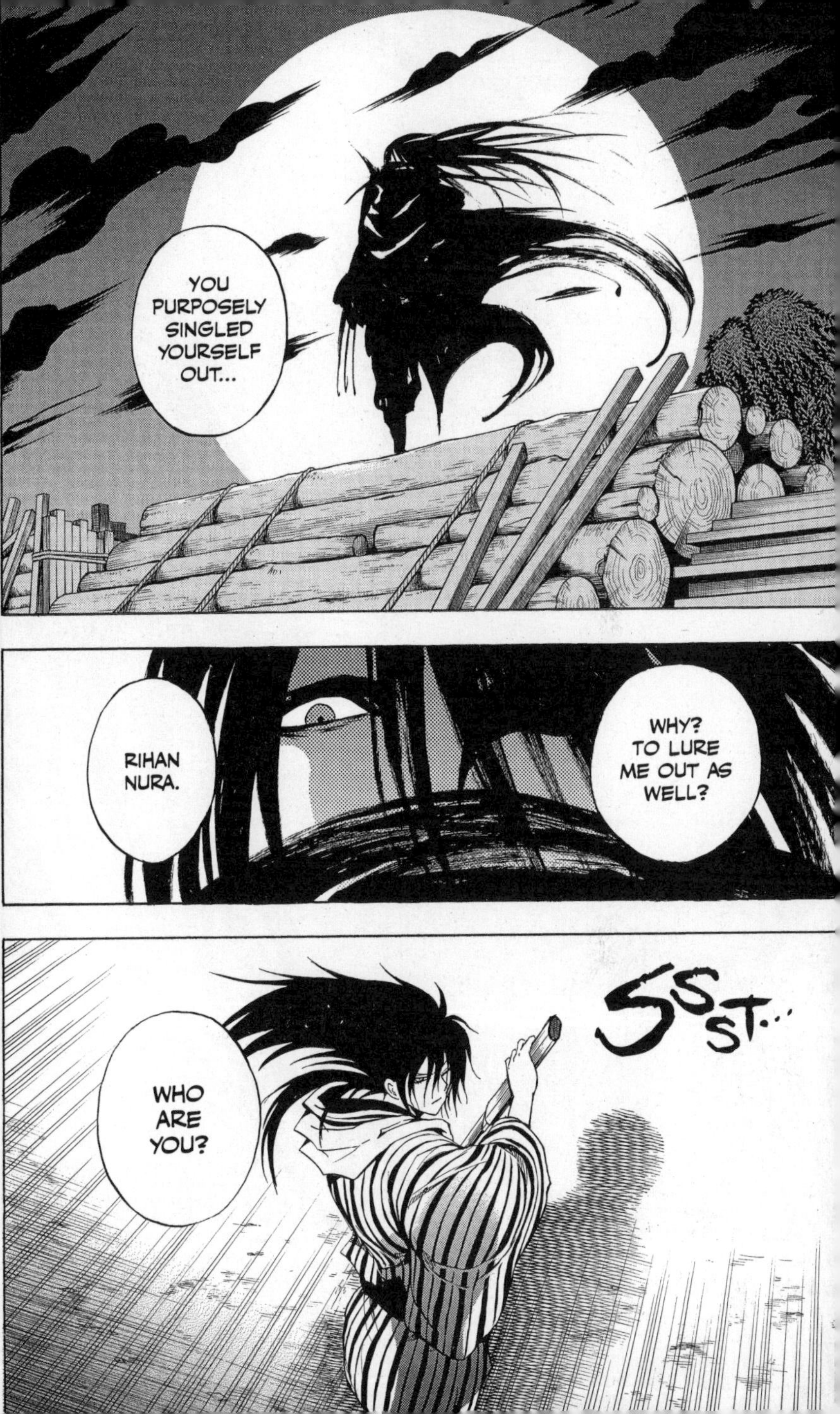
YOU PURPOSELY SINGLED YOURSELF OUT...
WHY? TO LURE ME OUT AS WELL?
RIHAN NURA.
SSST...
WHO ARE YOU?

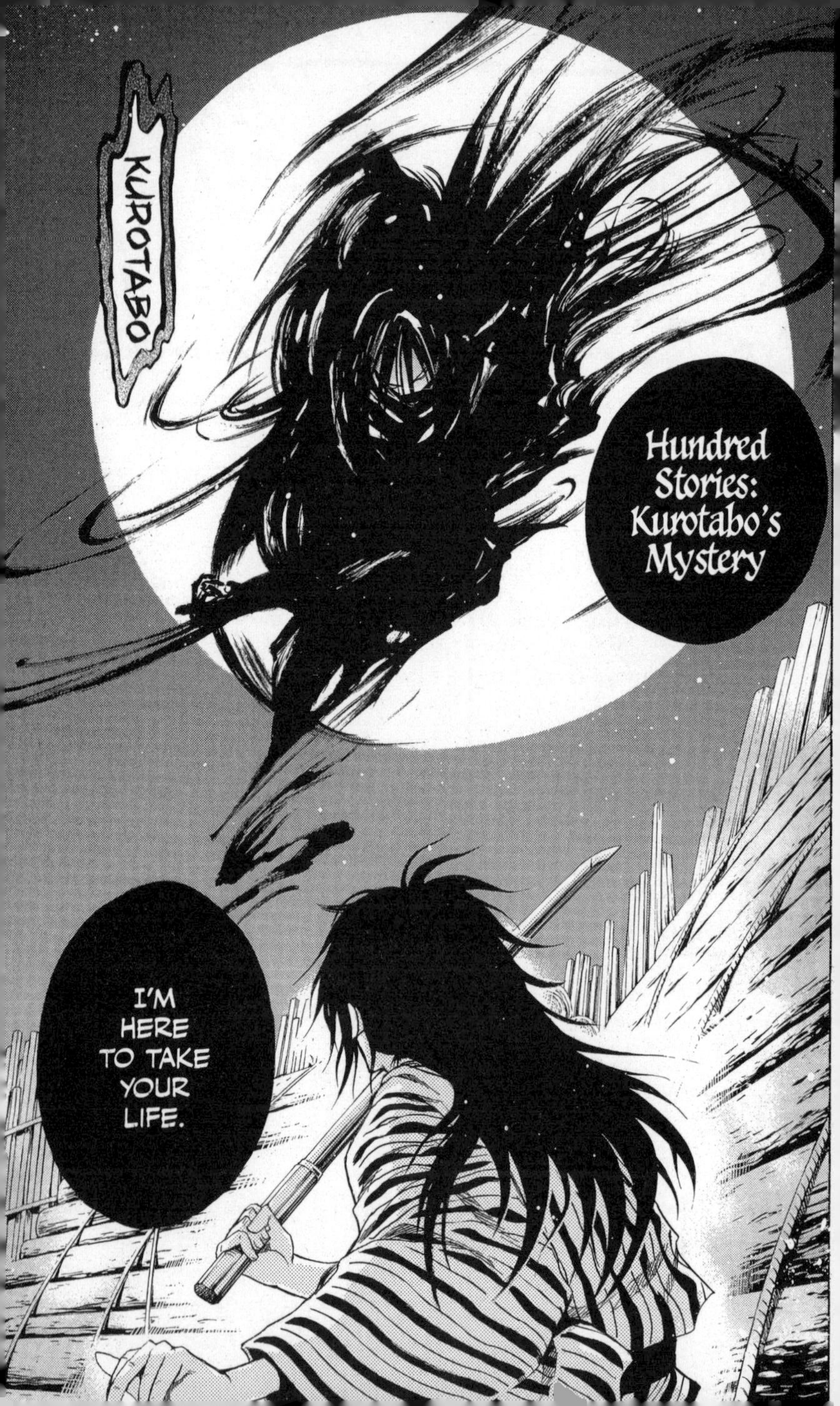
KUROTABO
Hundred Stories: Kurotabo's Mystery
I'M HERE TO TAKE YOUR LIFE.

KIYOTSUGU'S YOKAI BRAIN

#17 THE "JUST LOOK AT THOSE MUSCLES" SPECIAL

Q: WHY IS AMEZO SO MUSCULAR? ALSO, IS AMEZO NAKED? –K, CHIBA PREFECTURE

AMEZO: NAKED ON THE TOP!! AND DARNED PROUD OF THESE WELL-TRAINED MUSCLES!

SHIMA: CAN'T GET ANY CLOTHES ON OVER THAT SHELL OF YOURS, EH?

Q: WHEN NIGHT COMES AND RIKUO TRANSFORMS, HE HAS A SIX-PACK! DOES THE DAYTIME RIKUO ALSO HAVE A SIX-PACK? –YOKAI NANAHENGE, OKINAWA PREFECTURE

URARA: UHM, NOT REALLY.

RIKUO: WHY IS TSURARA ANSWERING? YEAH... WELL, DURING THE DAY, MY ABS ARE PROBABLY ABOUT THE SAME AS ANY REGULAR MIDDLE-SCHOOLER'S ABS... HA HA HA...

SO, UM, TODAY IT'S ALL ABOUT MUSCLES, HUH...?

Q: QUESTION FOR LORD GYUKI!! (FROM VOLUME 15.) DO YOU REMEMBER WHEN YOU WERE DRUNK? –AHO GOD'S MESSENGER, TOKYO

GYUKI: I DON'T KNOW WHAT YOU'RE TALKING ABOUT...

Q: QUESTION FOR GOZUMARU!! YOU ALWAYS HAVE YOUR HAIR TIED UP, BUT HOW LONG IS IT IF YOU LET IT DOWN? I SURE WOULD LOVE TO SEE YOUR HAIR DOWN! –HANTSUKI NAKAJIMA, IBARAKI PREFECTURE

UMARU: HUHH? WHAT'S YOUR POINT? IT GETS IN THE WAY, SO I TIE IT BACK. ENOUGH SAID.

MEZUMARU: WHEN YOU LET YOUR HAIR DOWN YOU LOOK LIKE A GIRL!

GOZUMARU: GET A LIFE!! (PUNCH) THAT'S SIMPLY NOT FOR PUBLIC VIEW-ING!

Q: I WANT TO JOIN THE OSHU TONO FAMILY! I'LL DO ANY-THING! PLEASE LET ME IN! –BAKENEKO, KAGOSHIMA PREFECTURE

ITAKU: THE POWER OF FEAR KEEPS THE LAND OF TONO HIDDEN... WITHOUT ANYONE WHO KNOWS THE WAY, YOU'LL PROBABLY NEVER FIND IT.

REIRA: DON'T BE SO STRICT, ITAKU. BAKENEKO WANTS TO ENTER, SO IF HE COMES, WHY NOT LET HIM IN?

ITAKU: IT'S ALL ABOUT TRAINING HARD... YOU SURE YOU CAN HANDLE IT? IF, AND ONLY IF, YOU CAN SHOW US THE SAME ROCK-SOLID FEAR AS ANYONE HERE, THEN TONO WELCOMES YOU.

YUKARI: YOU'RE SO TOUGH... ITAKU, SO TOUGH.

ITAKU: ... (CLEARS HIS THROAT NER-VOUSLY.)

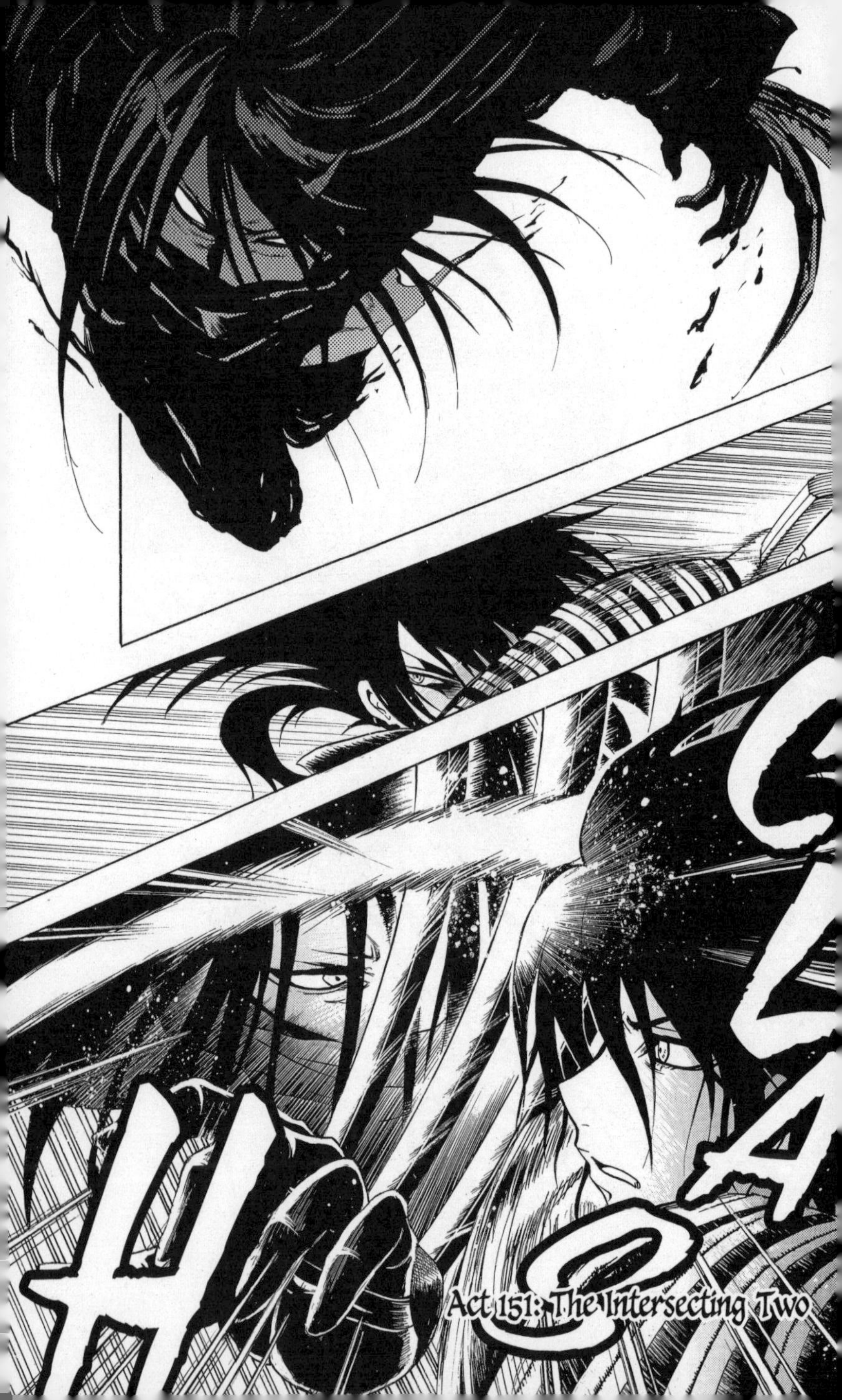
Act 151: The Intersecting Two

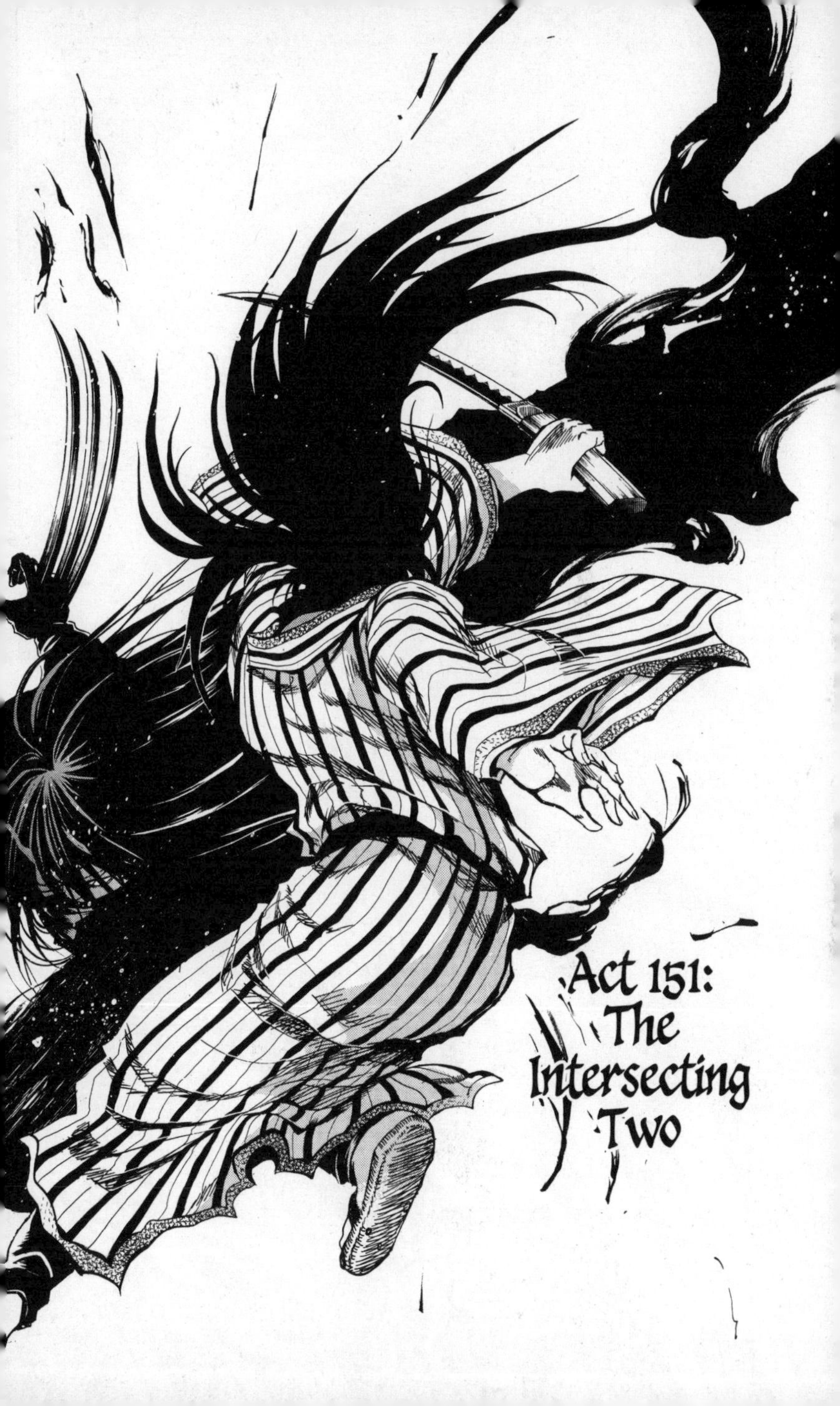
Act 151:
The Intersecting Two

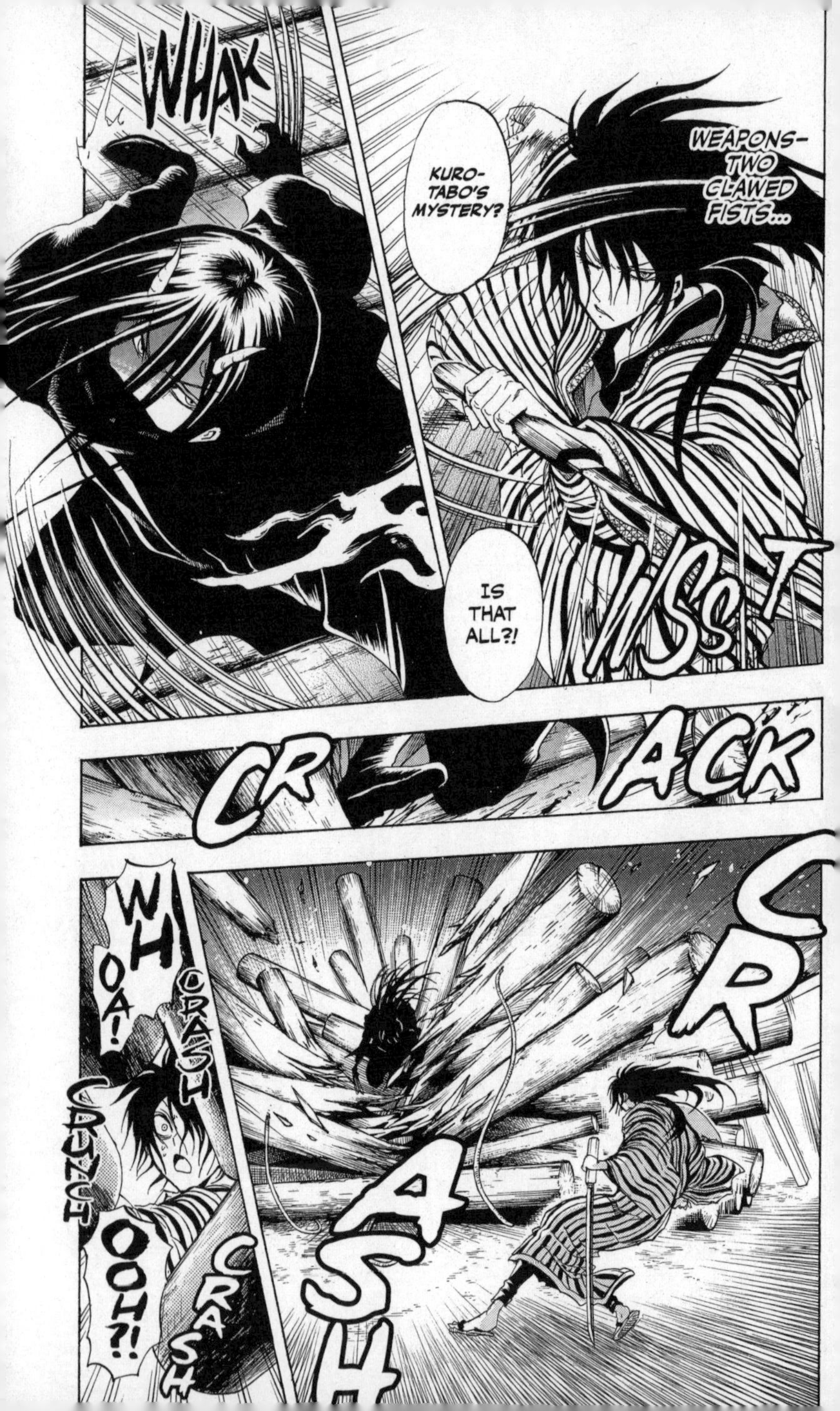
WEAPONS— TWO CLAWED FISTS...
KURO-TABO'S MYSTERY?
WHAK
IS THAT ALL?!
VISST
CR ACK
CRASH
WHOA!
CRASH
CRASH
CRUNCH
OOH?!

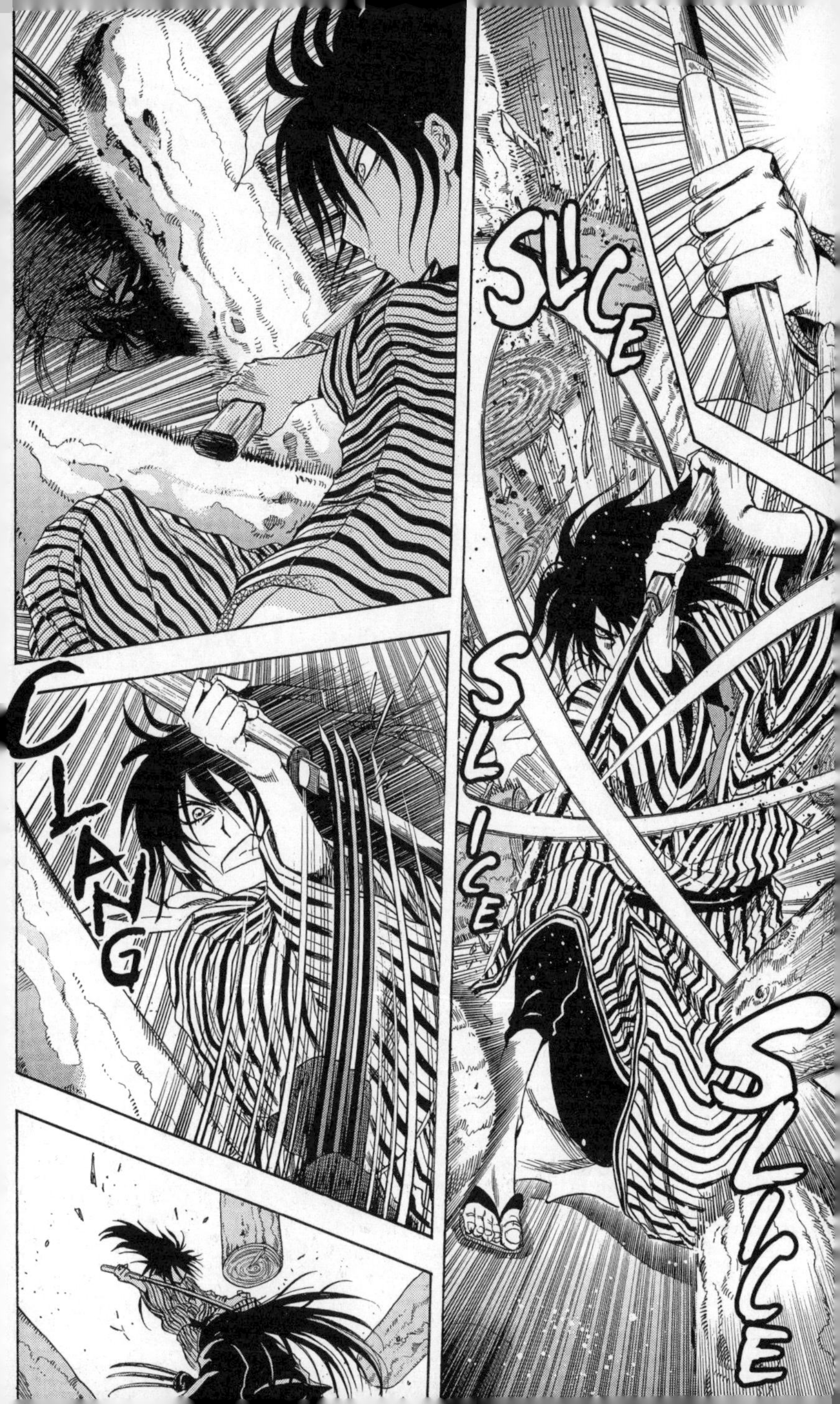
SLICE
SLICE
SLICE
CLANG

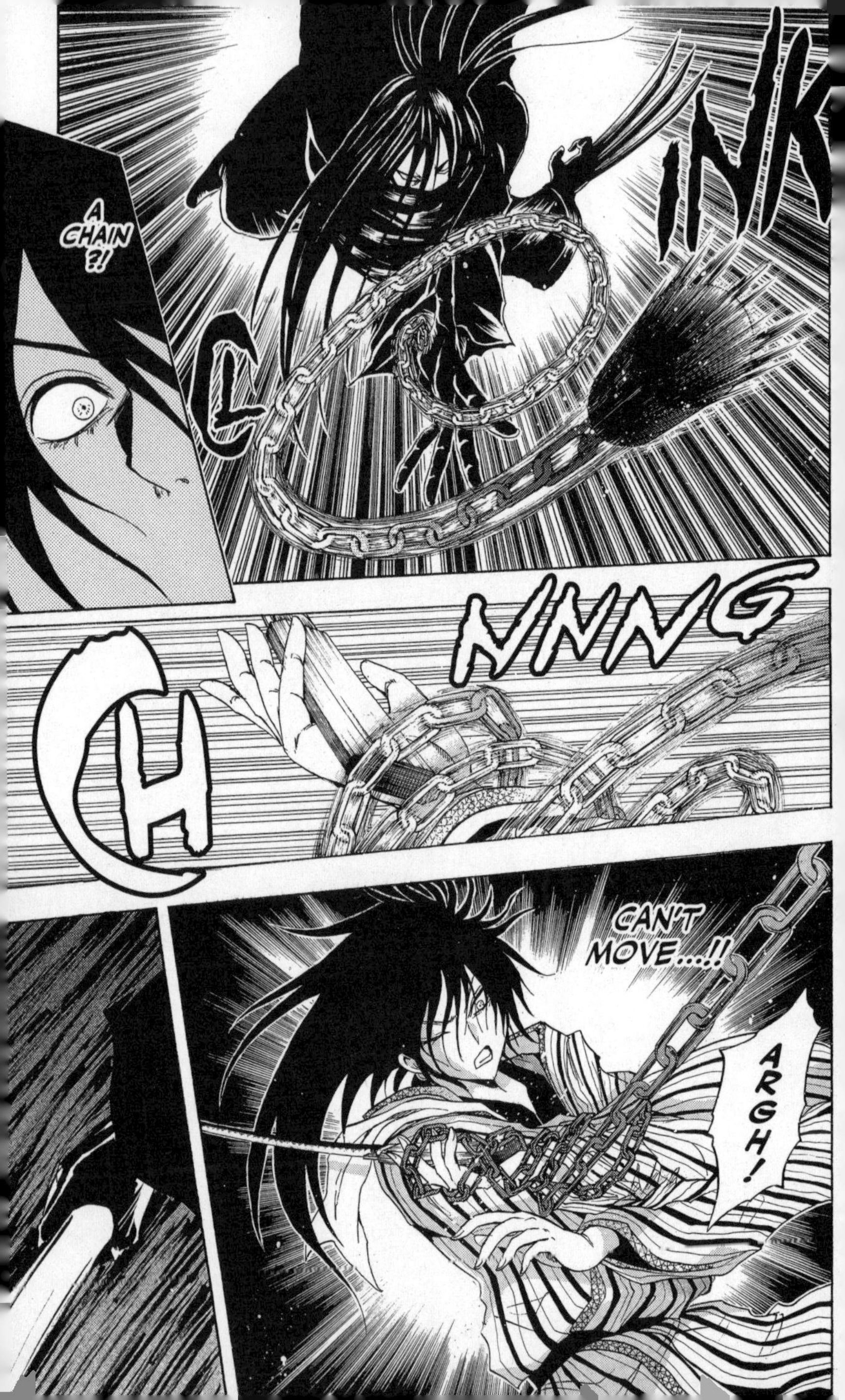
CLINK
A CHAIN ?!
CHNNNG
CAN'T MOVE...!!
ARGH!

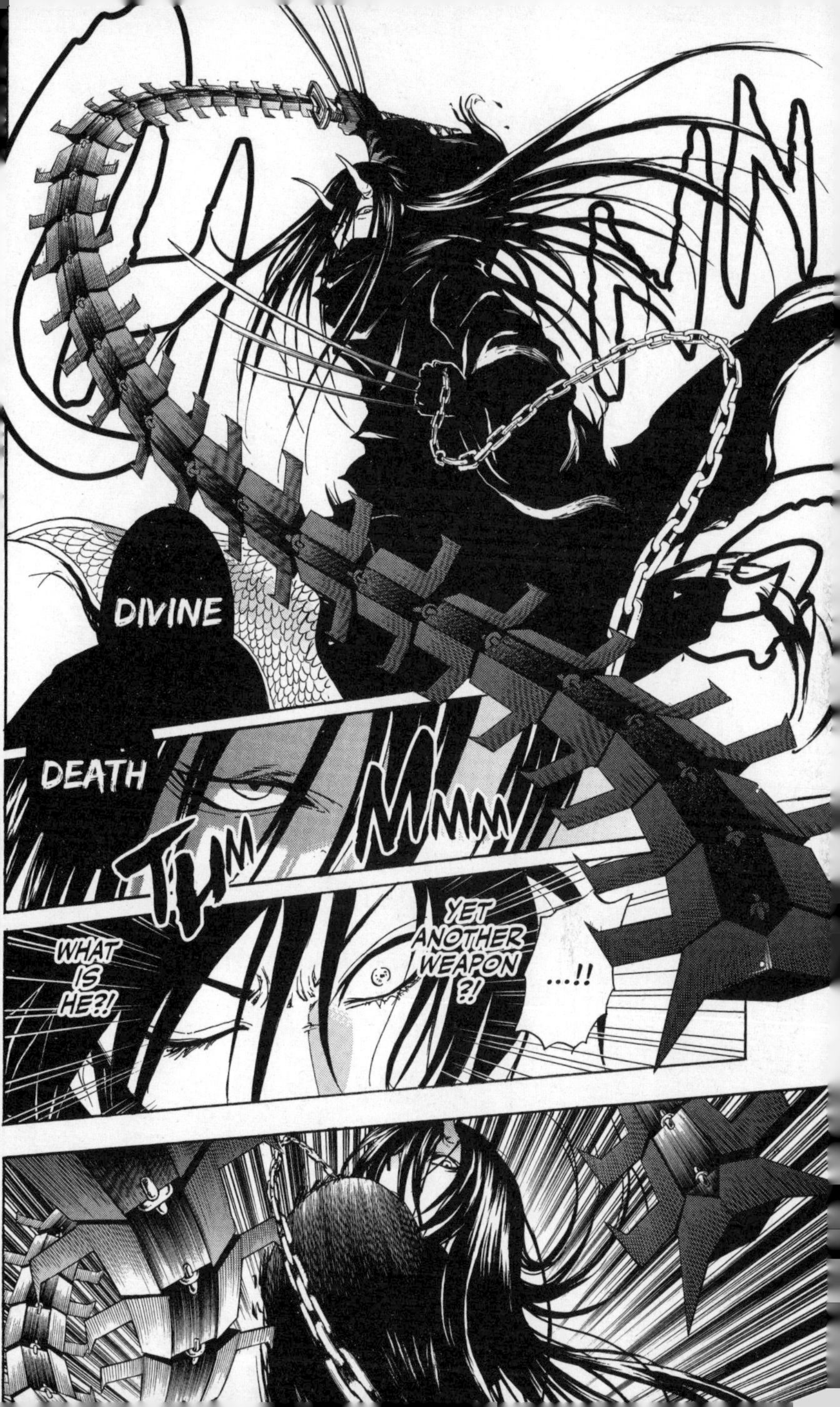
DIVINE
DEATH
...!!
YET ANOTHER WEAPON ?!
WHAT IS HE?!

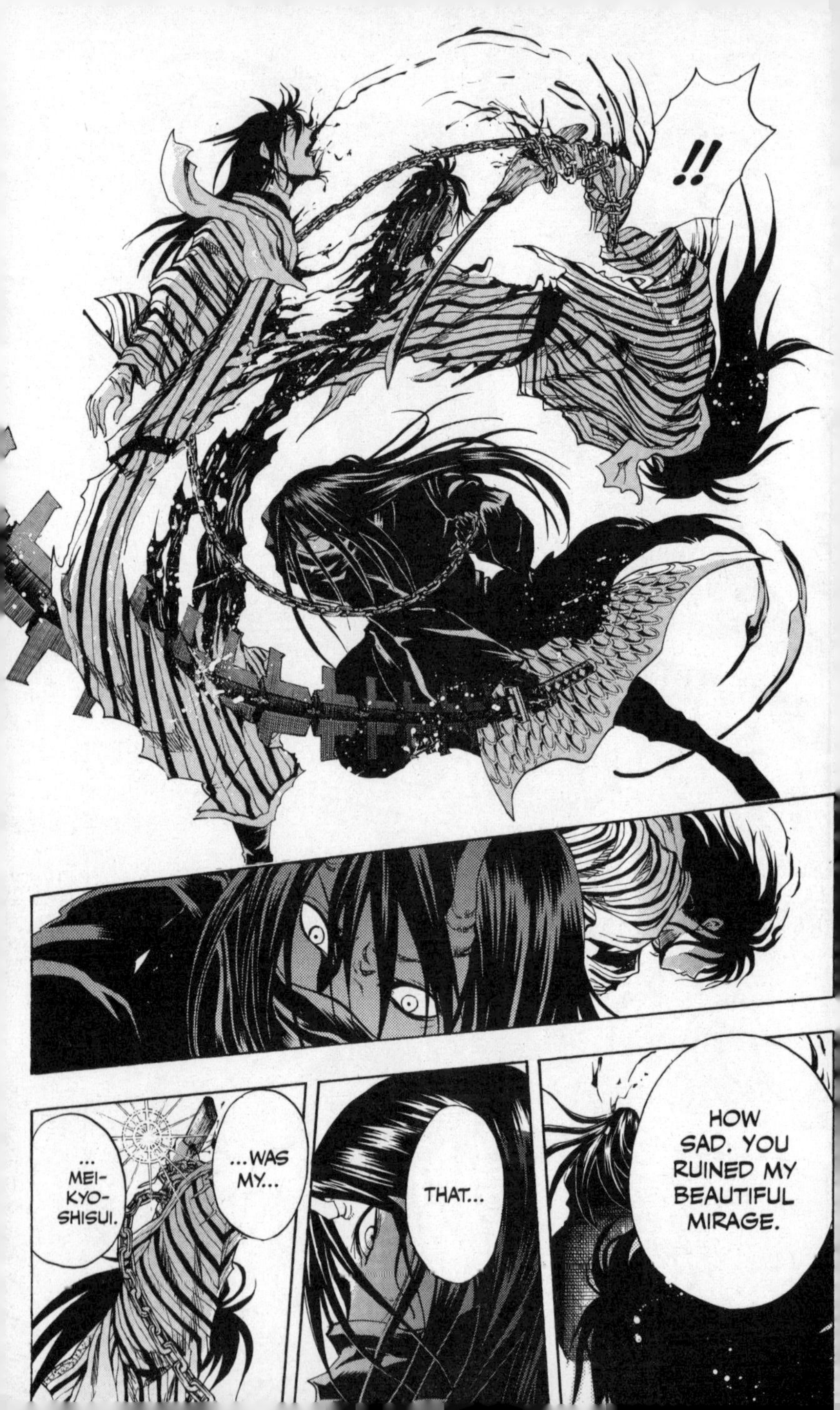
!!
HOW SAD. YOU RUINED MY BEAUTIFUL MIRAGE.
THAT...
...WAS MY...
...MEI-KYO-SHISUI.

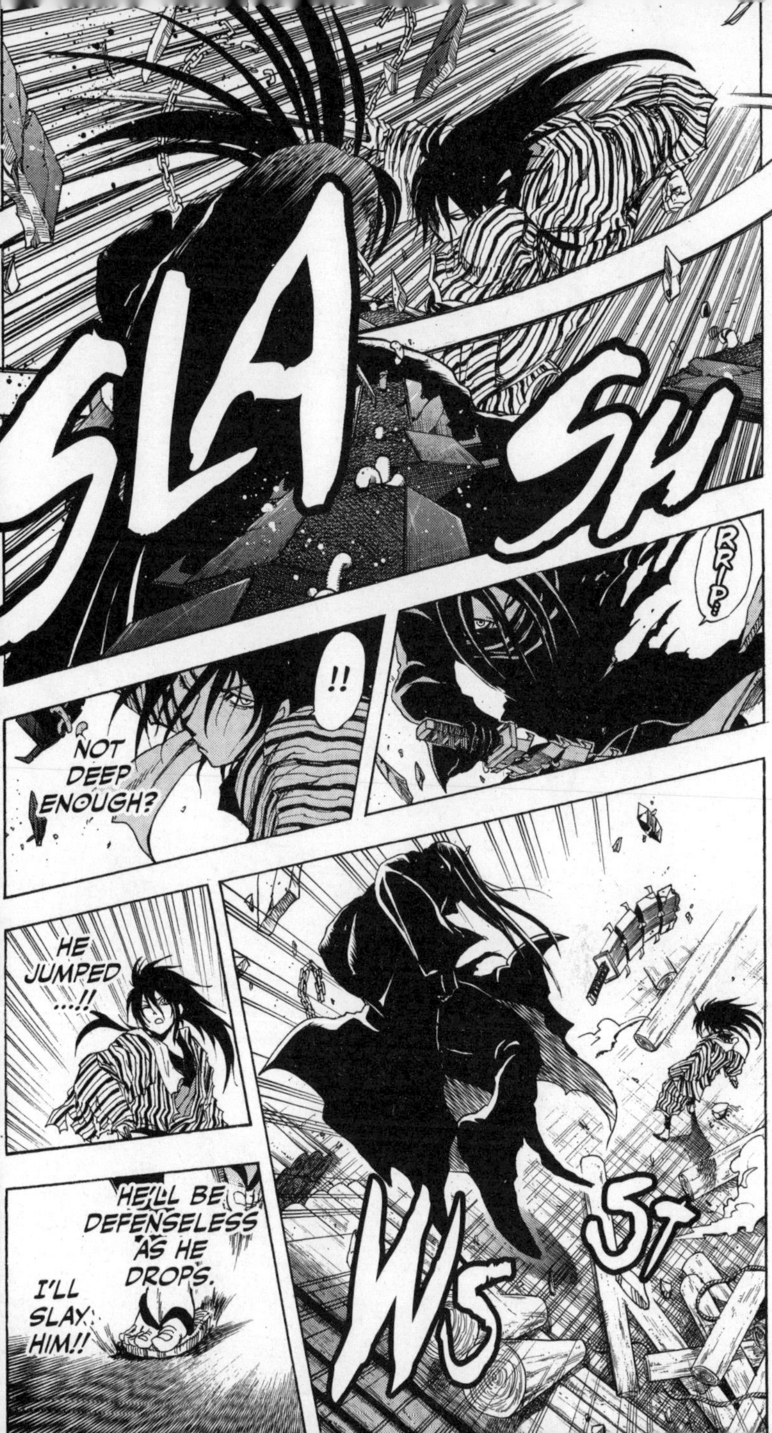
SLASH
RRIP.
!!
NOT DEEP ENOUGH?
WSST
HE JUMPED ...!!
HE'LL BE DEFENSELESS AS HE DROPS.
I'LL SLAY HIM!!

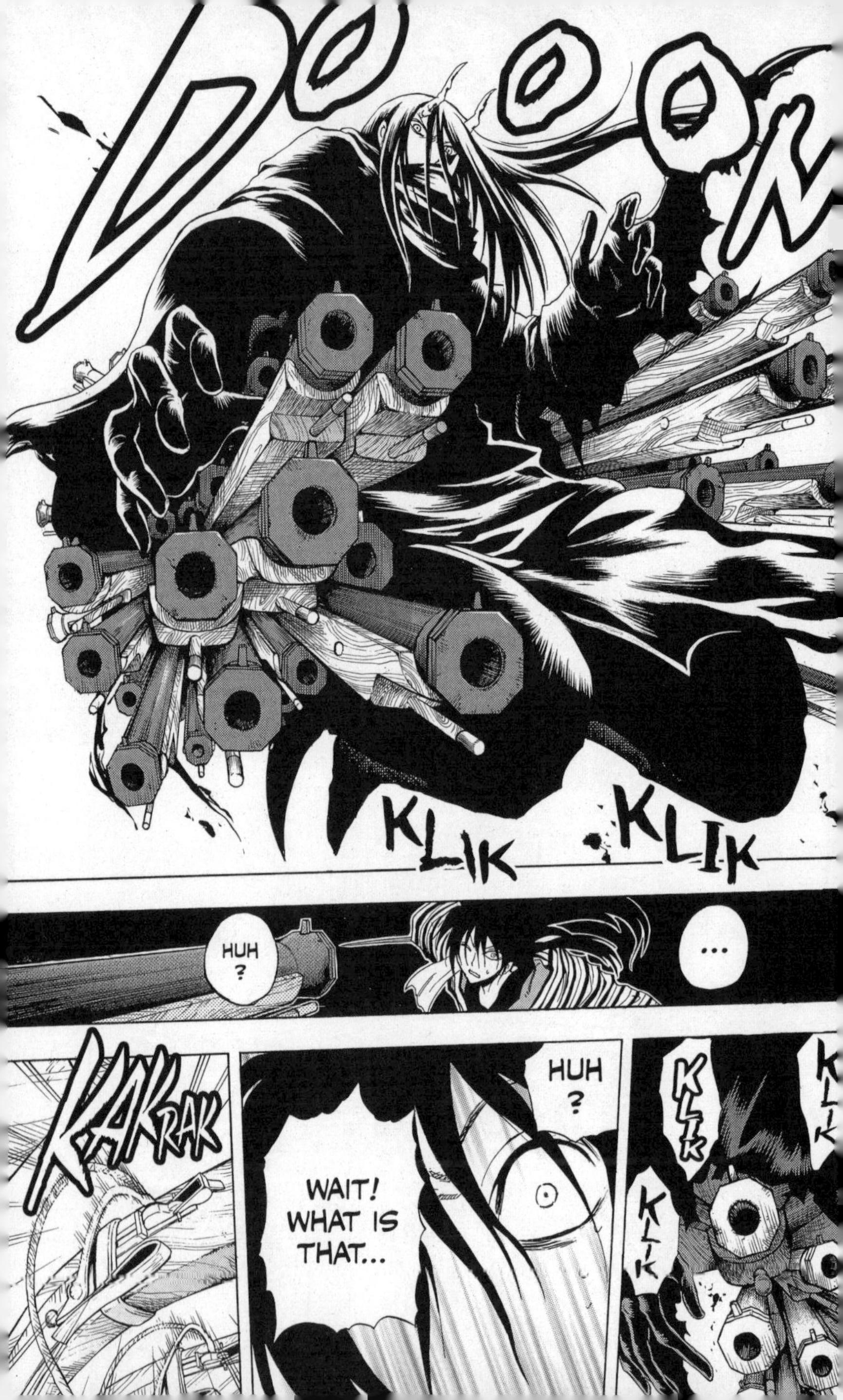
DOOON
KLIK
KLIK
...
HUH?
KLIK
KLIK
KLIK
HUH?
WAIT! WHAT IS THAT...
KAK RAK

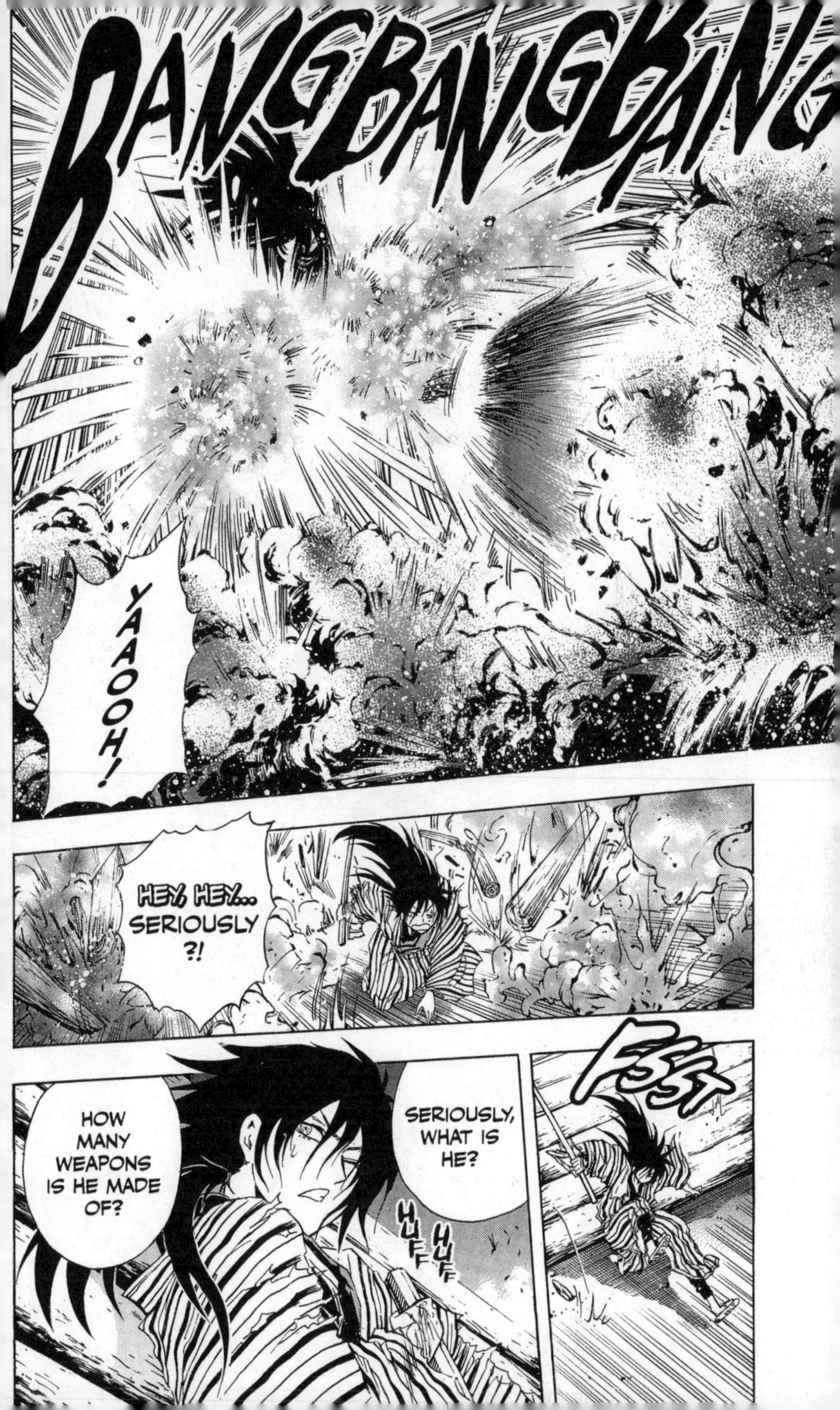
BANG BANG KANG
YAAAOOH!
HEY, HEY... SERIOUSLY?!
FSST
SERIOUSLY, WHAT IS HE?
HUFF HUFF
HOW MANY WEAPONS IS HE MADE OF?

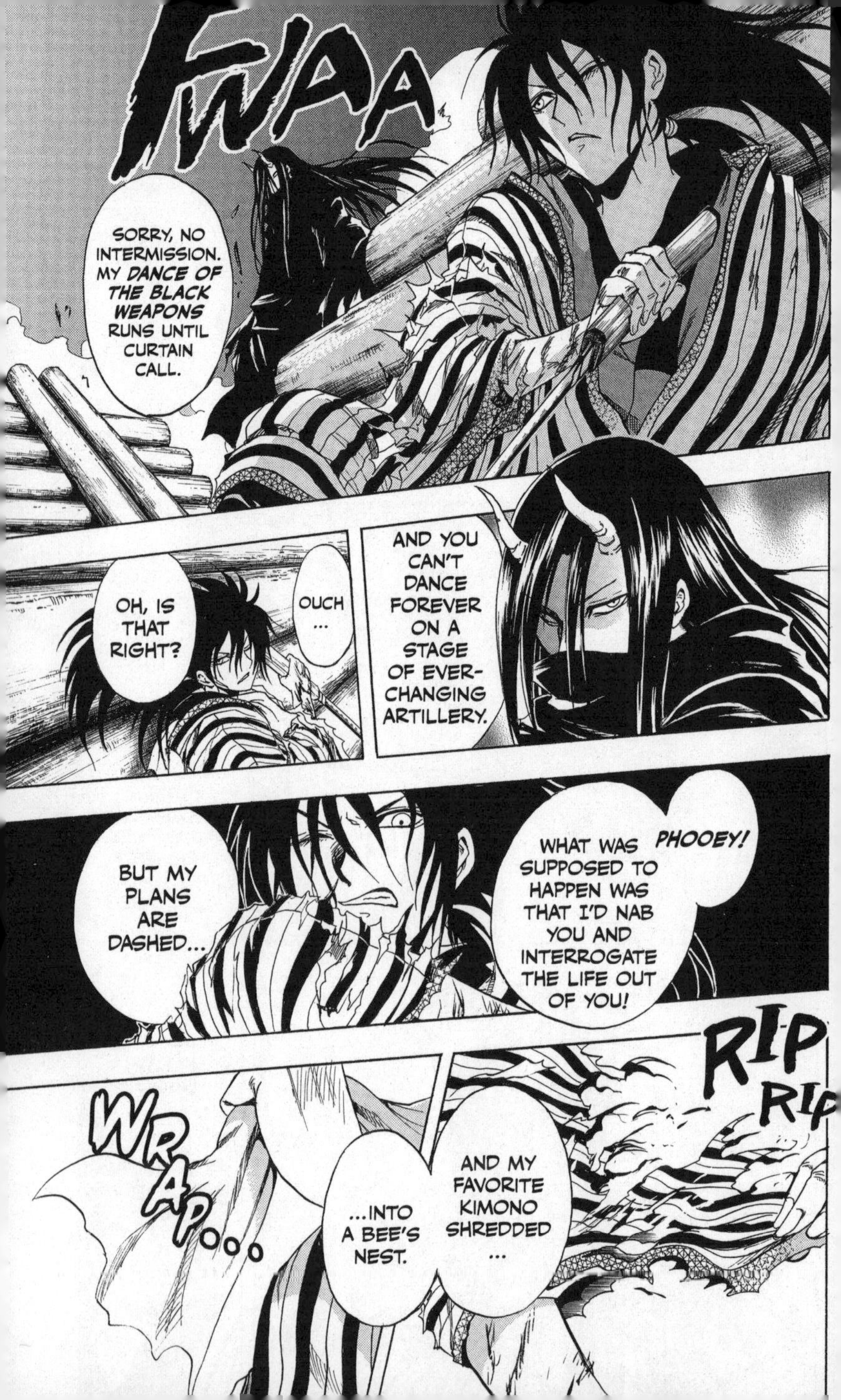
FWAA
SORRY, NO INTERMISSION. MY *DANCE OF THE BLACK WEAPONS* RUNS UNTIL CURTAIN CALL.
AND YOU CAN'T DANCE FOREVER ON A STAGE OF EVER-CHANGING ARTILLERY.
OUCH ...
OH, IS THAT RIGHT?
PHOOEY!
WHAT WAS SUPPOSED TO HAPPEN WAS THAT I'D NAB YOU AND INTERROGATE THE LIFE OUT OF YOU!
BUT MY PLANS ARE DASHED...
RIP RIP
AND MY FAVORITE KIMONO SHREDDED ...
...INTO A BEE'S NEST.
WRAPOOO

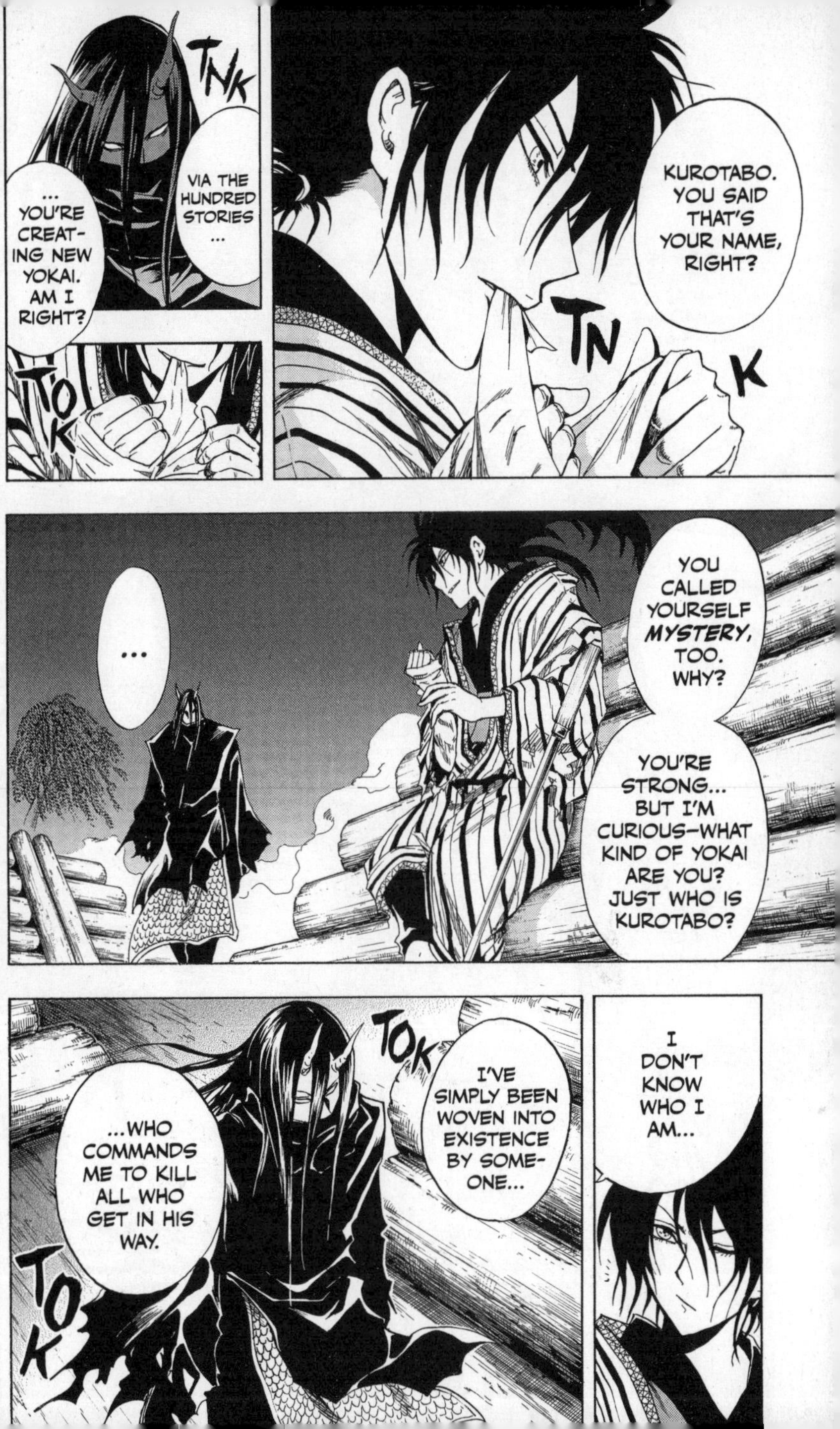
KUROTABO. YOU SAID THAT'S YOUR NAME, RIGHT?
TN K
TNK
VIA THE HUNDRED STORIES ...
... YOU'RE CREATING NEW YOKAI. AM I RIGHT?
TOK
YOU CALLED YOURSELF *MYSTERY*, TOO. WHY?
YOU'RE STRONG... BUT I'M CURIOUS—WHAT KIND OF YOKAI ARE YOU? JUST WHO IS KUROTABO?
...
I DON'T KNOW WHO I AM...
TOK
I'VE SIMPLY BEEN WOVEN INTO EXISTENCE BY SOMEONE...
...WHO COMMANDS ME TO KILL ALL WHO GET IN HIS WAY.
TOK

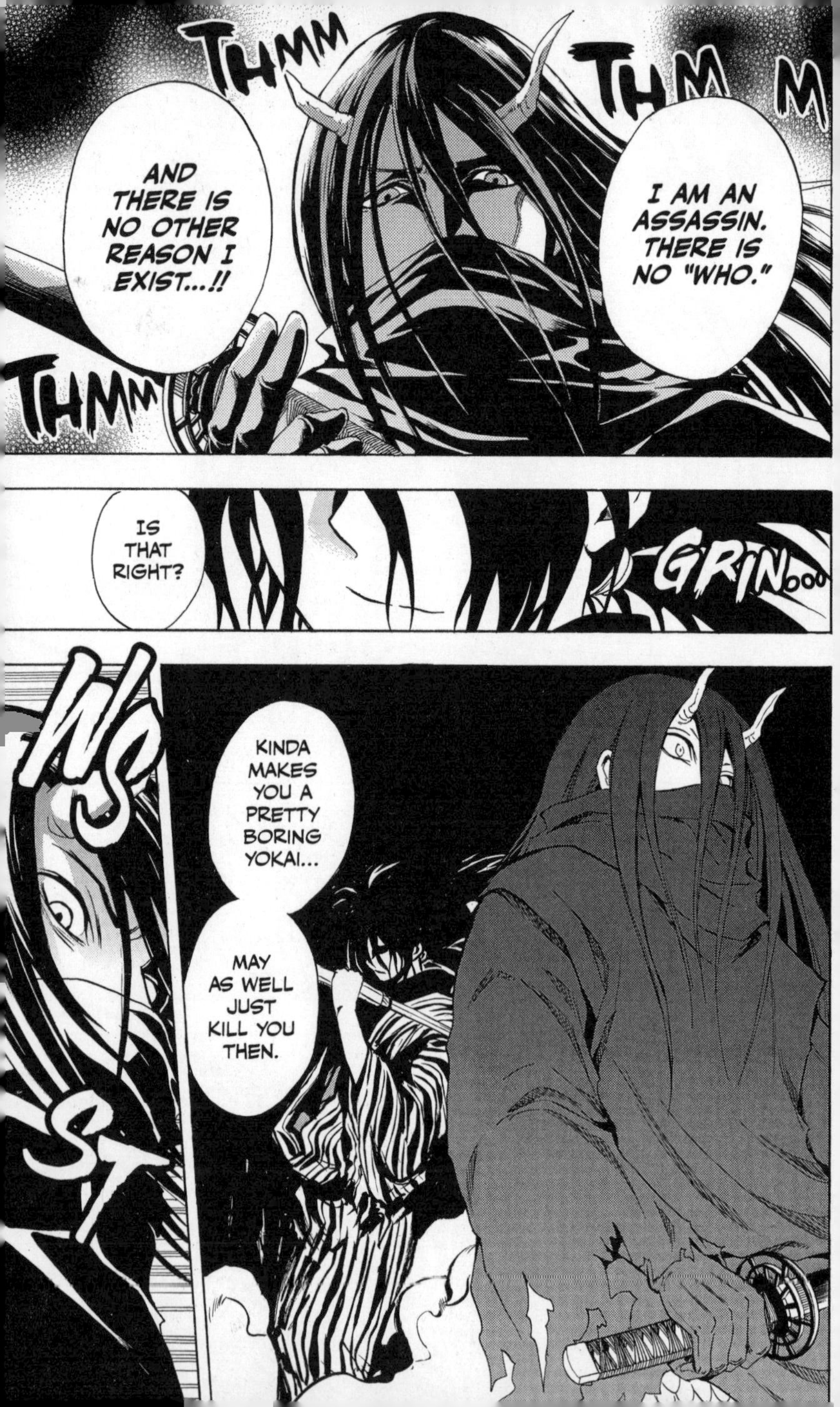
THM M
I AM AN ASSASSIN. THERE IS NO "WHO."
THMM
AND THERE IS NO OTHER REASON I EXIST...!!
THMM
GRIN
IS THAT RIGHT?
KINDA MAKES YOU A PRETTY BORING YOKAI...
MAY AS WELL JUST KILL YOU THEN.

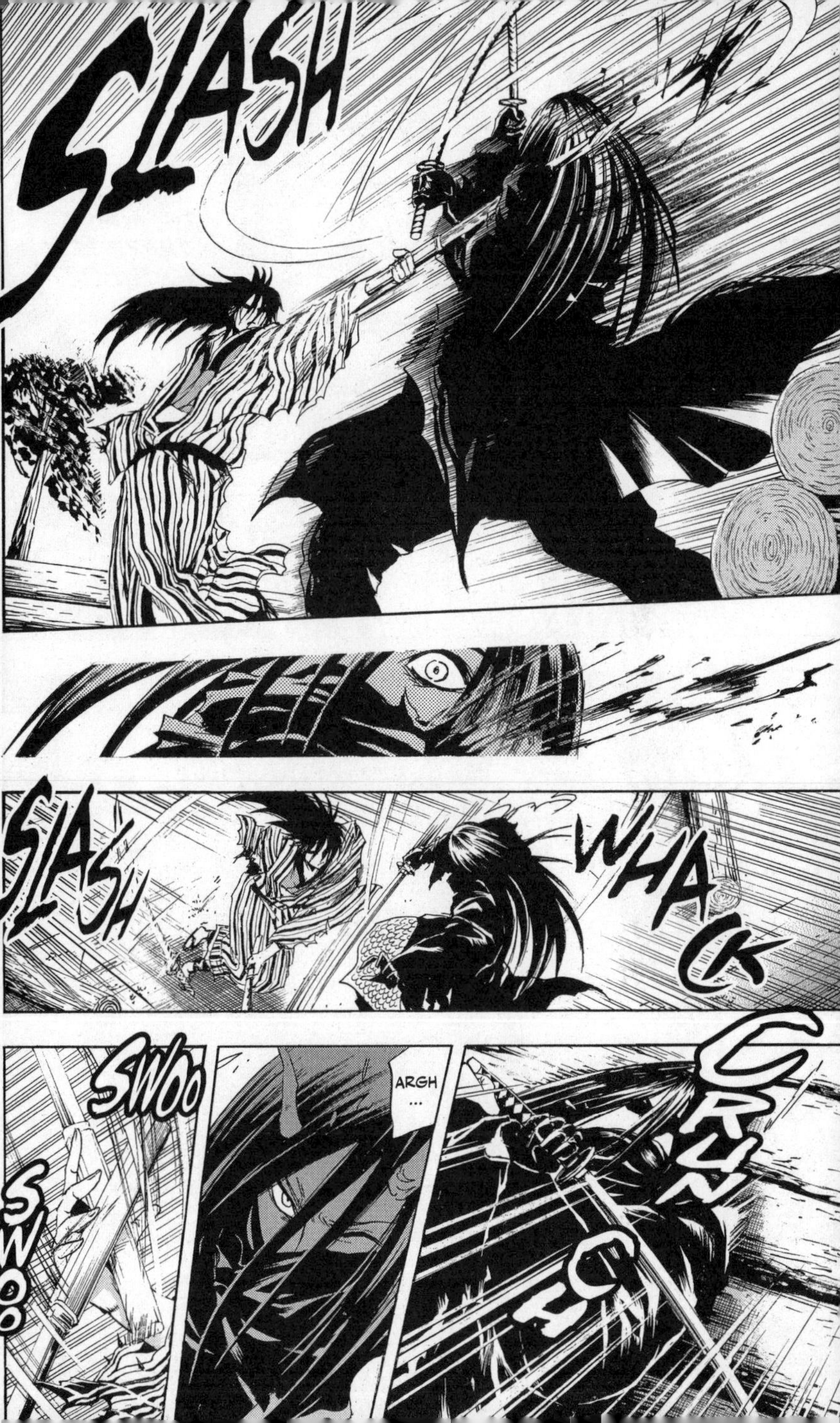
SLASH
WHACK
SLASH
CRUNCH
ARGH...
SWOO
SWOO

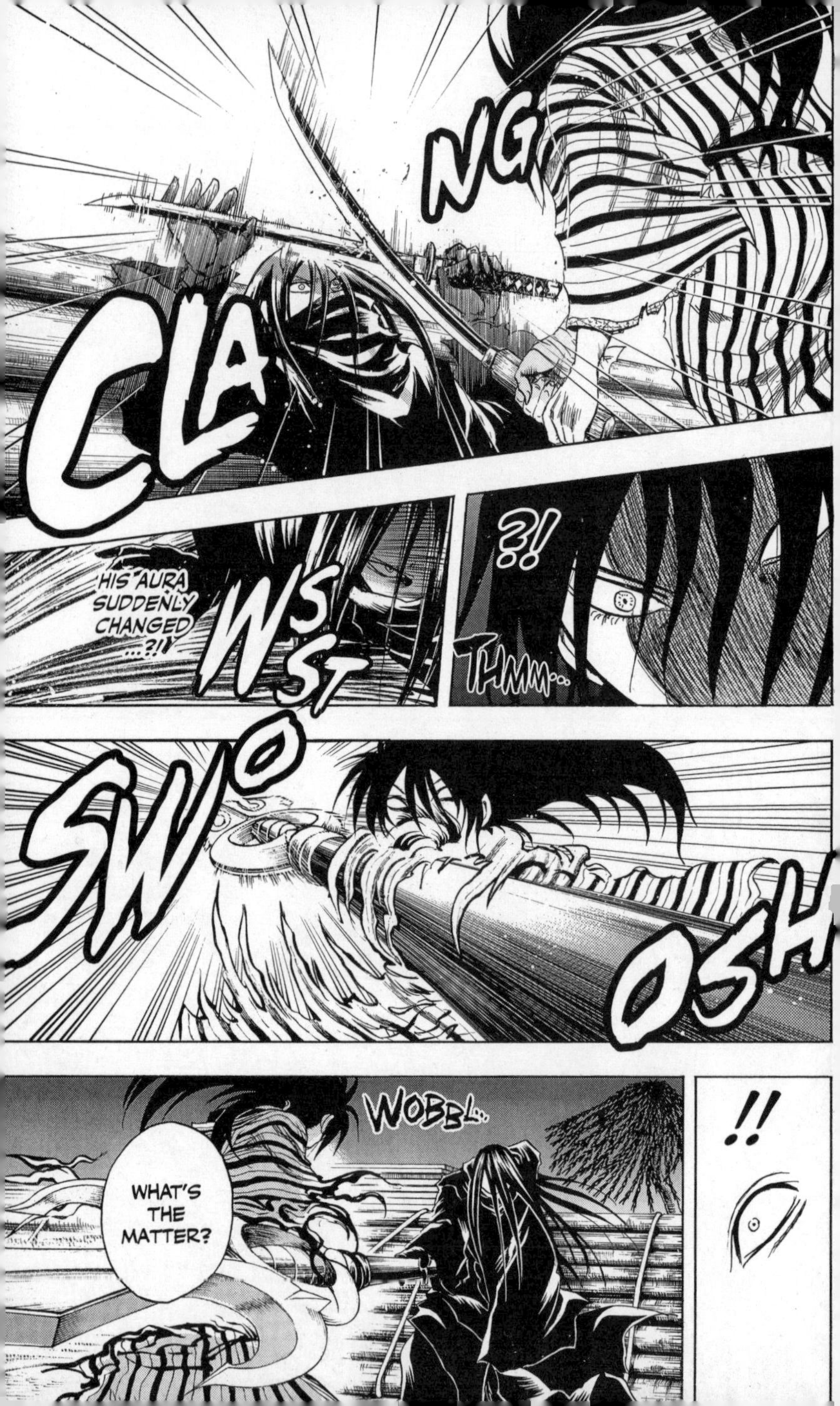
CLA
NG
?!
THMM...
HIS AURA SUDDENLY CHANGED ...?!
WS
ST
SWO
OSH
!!
WOBBL...
WHAT'S THE MATTER?

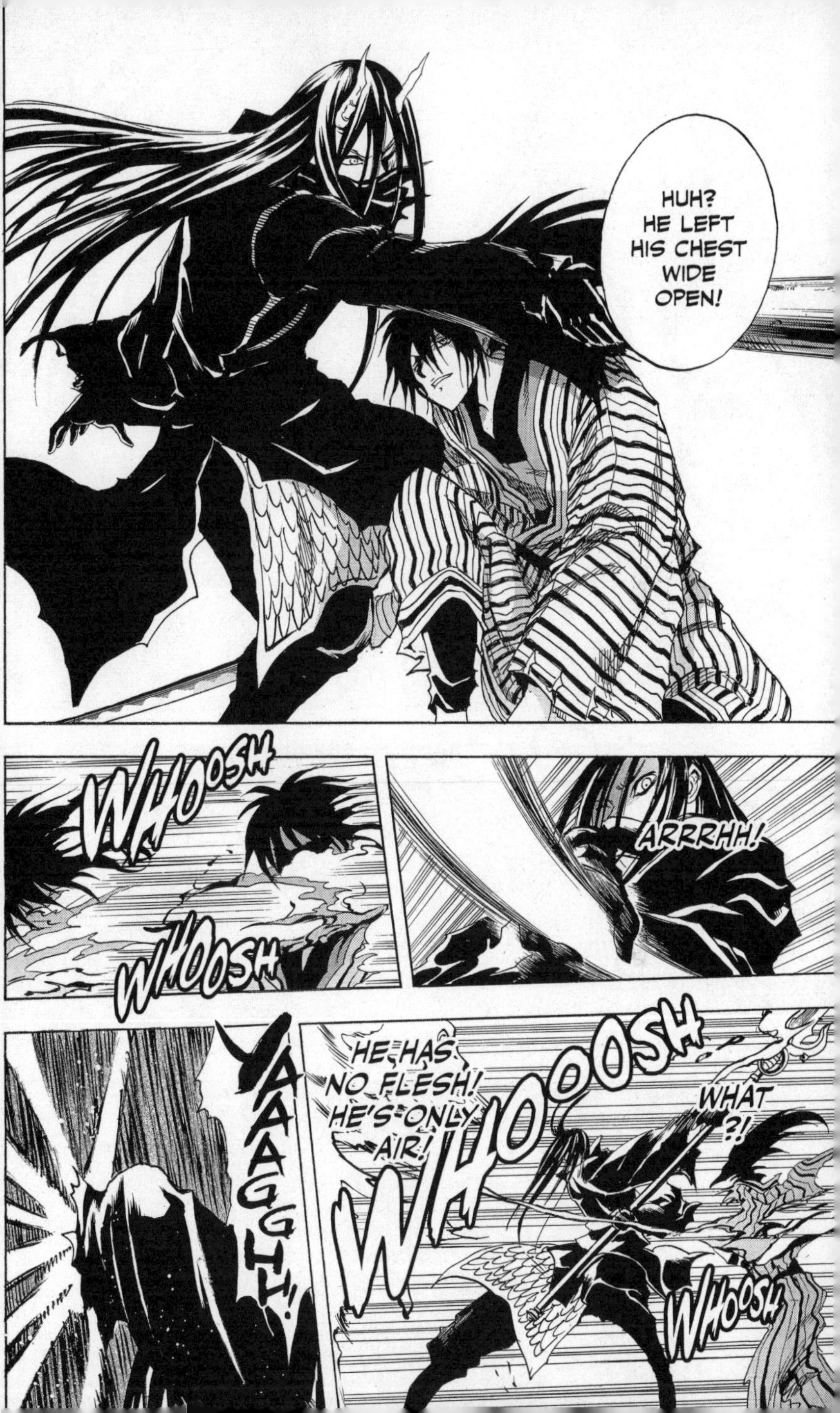
HUH? HE LEFT HIS CHEST WIDE OPEN!
ARRRHH!
WHOOSH
WHOOSH
WHAT?!
HE HAS NO FLESH! HE'S ONLY AIR!
WHOOOOSH
WHOOSH
YAAAGHH!!

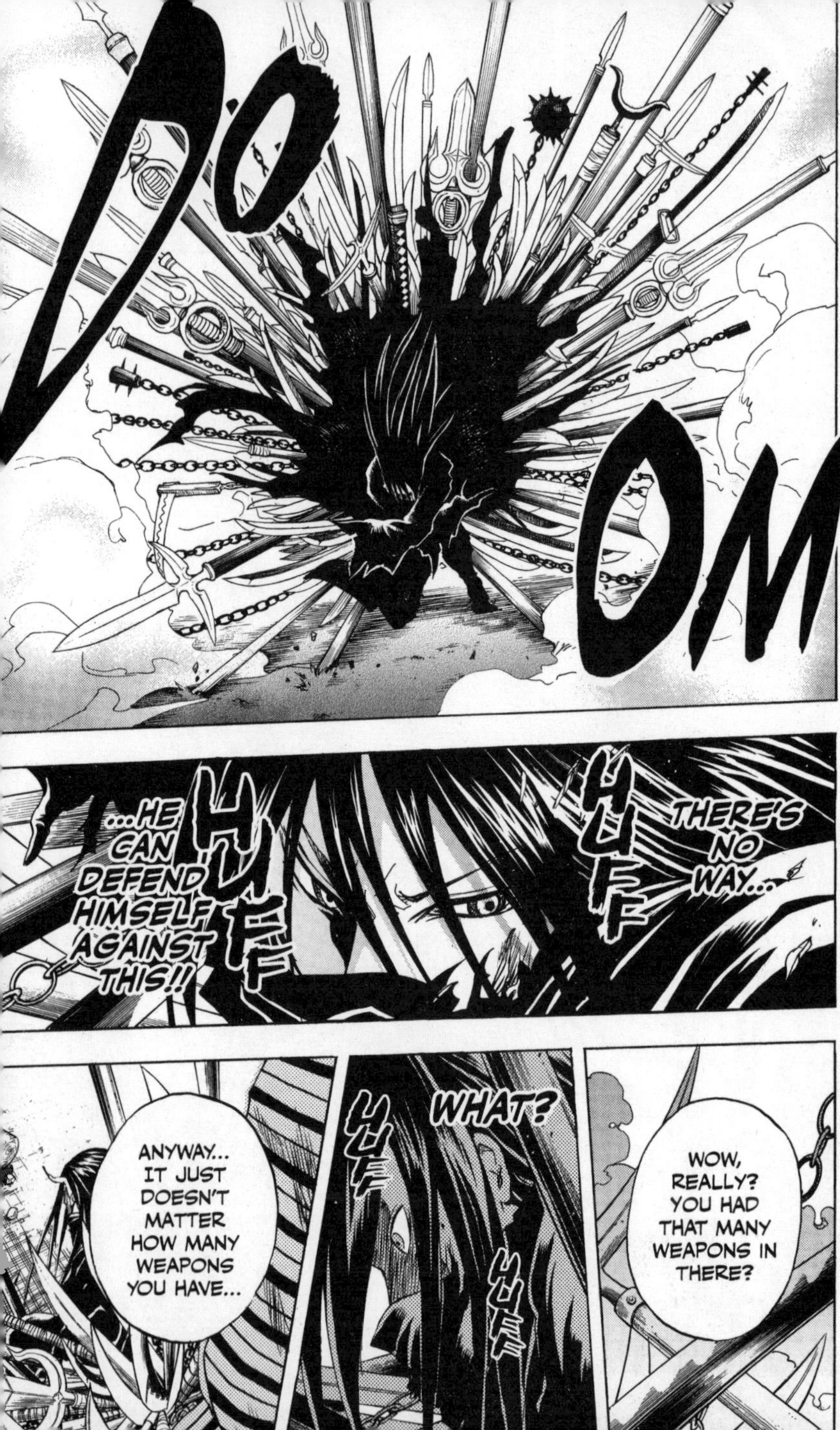
DOOM
HUFF
THERE'S NO WAY...
...HE CAN DEFEND HIMSELF AGAINST THIS!!
HUFF
WOW, REALLY? YOU HAD THAT MANY WEAPONS IN THERE?
WHAT?
HUF
HUF
ANYWAY... IT JUST DOESN'T MATTER HOW MANY WEAPONS YOU HAVE...

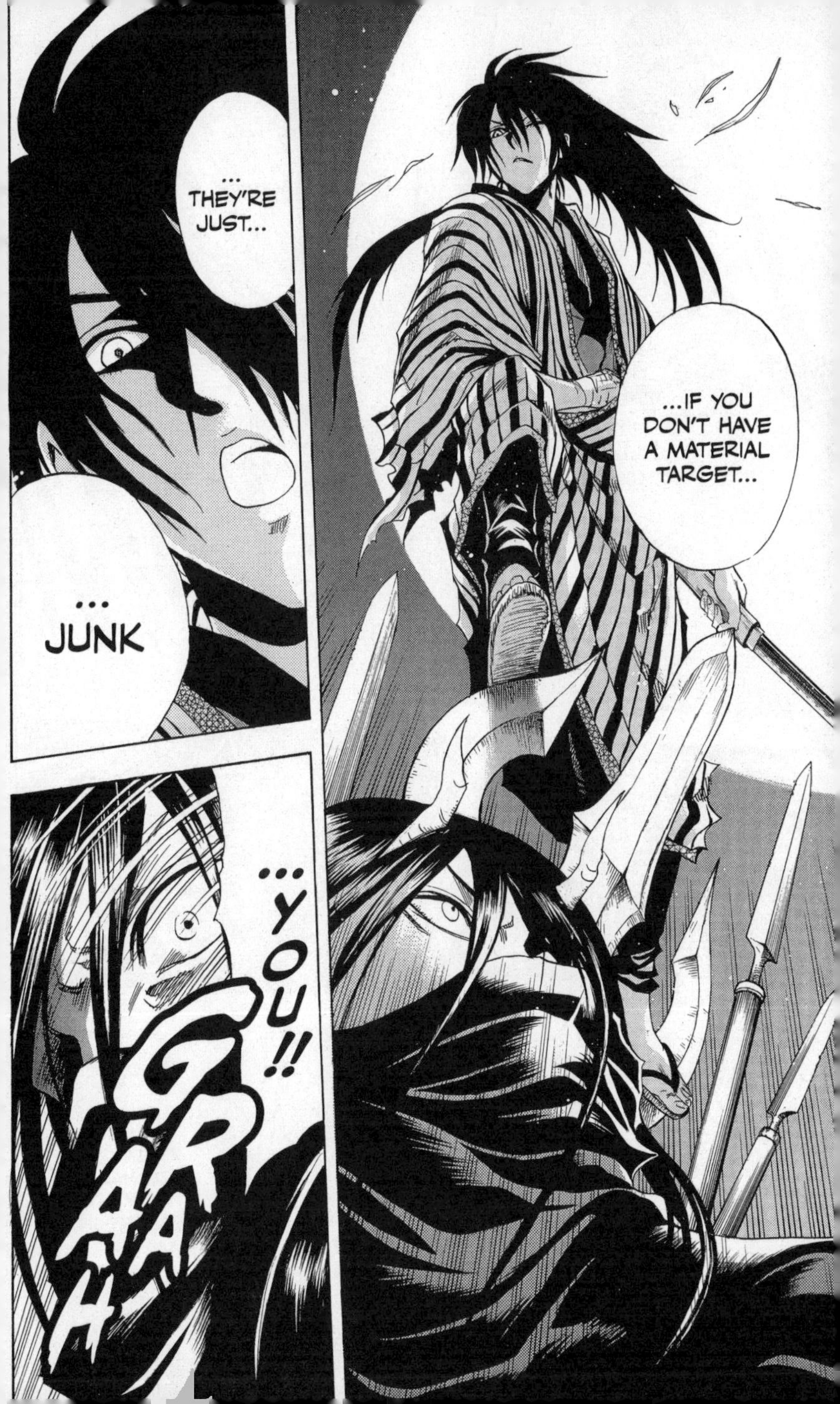
...IF YOU DON'T HAVE A MATERIAL TARGET...
... THEY'RE JUST...
... JUNK
...YOU!!
GRAAAH

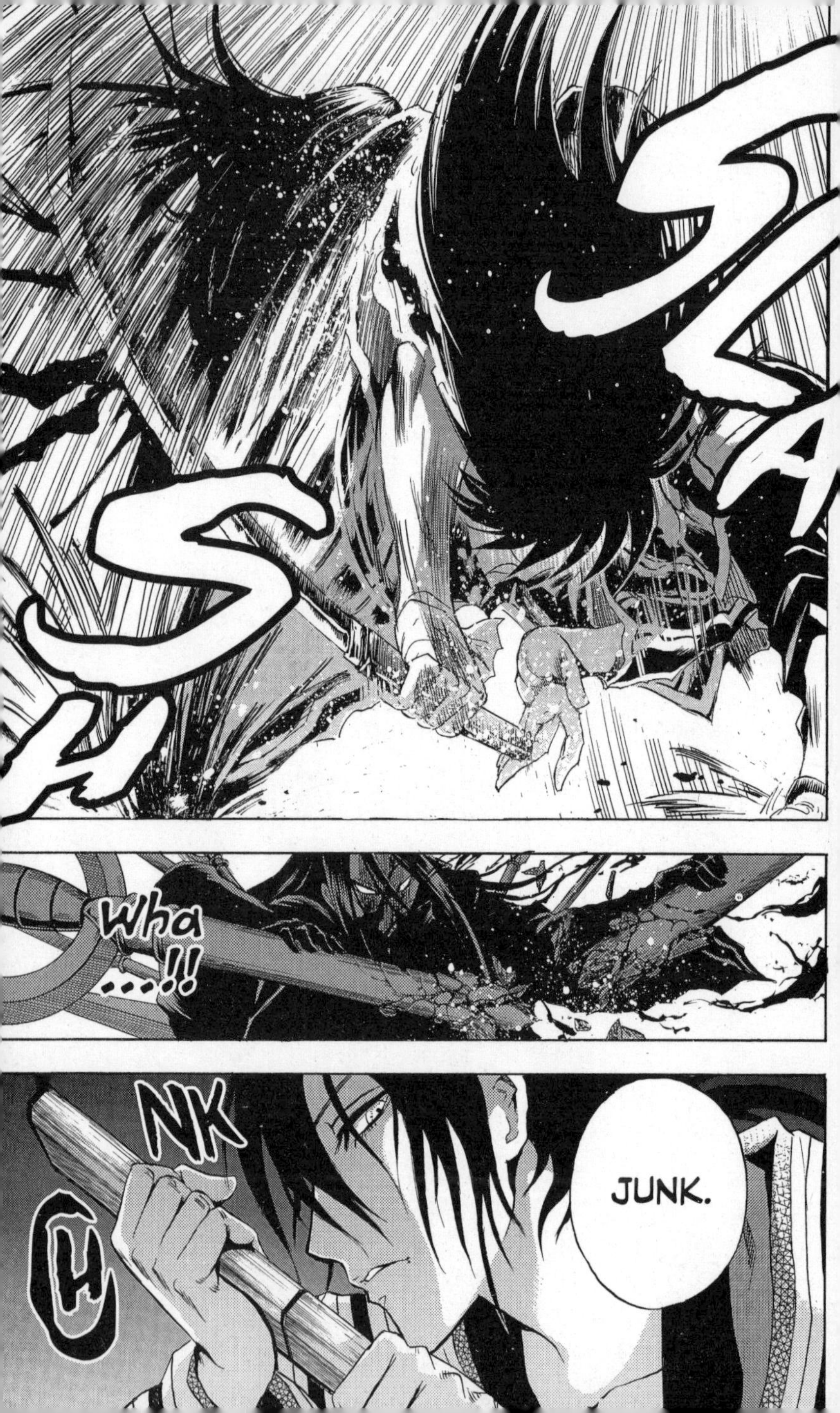
wha
...!!
JUNK.

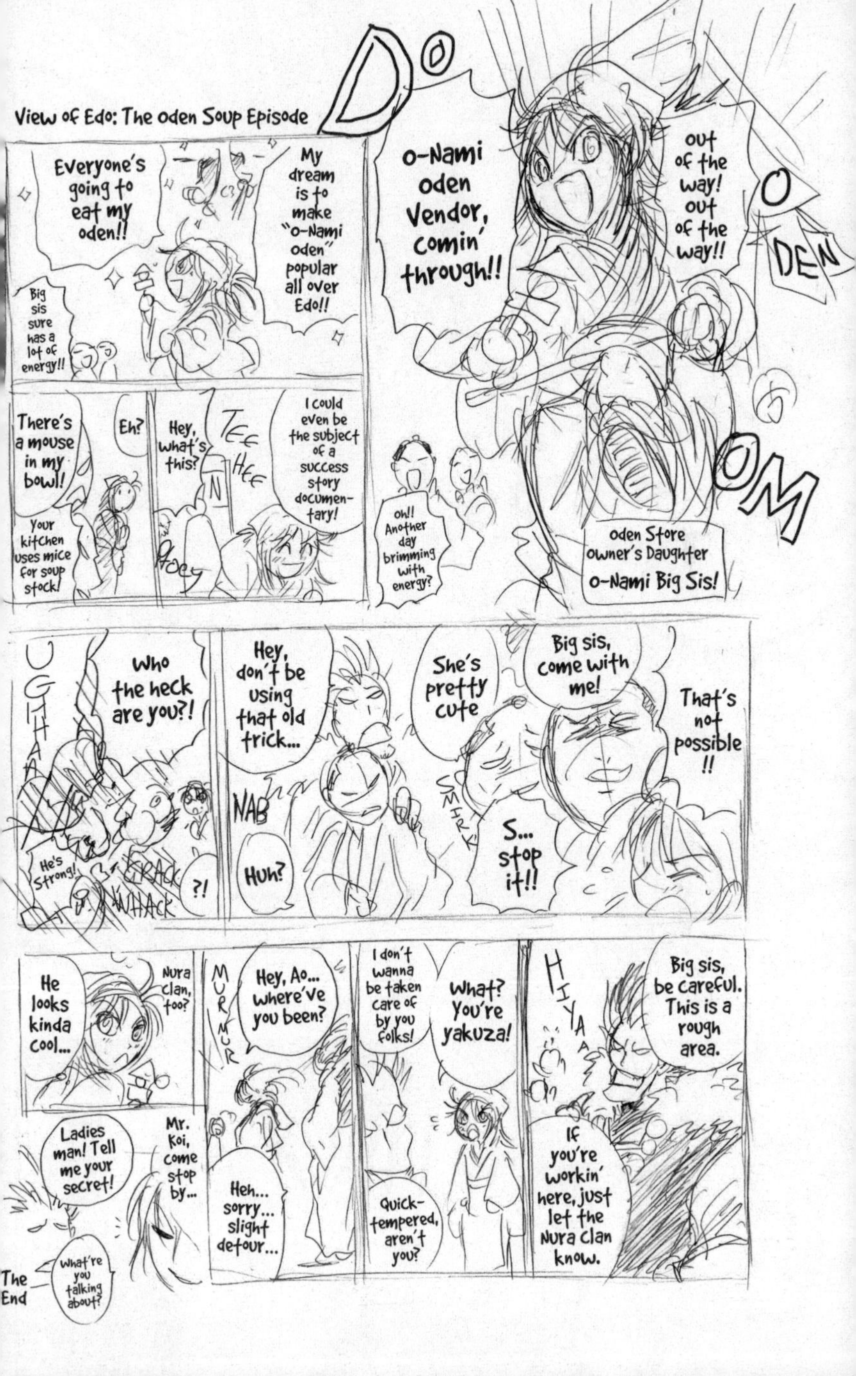
View of Edo: The oden Soup Episode
DO
O
DEN
OM
out of the way! out of the way!!
o-Nami oden Vendor, comin' through!!
Oh!! Another day brimming with energy?
oden Store owner's Daughter o-Nami Big Sis!
My dream is to make "o-Nami oden" popular all over Edo!!
Everyone's going to eat my oden!!
Big sis sure has a lot of energy!!
I could even be the subject of a success story documentary!
TEE HEE
Hey, what's this?
N
Eh?
There's a mouse in my bowl!
Your kitchen uses mice for soup stock!
Big sis, come with me!
That's not possible!!
She's pretty cute
SMIRK
S... stop it!!
Hey, don't be using that old trick...
NAB
Huh?
Who the heck are you?!
UGHHAA
He's Strong!
CRACK
WHACK
?!
HIYAAA
Big sis, be careful. This is a rough area.
If you're workin' here, just let the Nura Clan know.
What? You're yakuza!
I don't wanna be taken care of by you folks!
Quick-tempered, aren't you?
Hey, Ao... where've you been?
MUR MUR
Heh... sorry... slight detour...
Nura clan, too?
He looks kinda cool...
Mr. Koi, come stop by...
Ladies man! Tell me your secret!
What're you talking about?
The End

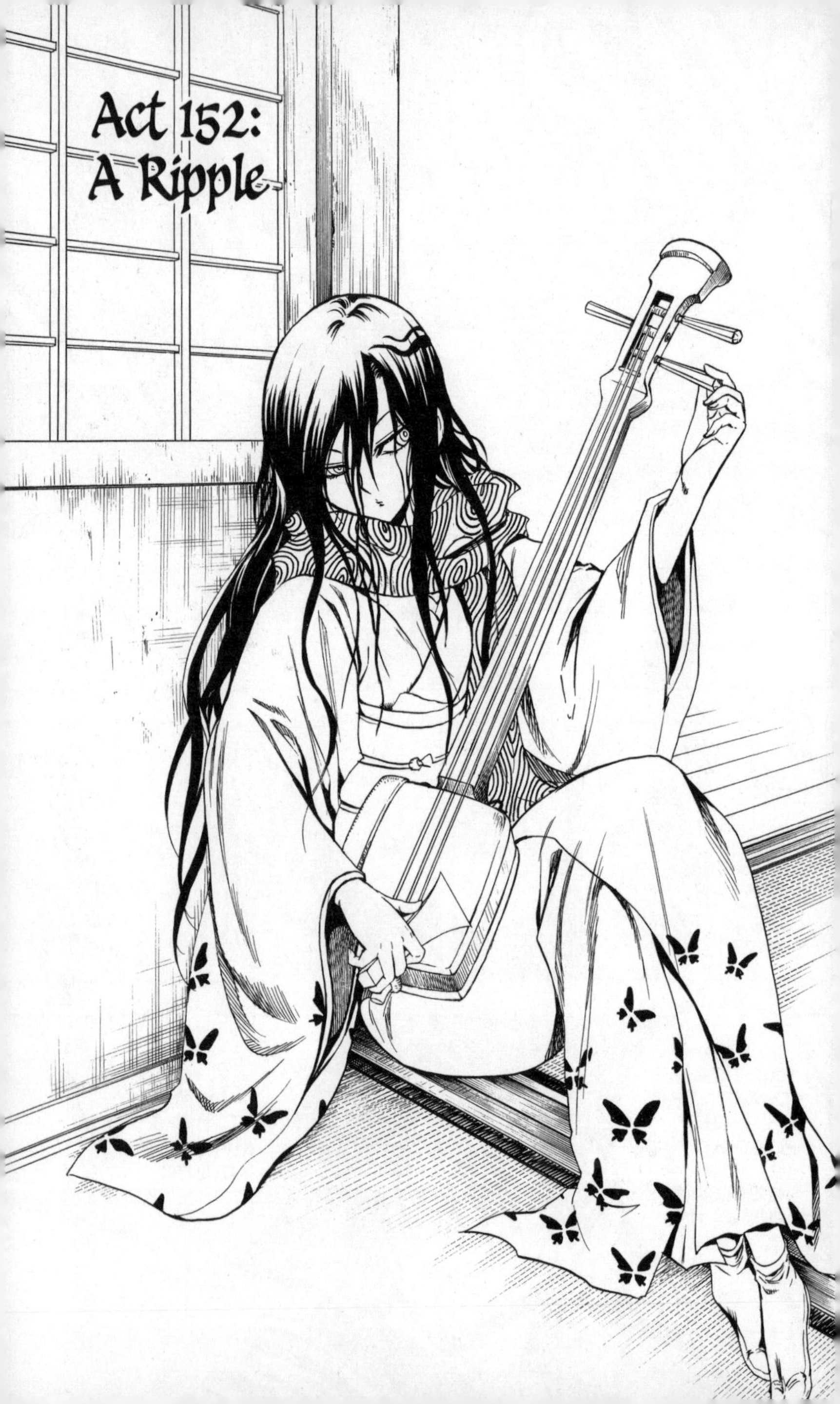
Act 152:
A Ripple

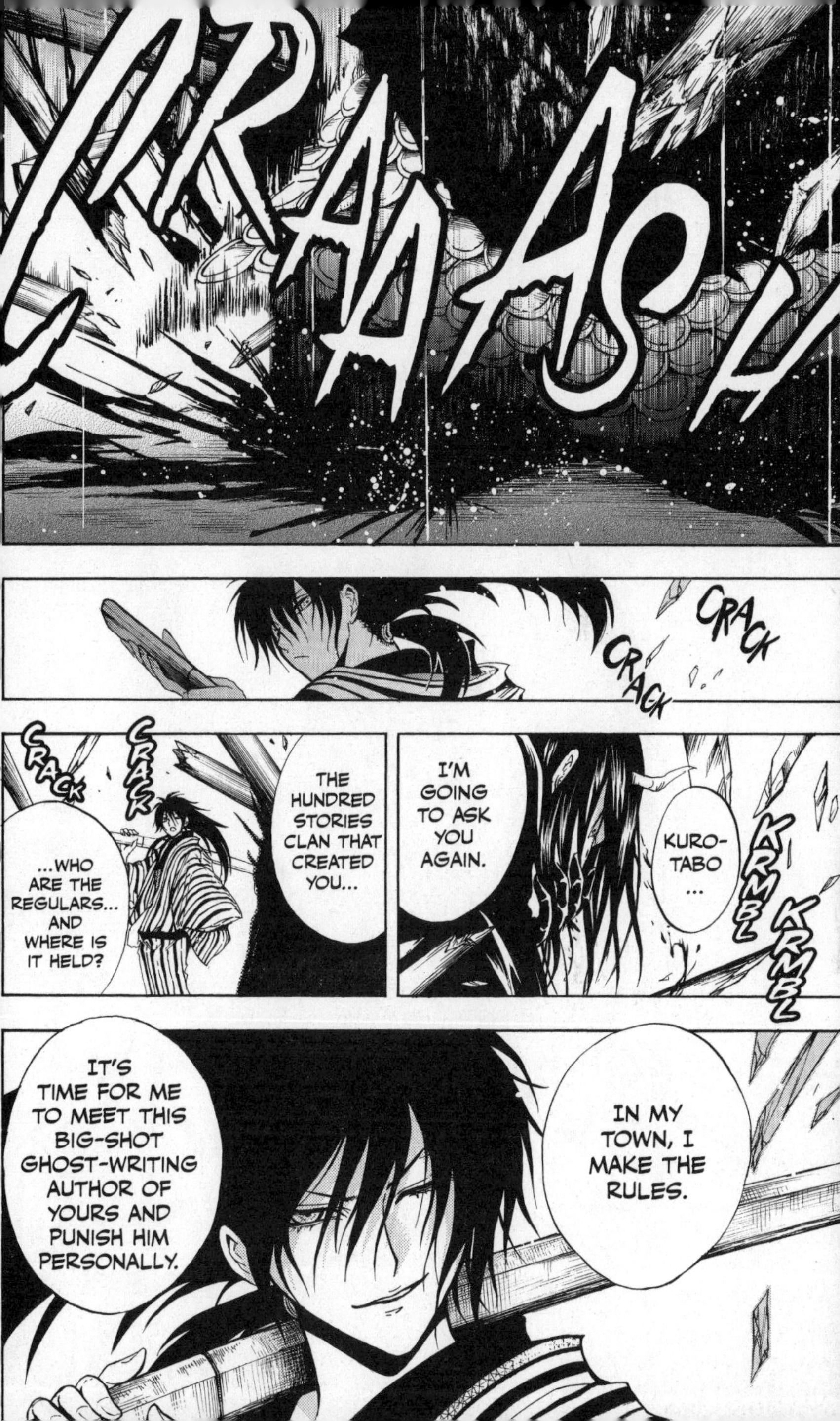
KRAASH
CRACK
CRACK
KRMBL
KRMBL
KURO-TABO ...
I'M GOING TO ASK YOU AGAIN.
THE HUNDRED STORIES CLAN THAT CREATED YOU...
...WHO ARE THE REGULARS... AND WHERE IS IT HELD?
CRACK
CRACK
IN MY TOWN, I MAKE THE RULES.
IT'S TIME FOR ME TO MEET THIS BIG-SHOT GHOST-WRITING AUTHOR OF YOURS AND PUNISH HIM PERSONALLY.

POIK
POIK

HEY.

DIDN'T YOU HEAR...

MY BRILLIANT PLAY ON WORDS?

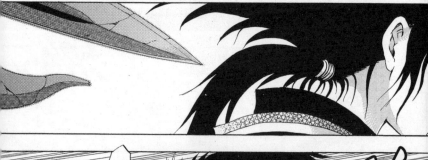

HEY, KNOCK IT OFF ALREADY!

OUCH!!

SLASH

SHUKSHHN

...KILL YOU ...!!

I...I... MUST...

Graah...

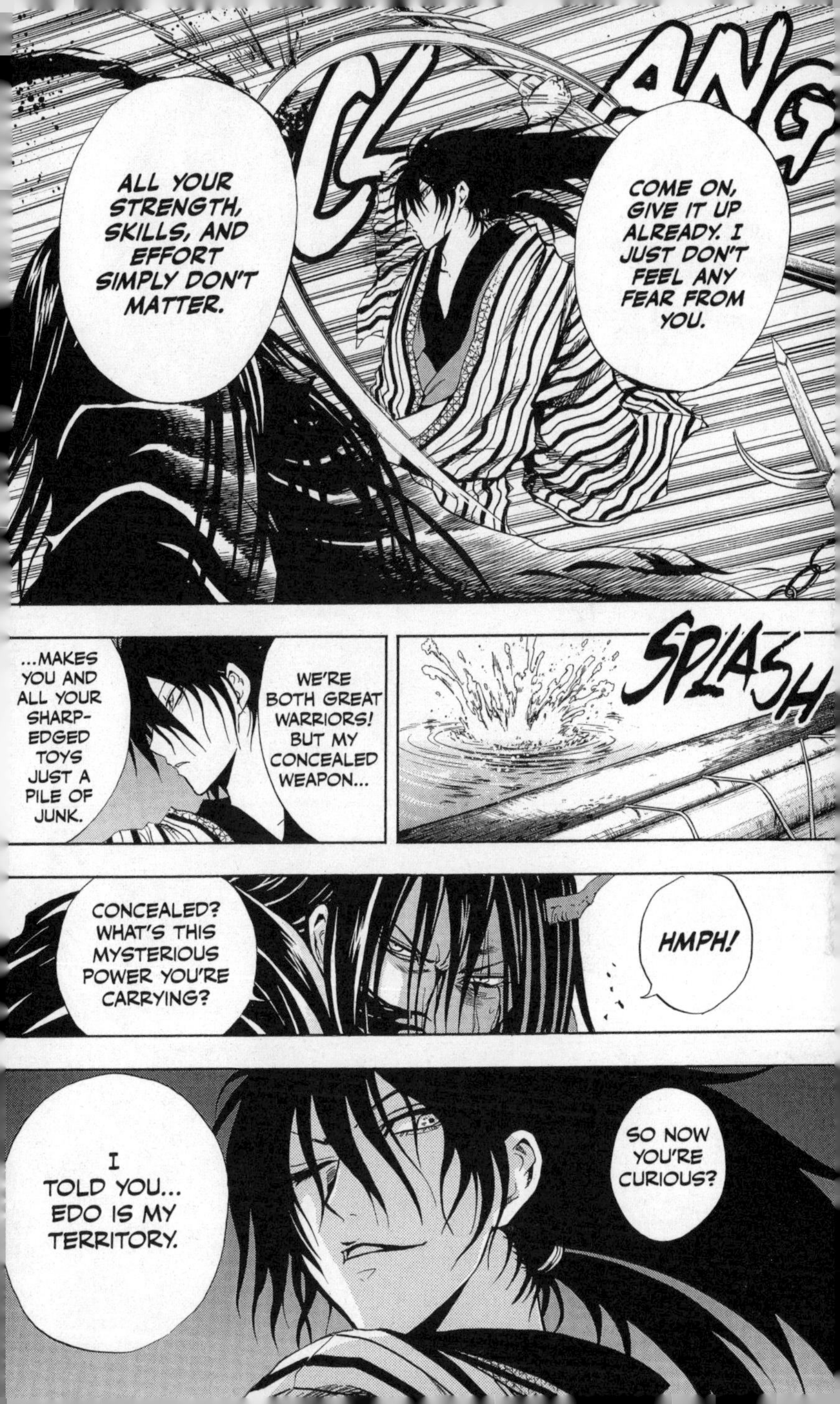
CLANG
COME ON, GIVE IT UP ALREADY. I JUST DON'T FEEL ANY FEAR FROM YOU.
ALL YOUR STRENGTH, SKILLS, AND EFFORT SIMPLY DON'T MATTER.
SPLASH
WE'RE BOTH GREAT WARRIORS! BUT MY CONCEALED WEAPON...
...MAKES YOU AND ALL YOUR SHARP-EDGED TOYS JUST A PILE OF JUNK.
HMPH!
CONCEALED? WHAT'S THIS MYSTERIOUS POWER YOU'RE CARRYING?
SO NOW YOU'RE CURIOUS?
I TOLD YOU... EDO IS MY TERRITORY.

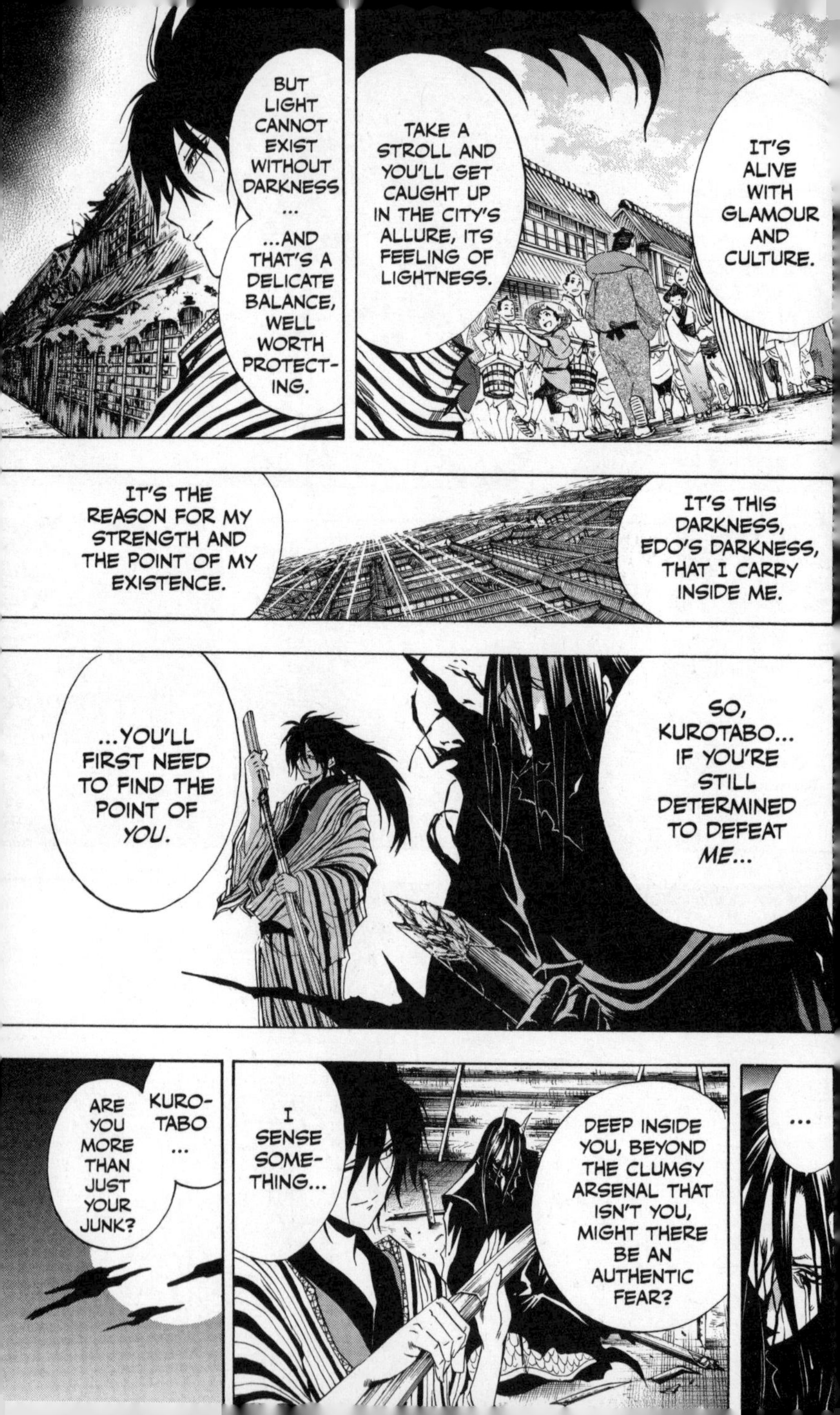
IT'S ALIVE WITH GLAMOUR AND CULTURE.
TAKE A STROLL AND YOU'LL GET CAUGHT UP IN THE CITY'S ALLURE, ITS FEELING OF LIGHTNESS.
BUT LIGHT CANNOT EXIST WITHOUT DARKNESS ...
...AND THAT'S A DELICATE BALANCE, WELL WORTH PROTECT-ING.
IT'S THIS DARKNESS, EDO'S DARKNESS, THAT I CARRY INSIDE ME.
IT'S THE REASON FOR MY STRENGTH AND THE POINT OF MY EXISTENCE.
SO, KUROTABO... IF YOU'RE STILL DETERMINED TO DEFEAT *ME*...
...YOU'LL FIRST NEED TO FIND THE POINT OF *YOU*.
...
I SENSE SOME-THING...
DEEP INSIDE YOU, BEYOND THE CLUMSY ARSENAL THAT ISN'T YOU, MIGHT THERE BE AN AUTHENTIC FEAR?
KURO-TABO ...
ARE YOU MORE THAN JUST YOUR JUNK?

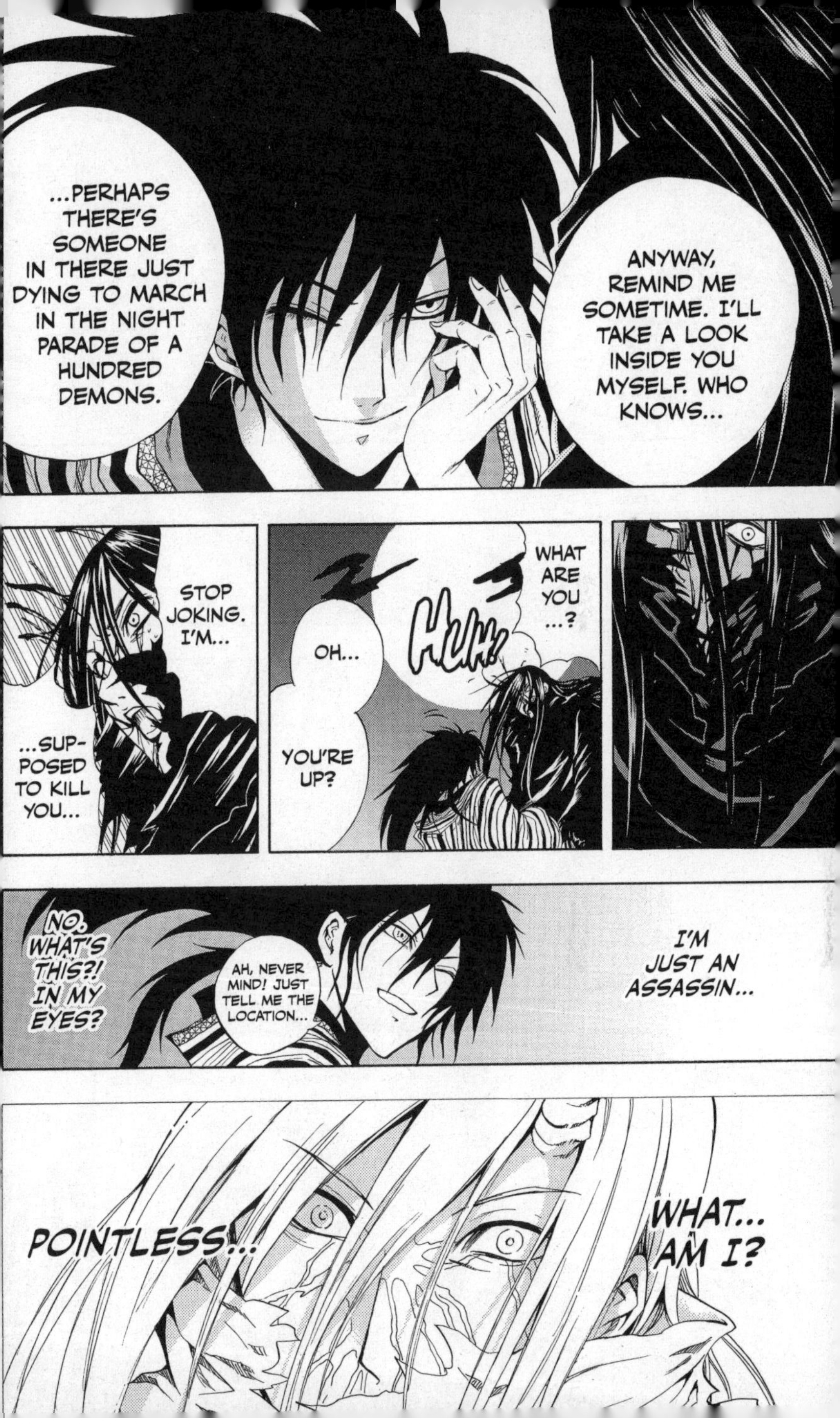
ANYWAY, REMIND ME SOMETIME. I'LL TAKE A LOOK INSIDE YOU MYSELF. WHO KNOWS...
...PERHAPS THERE'S SOMEONE IN THERE JUST DYING TO MARCH IN THE NIGHT PARADE OF A HUNDRED DEMONS.
WHAT ARE YOU ...?
HUH!
OH...
YOU'RE UP?
STOP JOKING. I'M...
...SUP-POSED TO KILL YOU...
I'M JUST AN ASSASSIN...
AH, NEVER MIND! JUST TELL ME THE LOCATION...
NO. WHAT'S THIS?! IN MY EYES?
WHAT... AM I?
POINTLESS...

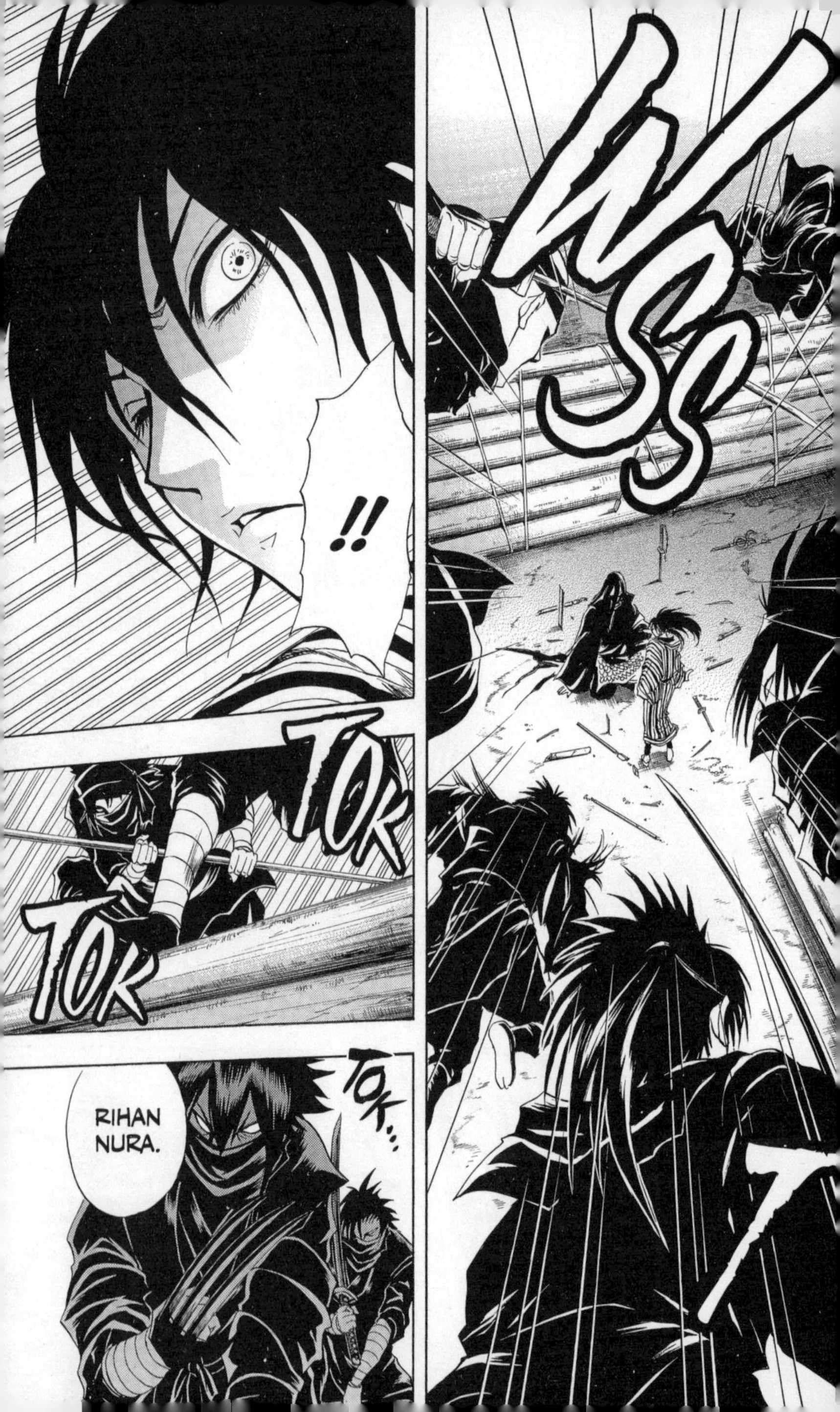
WHSS
!!
TOK
TOK
TOK...
RIHAN NURA.

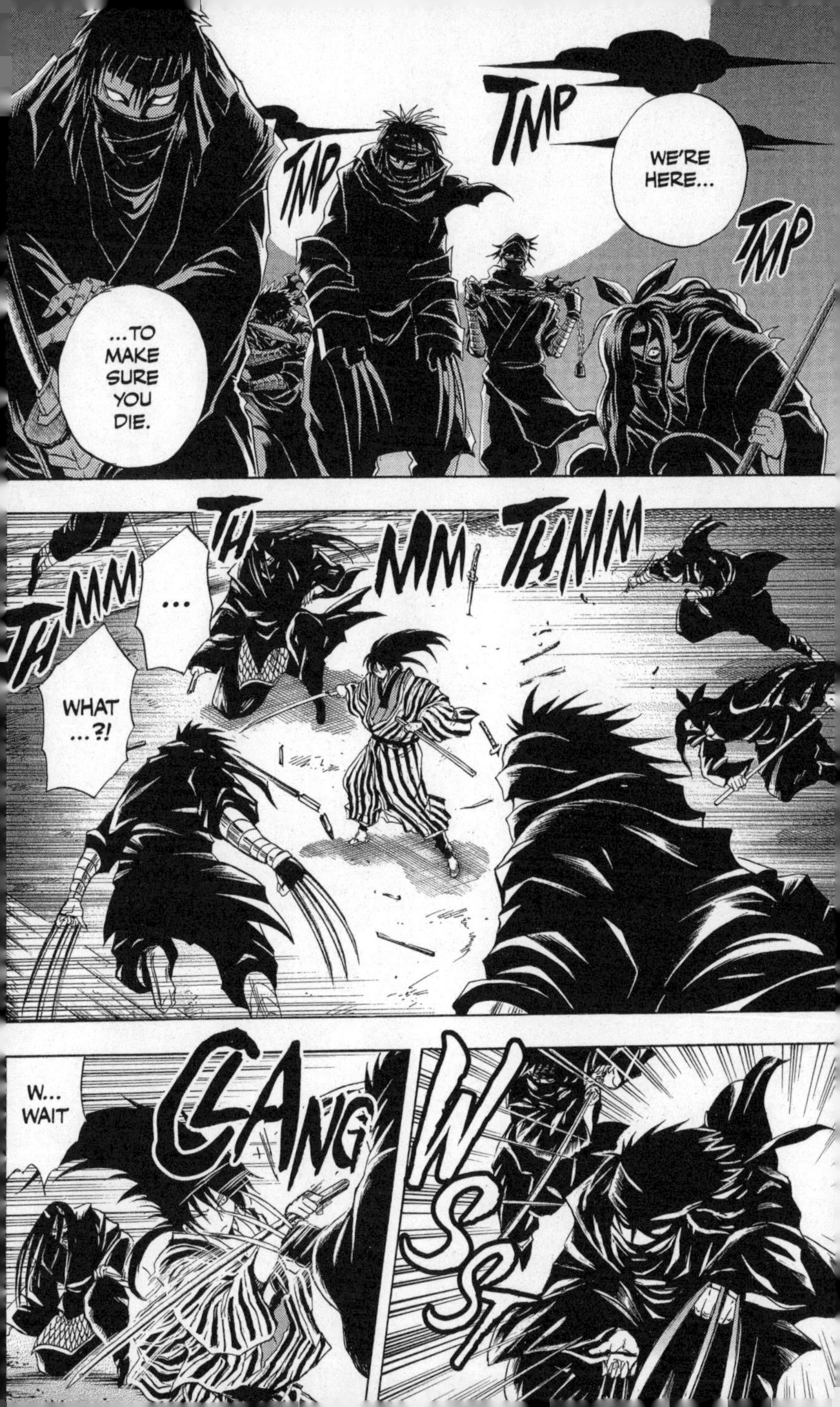
TMP
TMP
WE'RE HERE...
TMP
...TO MAKE SURE YOU DIE.
THMM
THMM
THMM
...
WHAT ...?!
CLANG
WSS
W... WAIT

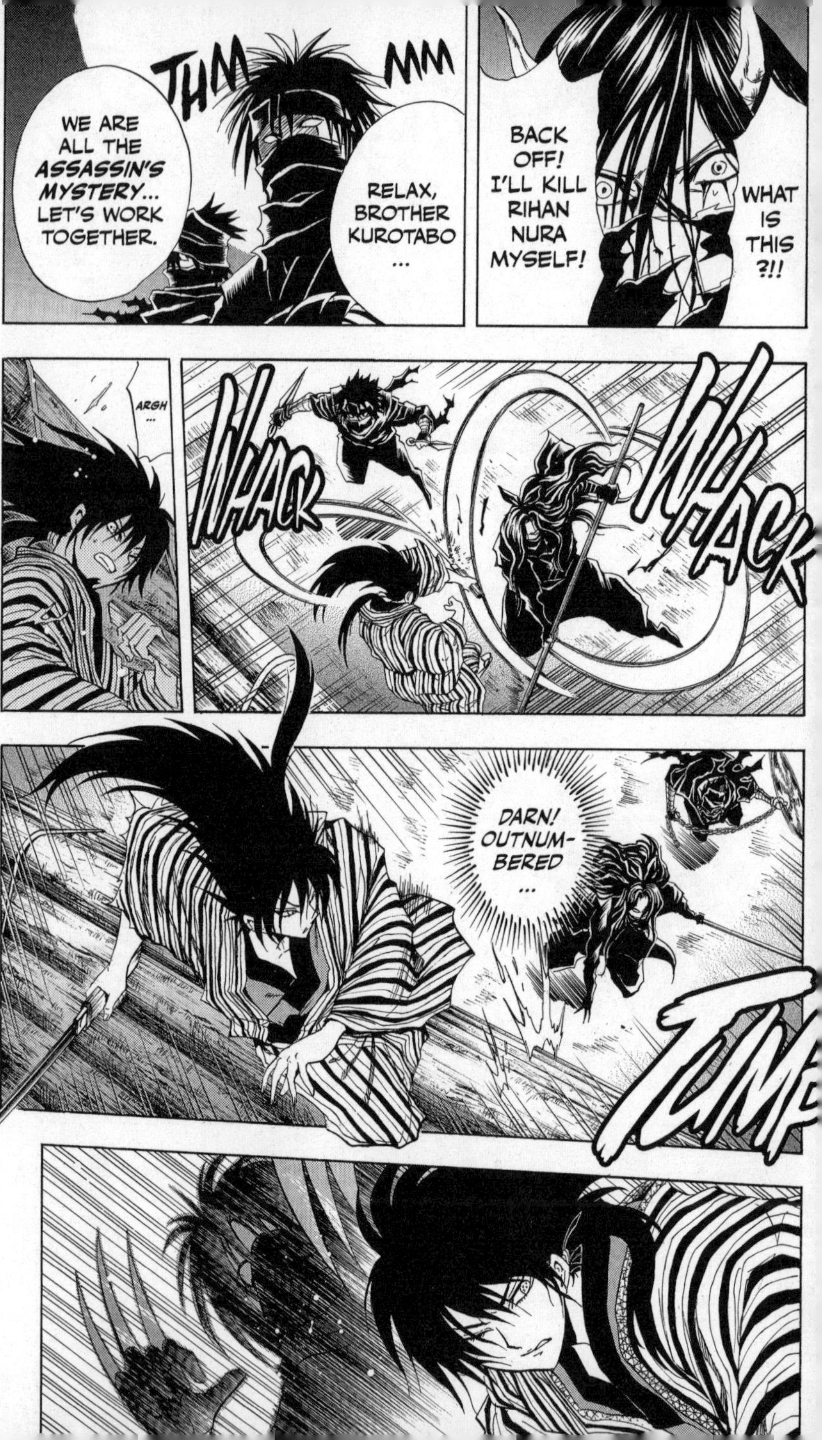
WHAT IS THIS ?!!
BACK OFF! I'LL KILL RIHAN NURA MYSELF!
THMMM
RELAX, BROTHER KUROTABO ...
WE ARE ALL THE ASSASSIN'S MYSTERY... LET'S WORK TOGETHER.
WHACK
WHACK
ARGH ...
TUMP
DARN! OUTNUMBERED ...

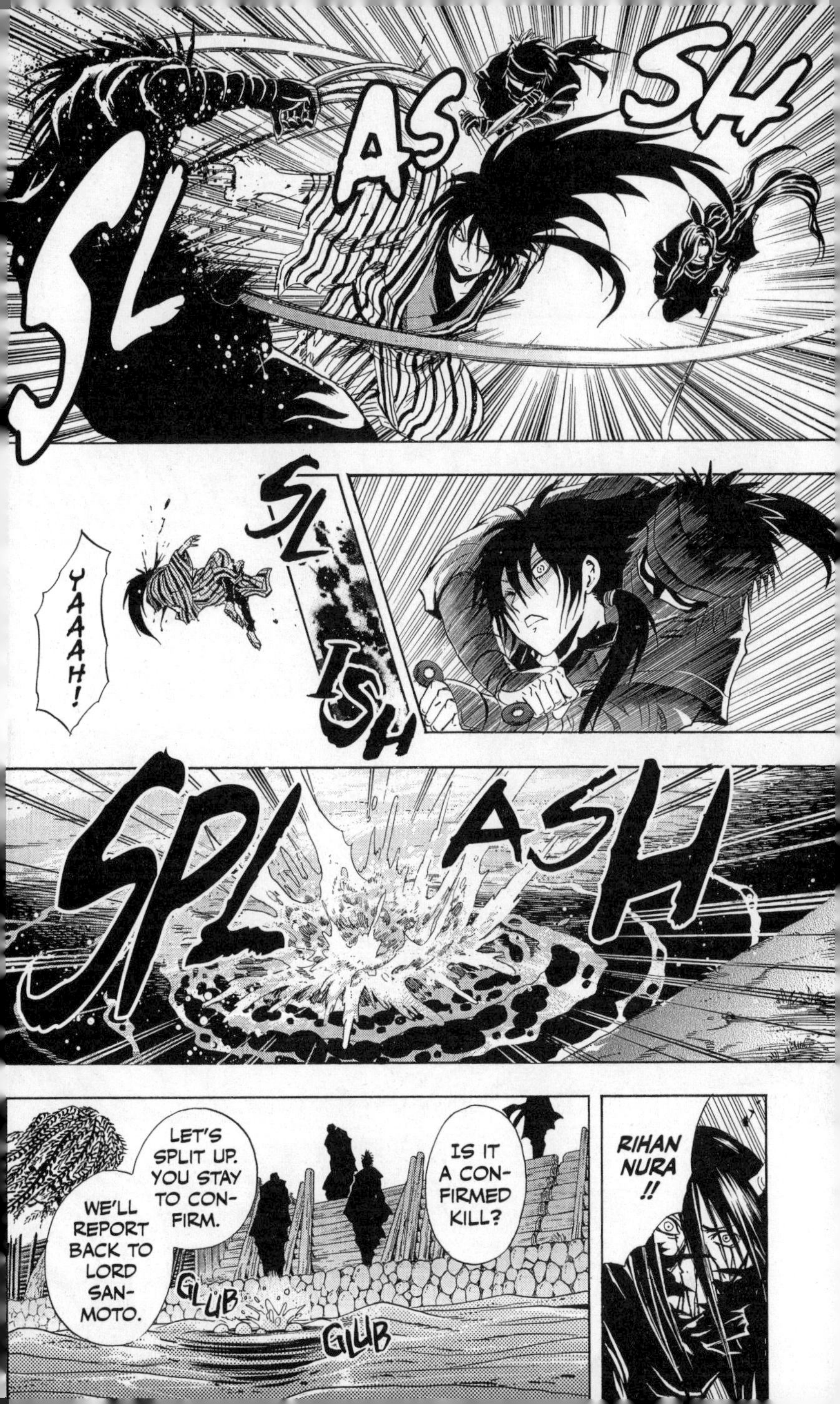

SLASH
SLISH
YAAAAH!
SPLASH
RIHAN NURA!!
IS IT A CONFIRMED KILL?
LET'S SPLIT UP. YOU STAY TO CONFIRM.
WE'LL REPORT BACK TO LORD SANMOTO.
GLUB
GLUB

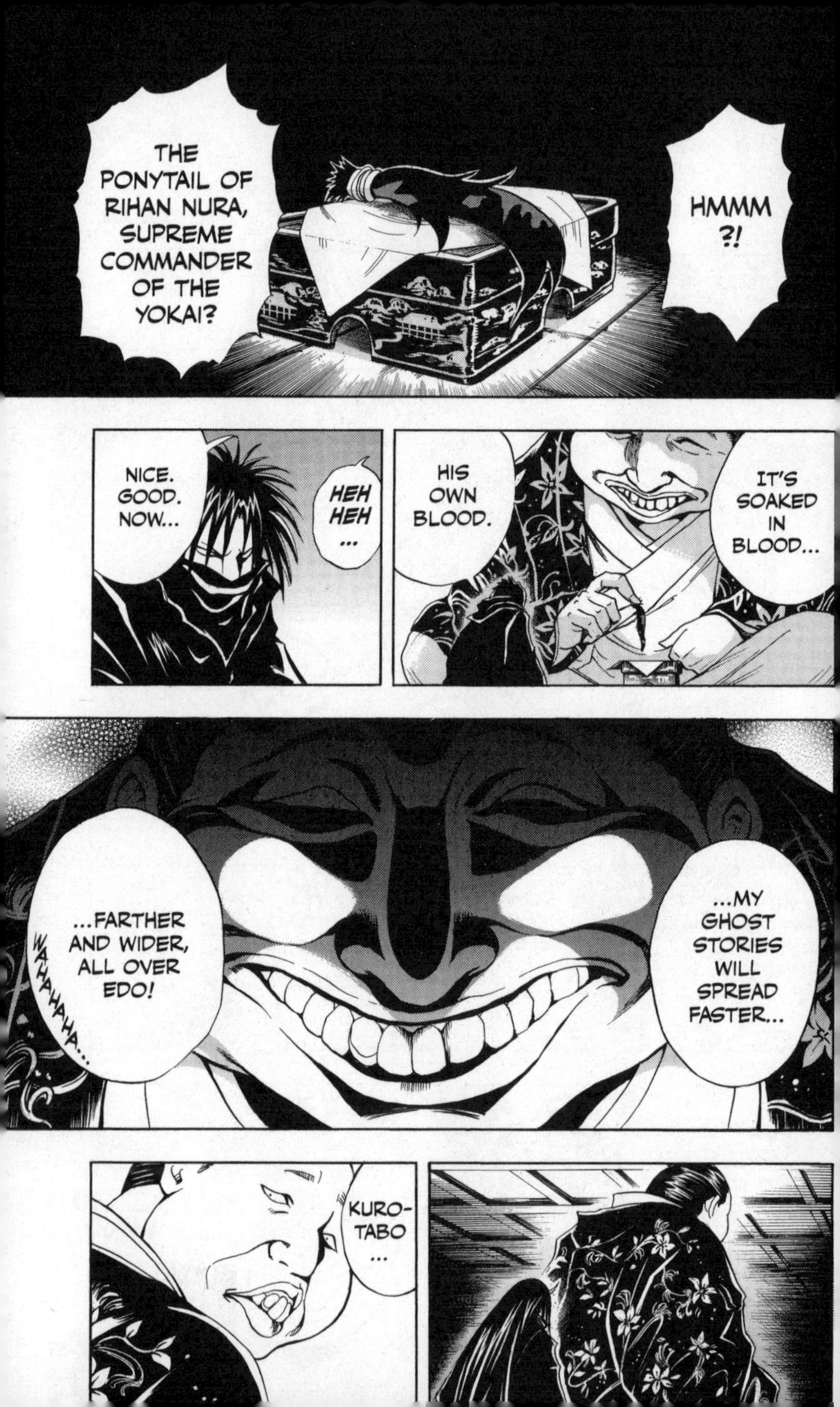
HMMM ?!
THE PONYTAIL OF RIHAN NURA, SUPREME COMMANDER OF THE YOKAI?
IT'S SOAKED IN BLOOD...
HIS OWN BLOOD.
HEH HEH ...
NICE. GOOD. NOW...
...MY GHOST STORIES WILL SPREAD FASTER...
...FARTHER AND WIDER, ALL OVER EDO!
WAHAHAHAHA...
KURO-TABO ...

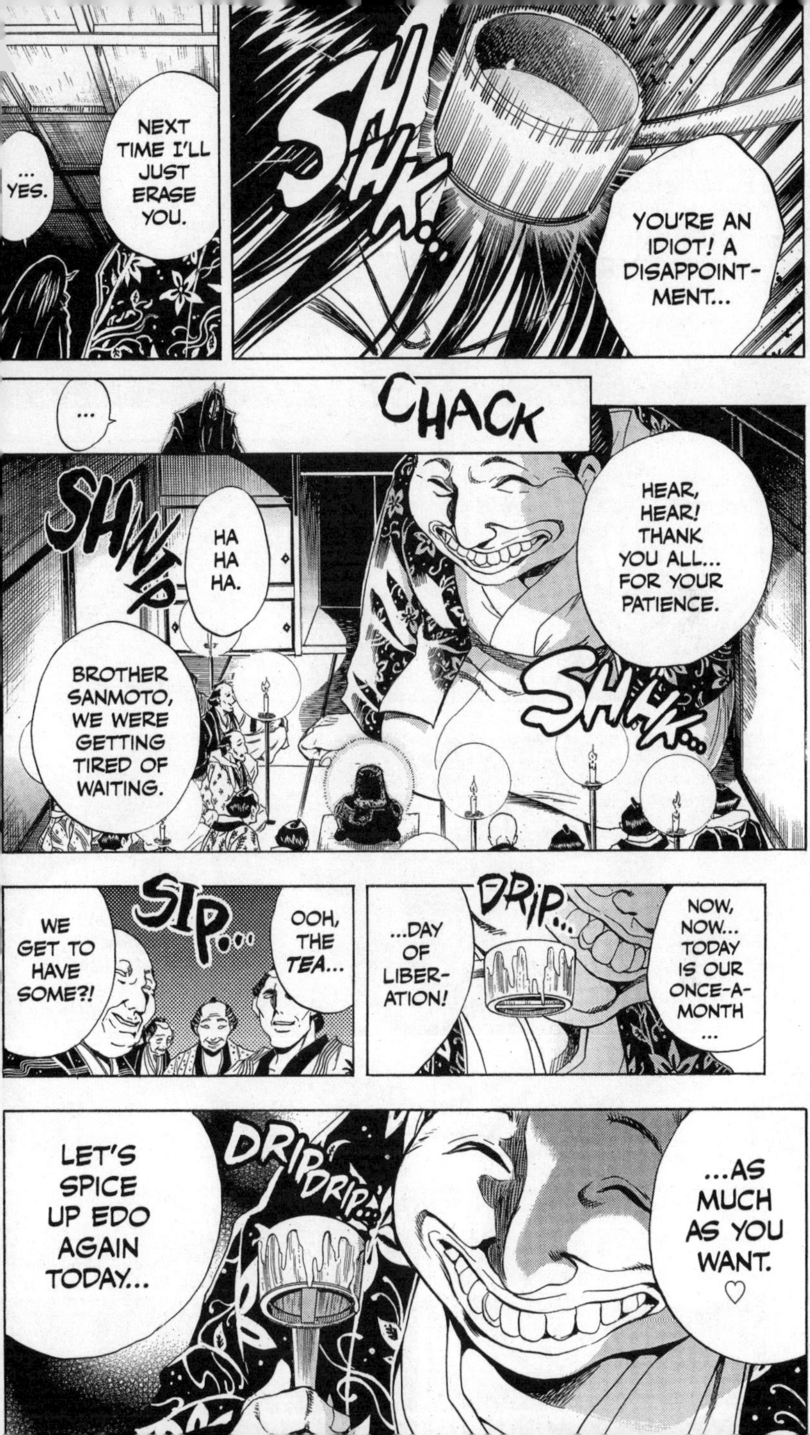
SHHK...
YOU'RE AN IDIOT! A DISAPPOINTMENT...
NEXT TIME I'LL JUST ERASE YOU.
... YES.
CHACK
...
HEAR, HEAR! THANK YOU ALL... FOR YOUR PATIENCE.
HA HA HA.
SHWIP
SHHK...
BROTHER SANMOTO, WE WERE GETTING TIRED OF WAITING.
NOW, NOW... TODAY IS OUR ONCE-A-MONTH ...
DRIP...
...DAY OF LIBERATION!
OOH, THE *TEA*...
SIP...
WE GET TO HAVE SOME?!
...AS MUCH AS YOU WANT. ♡
DRIPDRIP...
LET'S SPICE UP EDO AGAIN TODAY...

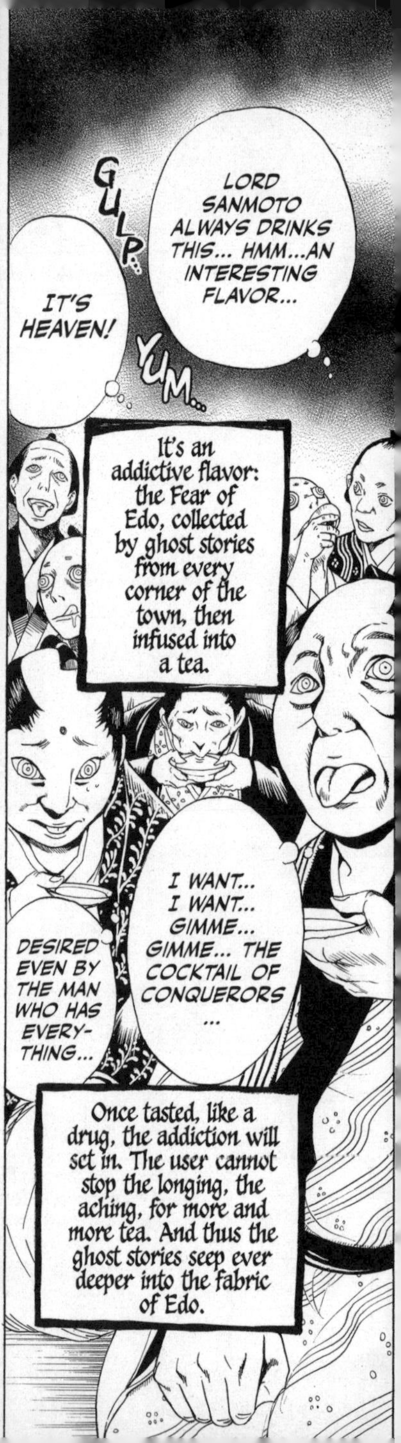
LORD SANMOTO ALWAYS DRINKS THIS... HMM...AN INTERESTING FLAVOR...
GULP...
IT'S HEAVEN!
YUM...
It's an addictive flavor: the Fear of Edo, collected by ghost stories from every corner of the town, then infused into a tea.
I WANT... I WANT... GIMME... GIMME... THE COCKTAIL OF CONQUERORS ...
DESIRED EVEN BY THE MAN WHO HAS EVERY-THING...
Once tasted, like a drug, the addiction will set in. The user cannot stop the longing, the aching, for more and more tea. And thus the ghost stories seep ever deeper into the fabric of Edo.

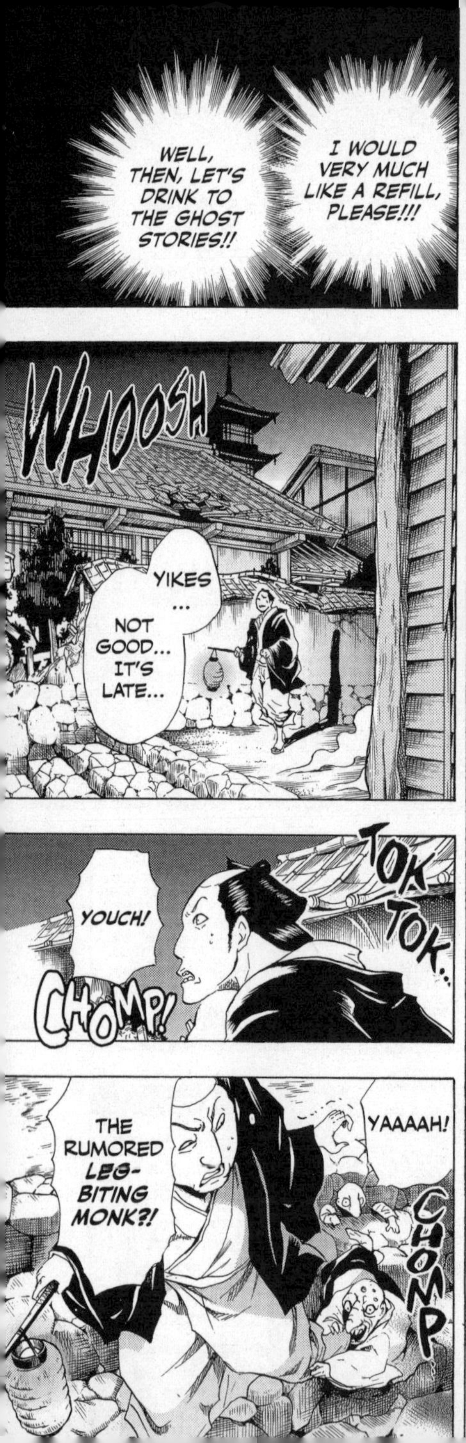
I WOULD VERY MUCH LIKE A REFILL, PLEASE!!!
WELL, THEN, LET'S DRINK TO THE GHOST STORIES!!
WHOOSH
YIKES ... NOT GOOD... IT'S LATE...
TOK TOK...
YOUCH!
CHOMP!
YAAAAH!
CHOMP
THE RUMORED LEG-BITING MONK?!

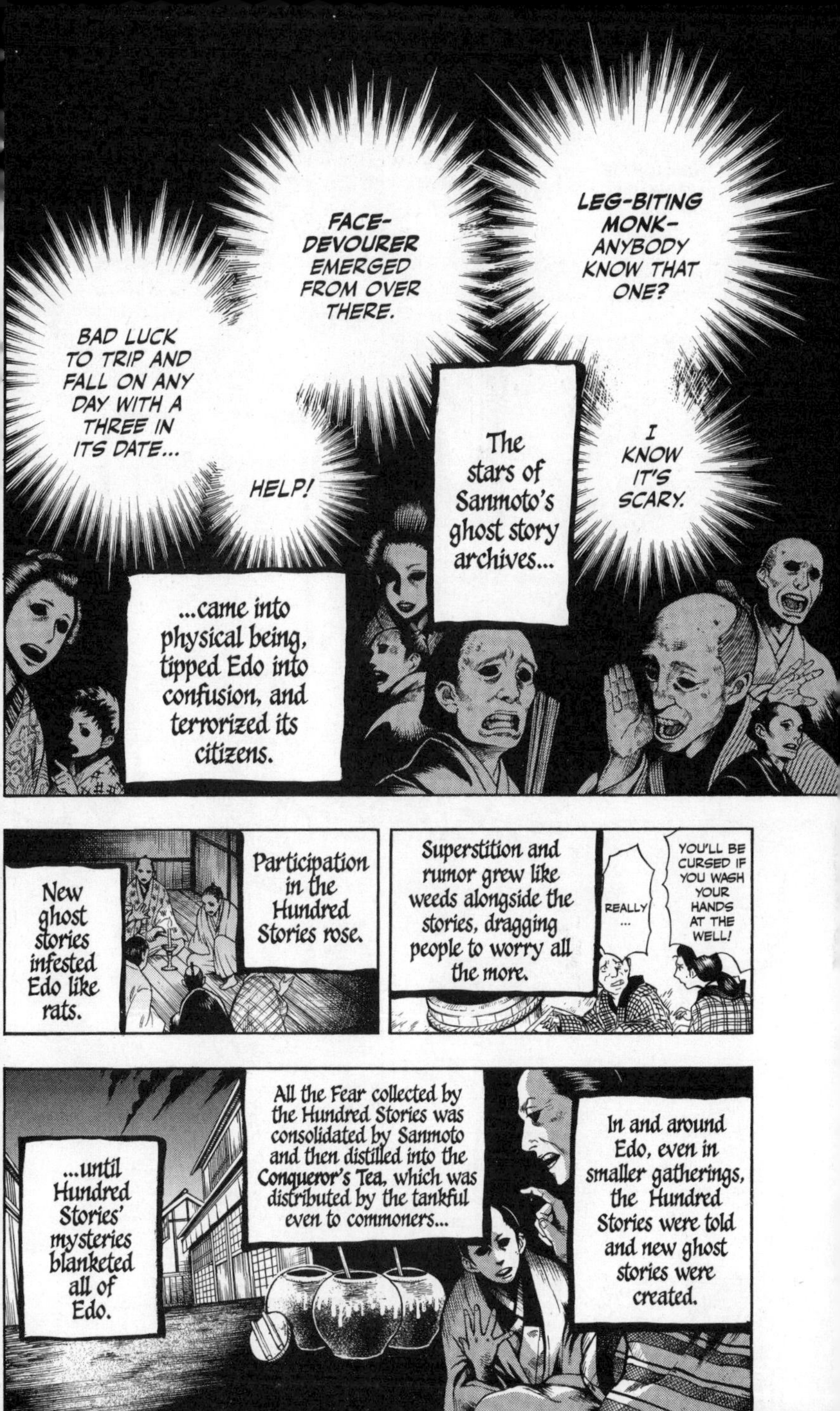
LEG-BITING MONK— ANYBODY KNOW THAT ONE?
I KNOW IT'S SCARY.
FACE-DEVOURER EMERGED FROM OVER THERE.
The stars of Sanmoto's ghost story archives...
HELP!
BAD LUCK TO TRIP AND FALL ON ANY DAY WITH A THREE IN ITS DATE...
...came into physical being, tipped Edo into confusion, and terrorized its citizens.
YOU'LL BE CURSED IF YOU WASH YOUR HANDS AT THE WELL!
REALLY...
Superstition and rumor grew like weeds alongside the stories, dragging people to worry all the more.
Participation in the Hundred Stories rose.
New ghost stories infested Edo like rats.
In and around Edo, even in smaller gatherings, the Hundred Stories were told and new ghost stories were created.
All the Fear collected by the Hundred Stories was consolidated by Sanmoto and then distilled into the Conqueror's Tea, which was distributed by the tankful even to commoners...
...until Hundred Stories' mysteries blanketed all of Edo.

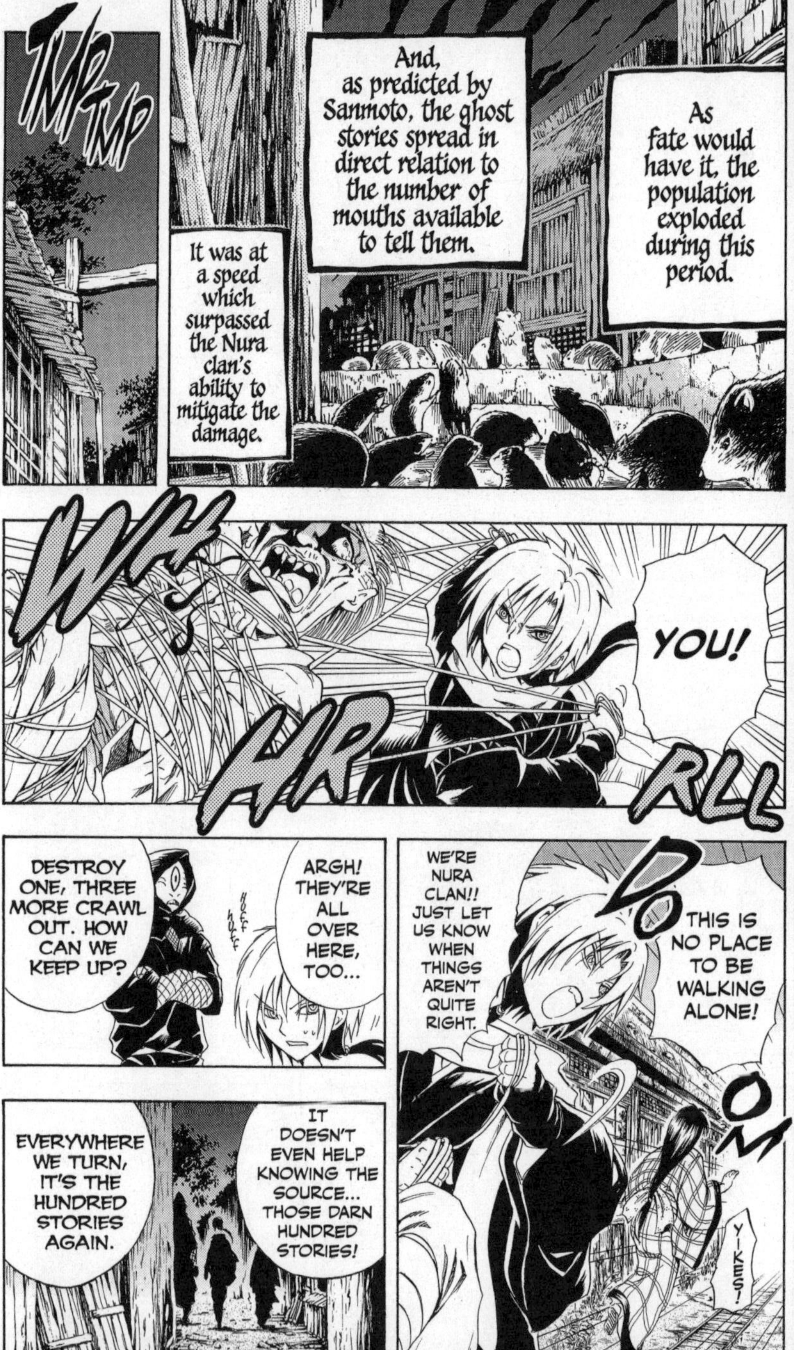
As fate would have it, the population exploded during this period.
And, as predicted by Sanmoto, the ghost stories spread in direct relation to the number of mouths available to tell them.
It was at a speed which surpassed the Nura clan's ability to mitigate the damage.
TMP TMP
YOU!
WH HR RLL
DO OM
THIS IS NO PLACE TO BE WALKING ALONE!
WE'RE NURA CLAN!! JUST LET US KNOW WHEN THINGS AREN'T QUITE RIGHT.
YIKES!
ARGH! THEY'RE ALL OVER HERE, TOO...
HUFF HUFF
DESTROY ONE, THREE MORE CRAWL OUT. HOW CAN WE KEEP UP?
IT DOESN'T EVEN HELP KNOWING THE SOURCE... THOSE DARN HUNDRED STORIES!
EVERYWHERE WE TURN, IT'S THE HUNDRED STORIES AGAIN.

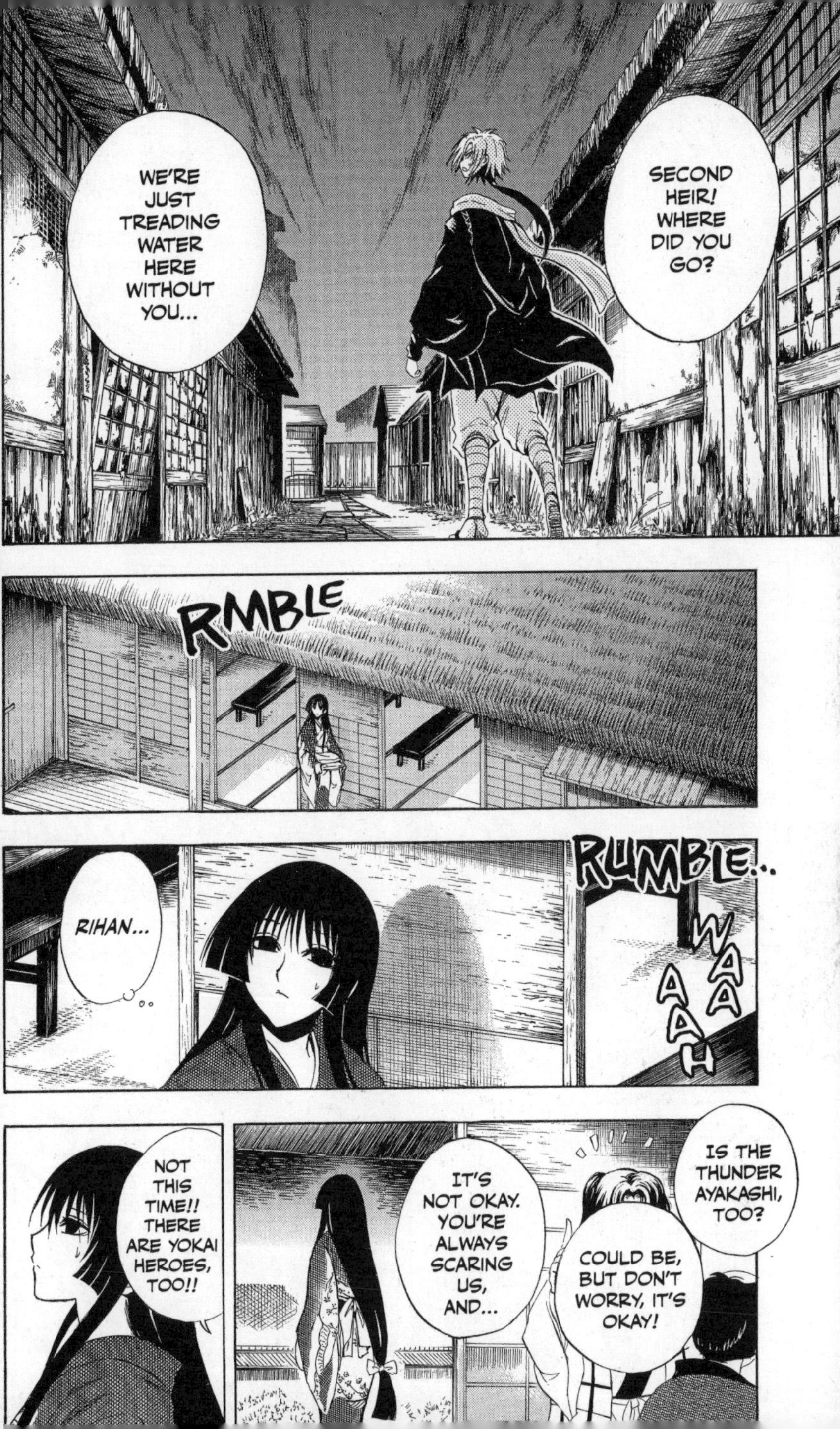
SECOND HEIR! WHERE DID YOU GO?
WE'RE JUST TREADING WATER HERE WITHOUT YOU...
RMBLE
RUMBLE...
WAAAAH
RIHAN...
IS THE THUNDER AYAKASHI, TOO?
COULD BE, BUT DON'T WORRY, IT'S OKAY!
IT'S NOT OKAY. YOU'RE ALWAYS SCARING US, AND...
NOT THIS TIME!! THERE ARE YOKAI HEROES, TOO!!

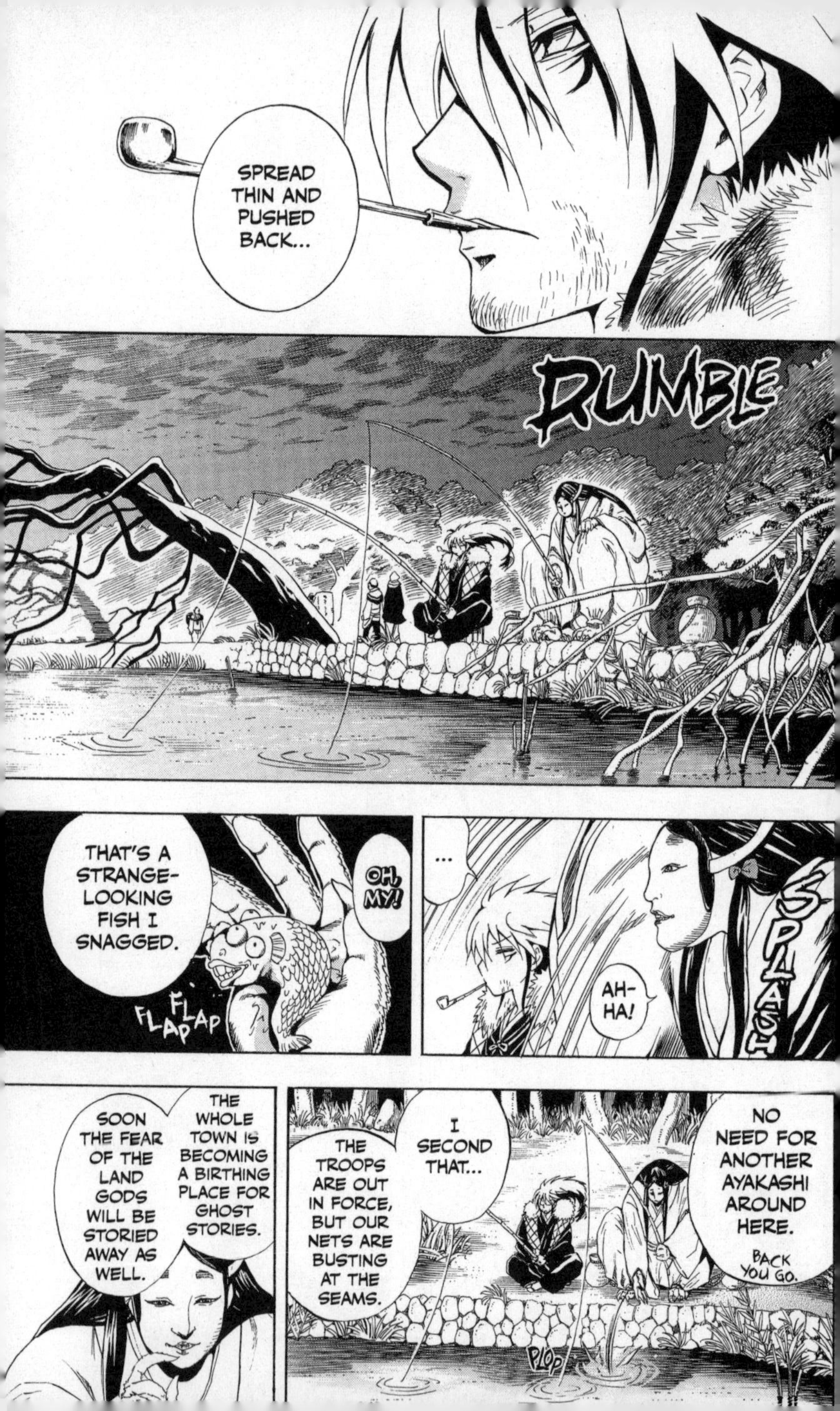
SPREAD THIN AND PUSHED BACK...
RUMBLE
...
AH-HA!
SPLASH
OH, MY!
THAT'S A STRANGE-LOOKING FISH I SNAGGED.
FLAP FLAP
NO NEED FOR ANOTHER AYAKASHI AROUND HERE.
BACK YOU GO.
I SECOND THAT...
THE TROOPS ARE OUT IN FORCE, BUT OUR NETS ARE BUSTING AT THE SEAMS.
PLOP
THE WHOLE TOWN IS BECOMING A BIRTHING PLACE FOR GHOST STORIES.
SOON THE FEAR OF THE LAND GODS WILL BE STORIED AWAY AS WELL.

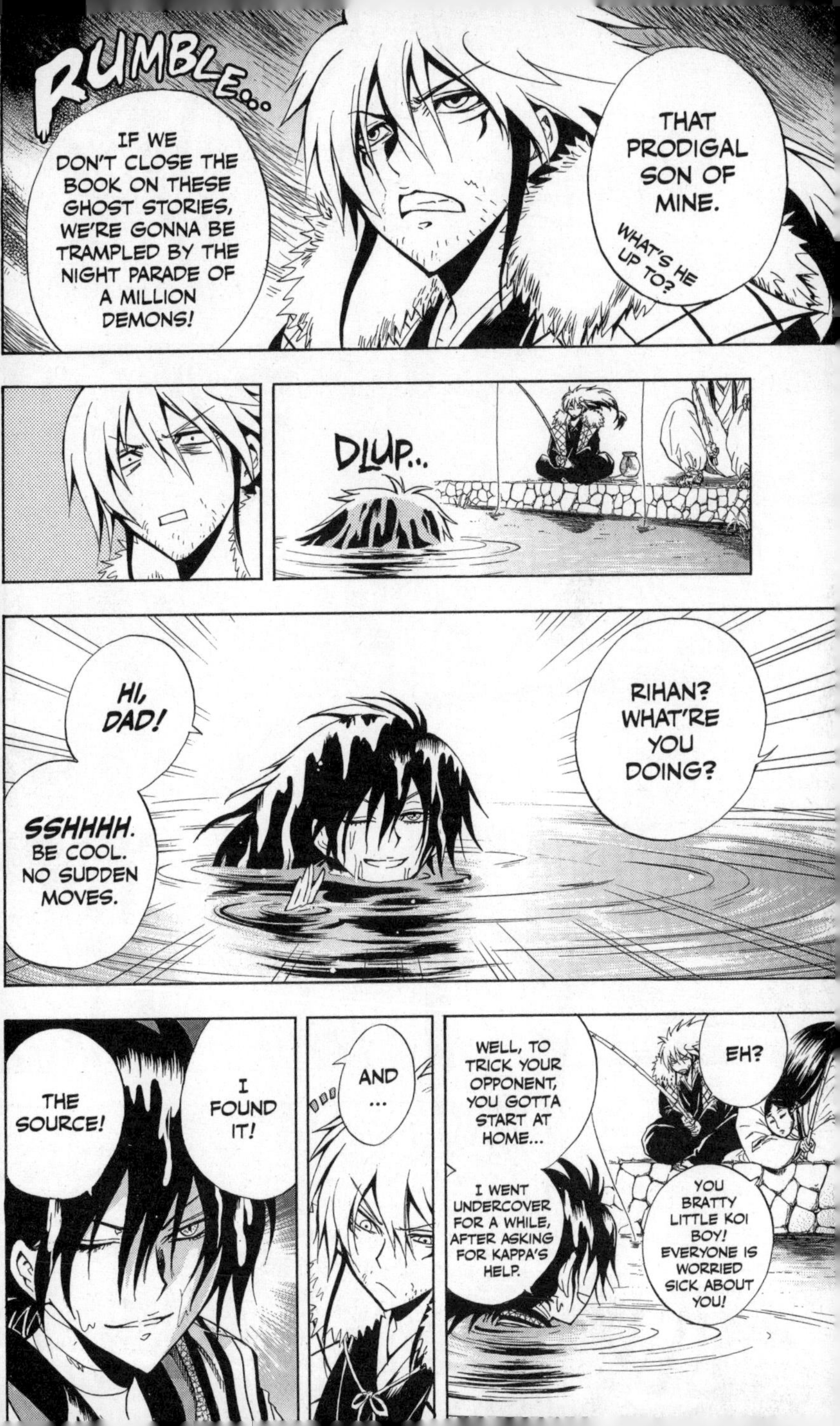
THAT PRODIGAL SON OF MINE.
WHAT'S HE UP TO?
RUMBLE...
IF WE DON'T CLOSE THE BOOK ON THESE GHOST STORIES, WE'RE GONNA BE TRAMPLED BY THE NIGHT PARADE OF A MILLION DEMONS!
DLUP...
RIHAN? WHAT'RE YOU DOING?
HI, DAD!
SSHHHH. BE COOL. NO SUDDEN MOVES.
EH?
WELL, TO TRICK YOUR OPPONENT, YOU GOTTA START AT HOME...
YOU BRATTY LITTLE KOI BOY! EVERYONE IS WORRIED SICK ABOUT YOU!
I WENT UNDERCOVER FOR A WHILE, AFTER ASKING FOR KAPPA'S HELP.
AND ...
I FOUND IT!
THE SOURCE!

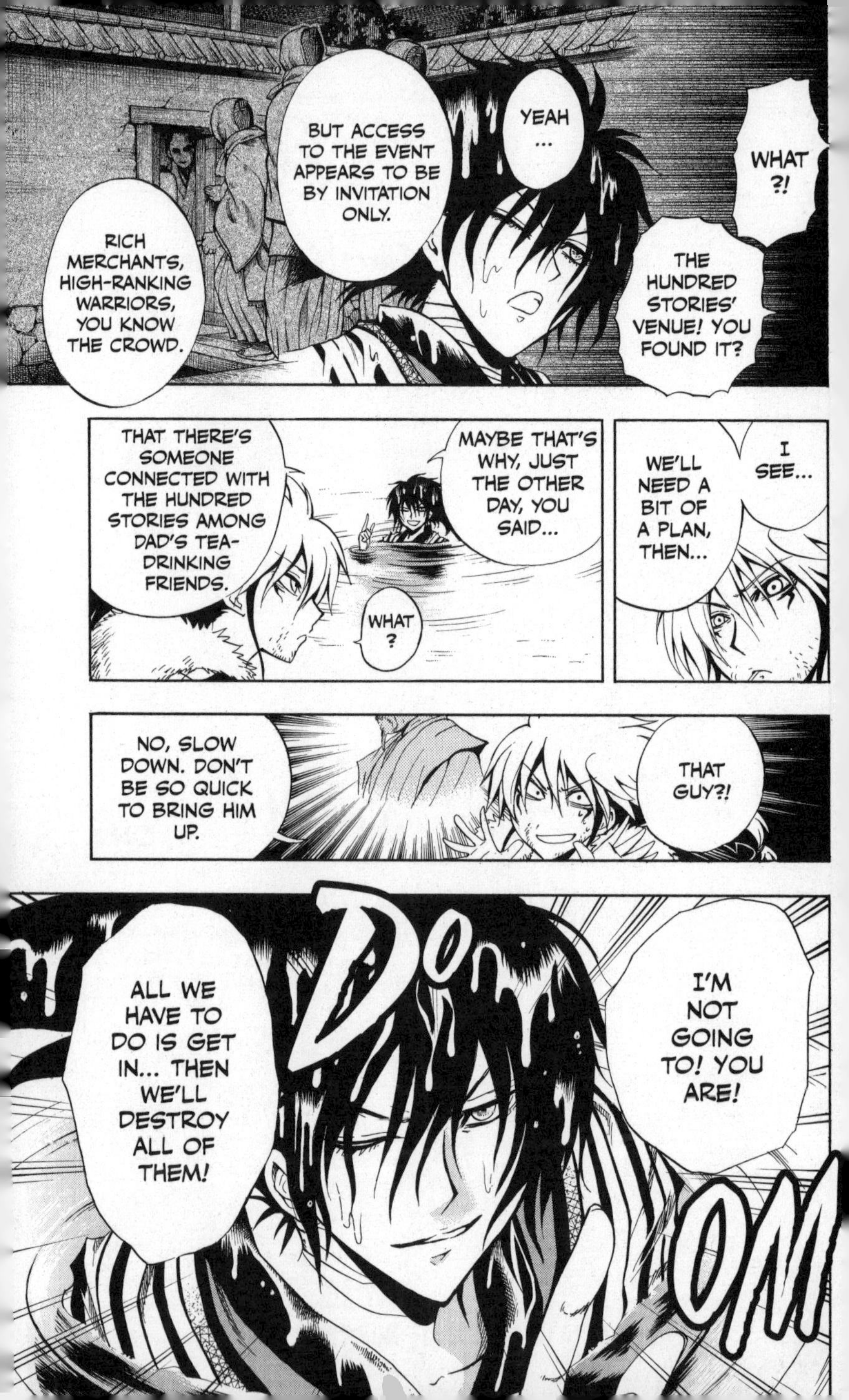
WHAT?!
THE HUNDRED STORIES' VENUE! YOU FOUND IT?
YEAH...
BUT ACCESS TO THE EVENT APPEARS TO BE BY INVITATION ONLY.
RICH MERCHANTS, HIGH-RANKING WARRIORS, YOU KNOW THE CROWD.
I SEE...
WE'LL NEED A BIT OF A PLAN, THEN...
MAYBE THAT'S WHY, JUST THE OTHER DAY, YOU SAID...
THAT THERE'S SOMEONE CONNECTED WITH THE HUNDRED STORIES AMONG DAD'S TEA-DRINKING FRIENDS.
WHAT?
THAT GUY?!
NO, SLOW DOWN. DON'T BE SO QUICK TO BRING HIM UP.
I'M NOT GOING TO! YOU ARE!
ALL WE HAVE TO DO IS GET IN... THEN WE'LL DESTROY ALL OF THEM!
DOOM

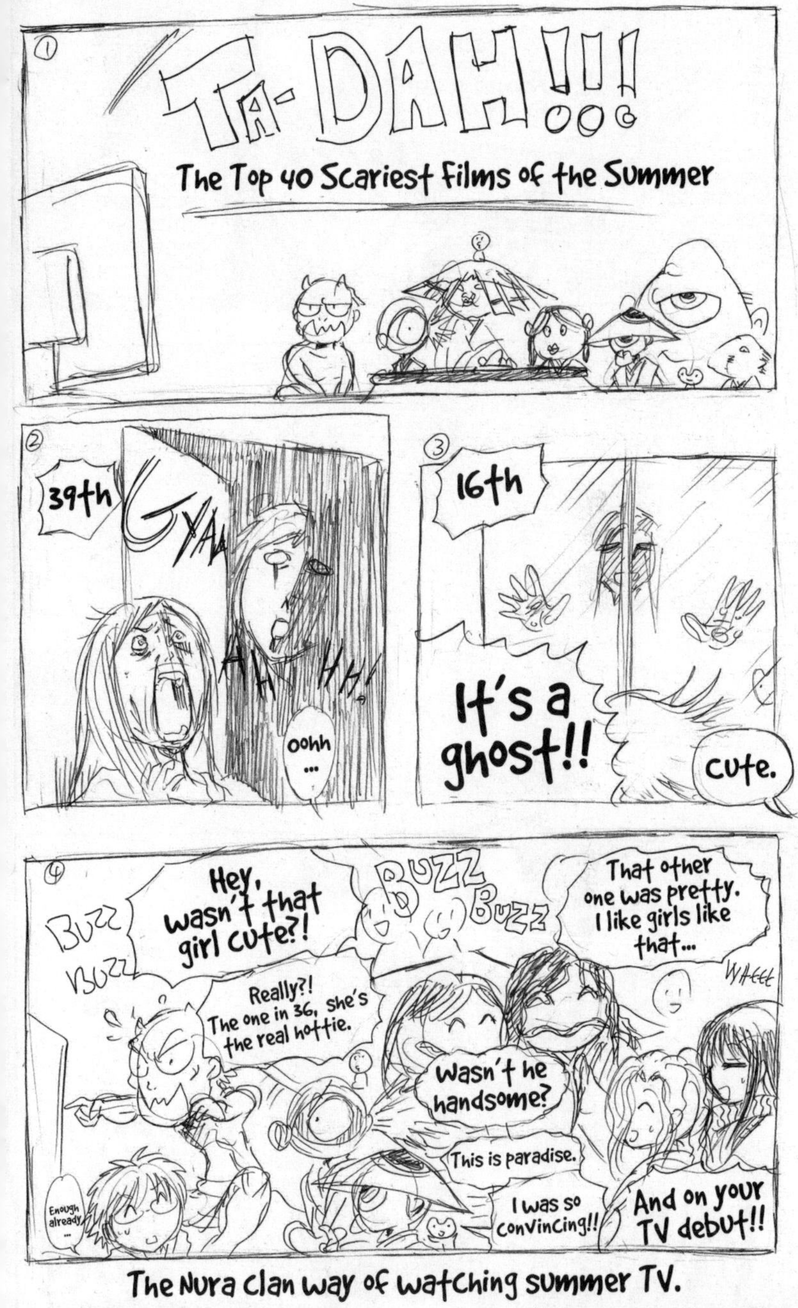
TA-DAH!!!
The Top 40 Scariest Films of the Summer
39th
GYAAAHH!
oohh ...
16th
It's a ghost!!
cute.
BUZZ BUZZ
Hey, wasn't that girl cute?!
BUZZ BUZZ
That other one was pretty. I like girls like that...
WAEEE
Really?! The one in 36, she's the real hottie.
Wasn't he handsome?
This is paradise.
Enough already ...
I was so convincing!!
And on your TV debut!!

The Nura Clan way of watching summer TV.

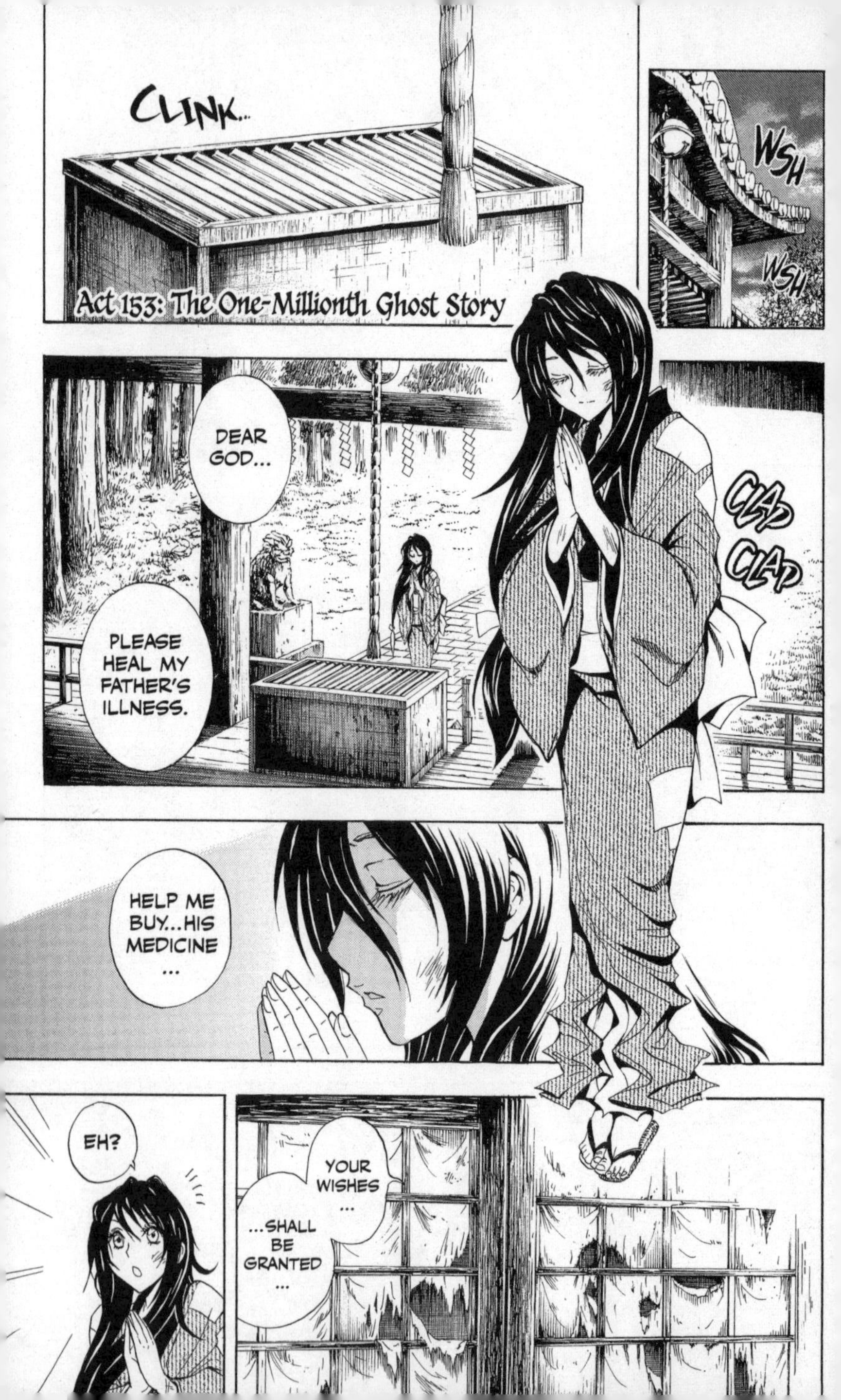
WSH
WSH
CLINK...
Act 153: The One-Millionth Ghost Story
CLAP
CLAP
DEAR GOD...
PLEASE HEAL MY FATHER'S ILLNESS.
HELP ME BUY...HIS MEDICINE ...
YOUR WISHES ...
...SHALL BE GRANTED ...
EH?

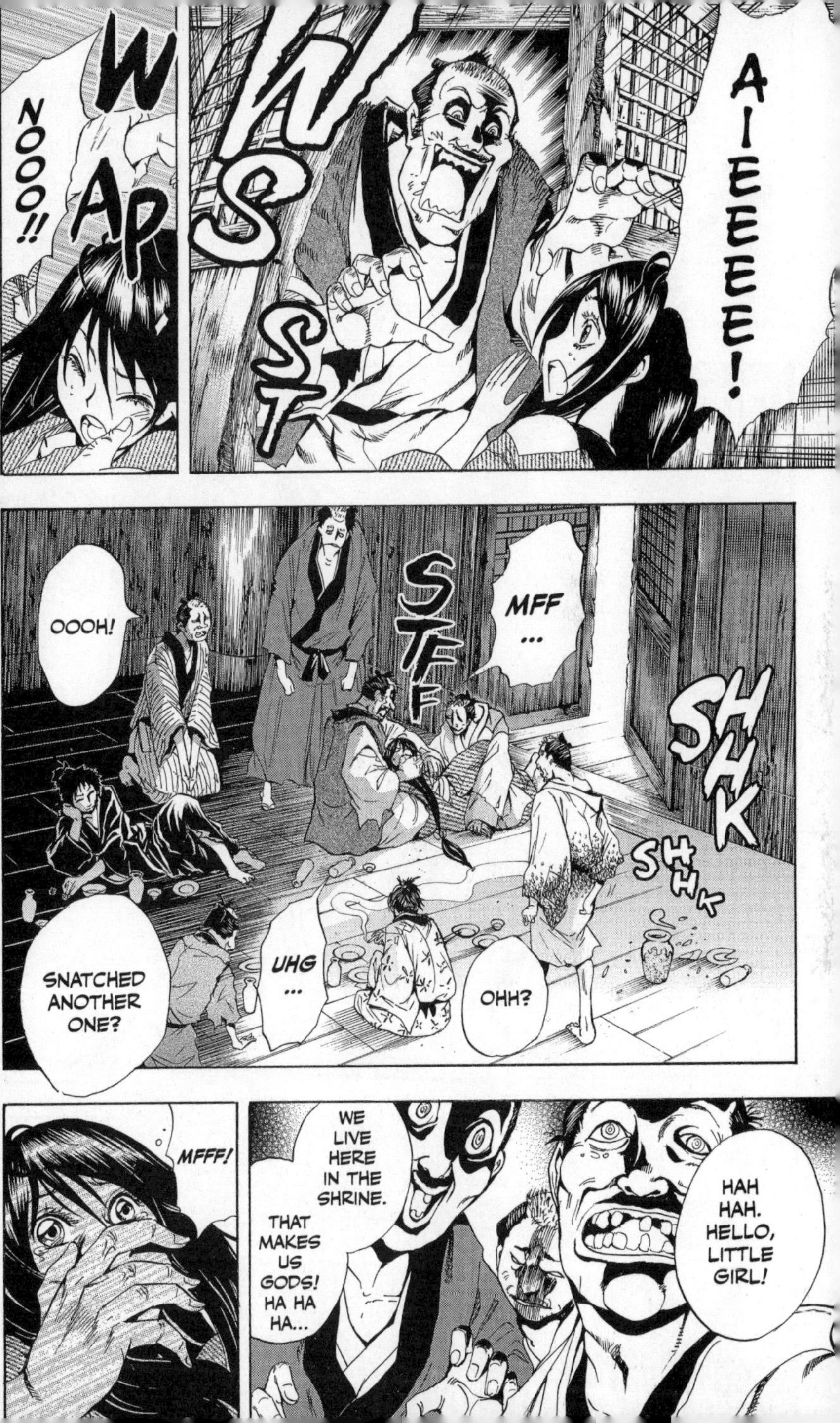
AIEEEE!
SST
NOOOO!!
WAP
SHHK
SHHK
MFF ...
STFF
OHH?
UHG ...
OOOH!
SNATCHED ANOTHER ONE?
HAH HAH. HELLO, LITTLE GIRL!
WE LIVE HERE IN THE SHRINE.
THAT MAKES US GODS! HA HA HA...
MFFF!

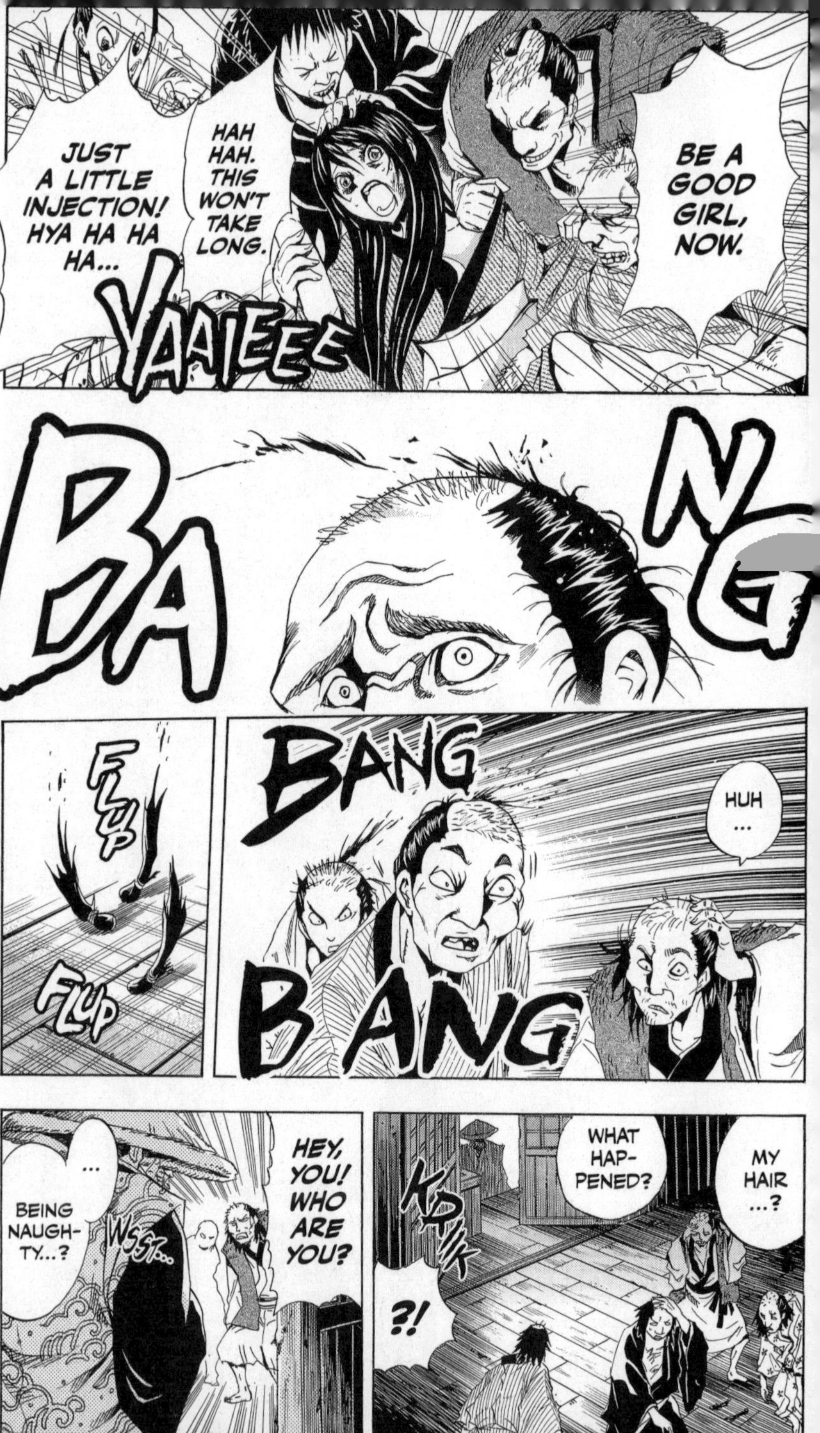
BE A GOOD GIRL, NOW.
HAH HAH. THIS WON'T TAKE LONG.
JUST A LITTLE INJECTION! HYA HA HA HA...
YAAIEEE
BANG
BANG
HUH ...
BANG
FLUP
FLUP
MY HAIR ...?
WHAT HAP-PENED?
KDRIK
?!
HEY, YOU! WHO ARE YOU?
...
WSST...
BEING NAUGH-TY...?

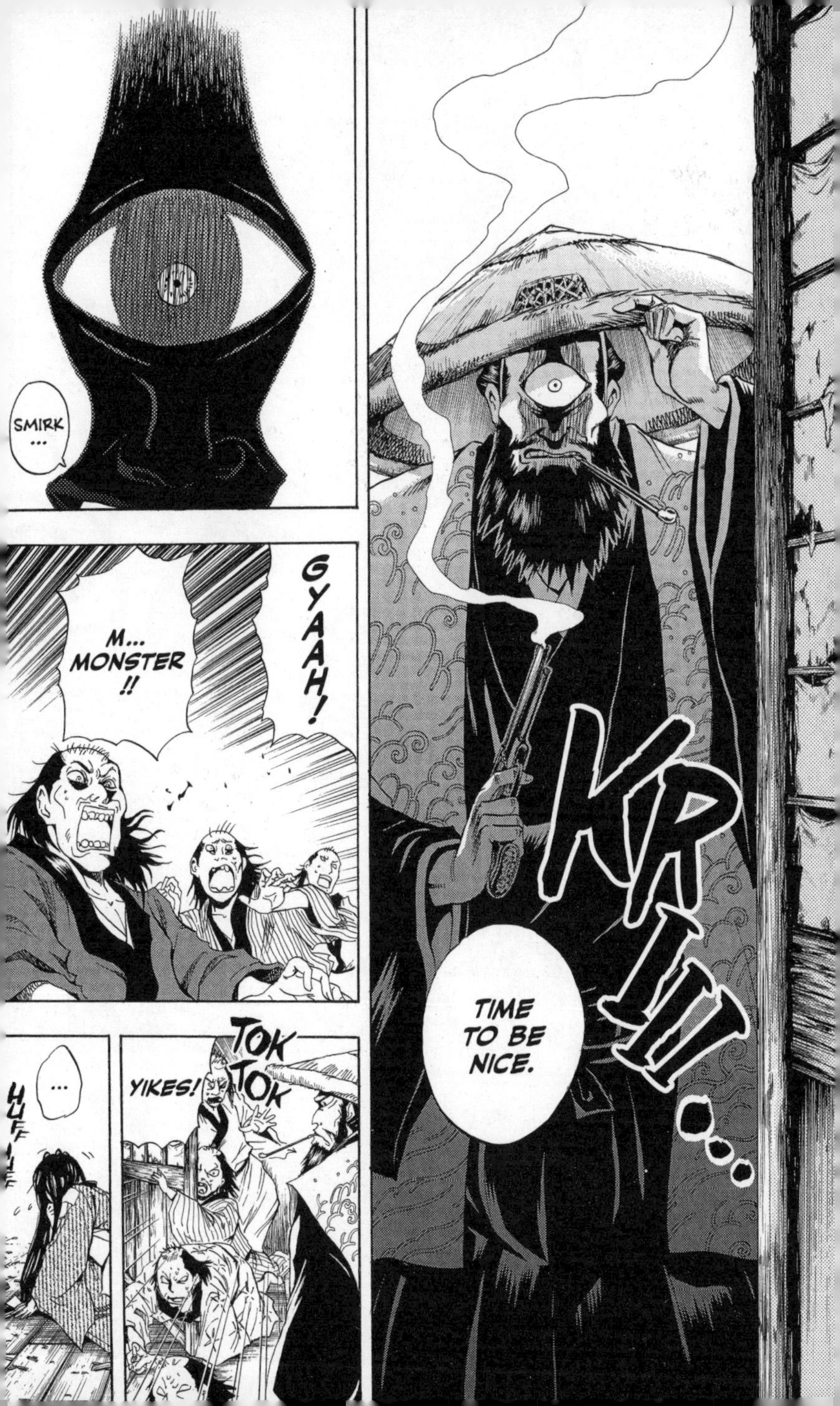

TIME TO BE NICE.
KRIIII...
SMIRK...
GYAAAH!
M... MONSTER!!
TOK TOK
YIKES!
...
HUFF

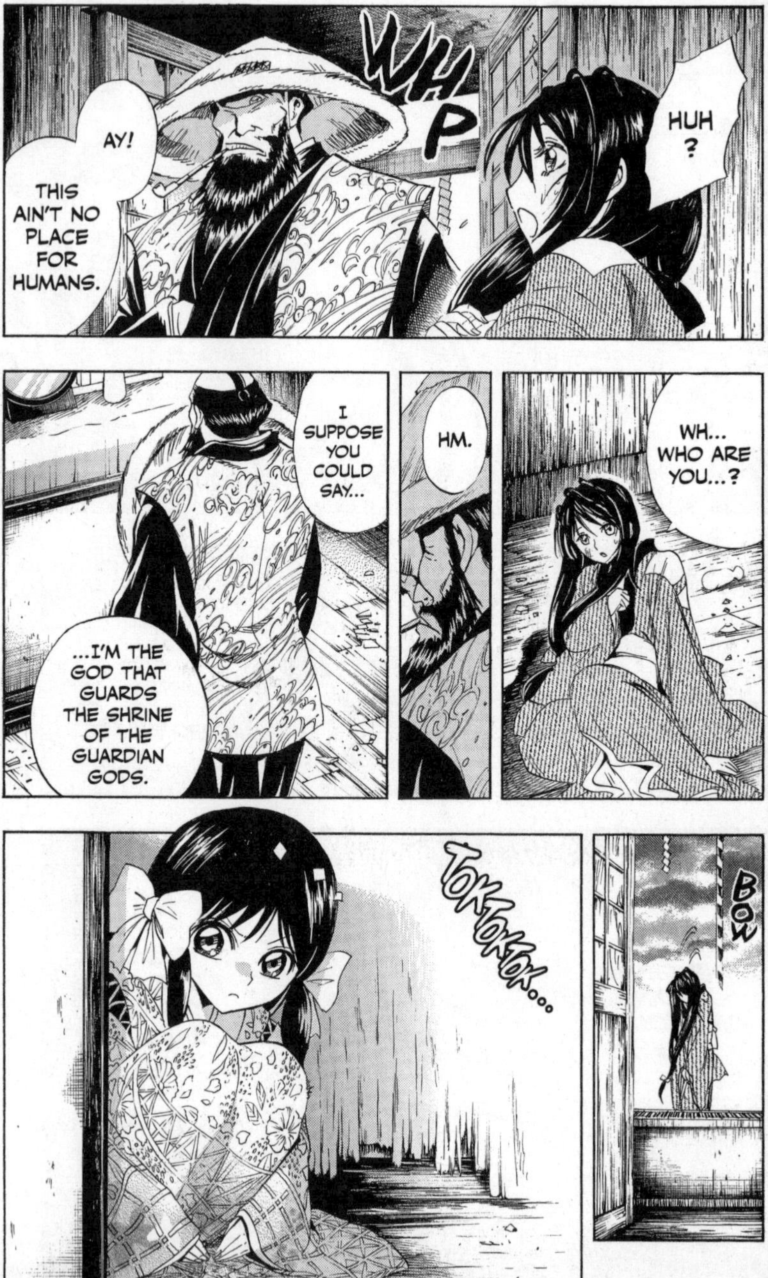
HUH?
WHP
AY!
THIS AIN'T NO PLACE FOR HUMANS.
WH... WHO ARE YOU...?
HM.
I SUPPOSE YOU COULD SAY...
...I'M THE GOD THAT GUARDS THE SHRINE OF THE GUARDIAN GODS.
BOW
TOKTOKTOK...

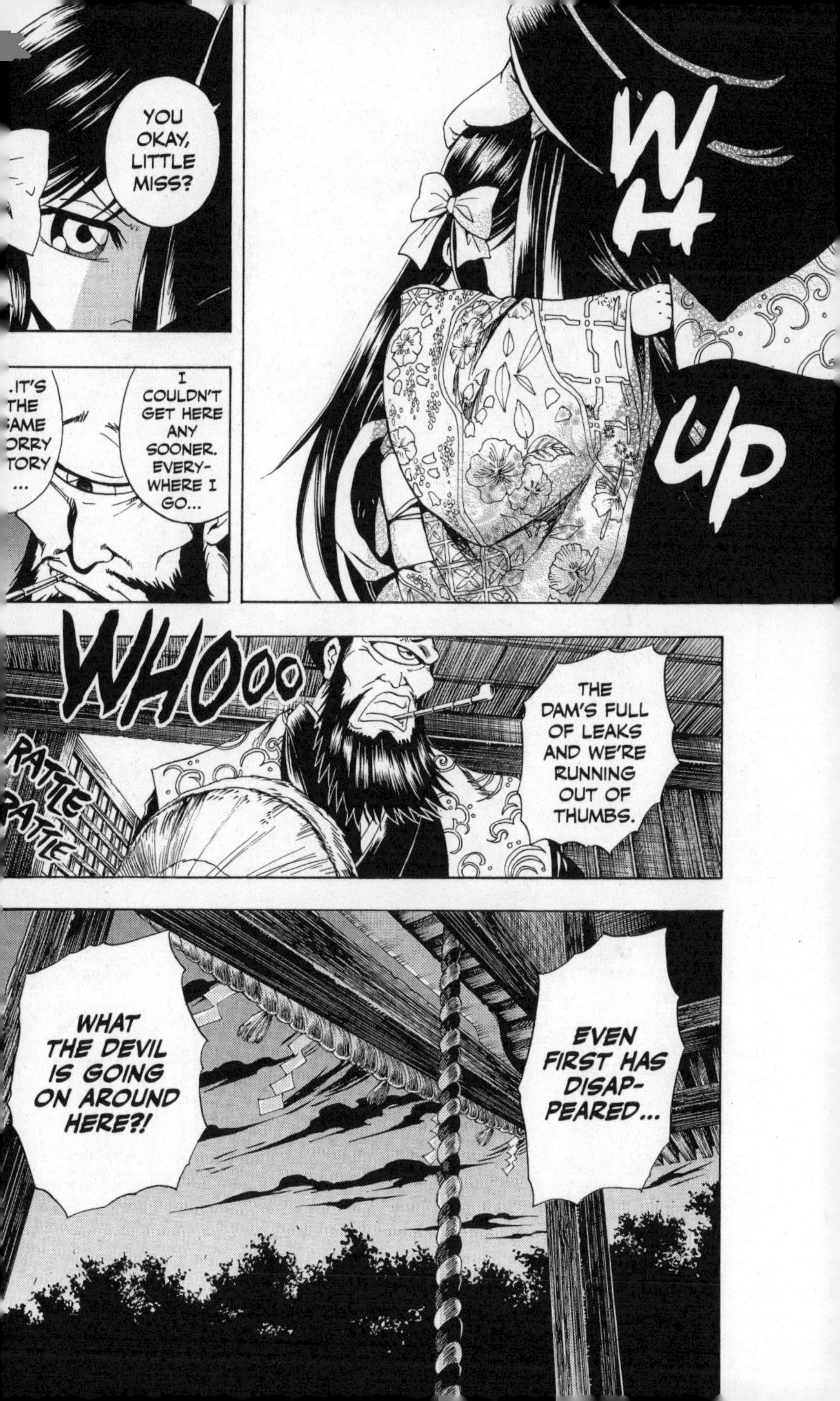
WH UP
YOU OKAY, LITTLE MISS?
I COULDN'T GET HERE ANY SOONER. EVERYWHERE I GO...
.IT'S THE AME ORRY TORY ...
THE DAM'S FULL OF LEAKS AND WE'RE RUNNING OUT OF THUMBS.
WHOOO
RATTLE RATTLE
EVEN FIRST HAS DISAPPEARED...
WHAT THE DEVIL IS GOING ON AROUND HERE?!

Act 153: The One-Millionth Ghost Story

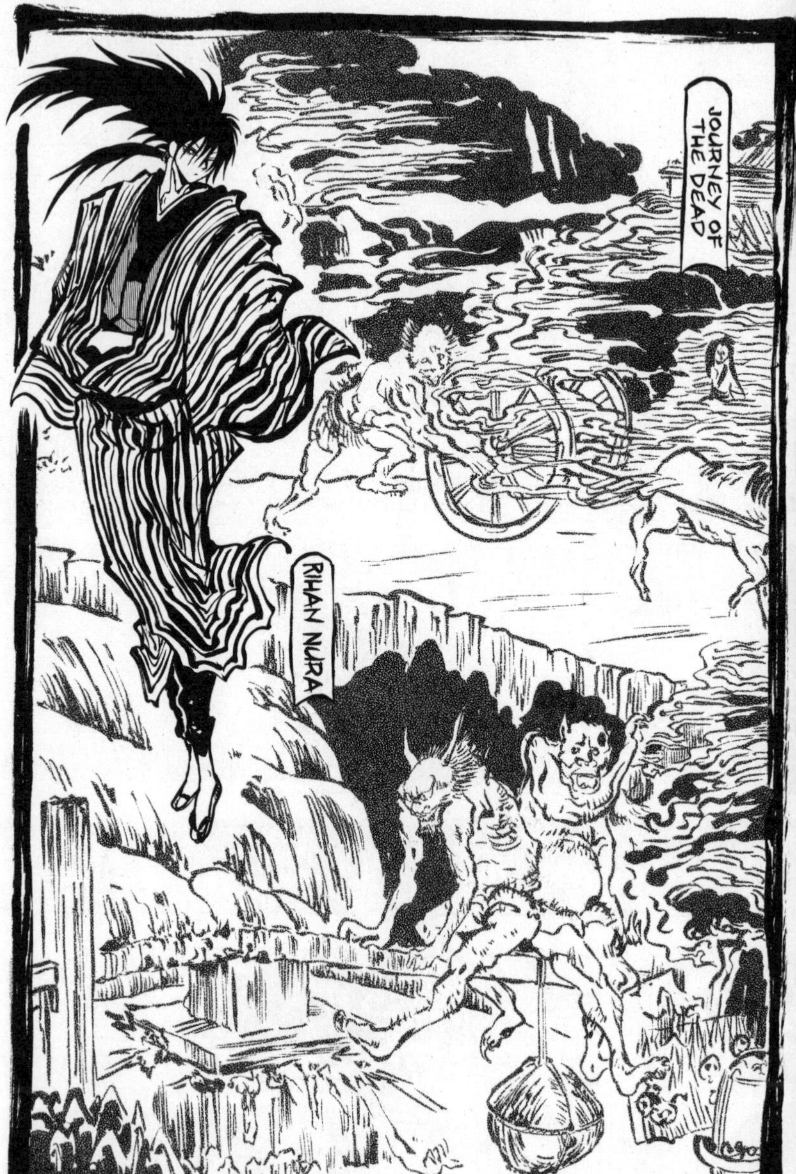
JOURNEY OF THE DEAD
RIHAN NURA

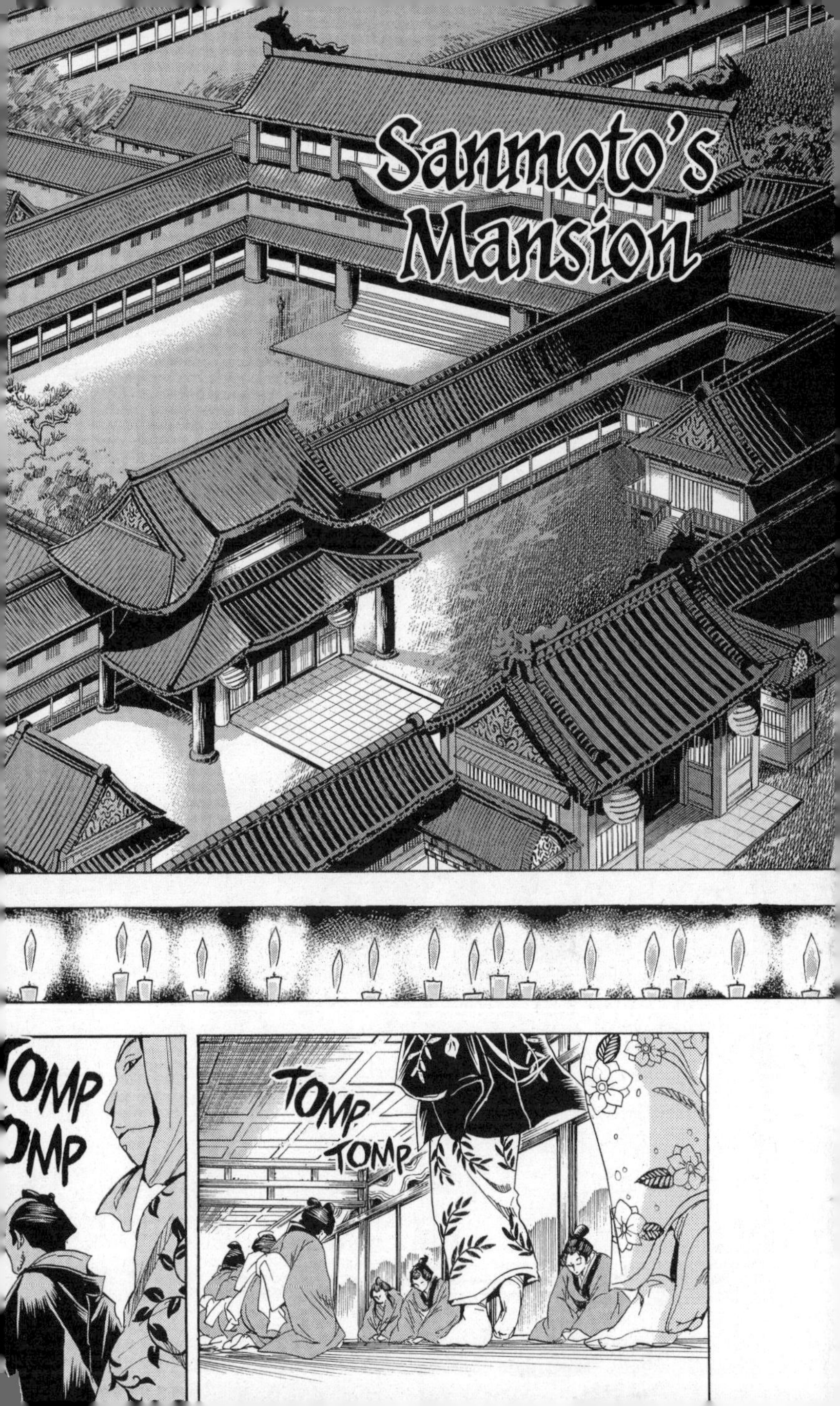
Sanmoto's Mansion
TOMP
TOMP
TOMP
OMP

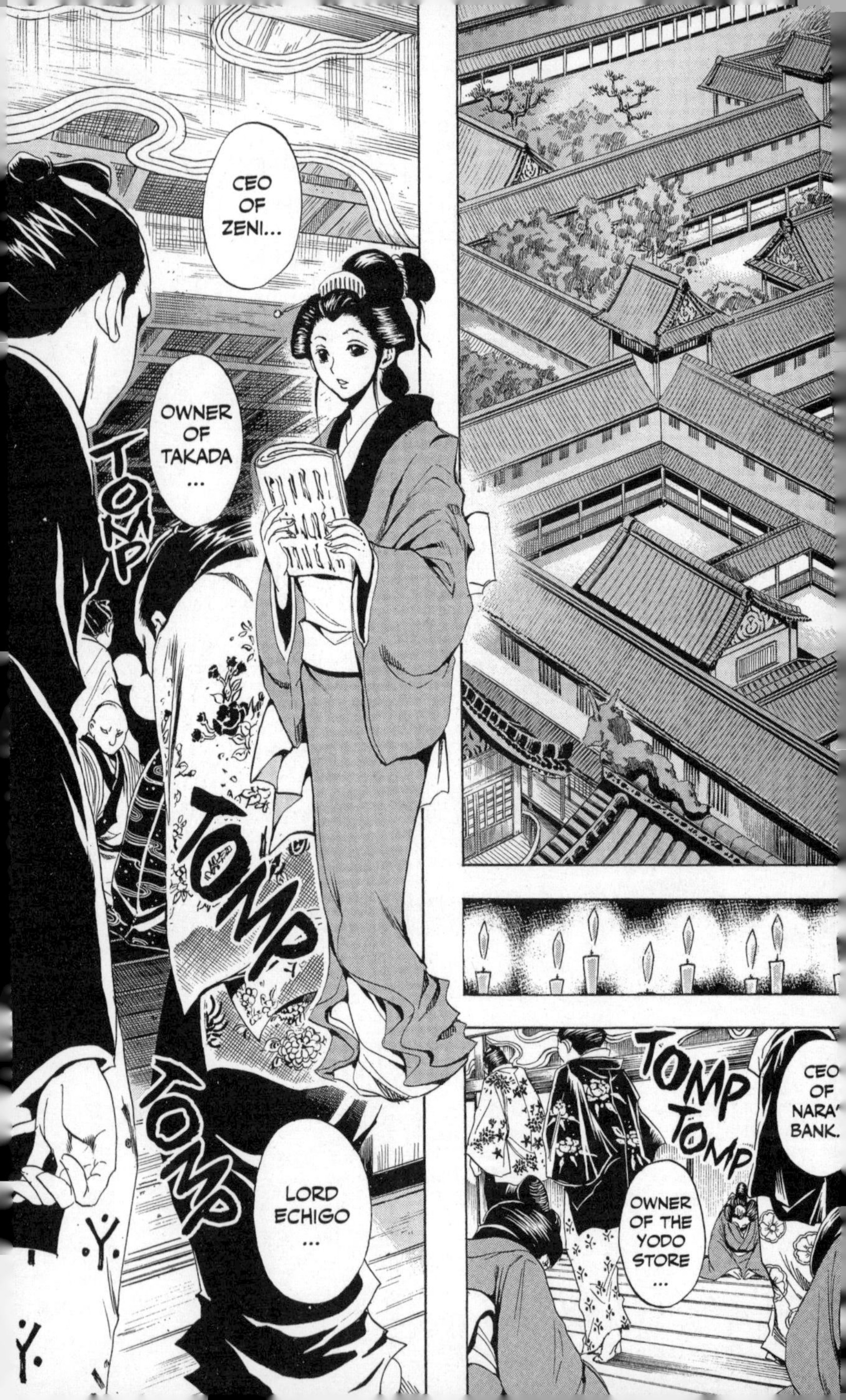
CEO OF NARA' BANK.
TOMP TOMP
OWNER OF THE YODO STORE ...
CEO OF ZENI...
OWNER OF TAKADA ...
TOMP
TOMP
LORD ECHIGO ...
TOMP

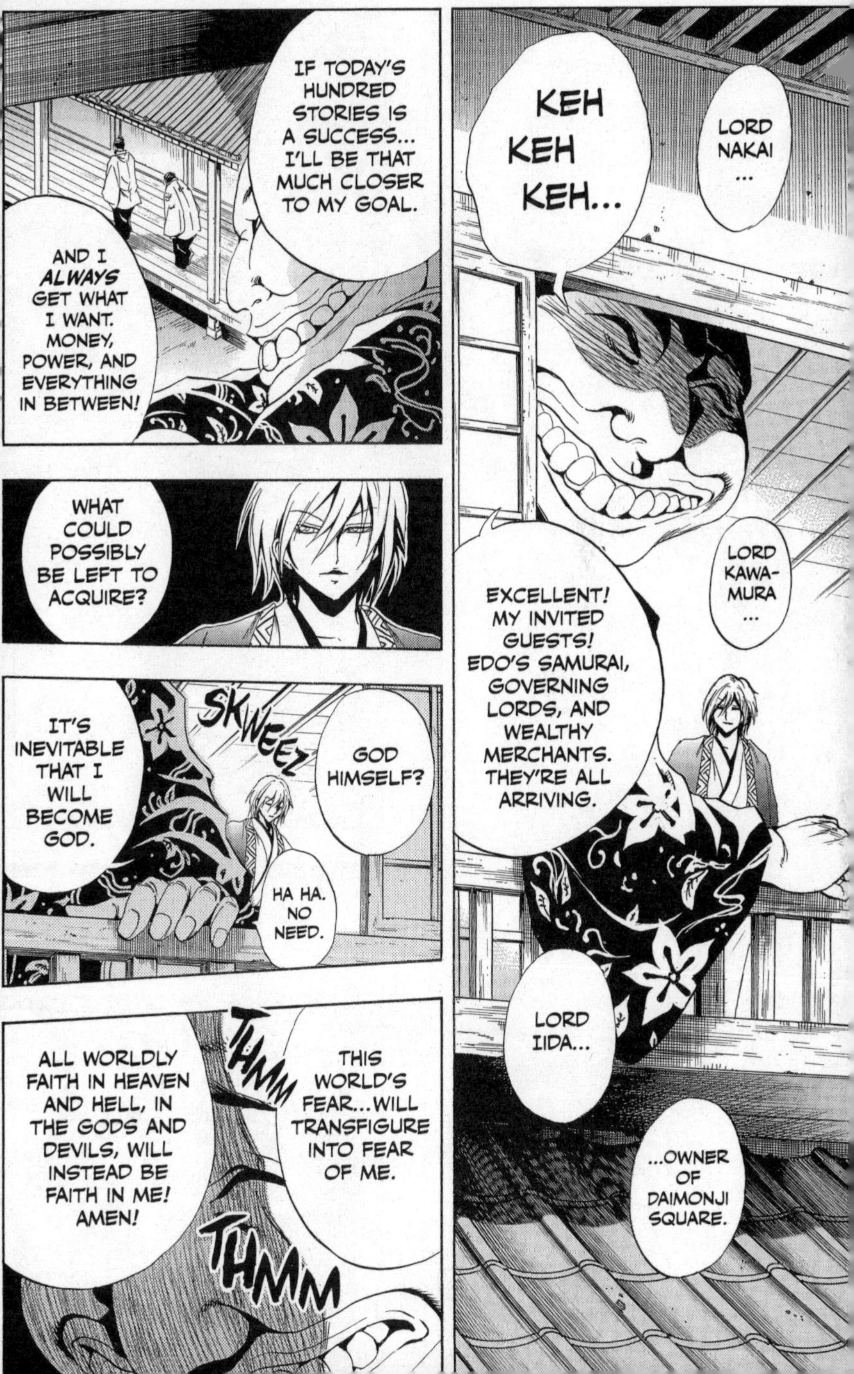
LORD NAKAI ...
KEH KEH KEH...
LORD KAWAMURA ...
EXCELLENT! MY INVITED GUESTS! EDO'S SAMURAI, GOVERNING LORDS, AND WEALTHY MERCHANTS. THEY'RE ALL ARRIVING.
LORD IIDA...
...OWNER OF DAIMONJI SQUARE.
IF TODAY'S HUNDRED STORIES IS A SUCCESS... I'LL BE THAT MUCH CLOSER TO MY GOAL.
AND I *ALWAYS* GET WHAT I WANT. MONEY, POWER, AND EVERYTHING IN BETWEEN!
WHAT COULD POSSIBLY BE LEFT TO ACQUIRE?
GOD HIMSELF?
SKWEEZ
IT'S INEVITABLE THAT I WILL BECOME GOD.
HA HA. NO NEED.
THIS WORLD'S FEAR...WILL TRANSFIGURE INTO FEAR OF ME.
THMM
ALL WORLDLY FAITH IN HEAVEN AND HELL, IN THE GODS AND DEVILS, WILL INSTEAD BE FAITH IN ME! AMEN!
THMM

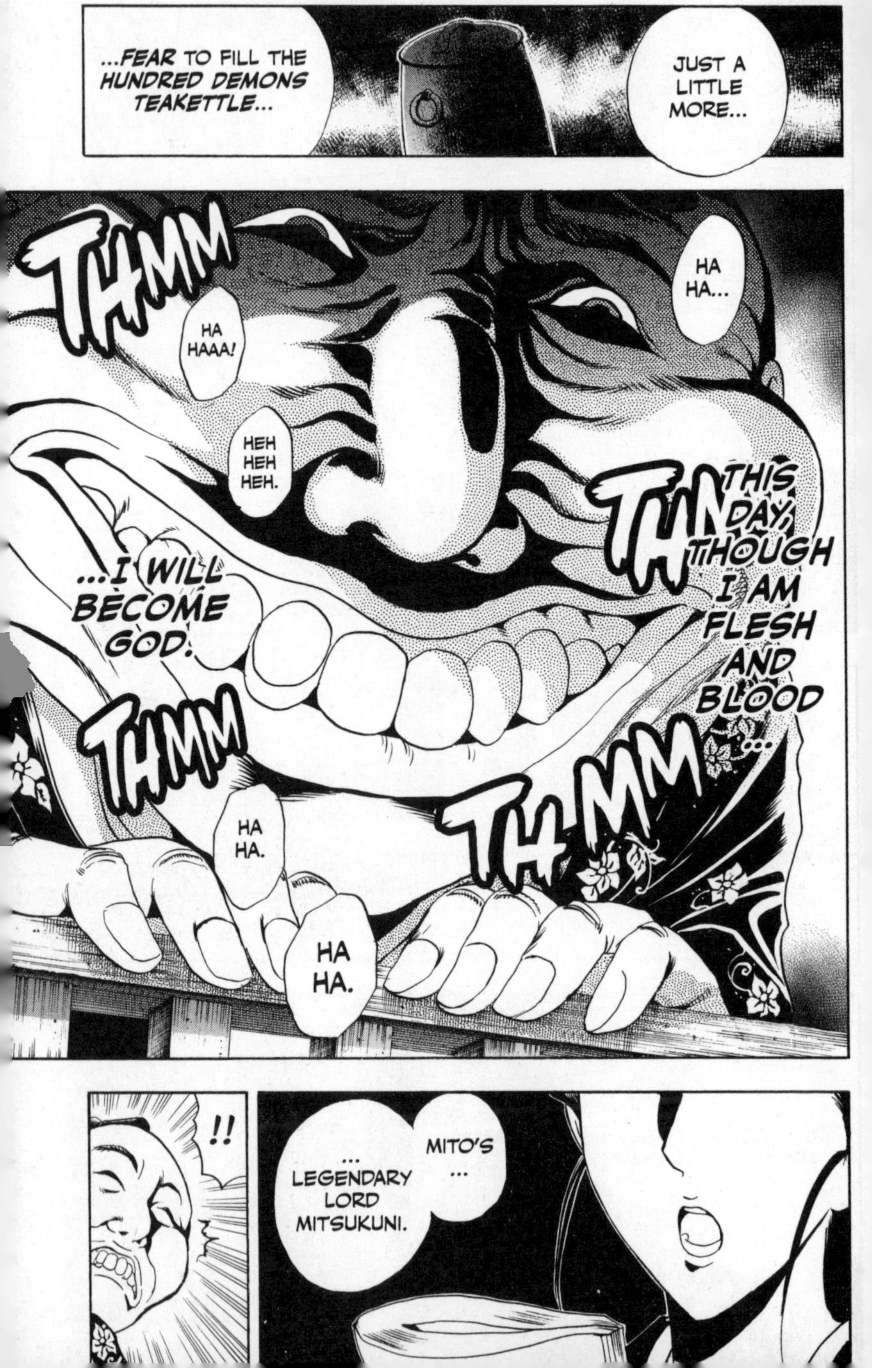
JUST A LITTLE MORE...
...FEAR TO FILL THE HUNDRED DEMONS TEAKETTLE...
HA HA...
THMM
THIS DAY, THOUGH I AM FLESH AND BLOOD...
THMM
HA HAAA!
HEH HEH HEH.
...I WILL BECOME GOD!
THMM
THMM
HA HA.
HA HA.
MITO'S ...
...LEGENDARY LORD MITSUKUNI.
!!

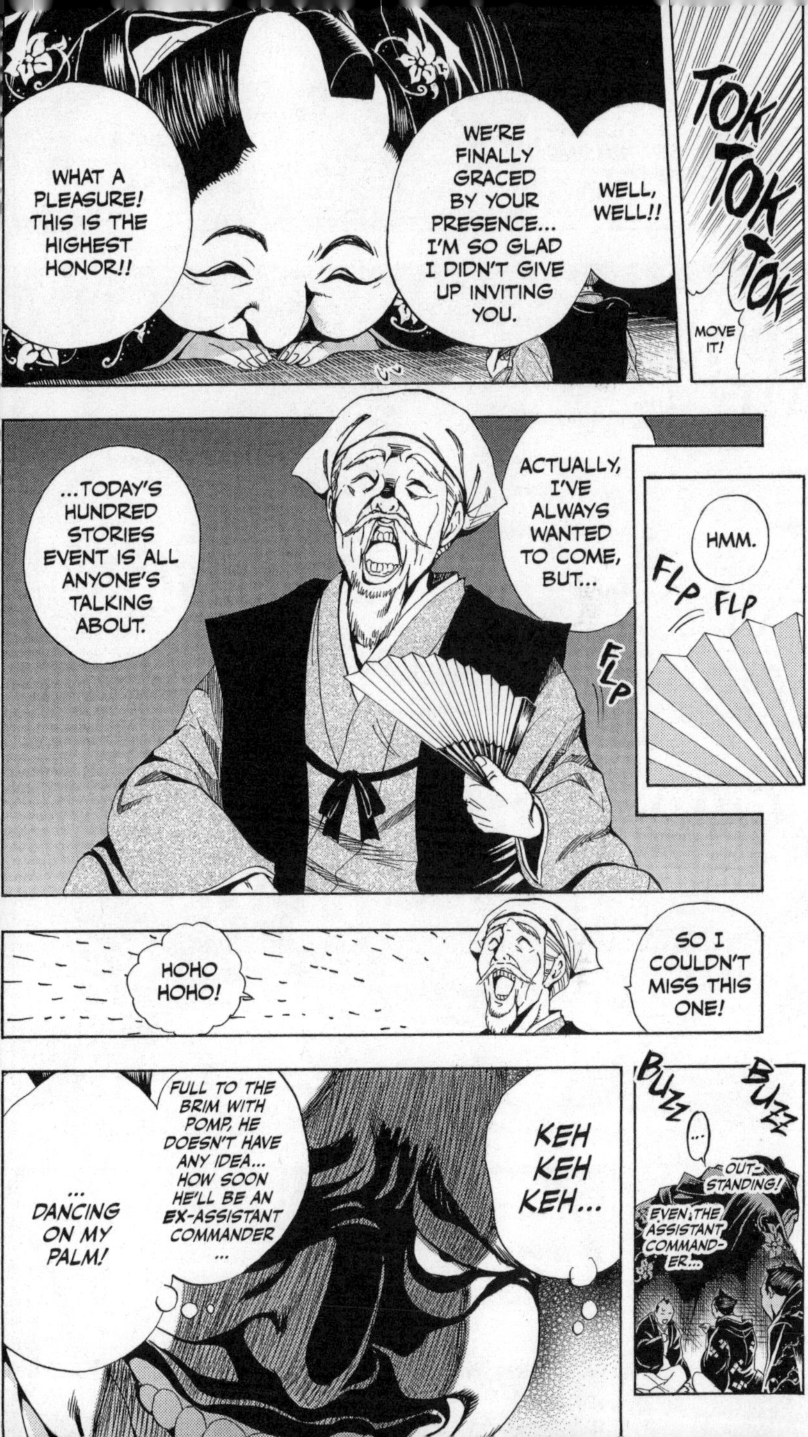
TOK TOK TOK TOK
MOVE IT!
WELL, WELL!!
WE'RE FINALLY GRACED BY YOUR PRESENCE... I'M SO GLAD I DIDN'T GIVE UP INVITING YOU.
WHAT A PLEASURE! THIS IS THE HIGHEST HONOR!!
HMM.
FLP FLP
ACTUALLY, I'VE ALWAYS WANTED TO COME, BUT...
...TODAY'S HUNDRED STORIES EVENT IS ALL ANYONE'S TALKING ABOUT.
FLP
SO I COULDN'T MISS THIS ONE!
HOHO HOHO!
BUZZ BUZZ
...
OUT-STANDING!
EVEN THE ASSISTANT COMMANDER...
KEH KEH KEH...
FULL TO THE BRIM WITH POMP, HE DOESN'T HAVE ANY IDEA... HOW SOON HE'LL BE AN EX-ASSISTANT COMMANDER ...
... DANCING ON MY PALM!

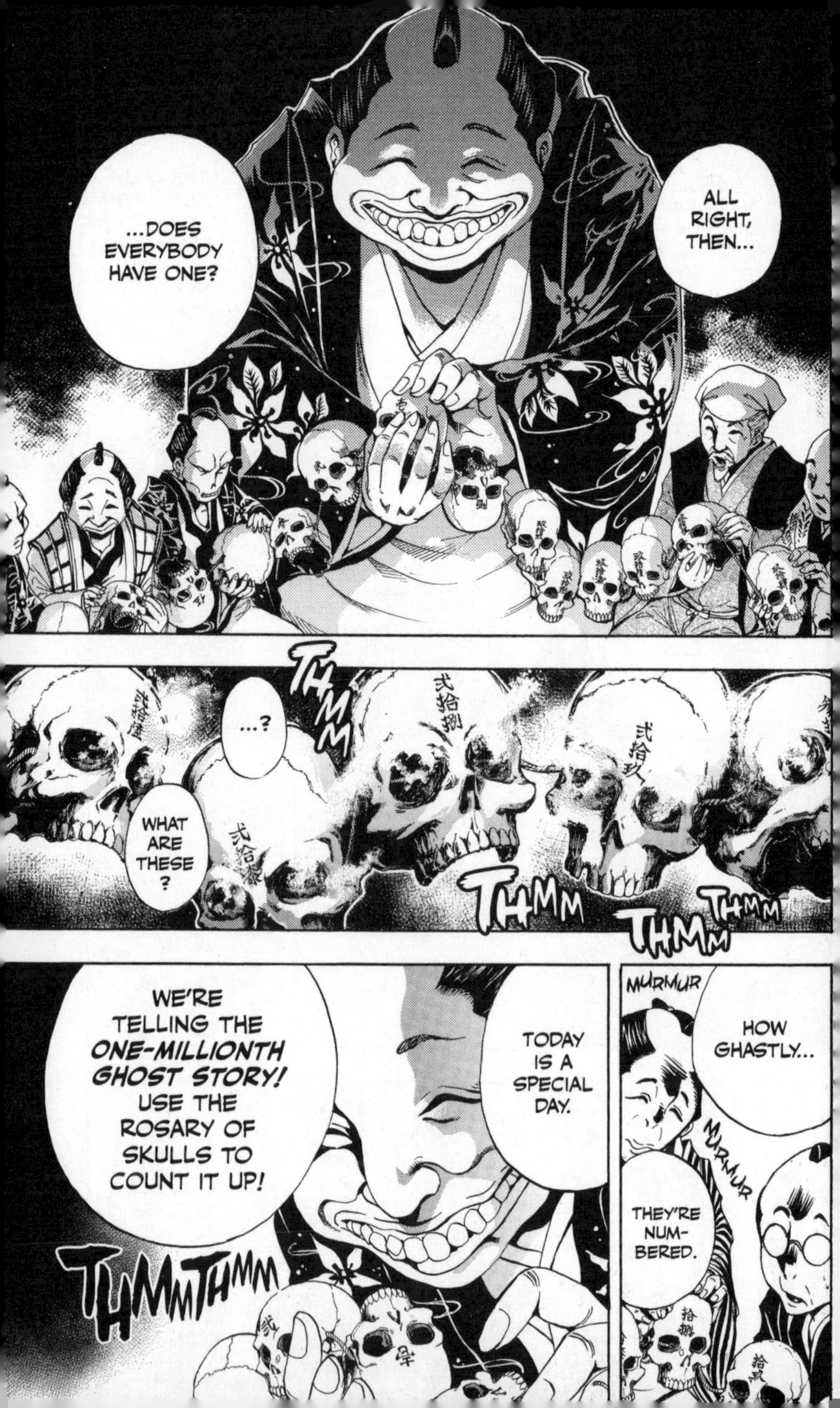
ALL RIGHT, THEN...
...DOES EVERYBODY HAVE ONE?
THMM
...?
WHAT ARE THESE ?
THMM
THMM
THMM
MURMUR
HOW GHASTLY...
MURMUR
THEY'RE NUM-BERED.
TODAY IS A SPECIAL DAY.
WE'RE TELLING THE *ONE-MILLIONTH GHOST STORY!* USE THE ROSARY OF SKULLS TO COUNT IT UP!
THMMTHMM

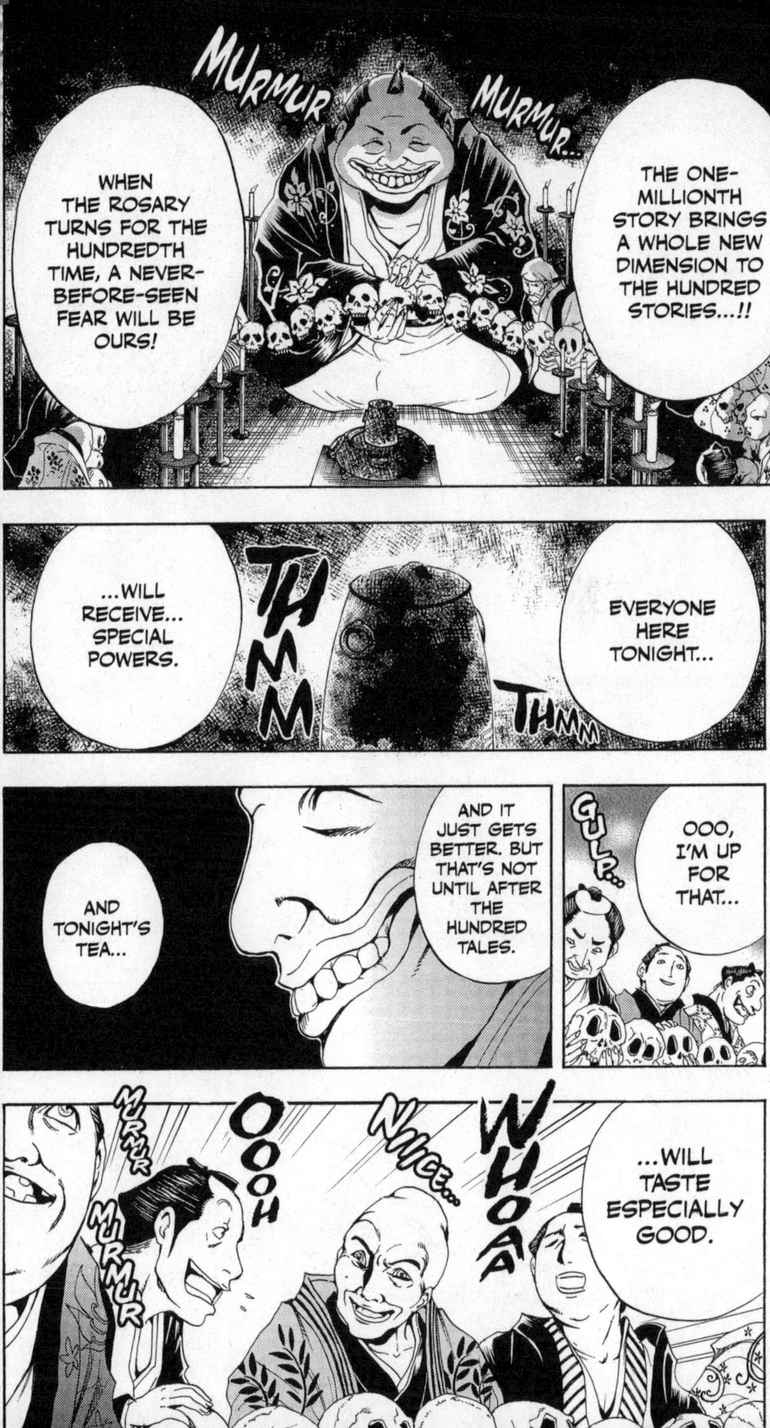
MURMUR...
MURMUR
THE ONE-MILLIONTH STORY BRINGS A WHOLE NEW DIMENSION TO THE HUNDRED STORIES...!!
WHEN THE ROSARY TURNS FOR THE HUNDREDTH TIME, A NEVER-BEFORE-SEEN FEAR WILL BE OURS!
EVERYONE HERE TONIGHT...
THMM
THMM
...WILL RECEIVE... SPECIAL POWERS.
GULP...
OOO, I'M UP FOR THAT...
AND IT JUST GETS BETTER. BUT THAT'S NOT UNTIL AFTER THE HUNDRED TALES.
AND TONIGHT'S TEA...
...WILL TASTE ESPECIALLY GOOD.
WHOA
NIICE...
OOOH
MURMUR
MURMUR

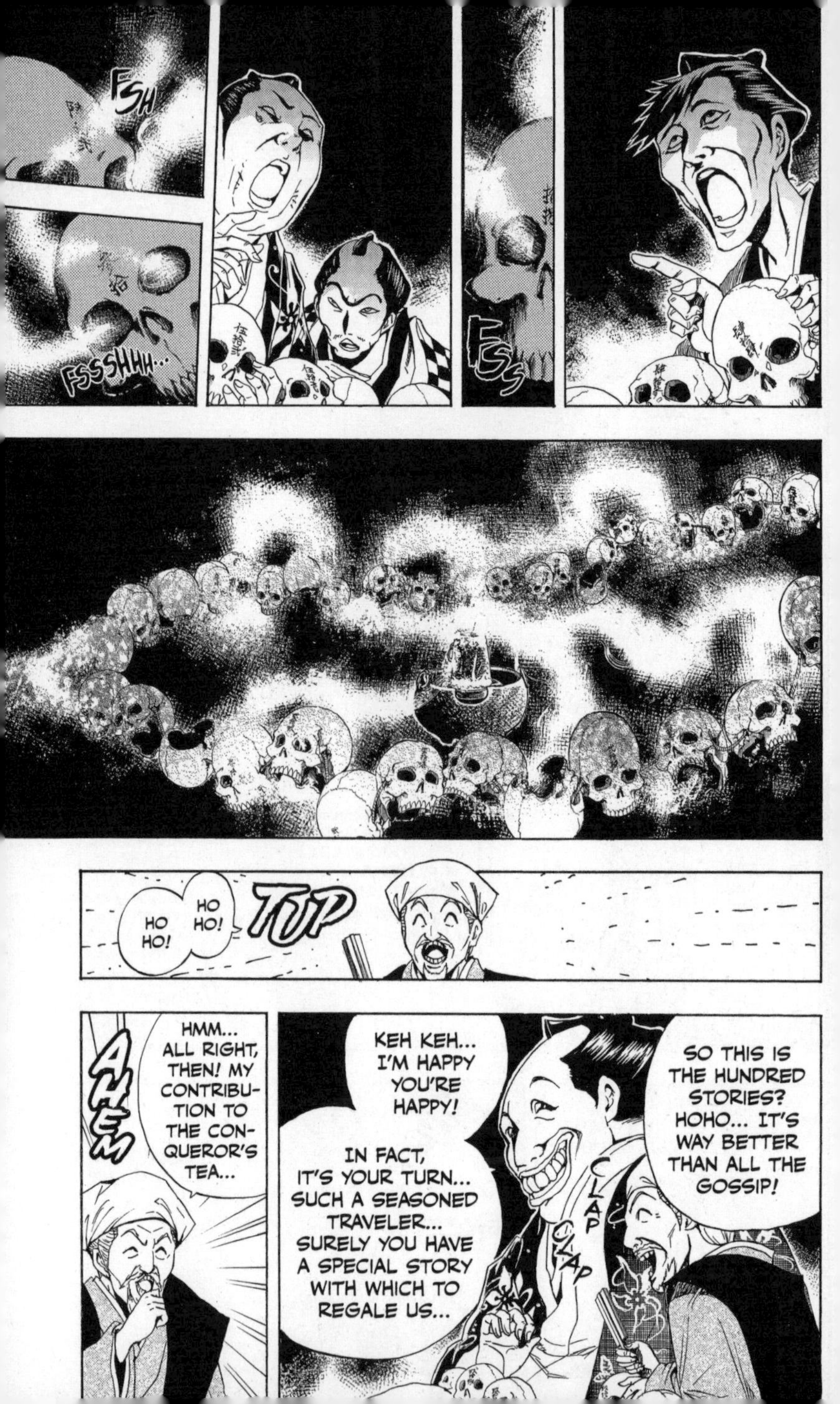
FSS
FSH
FSSSHHH...
TUP
HO HO!
HO HO!
SO THIS IS THE HUNDRED STORIES? HOHO... IT'S WAY BETTER THAN ALL THE GOSSIP!
KEH KEH... I'M HAPPY YOU'RE HAPPY!
IN FACT, IT'S YOUR TURN... SUCH A SEASONED TRAVELER... SURELY YOU HAVE A SPECIAL STORY WITH WHICH TO REGALE US...
CLAP
CLAP
HMM... ALL RIGHT, THEN! MY CONTRIBU-TION TO THE CON-QUEROR'S TEA...
AHEM

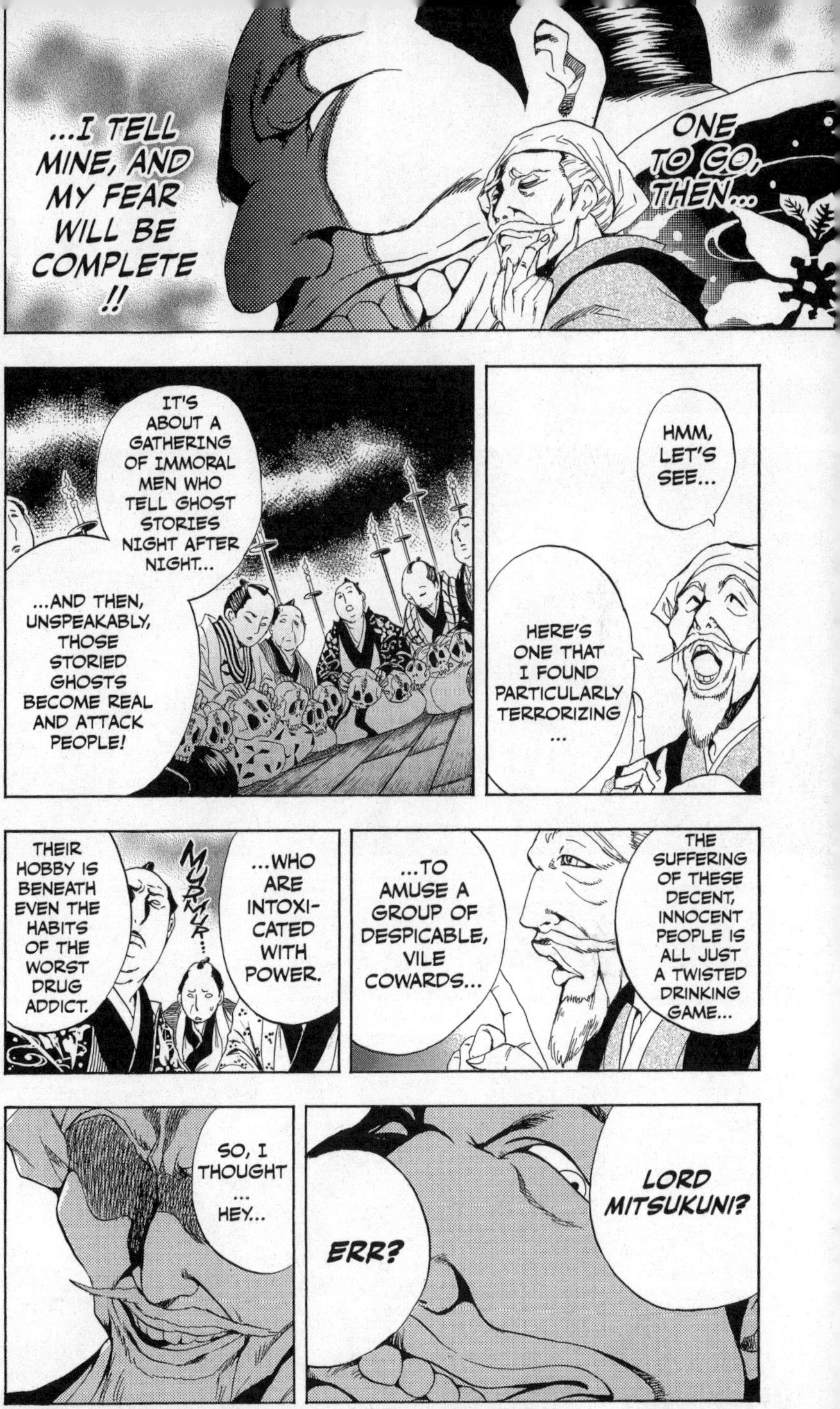
ONE TO GO, THEN...
...I TELL MINE, AND MY FEAR WILL BE COMPLETE !!
HMM, LET'S SEE...
HERE'S ONE THAT I FOUND PARTICULARLY TERRORIZING ...
IT'S ABOUT A GATHERING OF IMMORAL MEN WHO TELL GHOST STORIES NIGHT AFTER NIGHT...
...AND THEN, UNSPEAKABLY, THOSE STORIED GHOSTS BECOME REAL AND ATTACK PEOPLE!
THE SUFFERING OF THESE DECENT, INNOCENT PEOPLE IS ALL JUST A TWISTED DRINKING GAME...
...TO AMUSE A GROUP OF DESPICABLE, VILE COWARDS...
...WHO ARE INTOXI-CATED WITH POWER.
MURMUR...
THEIR HOBBY IS BENEATH EVEN THE HABITS OF THE WORST DRUG ADDICT.
LORD MITSUKUNI?
ERR?
SO, I THOUGHT ... HEY...

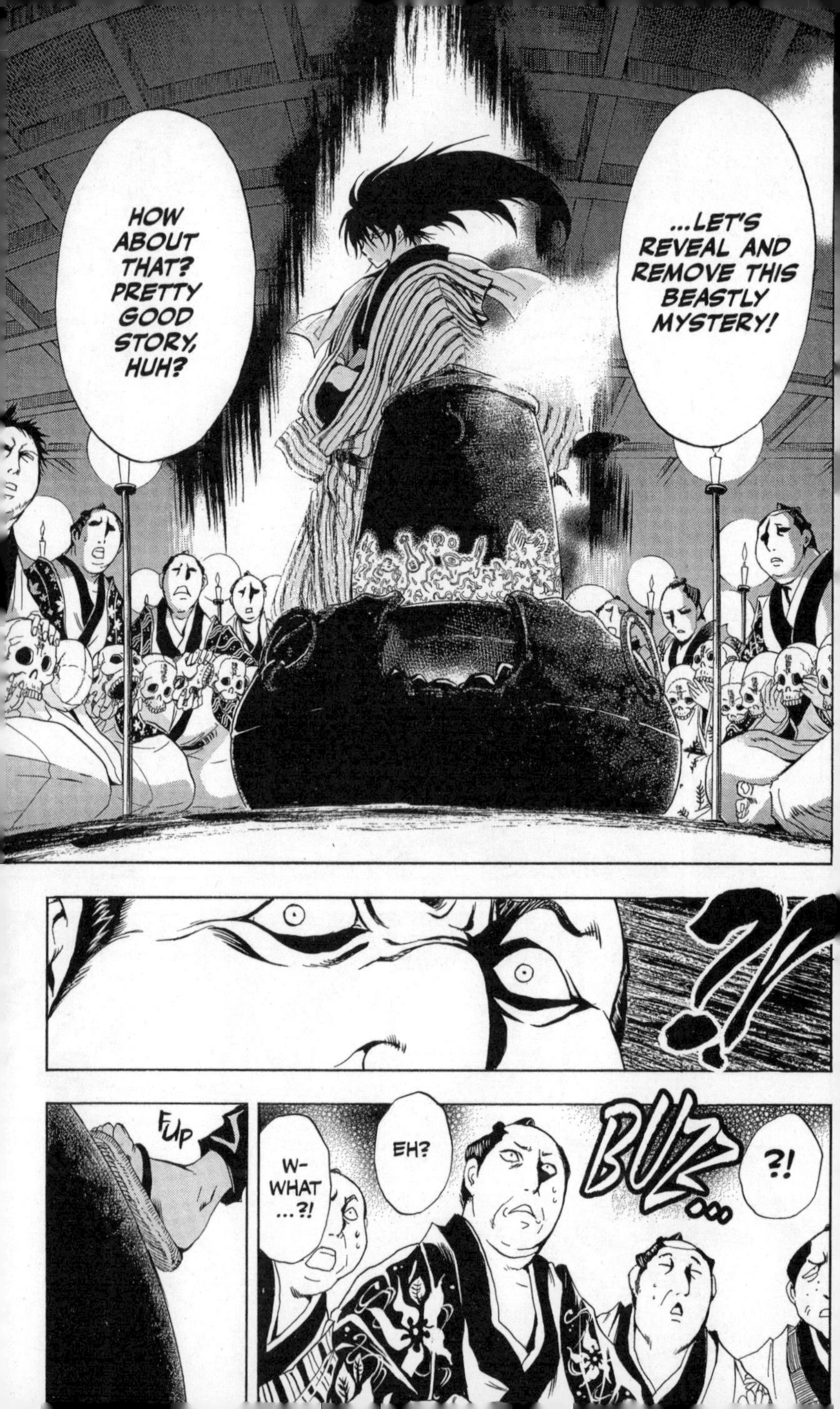
...LET'S REVEAL AND REMOVE THIS BEASTLY MYSTERY!
HOW ABOUT THAT? PRETTY GOOD STORY, HUH?
?!
?!
BUZ
EH?
W-WHAT...?!
FUP

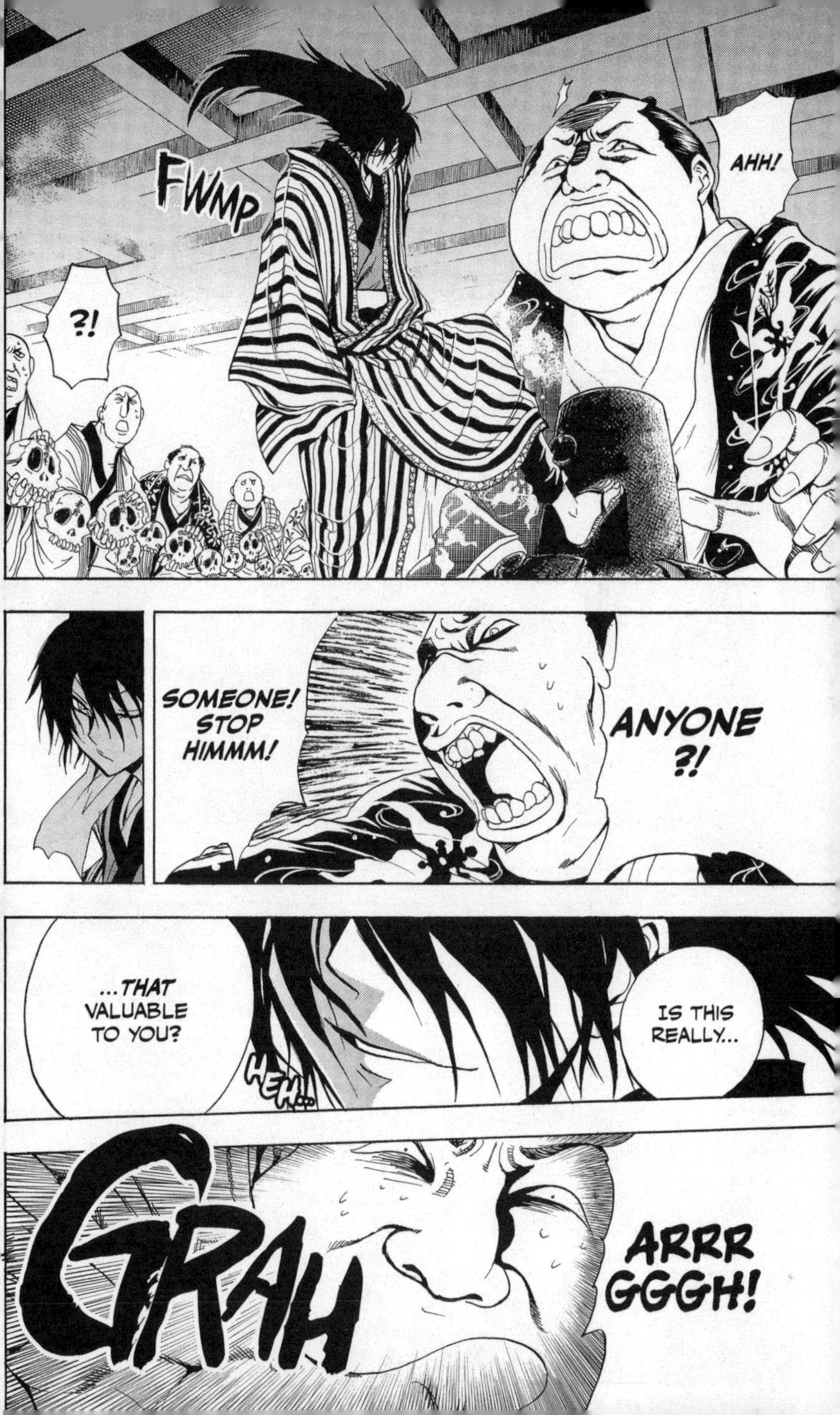
AHH!
FWMP
?!
ANYONE ?!
SOMEONE! STOP HIMMM!
IS THIS REALLY...
HEH...
...THAT VALUABLE TO YOU?
ARRR GGGH!
GRAH

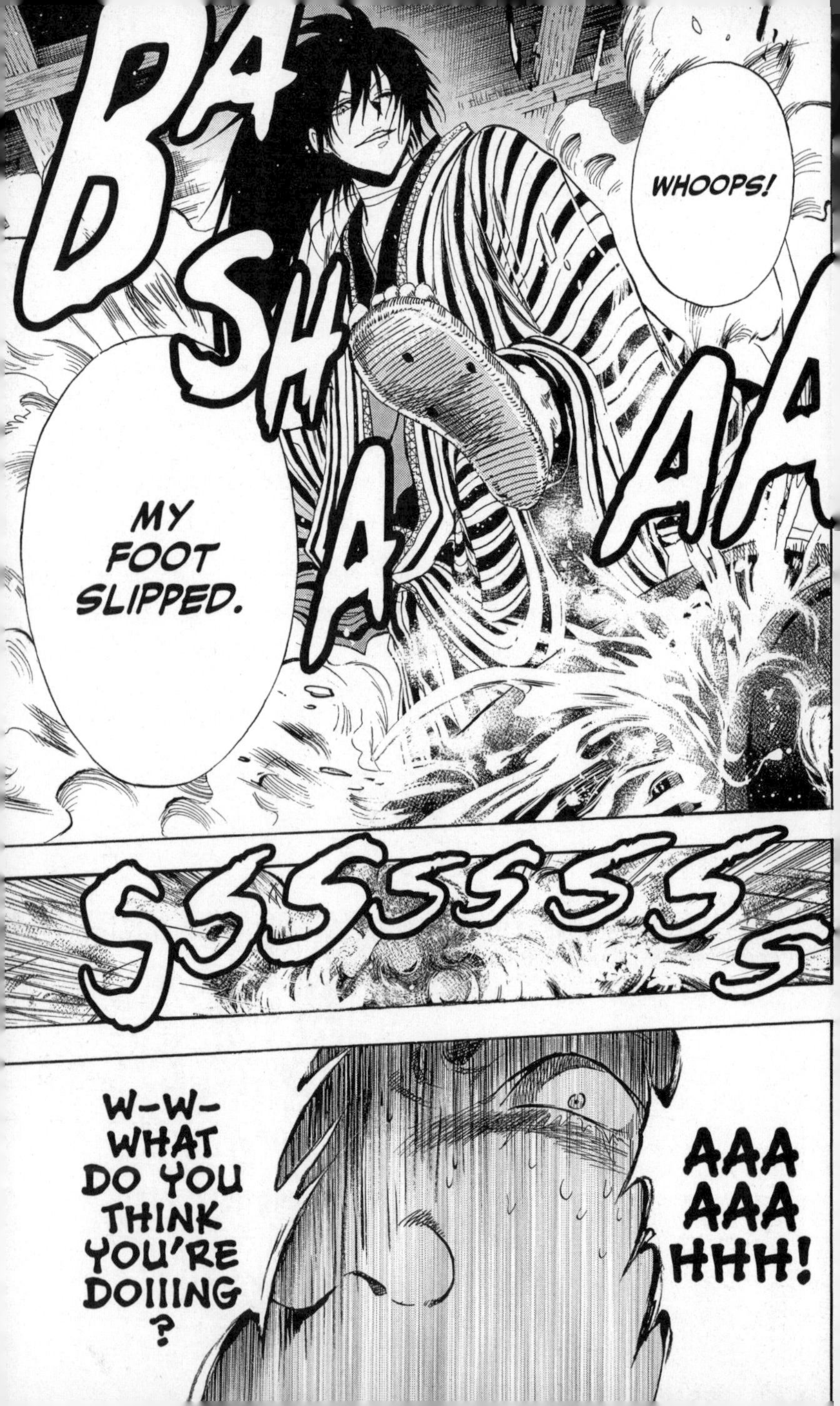
WHOOPS!
BASHAAA
MY FOOT SLIPPED.
SSSSSSSS
AAAAAAHHH!
W-W-WHAT DO YOU THINK YOU'RE DOIIING?

NURA: RISE OF THE YOKAI CLAN

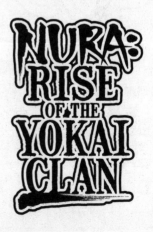

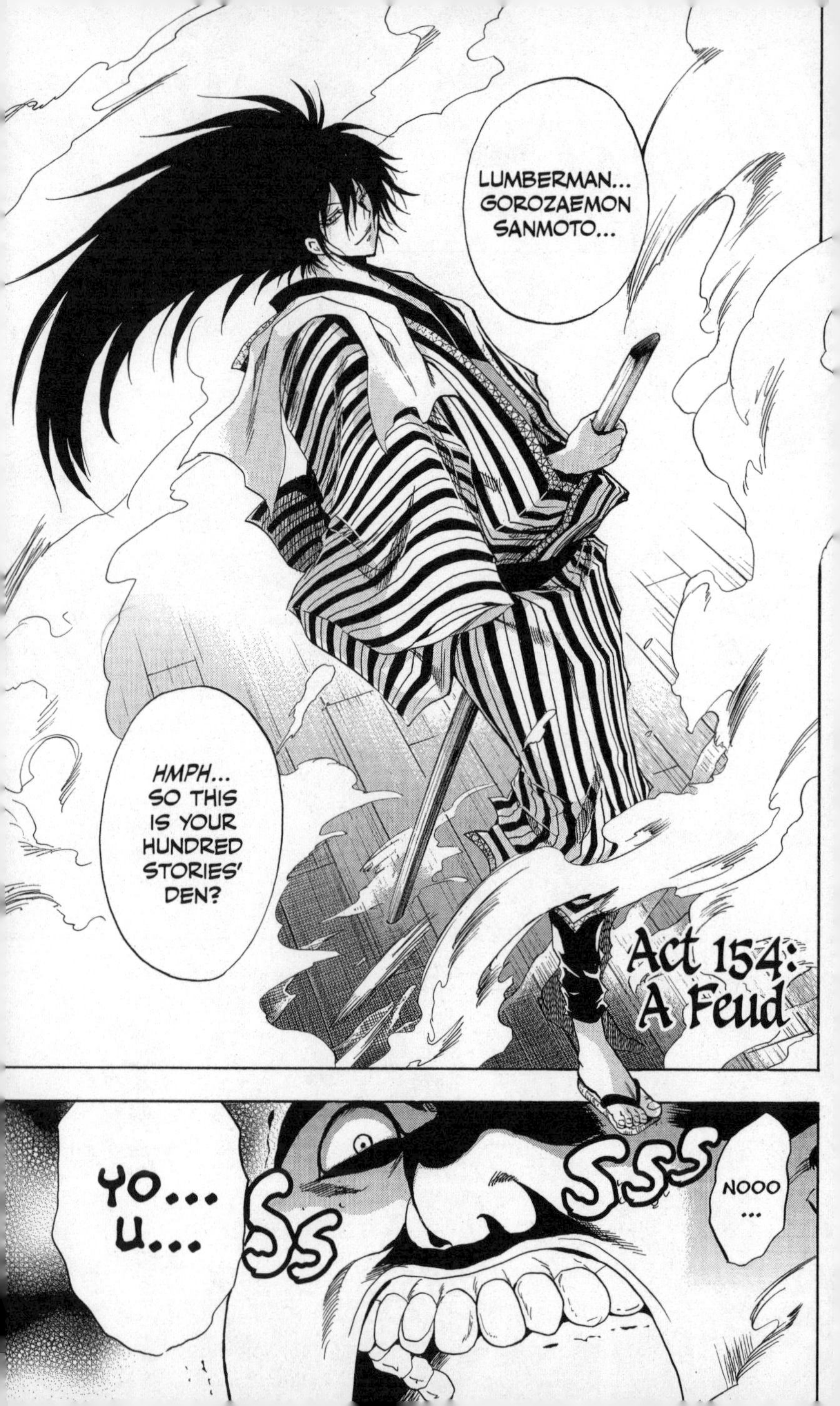
LUMBERMAN... GOROZAEMON SANMOTO...
HMPH... SO THIS IS YOUR HUNDRED STORIES' DEN?
Act 154: A Feud
NOOO ...
SSS
Ss
YO... U...

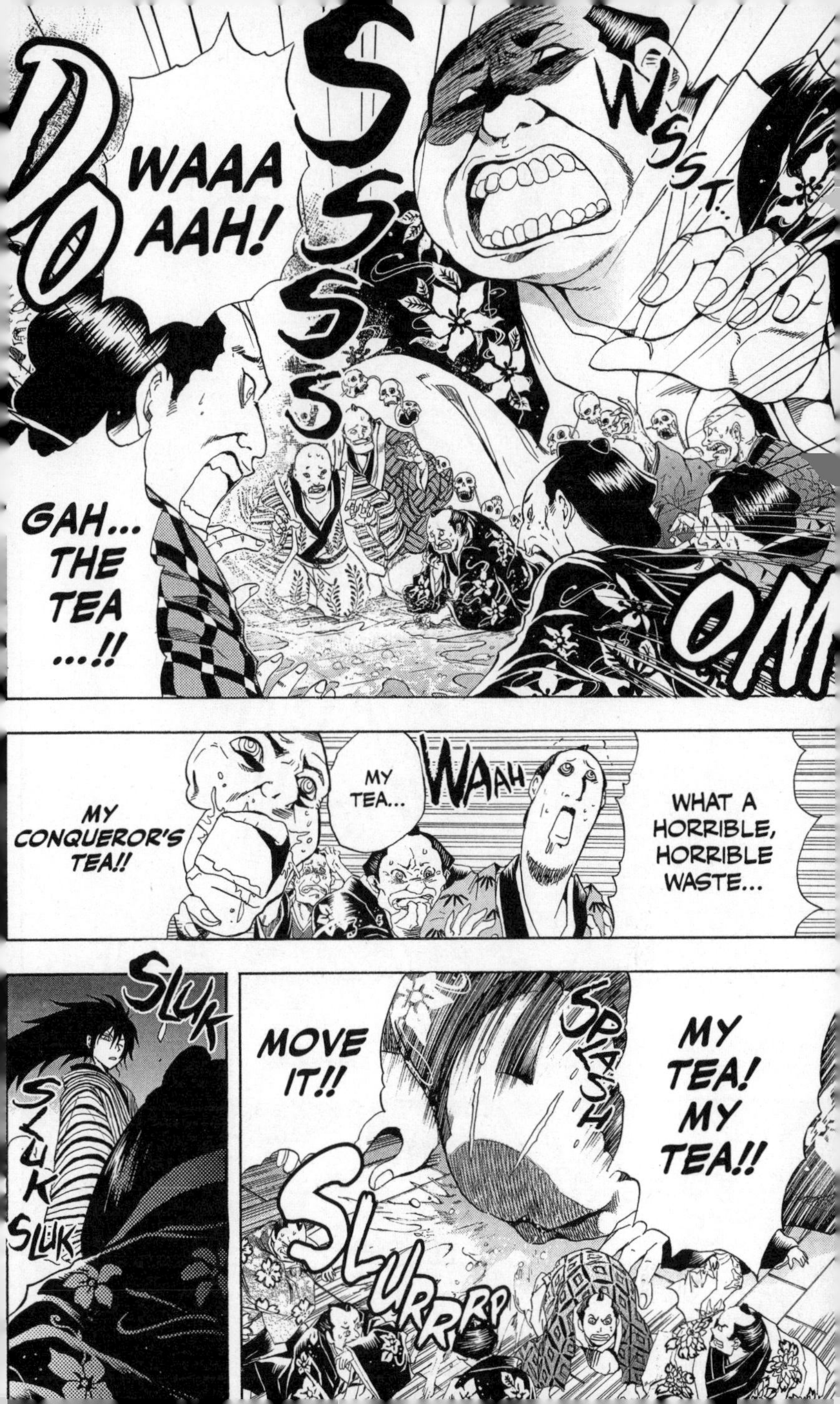
WSST...
SSSS
WAAA AAH!
DO
OM
GAH... THE TEA ...!!
WHAT A HORRIBLE, HORRIBLE WASTE...
WAAH
MY TEA...
MY CONQUEROR'S TEA!!
MY TEA! MY TEA!!
SPLASH
MOVE IT!!
SLURRRP
SLUK
SLUK
SLUK

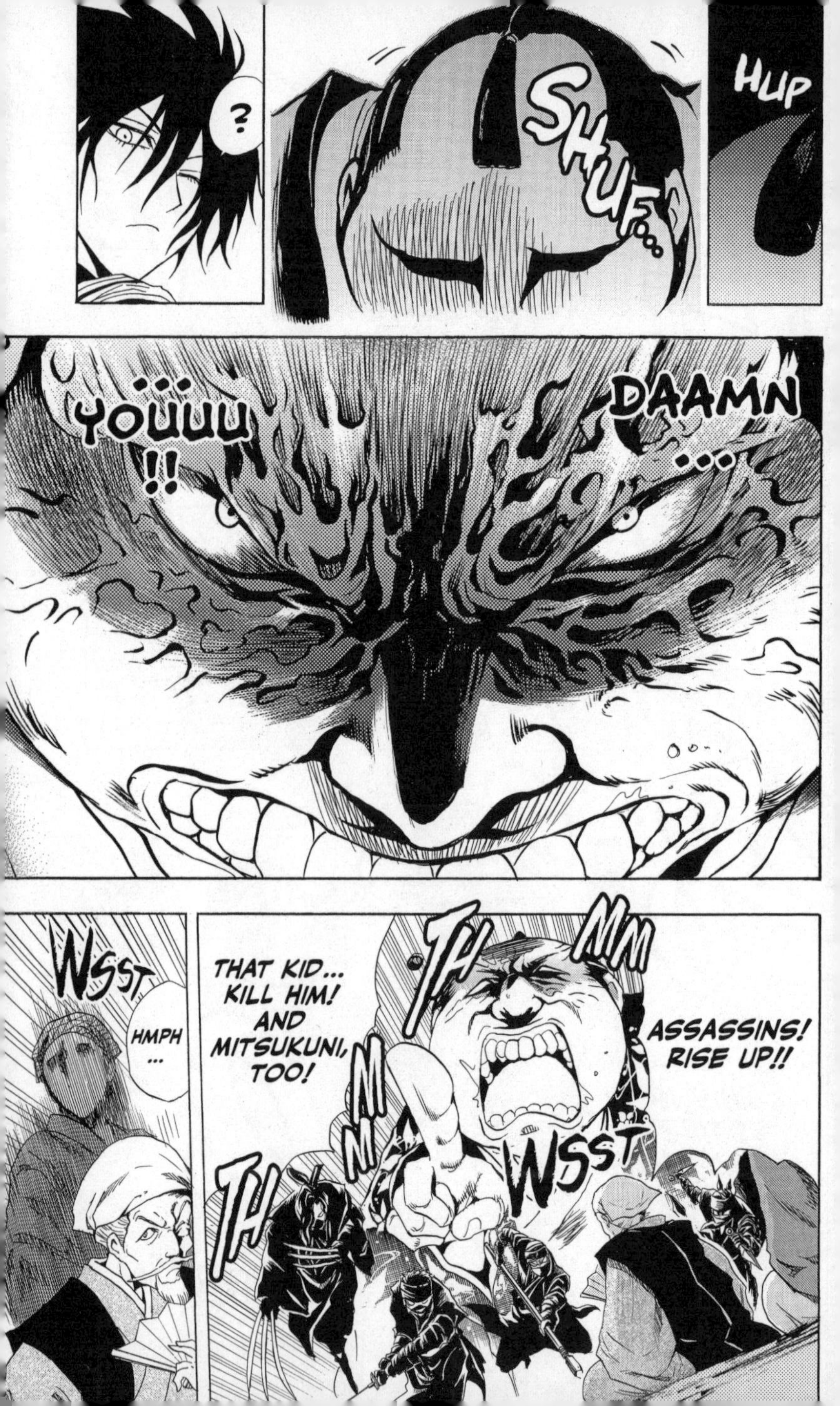
HUP
SHUF...
?
DAAMN ...
...YOUUU !!
THMM
ASSASSINS! RISE UP!!
THAT KID... KILL HIM! AND MITSUKUNI, TOO!
WSST
THMM
WSST
HMPH ...

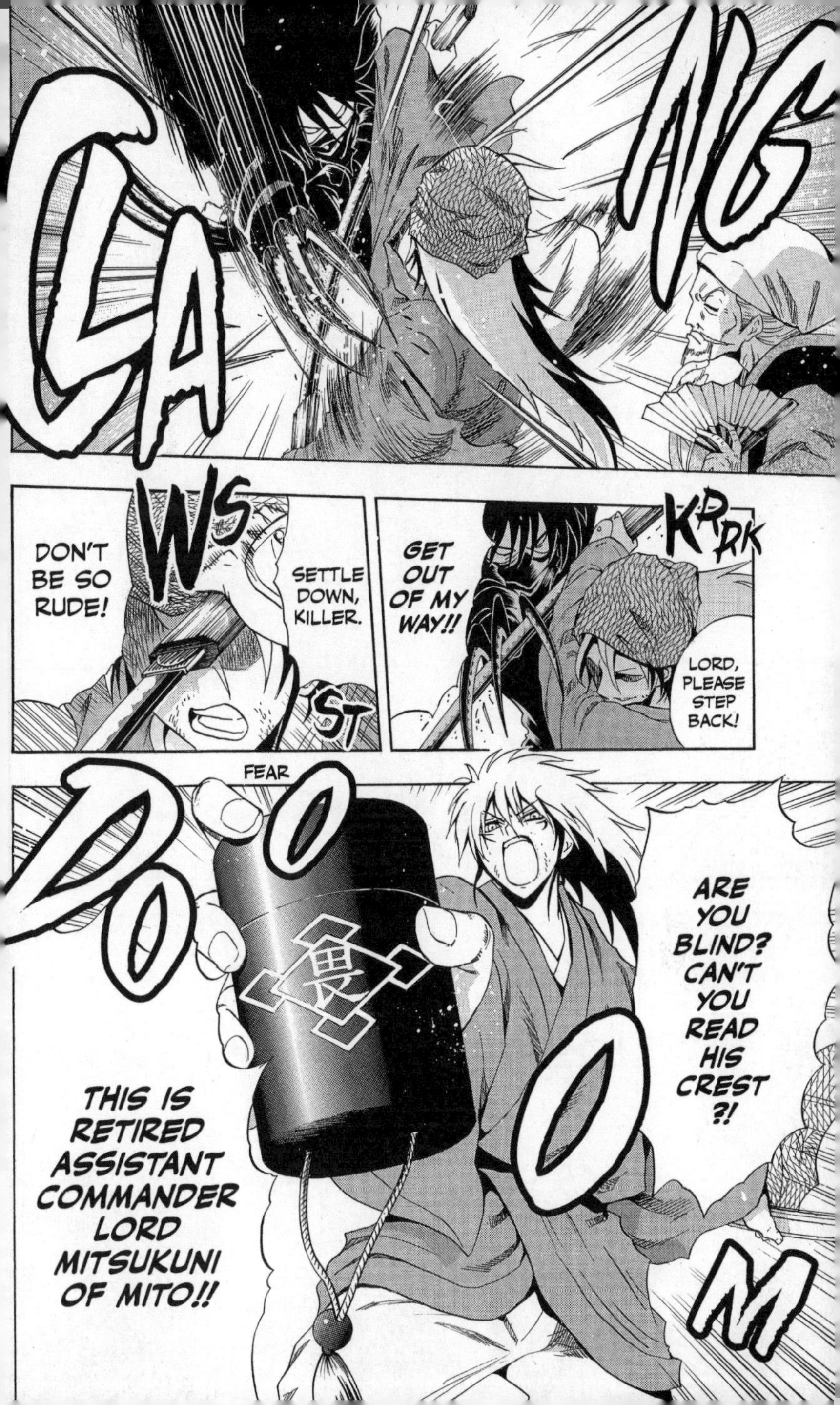
CLA
NG
KRDK
GET OUT OF MY WAY!!
LORD, PLEASE STEP BACK!
WS
SETTLE DOWN, KILLER.
DON'T BE SO RUDE!
ST
FEAR
DOOOOM
ARE YOU BLIND? CAN'T YOU READ HIS CREST?!
THIS IS RETIRED ASSISTANT COMMANDER LORD MITSUKUNI OF MITO!!

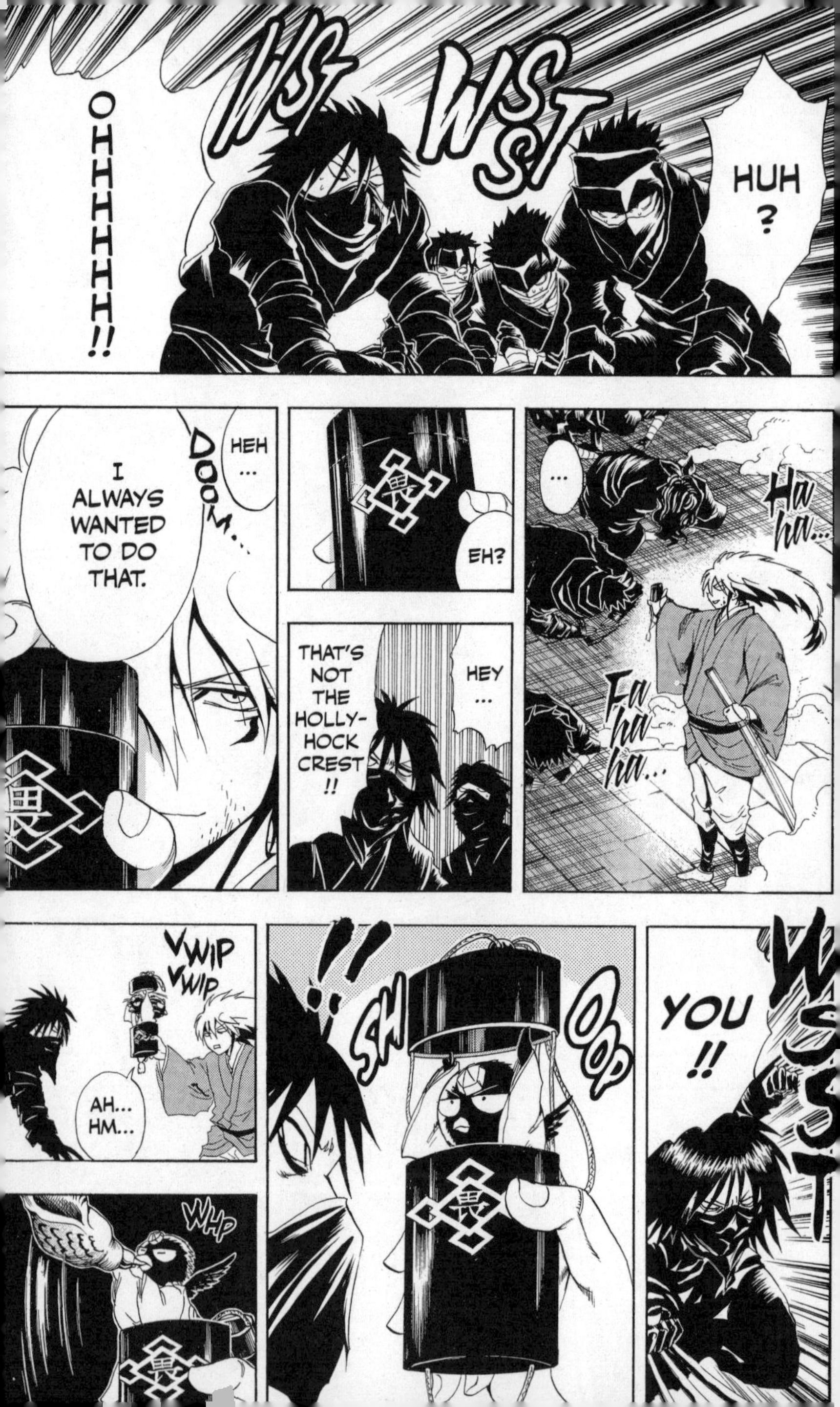
HUH ?
OHHHHHHH!!
...
Ha ha...
Fa ha ha...
EH?
HEY ...
THAT'S NOT THE HOLLY-HOCK CREST !!
HEH ...
DOOM...
I ALWAYS WANTED TO DO THAT.
YOU !!
!!
SHOOP
VWIP VWIP
AH... HM...
WHP

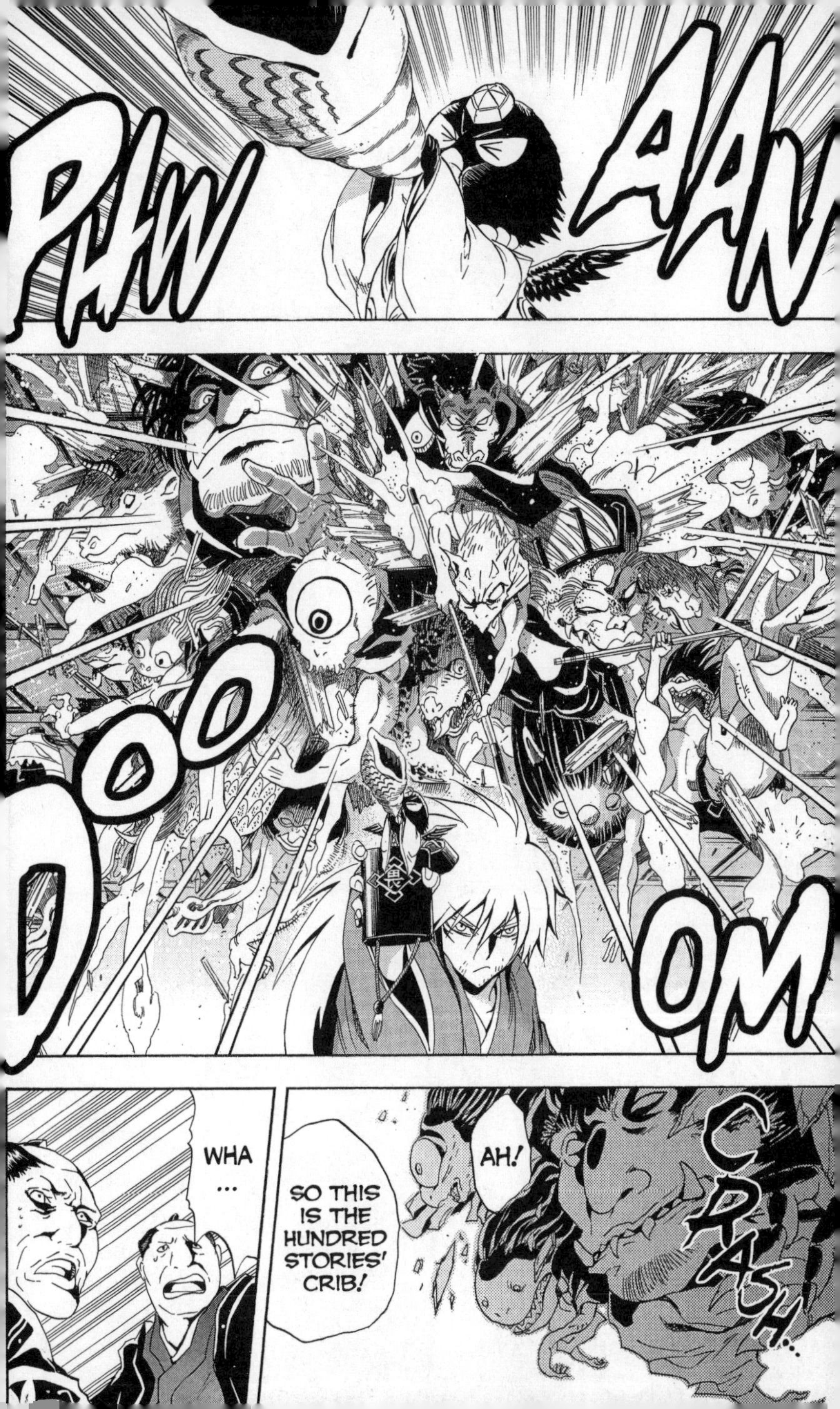

PAW
AAN
DOOOOM
AH!
SO THIS IS THE HUNDRED STORIES' CRIB!
CRASH...
WHA ...

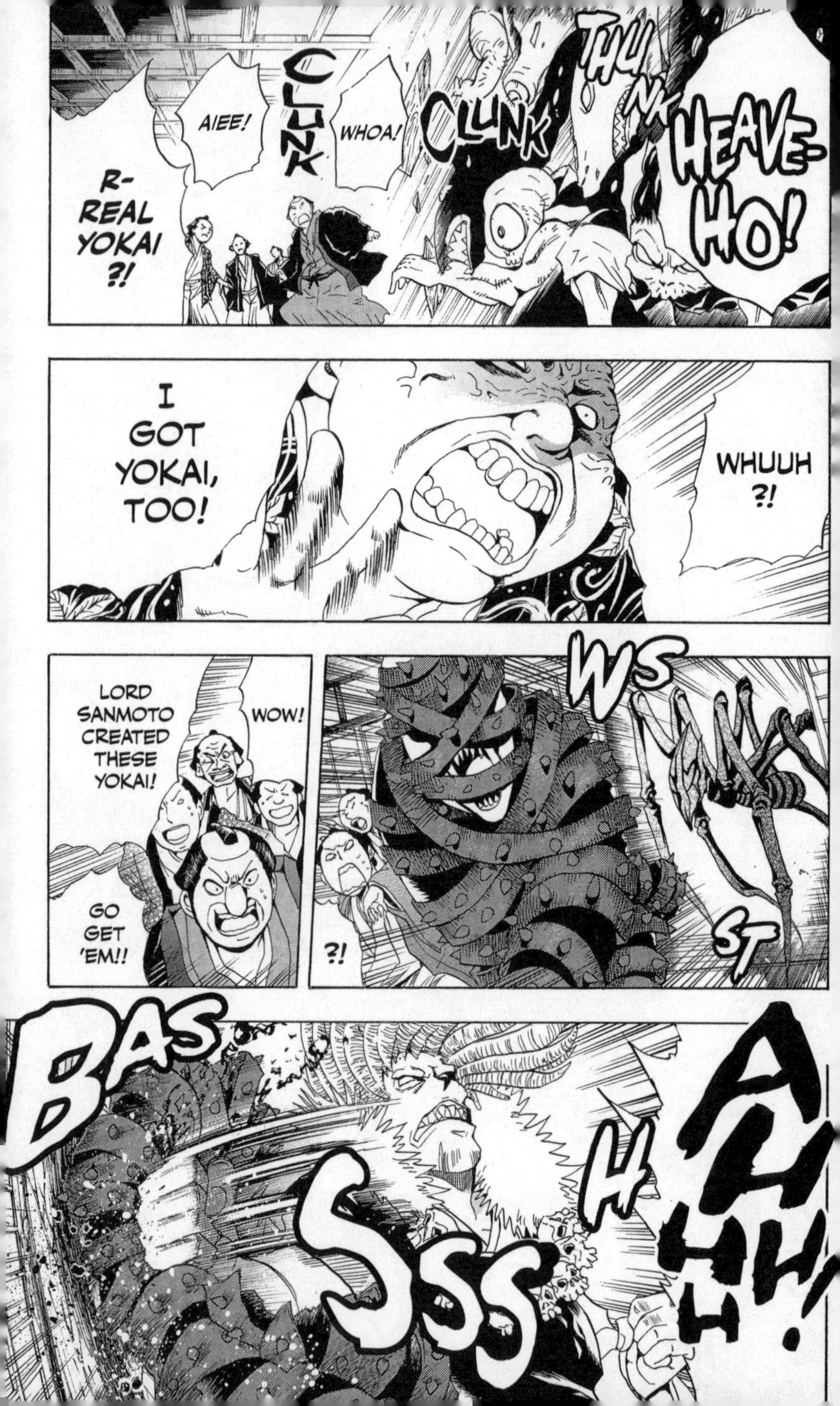
THUNK
HEAVE-HO!
CLUNK
WHOA!
CLUNK
AIEE!
R-REAL YOKAI?!
WHUUH?!
I GOT YOKAI, TOO!
WS
ST
?!
WOW!
LORD SANMOTO CREATED THESE YOKAI!
GO GET 'EM!!
AHHHH!!
BASSSSH

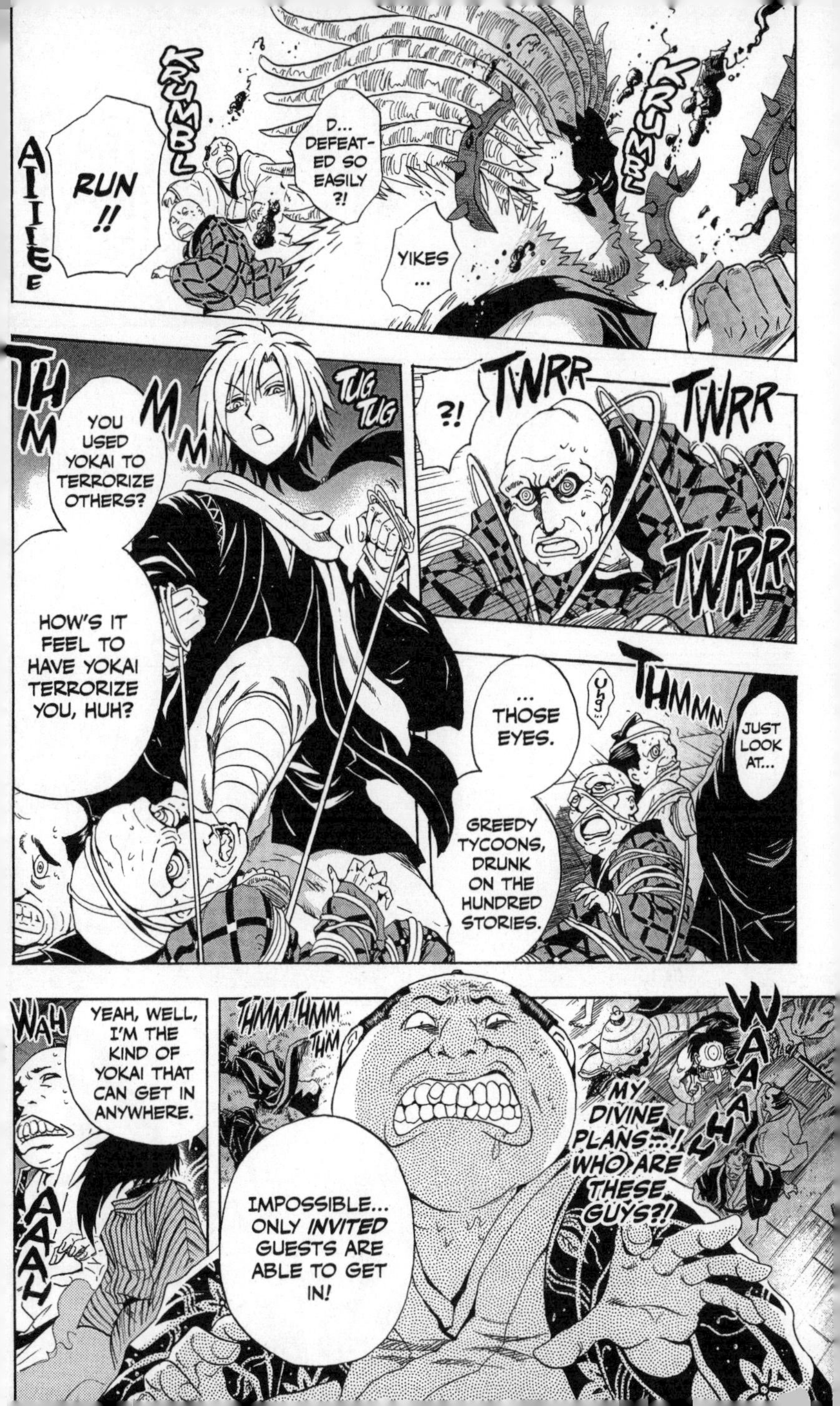
KRUMBL
YIKES ...
D... DEFEATED SO EASILY ?!
KRUMBL
RUN !!
AIIIEEE
TWRR
TWRR
?!
TWRR
THMMM
JUST LOOK AT...
Ugh...
... THOSE EYES.
GREEDY TYCOONS, DRUNK ON THE HUNDRED STORIES.
TUG TUG
THMMM
YOU USED YOKAI TO TERRORIZE OTHERS?
HOW'S IT FEEL TO HAVE YOKAI TERRORIZE YOU, HUH?
WAAAAH
MY DIVINE PLANS...! WHO ARE THESE GUYS?!
THMM THMM THM
IMPOSSIBLE... ONLY *INVITED* GUESTS ARE ABLE TO GET IN!
YEAH, WELL, I'M THE KIND OF YOKAI THAT CAN GET IN ANYWHERE.
WAH
AAAAH

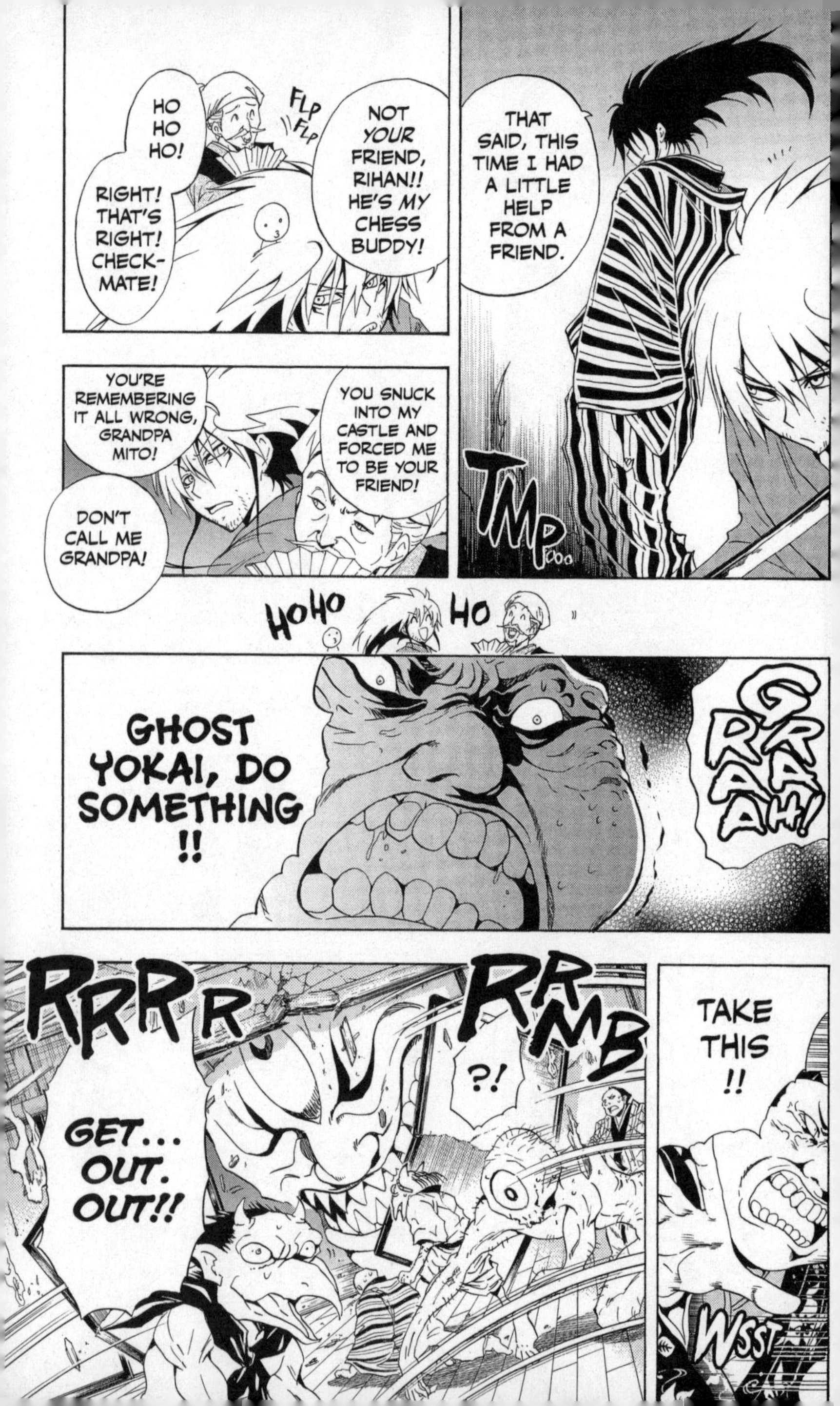
THAT SAID, THIS TIME I HAD A LITTLE HELP FROM A FRIEND.
TMP
FLP FLP
NOT YOUR FRIEND, RIHAN!! HE'S MY CHESS BUDDY!
HO HO HO!
RIGHT! THAT'S RIGHT! CHECKMATE!
YOU SNUCK INTO MY CASTLE AND FORCED ME TO BE YOUR FRIEND!
YOU'RE REMEMBERING IT ALL WRONG, GRANDPA MITO!
DON'T CALL ME GRANDPA!
HOHO HO
GRRAAH!
GHOST YOKAI, DO SOMETHING!!
TAKE THIS!!
WSST
RRRR RRMB
?!
GET... OUT. OUT!!

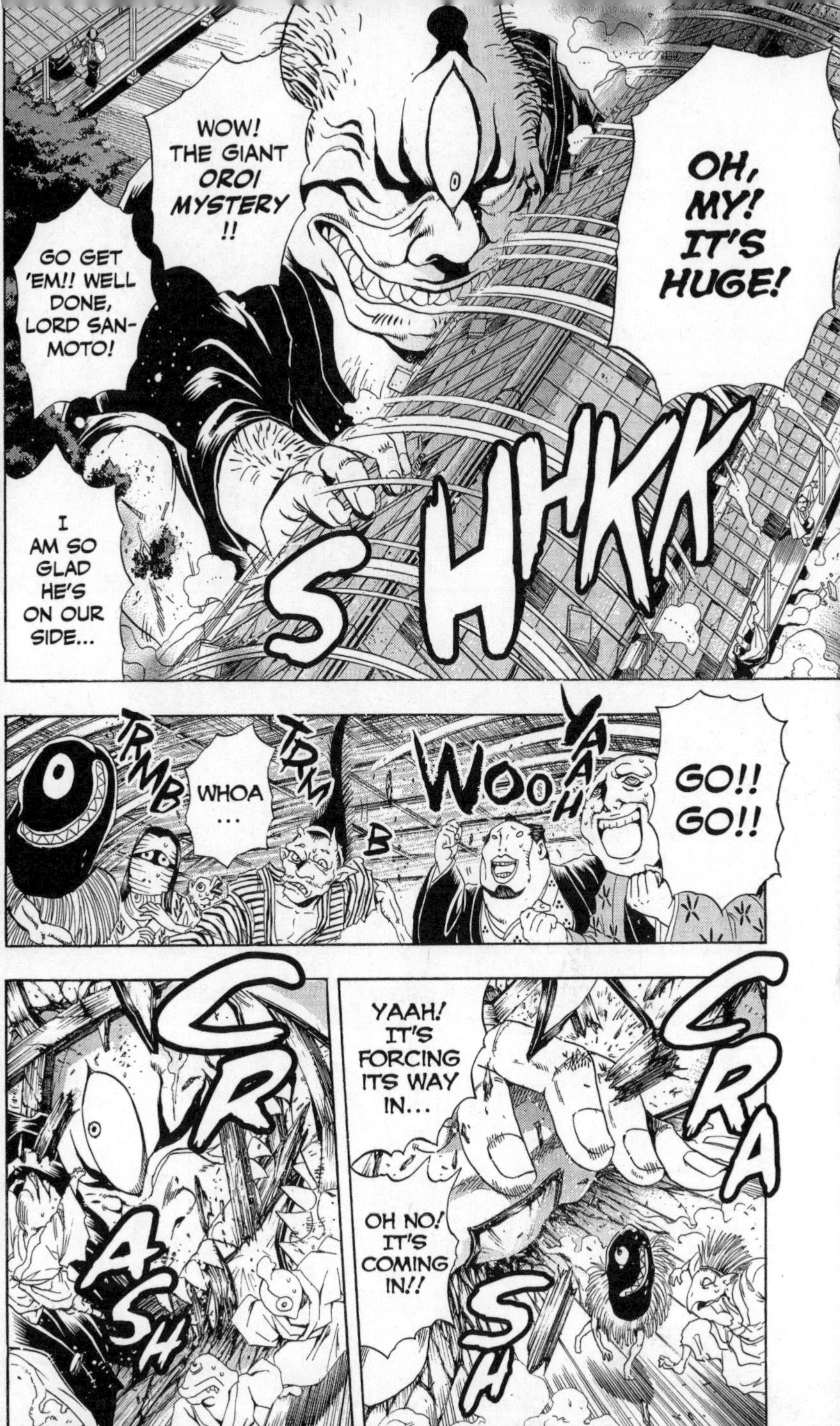

OH, MY! IT'S HUGE!
WOW! THE GIANT OROI MYSTERY!!
GO GET 'EM!! WELL DONE, LORD SAN-MOTO!
I AM SO GLAD HE'S ON OUR SIDE...
SHHKK
GO!! GO!!
YAAAH
WOOO
TRMB
WHOA...
TRMB
CRASH
YAAH! IT'S FORCING ITS WAY IN...
OH NO! IT'S COMING IN!!
CRASH

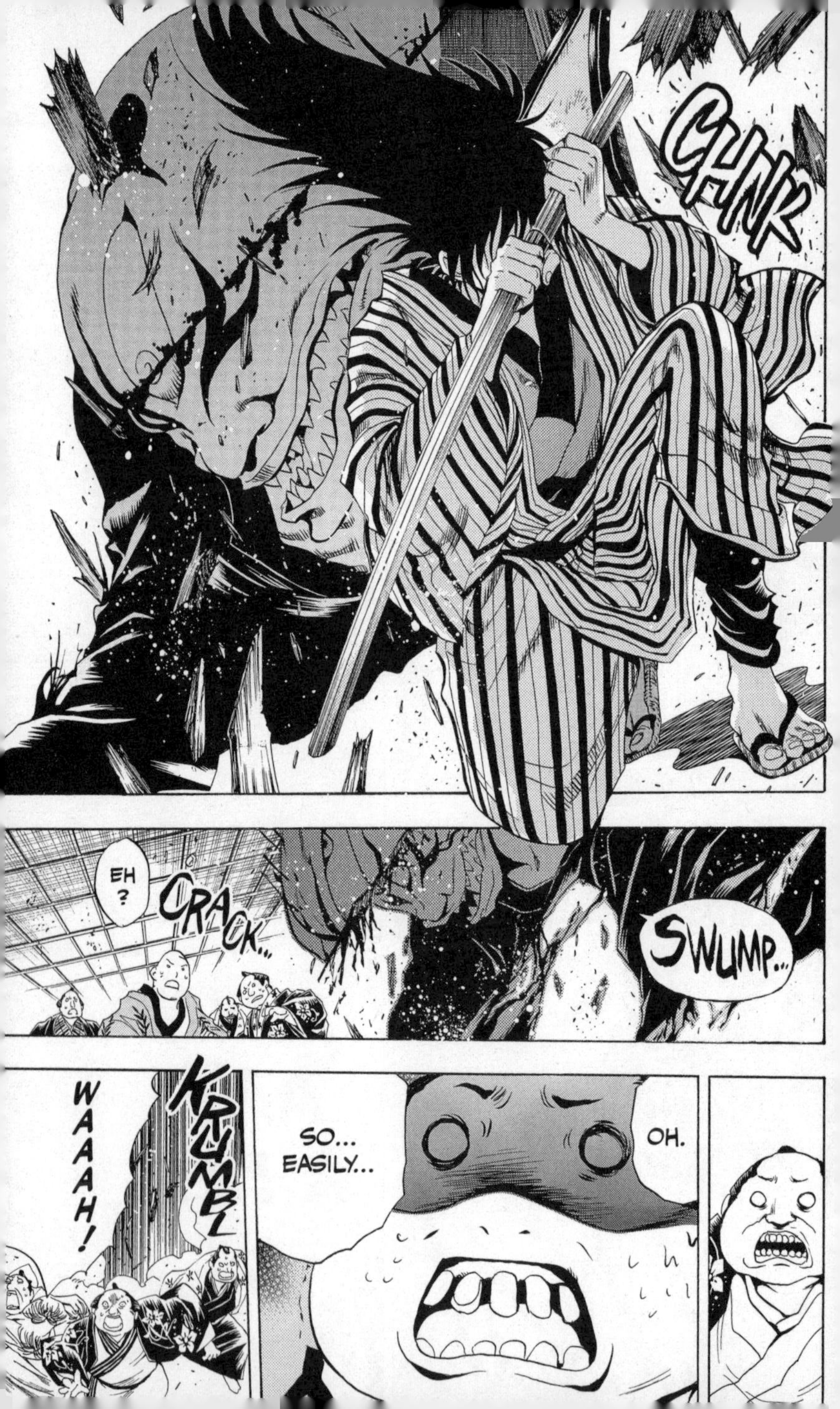
CHNK
SWUMP...
CRACK...
EH ?
OH.
SO... EASILY...
KRUMBL
WAAAAH!

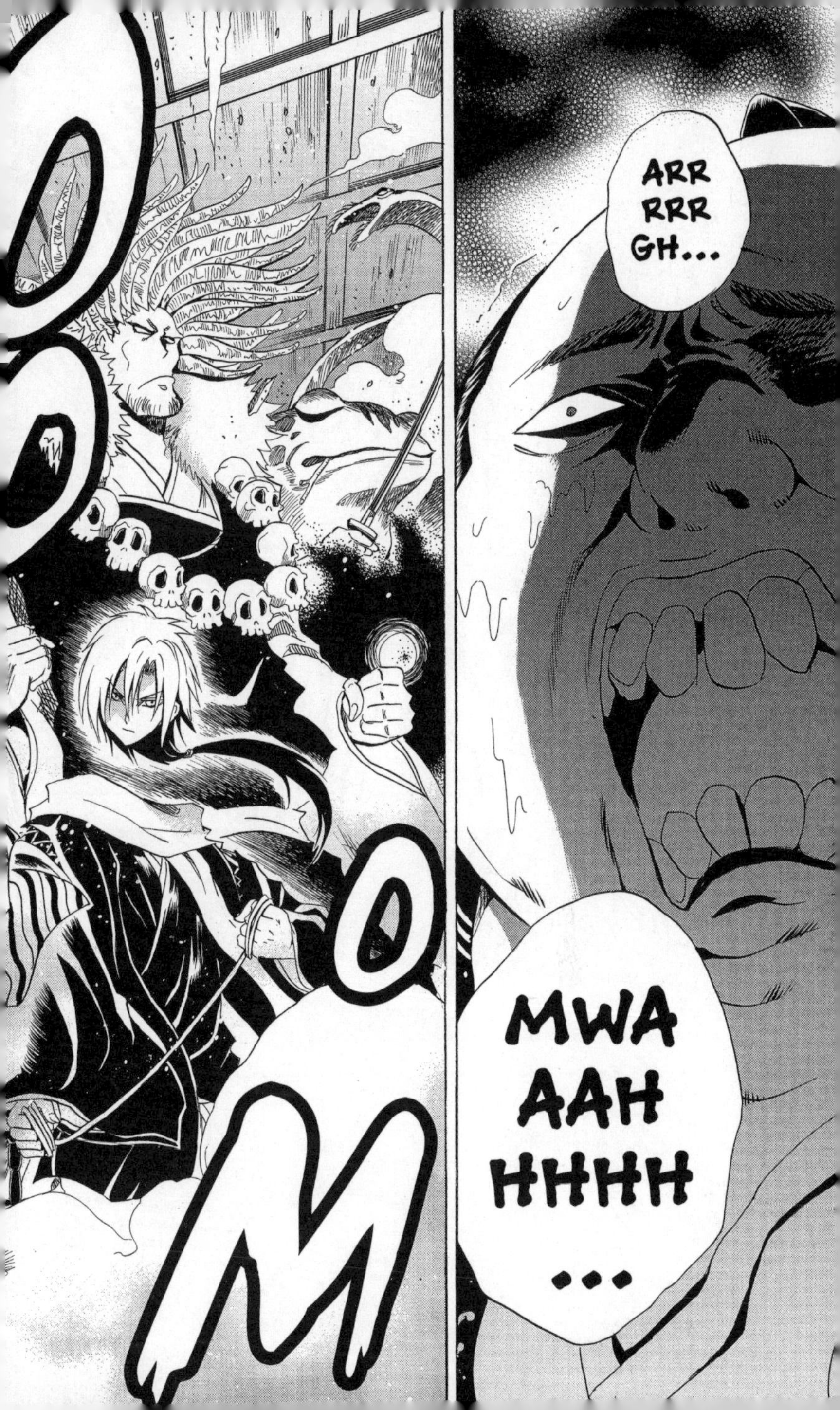
ARR RRR GH...
MWA AAH HHHH ...

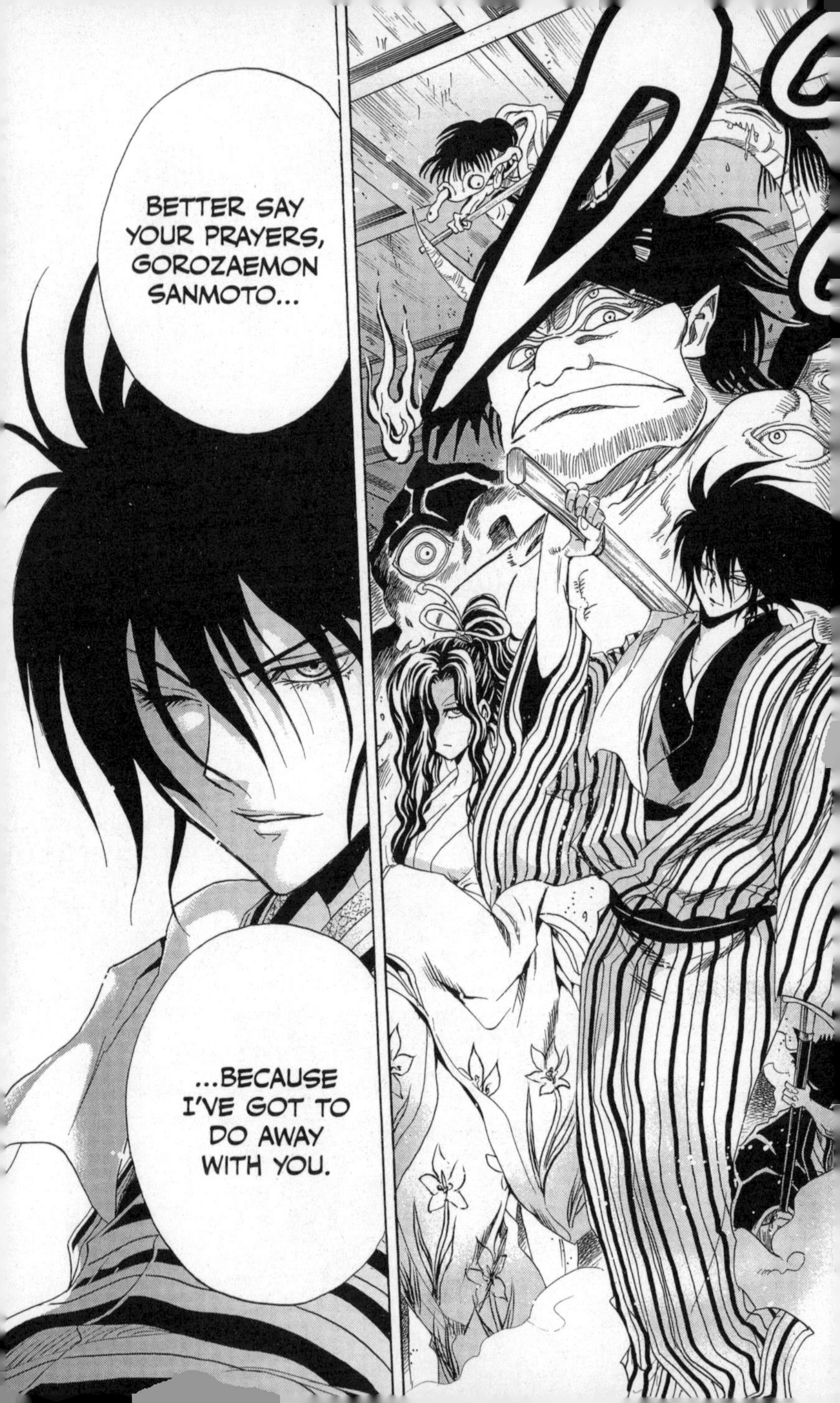
BETTER SAY YOUR PRAYERS, GOROZAEMON SANMOTO...
...BECAUSE I'VE GOT TO DO AWAY WITH YOU.

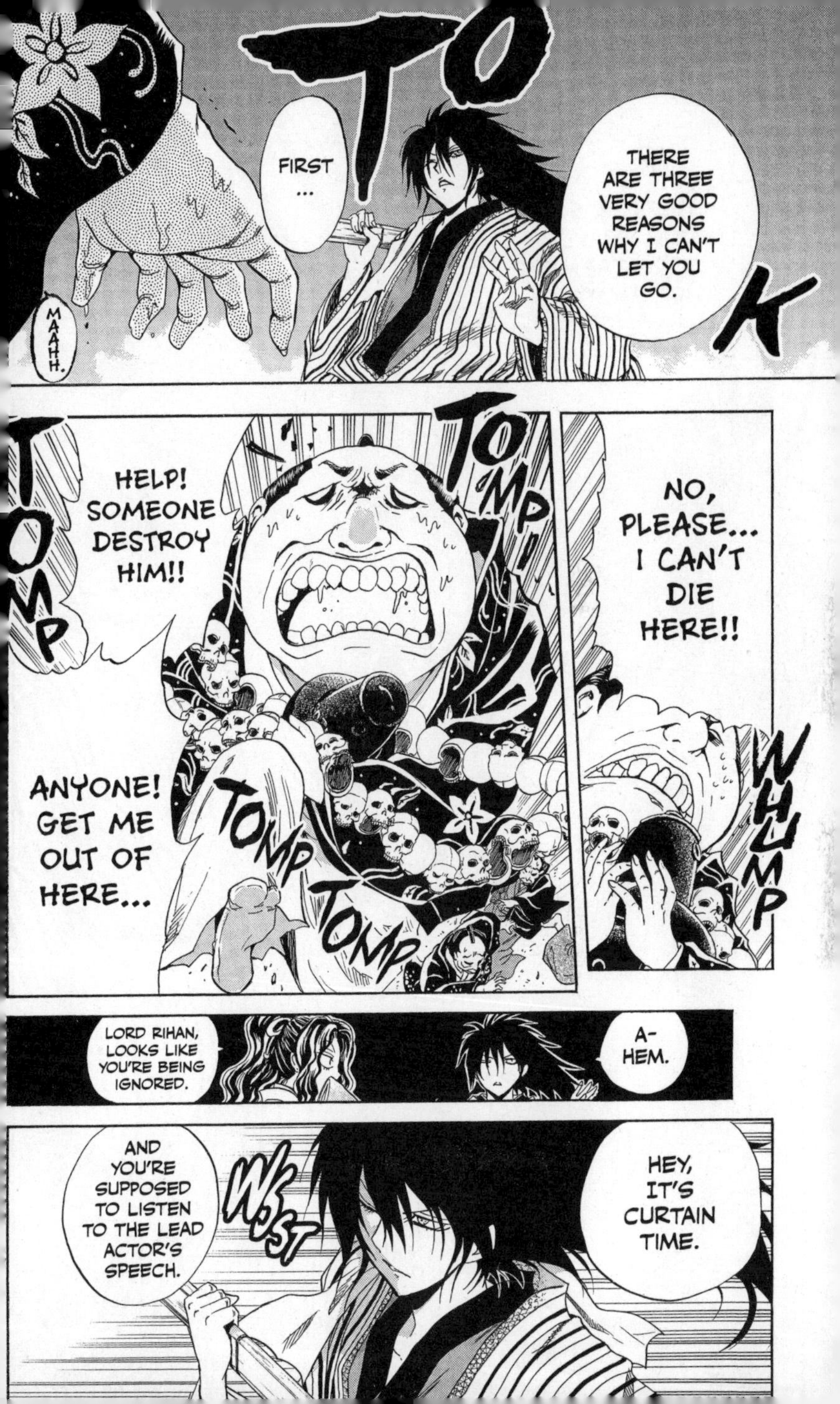
THERE ARE THREE VERY GOOD REASONS WHY I CAN'T LET YOU GO.
TOK
FIRST ...
MAAHH.
NO, PLEASE... I CAN'T DIE HERE!!
WHUMP
TOMP
HELP! SOMEONE DESTROY HIM!!
TOMP
ANYONE! GET ME OUT OF HERE...
TOMP
TOMP
A- HEM.
LORD RIHAN, LOOKS LIKE YOU'RE BEING IGNORED.
HEY, IT'S CURTAIN TIME.
AND YOU'RE SUPPOSED TO LISTEN TO THE LEAD ACTOR'S SPEECH.

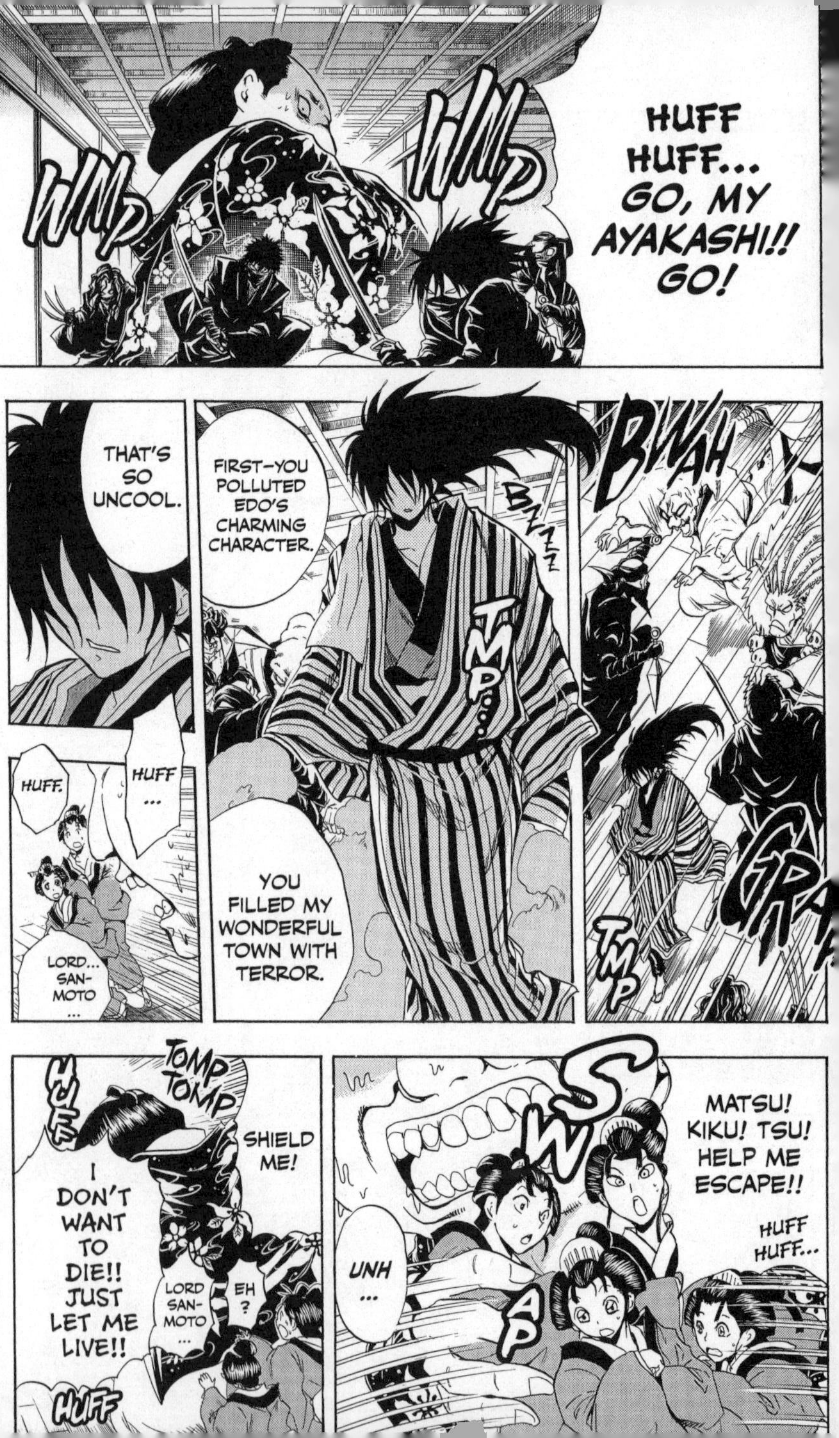
WMP
WMP
HUFF HUFF... GO, MY AYAKASHI!! GO!
BWAH
GRA
TMP
BZZZZ
FIRST—YOU POLLUTED EDO'S CHARMING CHARACTER.
TMP...
YOU FILLED MY WONDERFUL TOWN WITH TERROR.
THAT'S SO UNCOOL.
HUFF ...
HUFF.
LORD... SAN-MOTO ...
SWAP
MATSU! KIKU! TSU! HELP ME ESCAPE!!
HUFF HUFF...
UNH ...
TOMP TOMP
HUFF
SHIELD ME!
I DON'T WANT TO DIE!! JUST LET ME LIVE!!
EH ?
LORD SAN-MOTO ...
HUFF

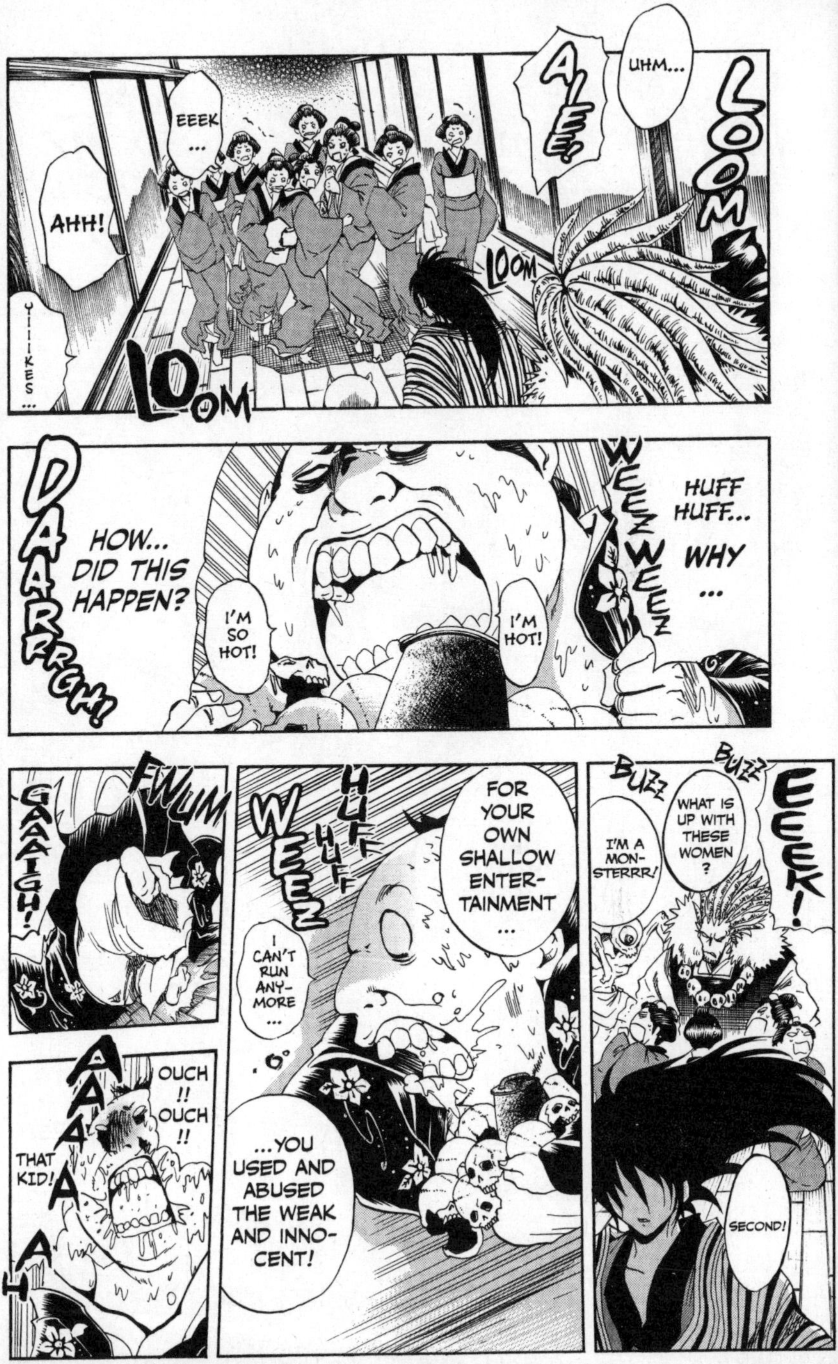

UHM...
AIEE!
LOOOM
LOOM
EEEK...
AHH!
YIIIKES...
LOOM
WEEZ WEEZ
HUFF HUFF... WHY...
I'M HOT!
HOW... DID THIS HAPPEN?
I'M SO HOT!
DAAARRGH!
BUZZ
BUZZ
EEEK!
WHAT IS UP WITH THESE WOMEN?
I'M A MONSTERRR!
SECOND!
HUFF HUFF
WEEZ
FOR YOUR OWN SHALLOW ENTERTAINMENT...
I CAN'T RUN ANYMORE...
...YOU USED AND ABUSED THE WEAK AND INNOCENT!
FWUM
GAAAIGH!
OUCH!! OUCH!!
AAAAAH
THAT KID!

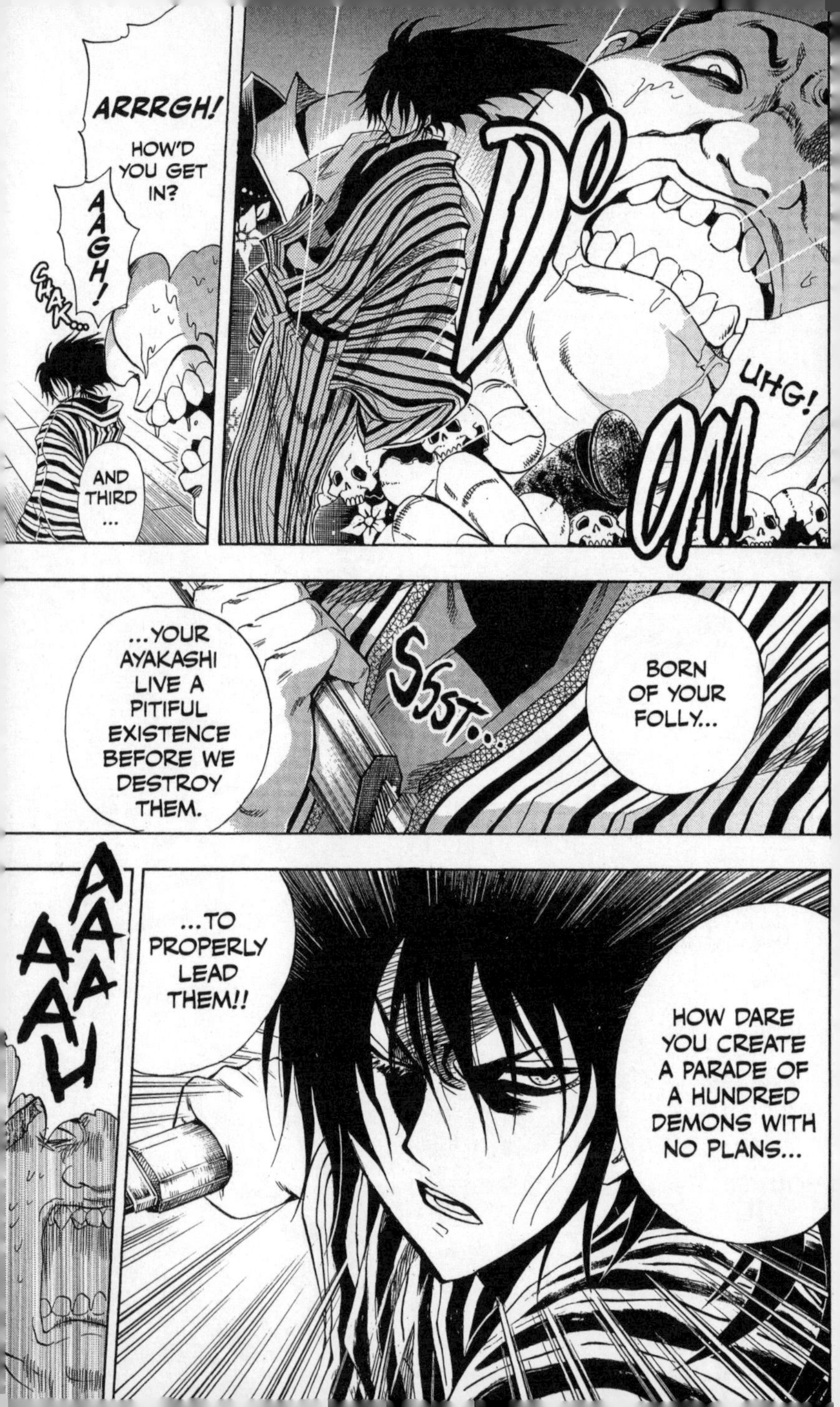
DOOM
UHG!
ARRRGH!
HOW'D YOU GET IN?
AAGH!
CHAK...
AND THIRD ...
BORN OF YOUR FOLLY...
SSST...
...YOUR AYAKASHI LIVE A PITIFUL EXISTENCE BEFORE WE DESTROY THEM.
HOW DARE YOU CREATE A PARADE OF A HUNDRED DEMONS WITH NO PLANS...
...TO PROPERLY LEAD THEM!!
AAAAAH

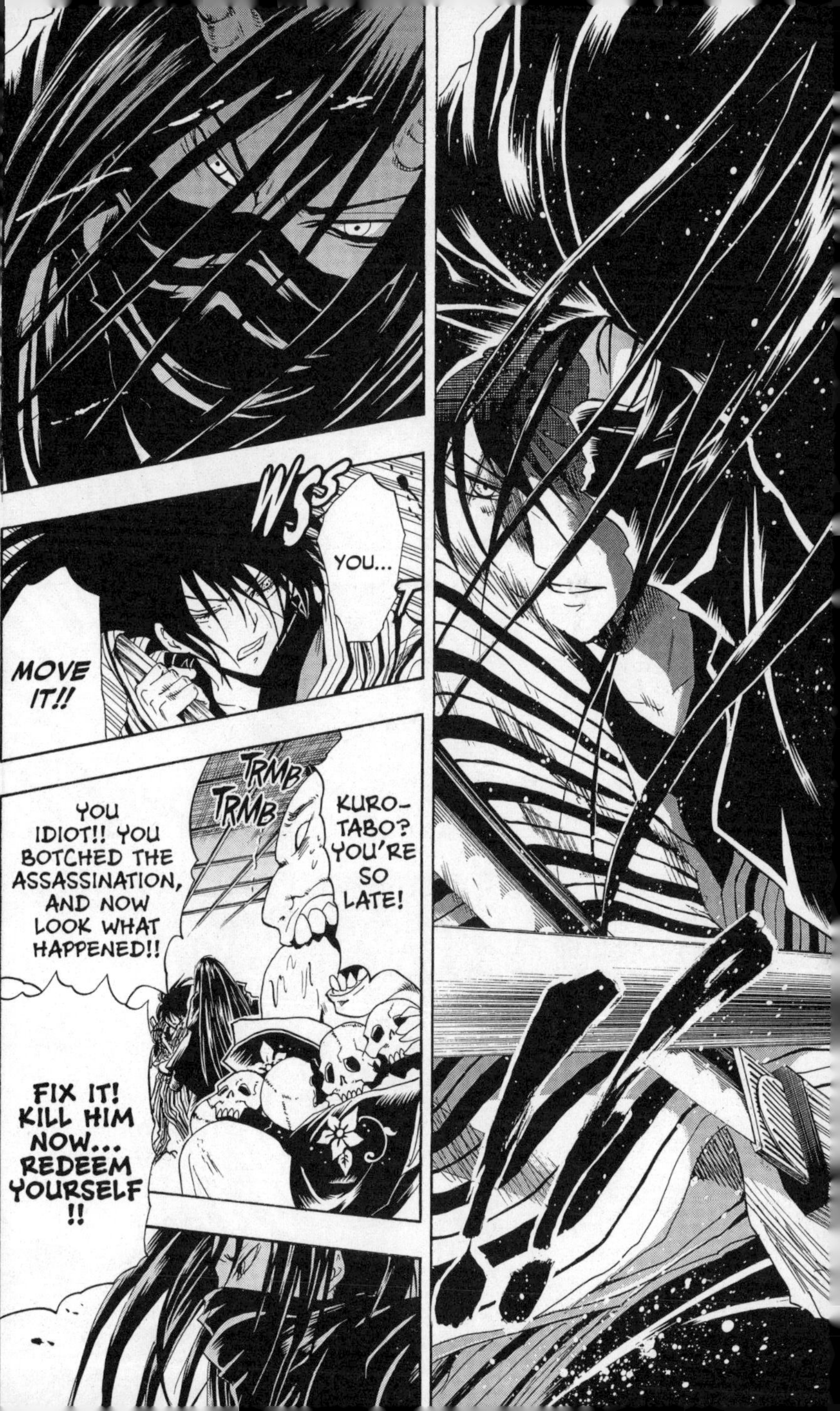
WSS
YOU...
MOVE IT!!
TRMB TRMB
KURO-TABO? YOU'RE SO LATE!
YOU IDIOT!! YOU BOTCHED THE ASSASSINATION, AND NOW LOOK WHAT HAPPENED!!
FIX IT! KILL HIM NOW... REDEEM YOURSELF!!

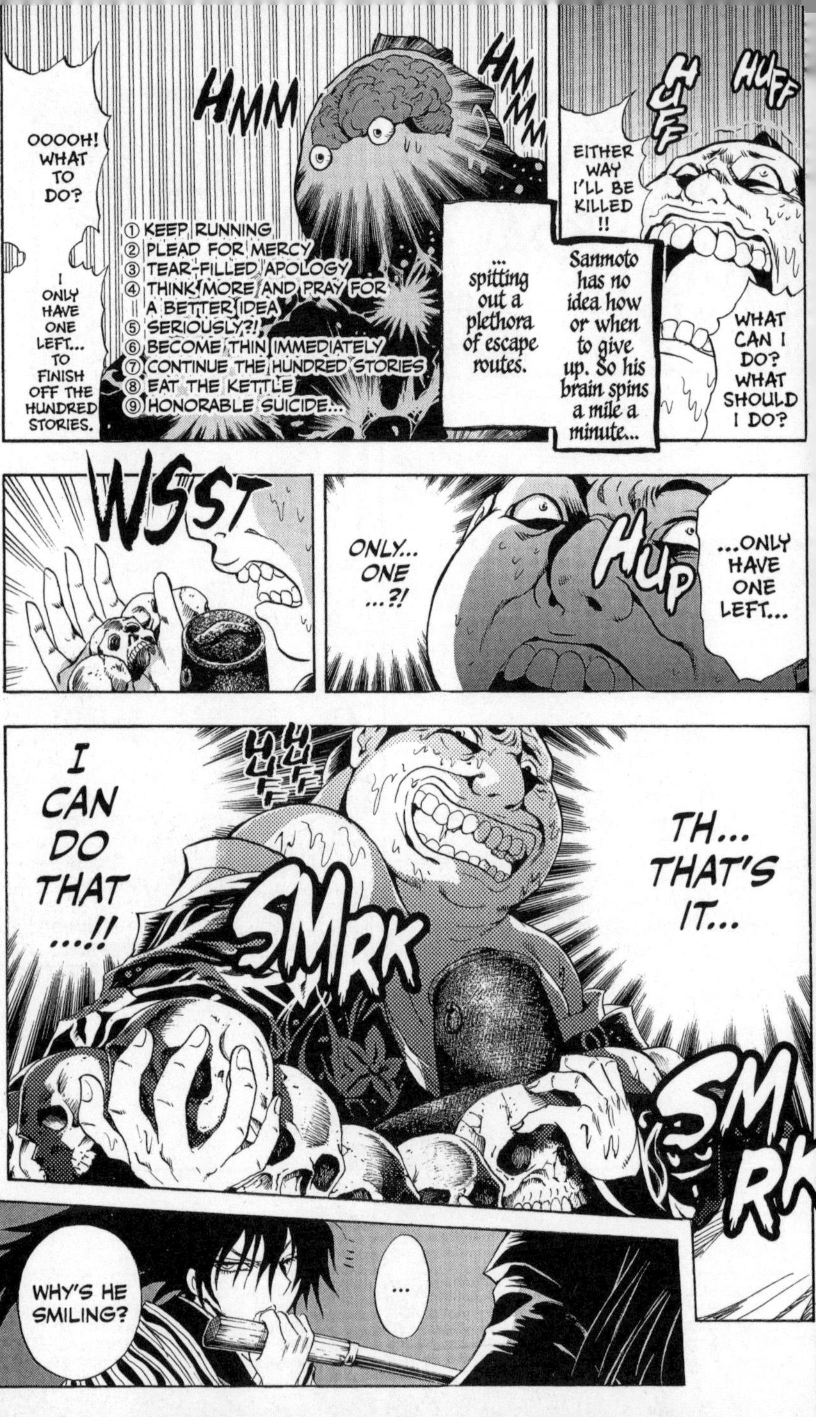
HUFF
HUFF
EITHER WAY I'LL BE KILLED !!
WHAT CAN I DO? WHAT SHOULD I DO?
Sanmoto has no idea how or when to give up. So his brain spins a mile a minute...
... spitting out a plethora of escape routes.
HMMMM
HMM
OOOOH! WHAT TO DO?
① KEEP RUNNING
② PLEAD FOR MERCY
③ TEAR-FILLED APOLOGY
④ THINK MORE AND PRAY FOR A BETTER IDEA
⑤ SERIOUSLY?!
⑥ BECOME THIN IMMEDIATELY
⑦ CONTINUE THE HUNDRED STORIES
⑧ EAT THE KETTLE
⑨ HONORABLE SUICIDE...
I ONLY HAVE ONE LEFT... TO FINISH OFF THE HUNDRED STORIES.
...ONLY HAVE ONE LEFT...
HUP
ONLY... ONE ...?!
WSST
TH... THAT'S IT...
SMRK
SMRK
I CAN DO THAT ...!!
...
WHY'S HE SMILING?

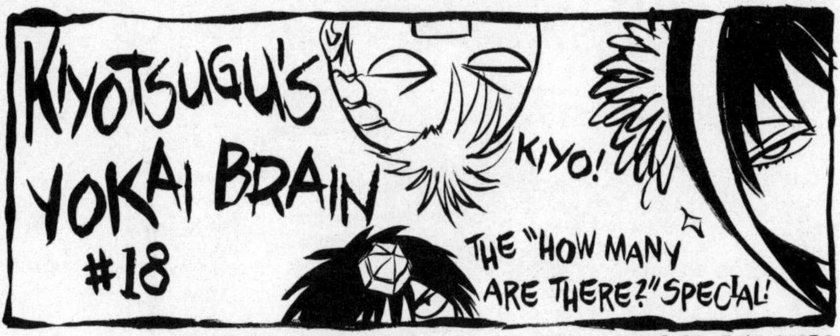
KIYOTSUGU'S
YOKAI BRAIN
#18
KIYO!
THE "HOW MANY ARE THERE?" SPECIAL!

Q: WHY DOES KARASU-TENGU ADDRESS GYUKI AND HITOTSUME AS LORD? IS IT POSSIBLE THAT KARASU-TENGU IS WEAKER THAN GYUKI? *–YUSUKE YAMADA, GIFU PREFECTURE*

KARASU-TENGU: EH... *KOFF*. DO I...? I HAVEN'T BEEN PAYING ATTENTION TO IT. BUT IN PUBLIC, SAY AT A FORMAL MEETING, I TRY TO SHOW RESPECT TO THE EXECUTIVE MEMBERS. THAT SAID, I DON'T THINK THAT I'D LOSE IF I WERE TO FIGHT MASTER GYUKI!!

Q: THOSE FOUR CHILDREN BEING CARRIED IN NURE-GARASU'S KIMONO... ARE THEY KARASU-TENGU'S CHILDREN? *–HORSEHEAD BONE, TOKYO*

NURE-GARASU: YES...! AS A MATTER OF FACT. TEEHEE! *(BLUSH)*

KUROMARU: UM, DAD ONLY GETS BACK ONCE A YEAR, SO...

TOSAKAMARU: DON'T DO IT, KUROMARU!! DON'T EVEN TRY TO DO THE MATH!!

Q: SO, NURE-GARASU, HOW MANY CHILDREN DO YOU HAVE, THEN? *–M-M, HYOGO PREFECTURE*

SASAMI: HMM? SO, IF HE STOPS BACK ONCE A YEAR... THEN ARE THERE OTHERS, TOO? YOUNGER BROTHERS AND SISTERS THAT I DON'T KNOW ABOUT...

TOSAKAMARU: STOP THINKING ABOUT IT!!

NURE-GARASU: HAHA! YOU ALL ONLY KNOW ABOUT THE MAIN HOUSE AND NOTHING ABOUT TAKAO!! I'LL TELL YOU ALL ABOUT IT NEXT TIME...

SANBA-GARASU: *GULP... (SCARY...)*

Q: HOW MANY ARE THERE IN THE TSURARA CLAN?! *–COLOGNE, TOKUSHIMA PREFECTURE*

TSURARA: YEAH, SO... I BOUGHT APPROXIMATELY 20 PLATES... UHM, SO... ABOUT 20!!

GET IN TOUCH!

MAILING ADDRESS: NURA EDITOR
VIZ MEDIA
P.O. BOX 77010
SAN FRANCISCO, CA 94107

*PLEASE INCLUDE YOUR NAME, AGE, ADDRESS AND PHONE NUMBER IN THE LETTER. IF YOU DO NOT WANT TO INCLUDE YOUR NAME, PLEASE USE A HANDLE OR NICKNAME. LETTERS AND ILLUSTRATIONS MAILED TO US WILL BE STORED FOR A CERTAIN PERIOD, THEN DISCARDED. IF YOU WISH TO KEEP A COPY, PLEASE MAKE ONE YOURSELF BEFORE MAILING IT IN. IF YOU'D LIKE TO HAVE YOUR NAME AND ADDRESS REMAIN ANONYMOUS, PLEASE INDICATE THAT IN YOUR LETTER.

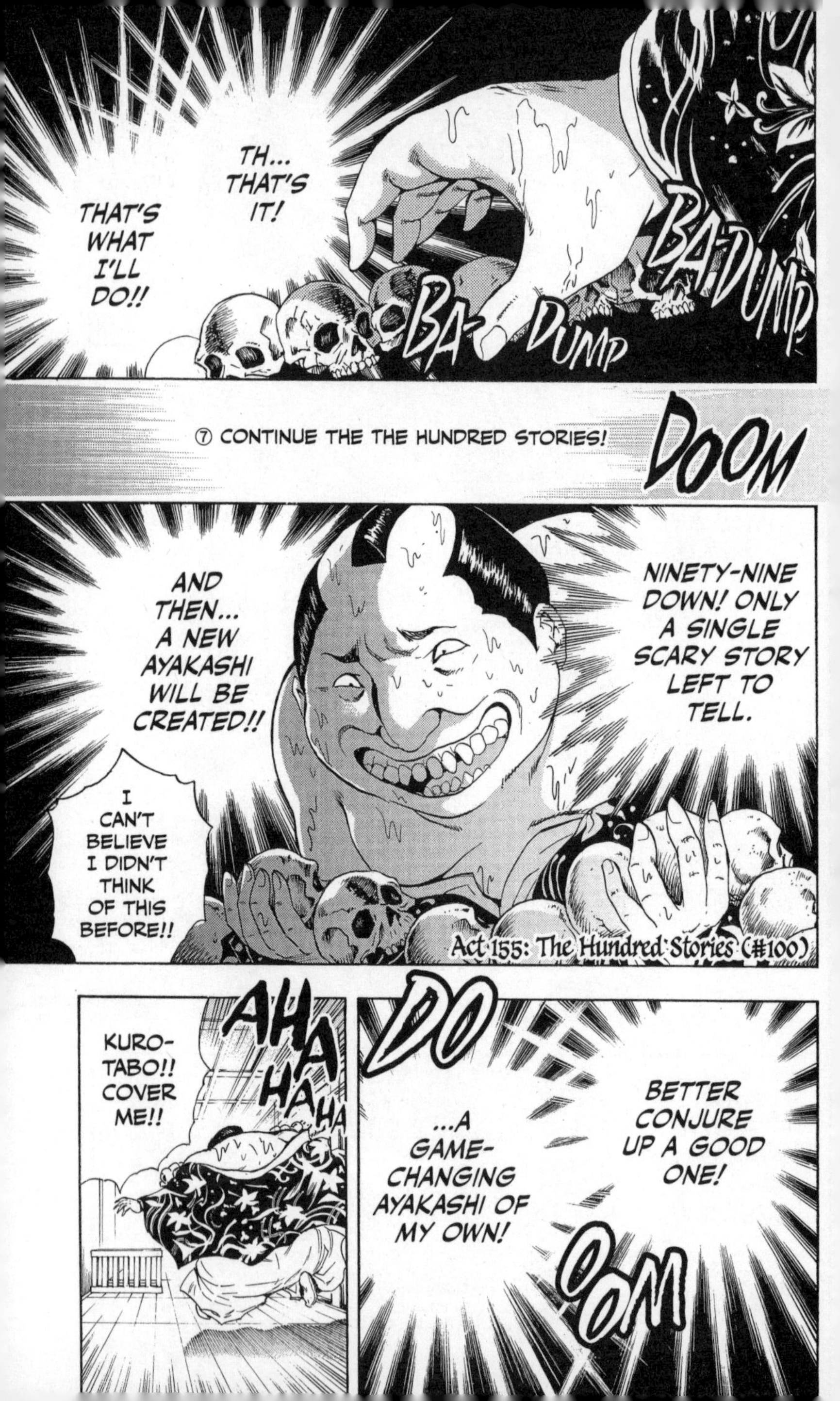

TH... THAT'S IT!
THAT'S WHAT I'LL DO!!
BADUMP
BA-DUMP
DOOM
⑦ CONTINUE THE THE HUNDRED STORIES!
NINETY-NINE DOWN! ONLY A SINGLE SCARY STORY LEFT TO TELL.
AND THEN... A NEW AYAKASHI WILL BE CREATED!!
I CAN'T BELIEVE I DIDN'T THINK OF THIS BEFORE!!
Act 155: The Hundred Stories (#100)
DO
BETTER CONJURE UP A GOOD ONE!
...A GAME-CHANGING AYAKASHI OF MY OWN!
OOM
AHAHAHA
KURO-TABO!! COVER ME!!

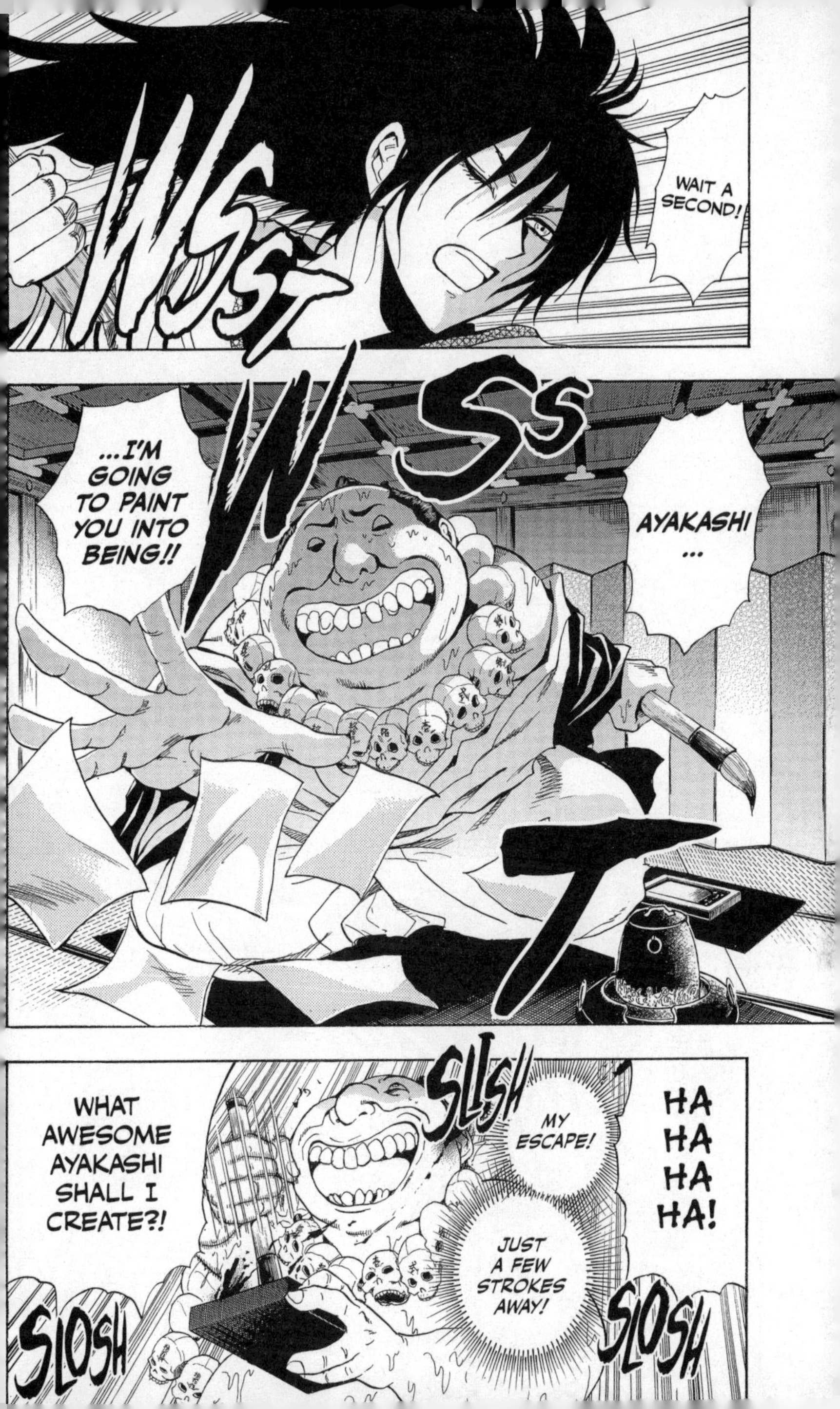

WAIT A SECOND!
WSSST
AYAKASHI ...
...I'M GOING TO PAINT YOU INTO BEING!!
SLISH
HA HA HA HA!
MY ESCAPE!
JUST A FEW STROKES AWAY!
WHAT AWESOME AYAKASHI SHALL I CREATE?!
SLOSH
SLOSH

Act 155: The Hundred Stories (#100)

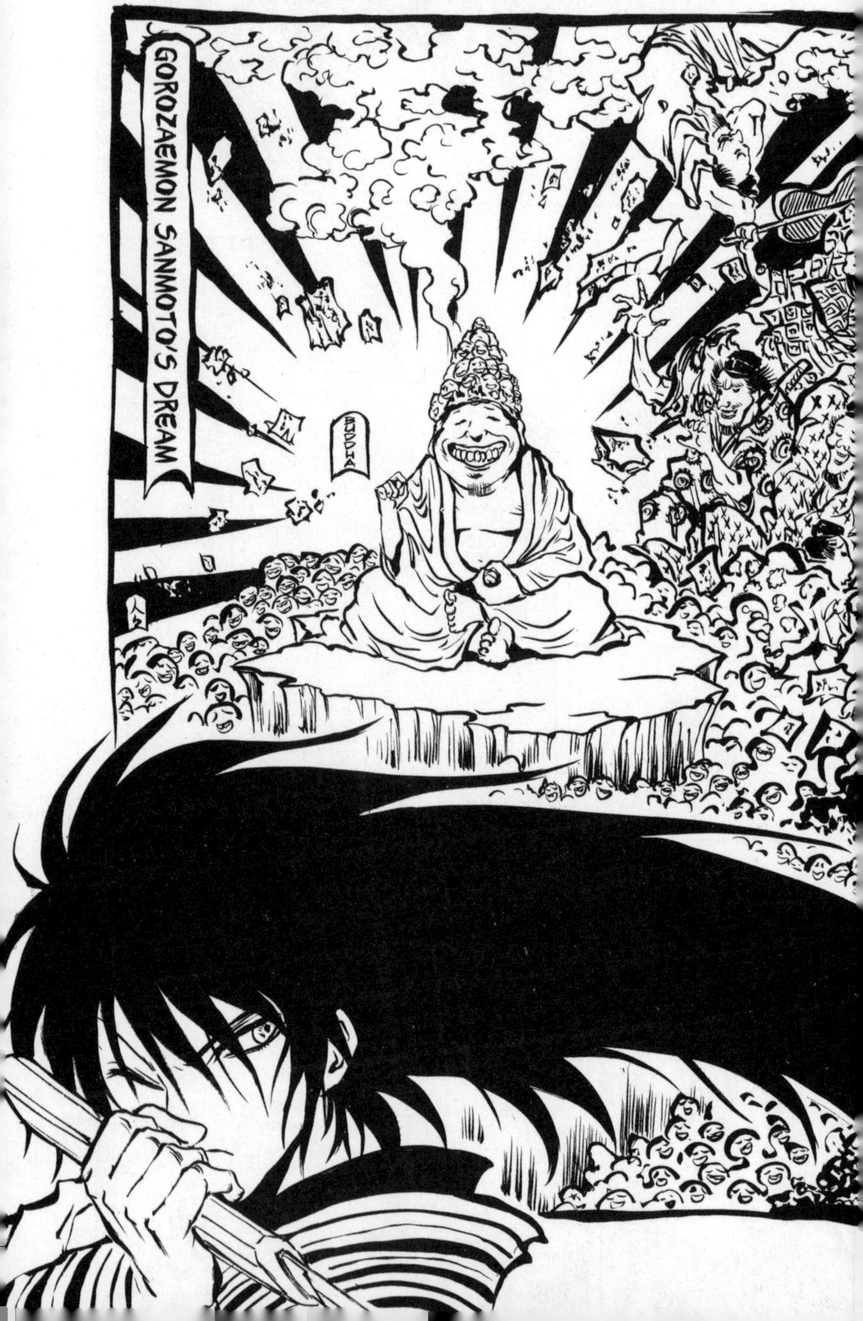
GOROZAEMON SANMOTO'S DREAM
BUDDHA

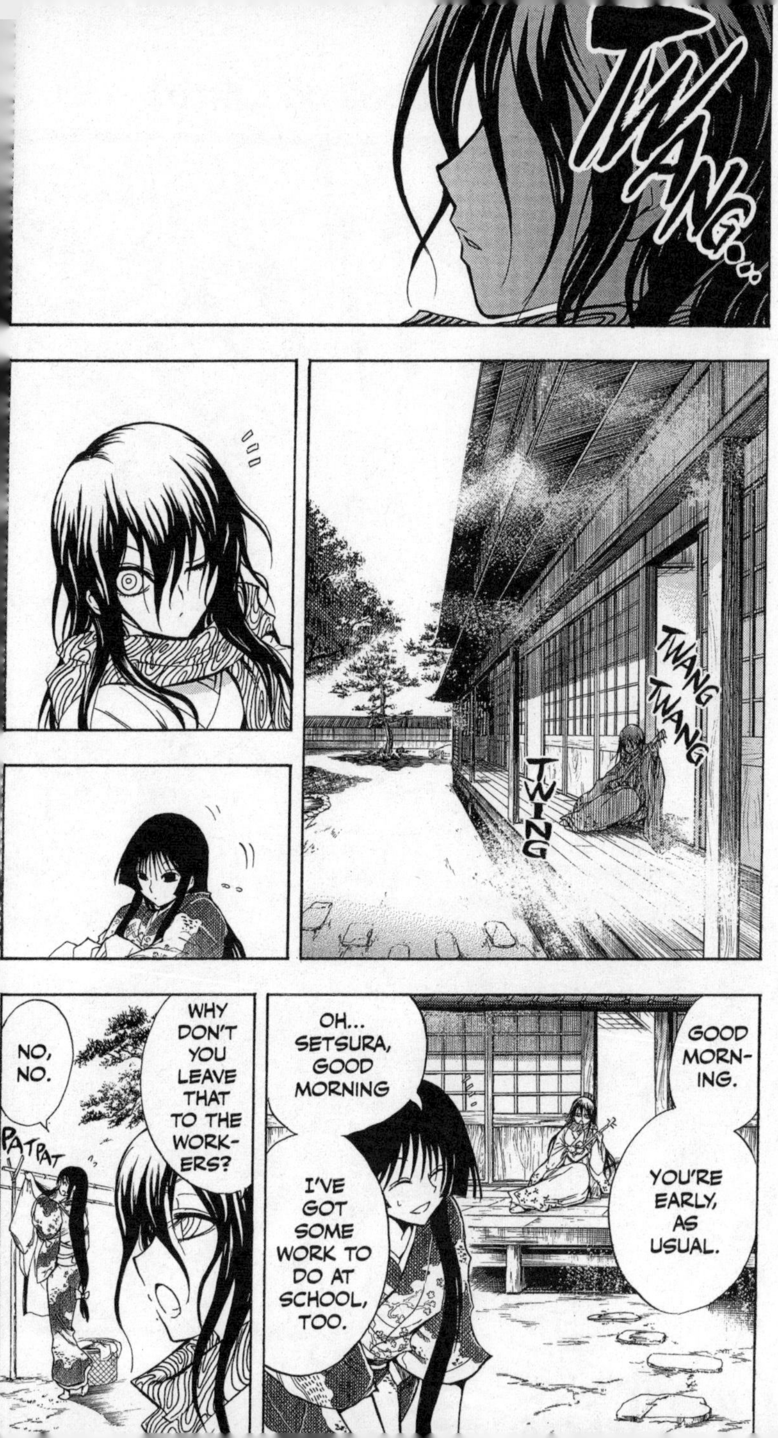
TWANG...
TWANG
TWANG
TWING
GOOD MORN-ING.
OH... SETSURA, GOOD MORNING
YOU'RE EARLY, AS USUAL.
I'VE GOT SOME WORK TO DO AT SCHOOL, TOO.
WHY DON'T YOU LEAVE THAT TO THE WORK-ERS?
NO, NO.
PATPAT

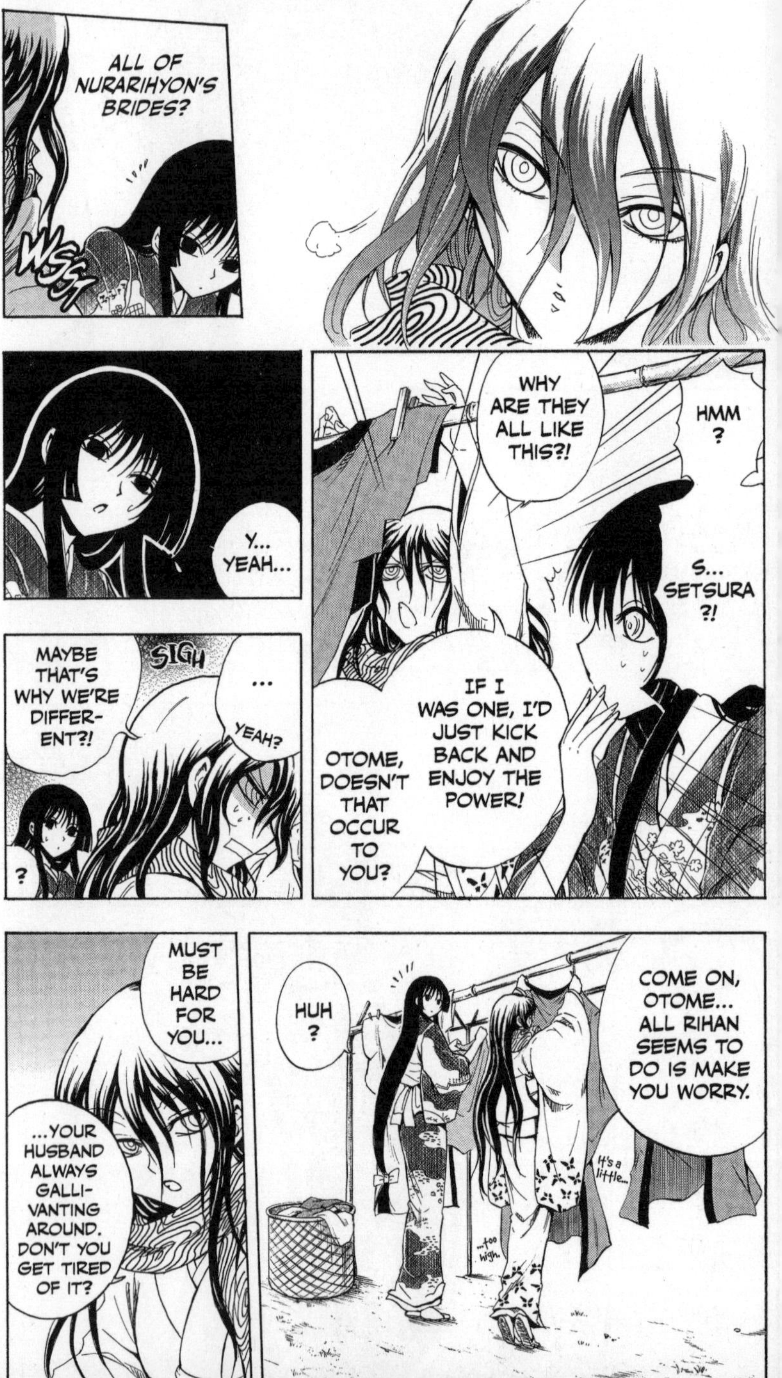

ALL OF NURARIHYON'S BRIDES?
WSSH
WHY ARE THEY ALL LIKE THIS?!
HMM ?
S... SETSURA ?!
IF I WAS ONE, I'D JUST KICK BACK AND ENJOY THE POWER!
OTOME, DOESN'T THAT OCCUR TO YOU?
Y... YEAH...
SIGH
...
YEAH?
MAYBE THAT'S WHY WE'RE DIFFER-ENT?!
?
COME ON, OTOME... ALL RIHAN SEEMS TO DO IS MAKE YOU WORRY.
HUH ?
It's a little...
...too high.
MUST BE HARD FOR YOU...
...YOUR HUSBAND ALWAYS GALLI-VANTING AROUND. DON'T YOU GET TIRED OF IT?

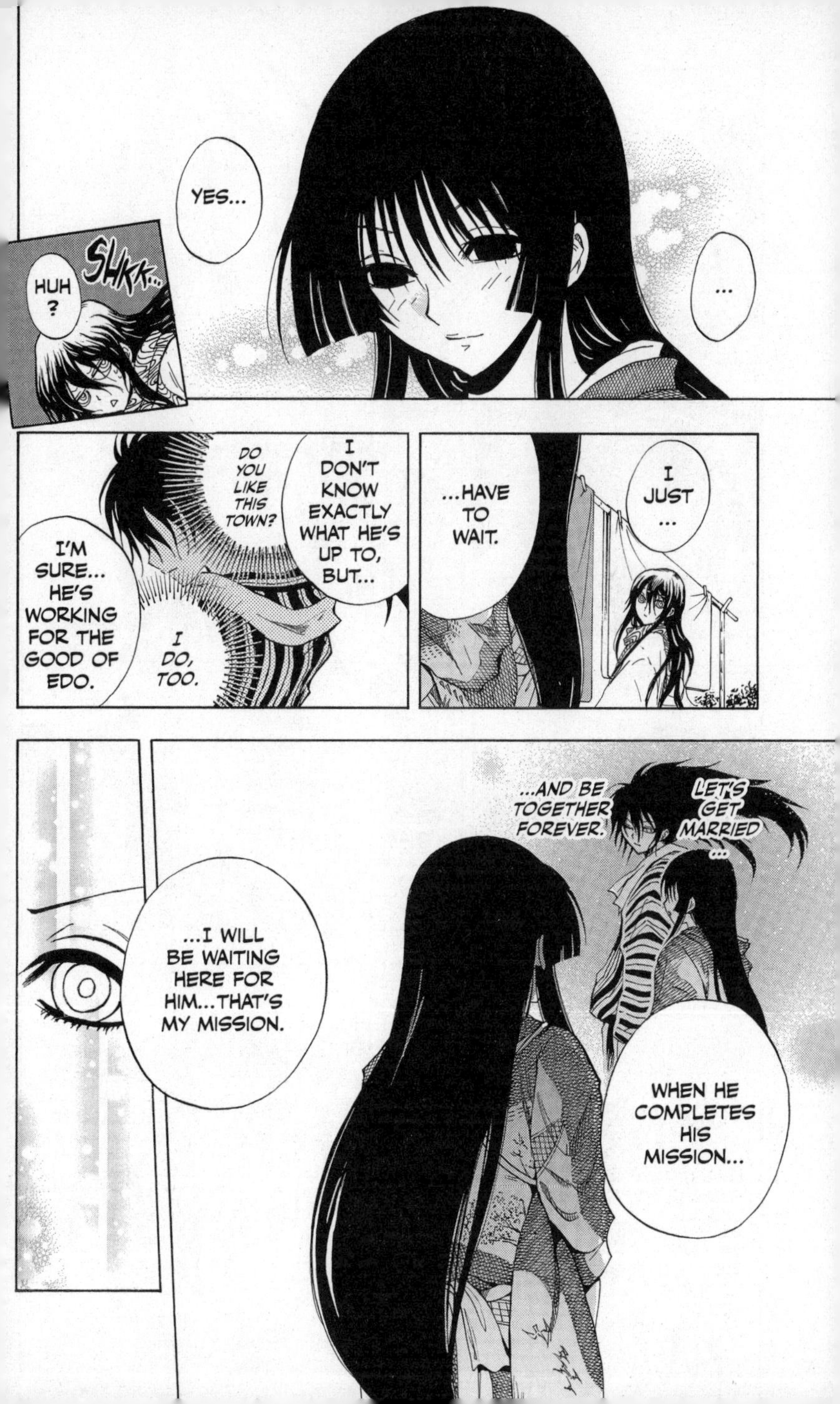
...
YES...
SHKK...
HUH ?
I JUST ...
...HAVE TO WAIT.
I DON'T KNOW EXACTLY WHAT HE'S UP TO, BUT...
DO YOU LIKE THIS TOWN?
I'M SURE... HE'S WORKING FOR THE GOOD OF EDO.
I DO, TOO.
LET'S GET MARRIED ...
...AND BE TOGETHER FOREVER.
WHEN HE COMPLETES HIS MISSION...
...I WILL BE WAITING HERE FOR HIM...THAT'S MY MISSION.

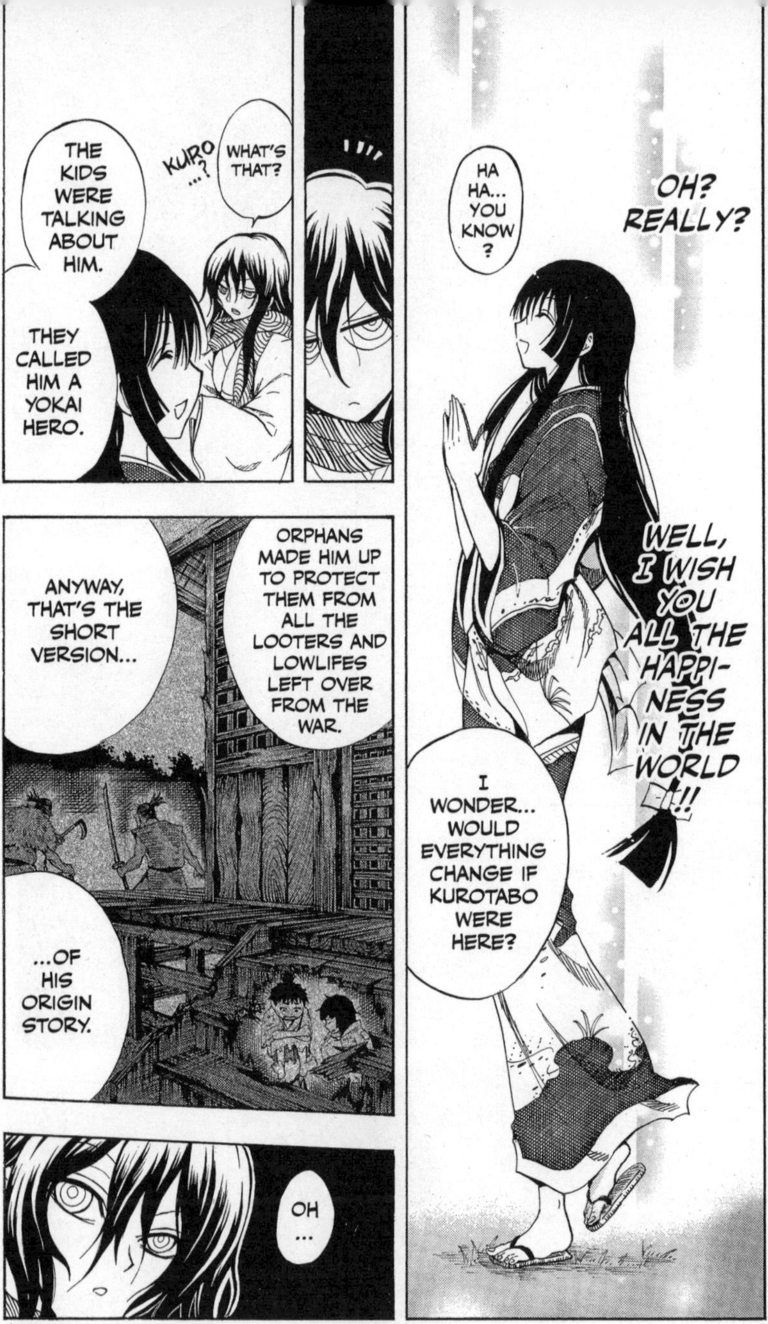
OH? REALLY?
HA HA... YOU KNOW?
WELL, I WISH YOU ALL THE HAPPINESS IN THE WORLD!!
I WONDER... WOULD EVERYTHING CHANGE IF KUROTABO WERE HERE?
WHAT'S THAT?
KURO...?
THE KIDS WERE TALKING ABOUT HIM.
THEY CALLED HIM A YOKAI HERO.
ORPHANS MADE HIM UP TO PROTECT THEM FROM ALL THE LOOTERS AND LOWLIFES LEFT OVER FROM THE WAR.
ANYWAY, THAT'S THE SHORT VERSION...
...OF HIS ORIGIN STORY.
OH...

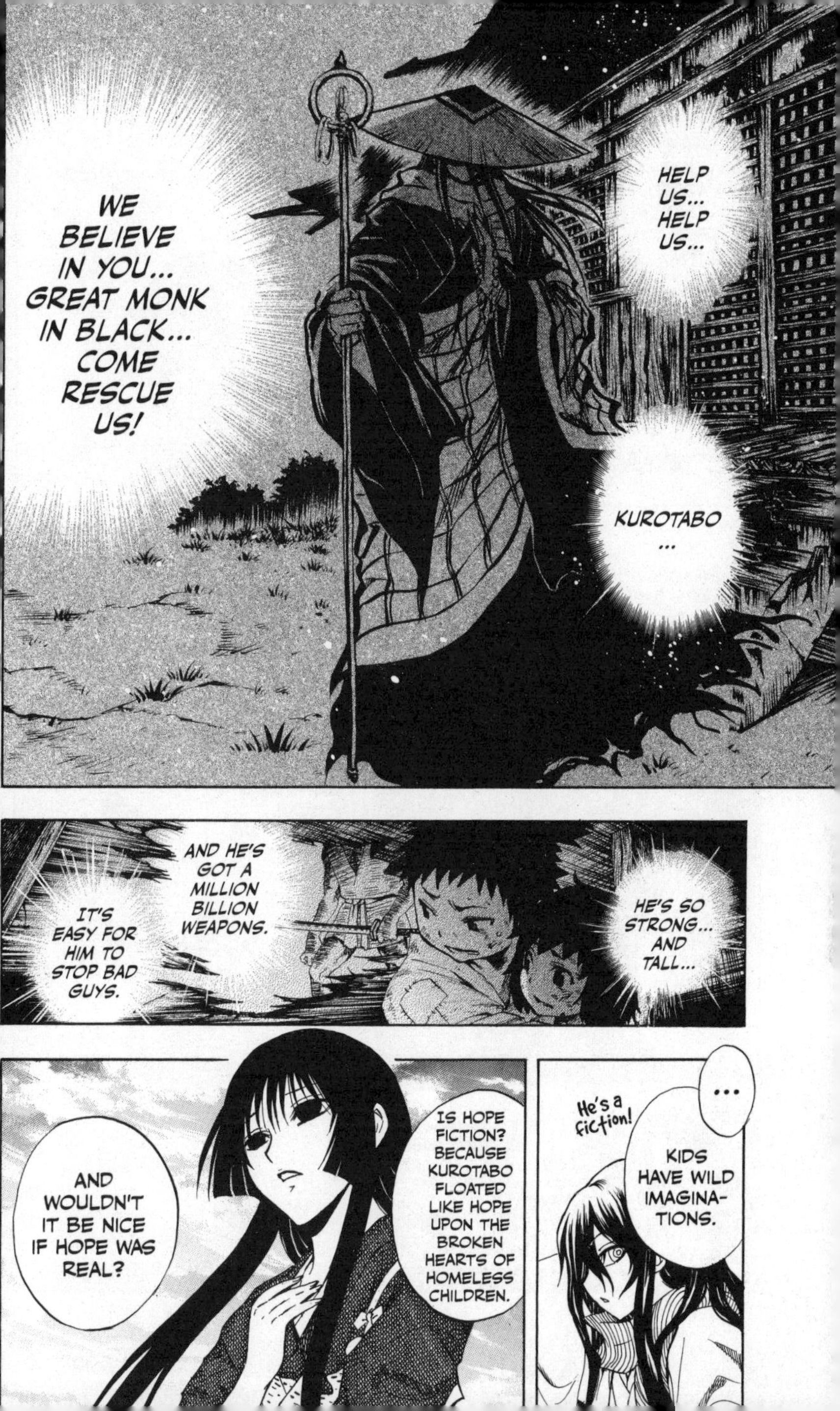
HELP US... HELP US...
WE BELIEVE IN YOU... GREAT MONK IN BLACK... COME RESCUE US!
KUROTABO...
HE'S SO STRONG... AND TALL...
AND HE'S GOT A MILLION BILLION WEAPONS.
IT'S EASY FOR HIM TO STOP BAD GUYS.
...
He's a fiction!
KIDS HAVE WILD IMAGINA-TIONS.
IS HOPE FICTION? BECAUSE KUROTABO FLOATED LIKE HOPE UPON THE BROKEN HEARTS OF HOMELESS CHILDREN.
AND WOULDN'T IT BE NICE IF HOPE WAS REAL?

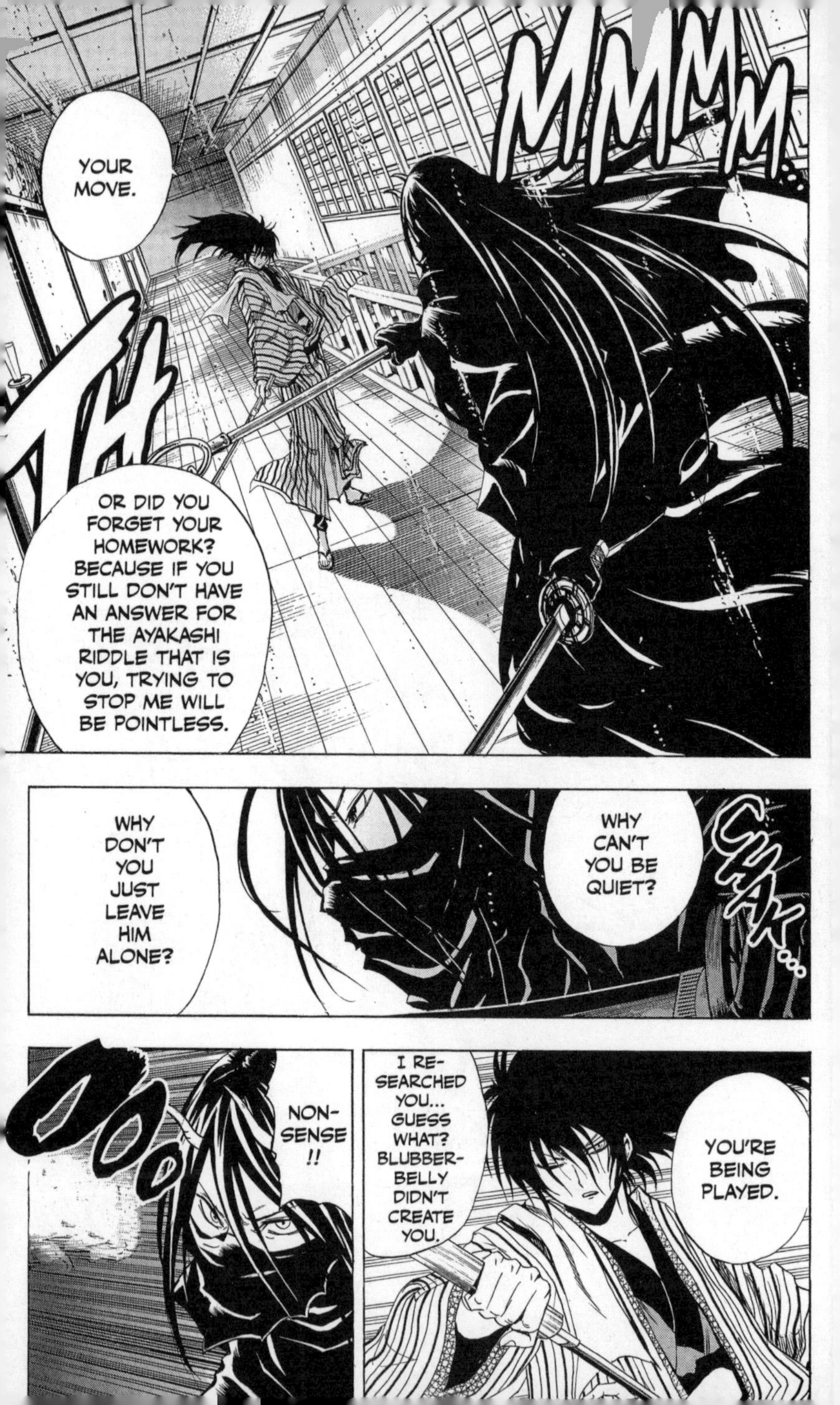
MMMM...
YOUR MOVE.
OR DID YOU FORGET YOUR HOMEWORK? BECAUSE IF YOU STILL DON'T HAVE AN ANSWER FOR THE AYAKASHI RIDDLE THAT IS YOU, TRYING TO STOP ME WILL BE POINTLESS.
CHAK...
WHY CAN'T YOU BE QUIET?
WHY DON'T YOU JUST LEAVE HIM ALONE?
YOU'RE BEING PLAYED.
I RE-SEARCHED YOU... GUESS WHAT? BLUBBER-BELLY DIDN'T CREATE YOU.
NON-SENSE!!
OOO

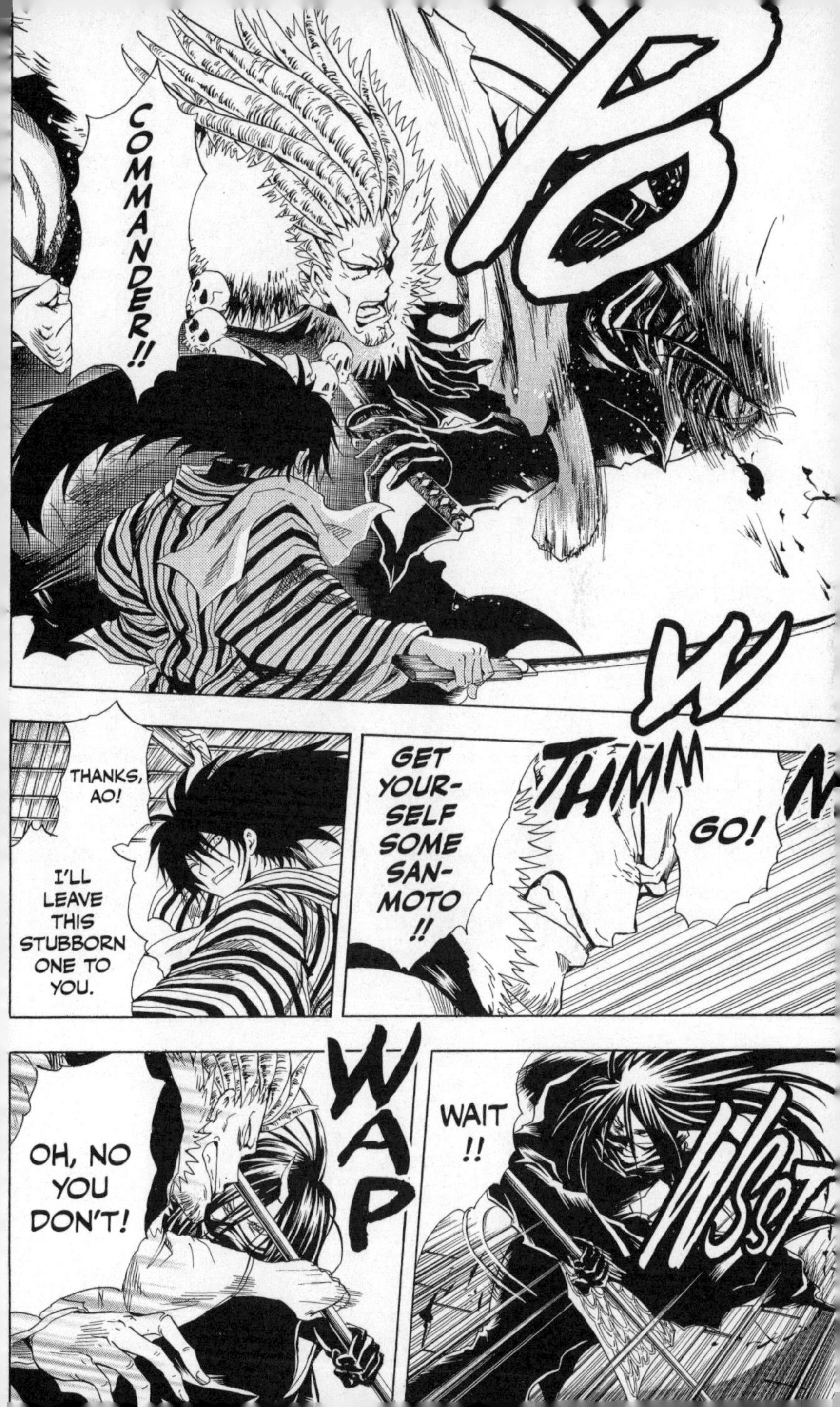

COMMANDER!!
THMM
GO!
GET YOURSELF SOME SAN-MOTO!!
THANKS, AO!
I'LL LEAVE THIS STUBBORN ONE TO YOU.
WAIT!!
WAP
OH, NO YOU DON'T!

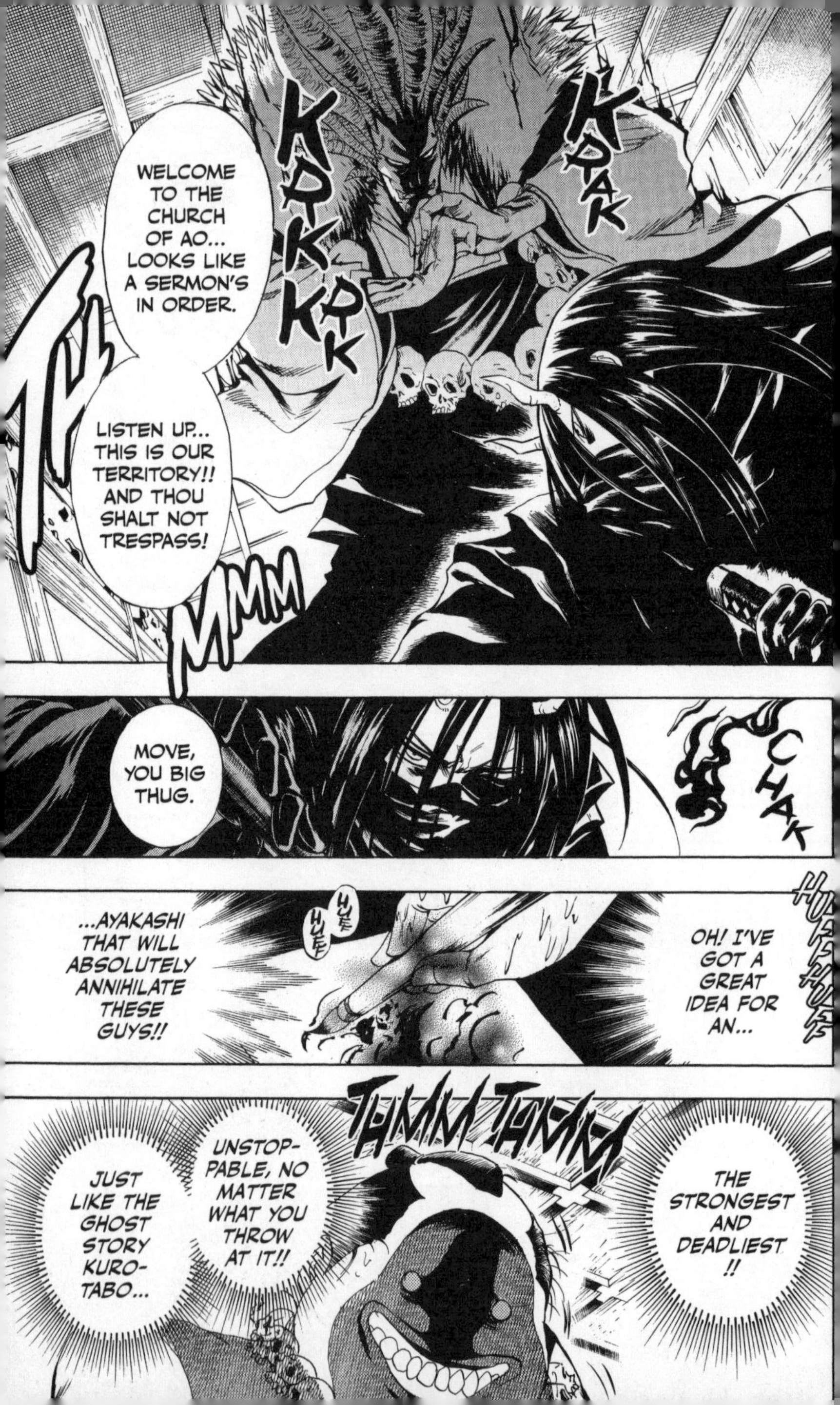

KDRAK
KRRK KRRK
WELCOME TO THE CHURCH OF AO... LOOKS LIKE A SERMON'S IN ORDER.
LISTEN UP... THIS IS OUR TERRITORY!! AND THOU SHALT NOT TRESPASS!
THMMM
CHAK
MOVE, YOU BIG THUG.
HUFF HUFF
OH! I'VE GOT A GREAT IDEA FOR AN...
HUFF HUFF
...AYAKASHI THAT WILL ABSOLUTELY ANNIHILATE THESE GUYS!!
THMM THMM
THE STRONGEST AND DEADLIEST !!
UNSTOP-PABLE, NO MATTER WHAT YOU THROW AT IT!!
JUST LIKE THE GHOST STORY KURO-TABO...

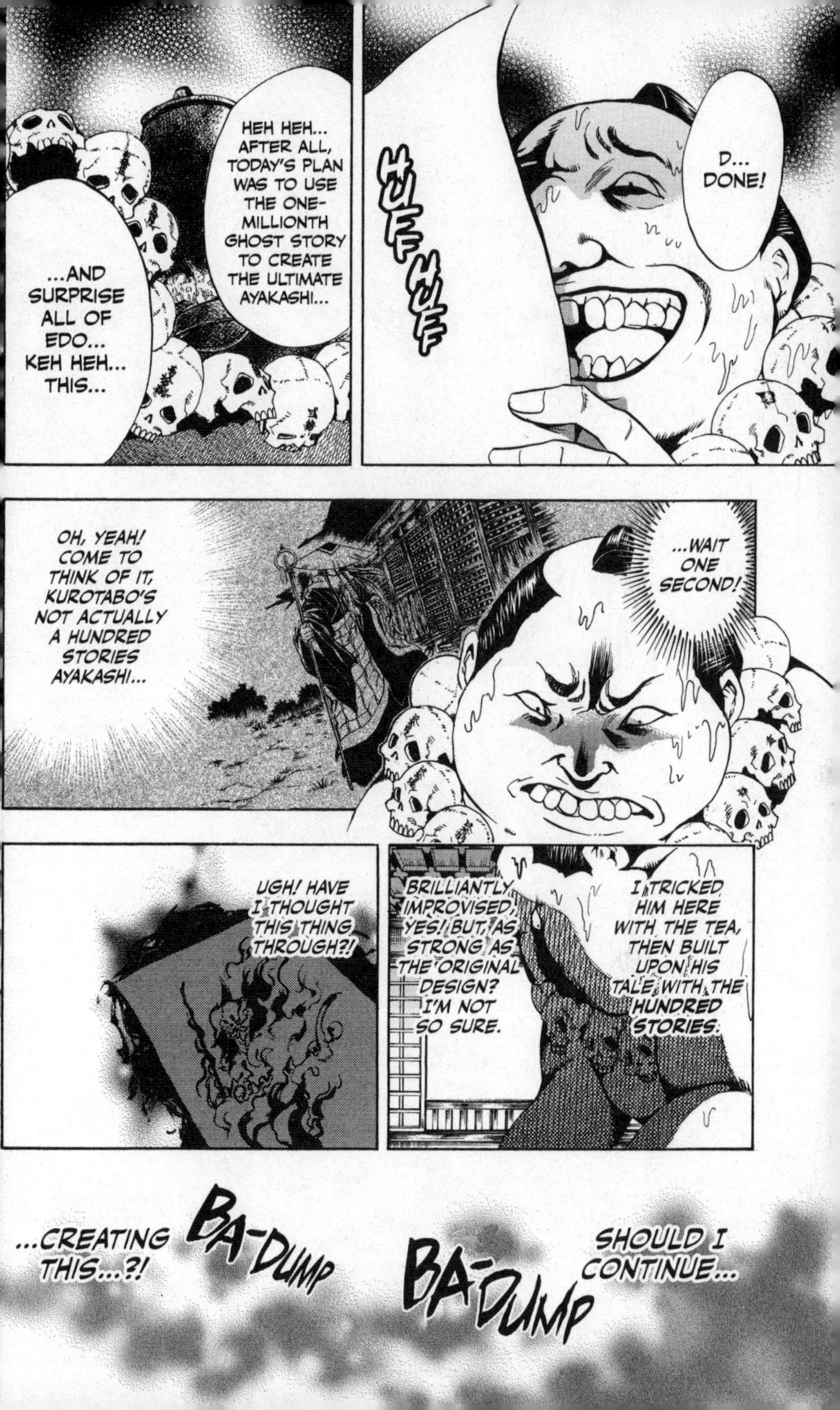
D... DONE!
HUFF HUFF
HEH HEH... AFTER ALL, TODAY'S PLAN WAS TO USE THE ONE-MILLIONTH GHOST STORY TO CREATE THE ULTIMATE AYAKASHI...
...AND SURPRISE ALL OF EDO... KEH HEH... THIS...
...WAIT ONE SECOND!
OH, YEAH! COME TO THINK OF IT, KUROTABO'S NOT ACTUALLY A HUNDRED STORIES AYAKASHI...
I TRICKED HIM HERE WITH THE TEA, THEN BUILT UPON HIS TALE WITH THE HUNDRED STORIES.
BRILLIANTLY IMPROVISED, YES! BUT, AS STRONG AS THE ORIGINAL DESIGN? I'M NOT SO SURE.
UGH! HAVE I THOUGHT THIS THING THROUGH?!
SHOULD I CONTINUE...
BA-DUMP
BA-DUMP
...CREATING THIS...?!

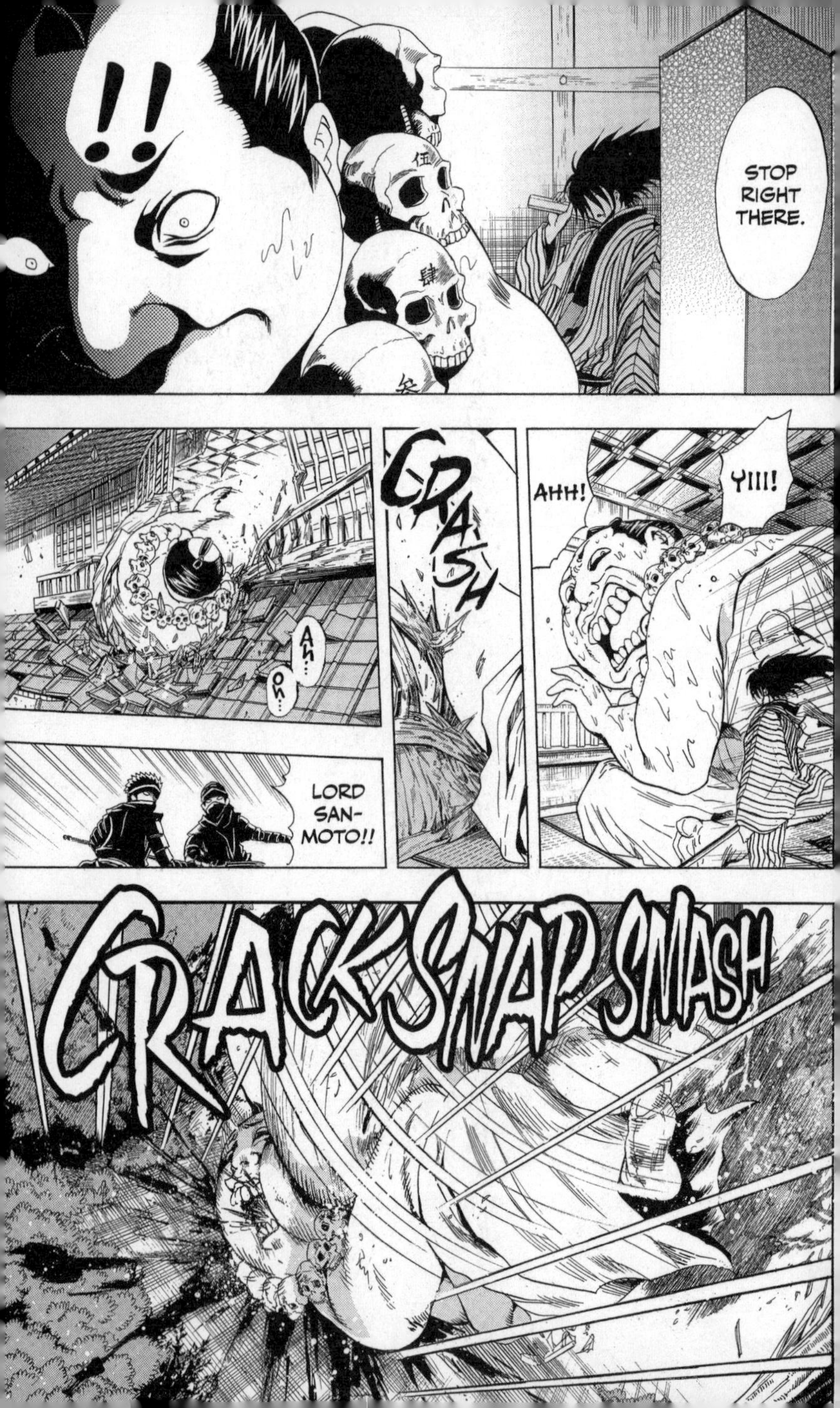

STOP RIGHT THERE.
!!
YIII!
AHH!
CRASH
Ah...
oh...
LORD SAN-MOTO!!
CRACK SNAP SMASH

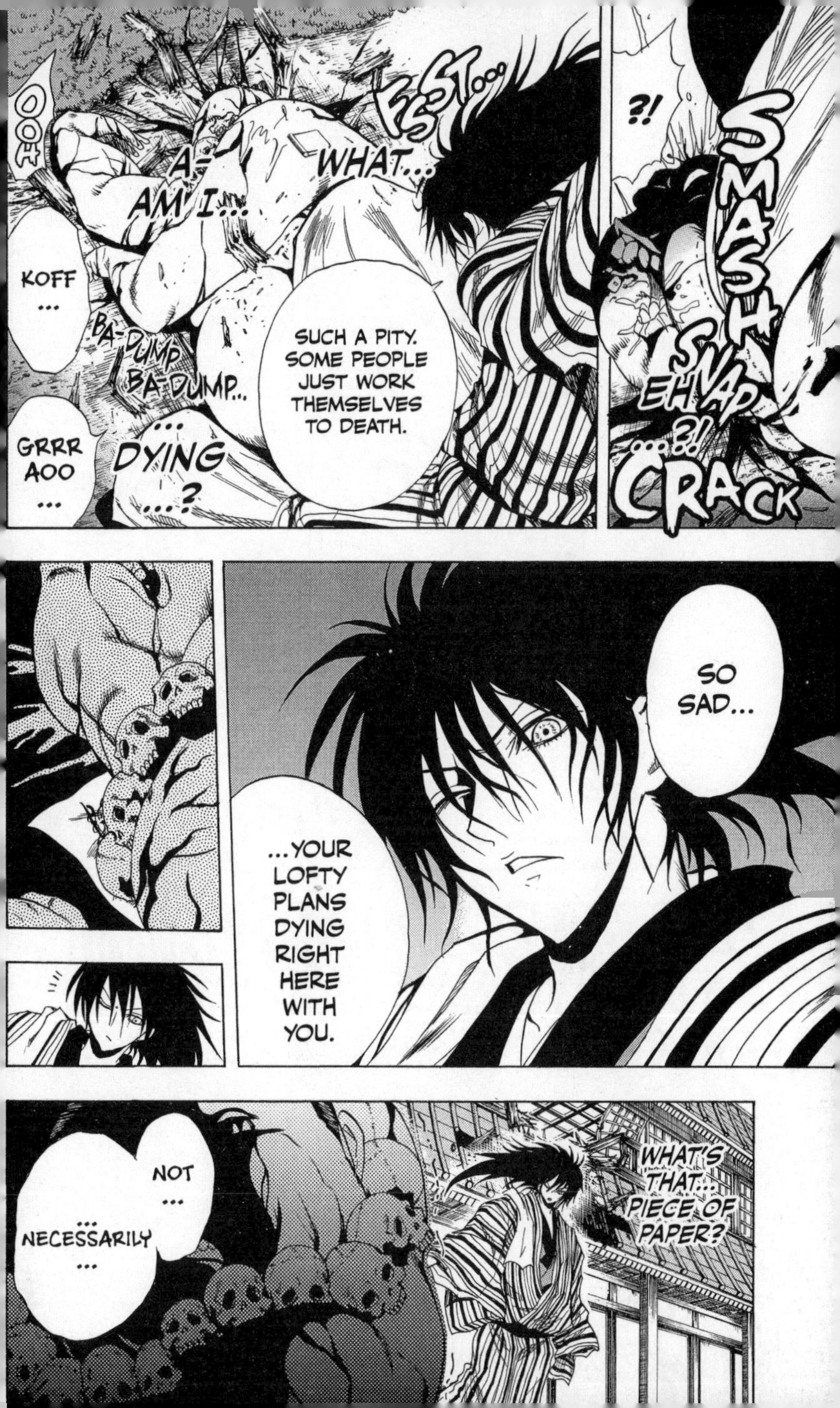
?!
SMASH
SNAP
EH ...?!
CRACK
FSST...
WHAT...
A- AM I...
OOH
SUCH A PITY. SOME PEOPLE JUST WORK THEMSELVES TO DEATH.
BA-DUMP BA-DUMP...
KOFF ...
... DYING ...?
GRRR AOO ...
SO SAD...
...YOUR LOFTY PLANS DYING RIGHT HERE WITH YOU.
WHAT'S THAT... PIECE OF PAPER?
NOT ... ... NECESSARILY ...

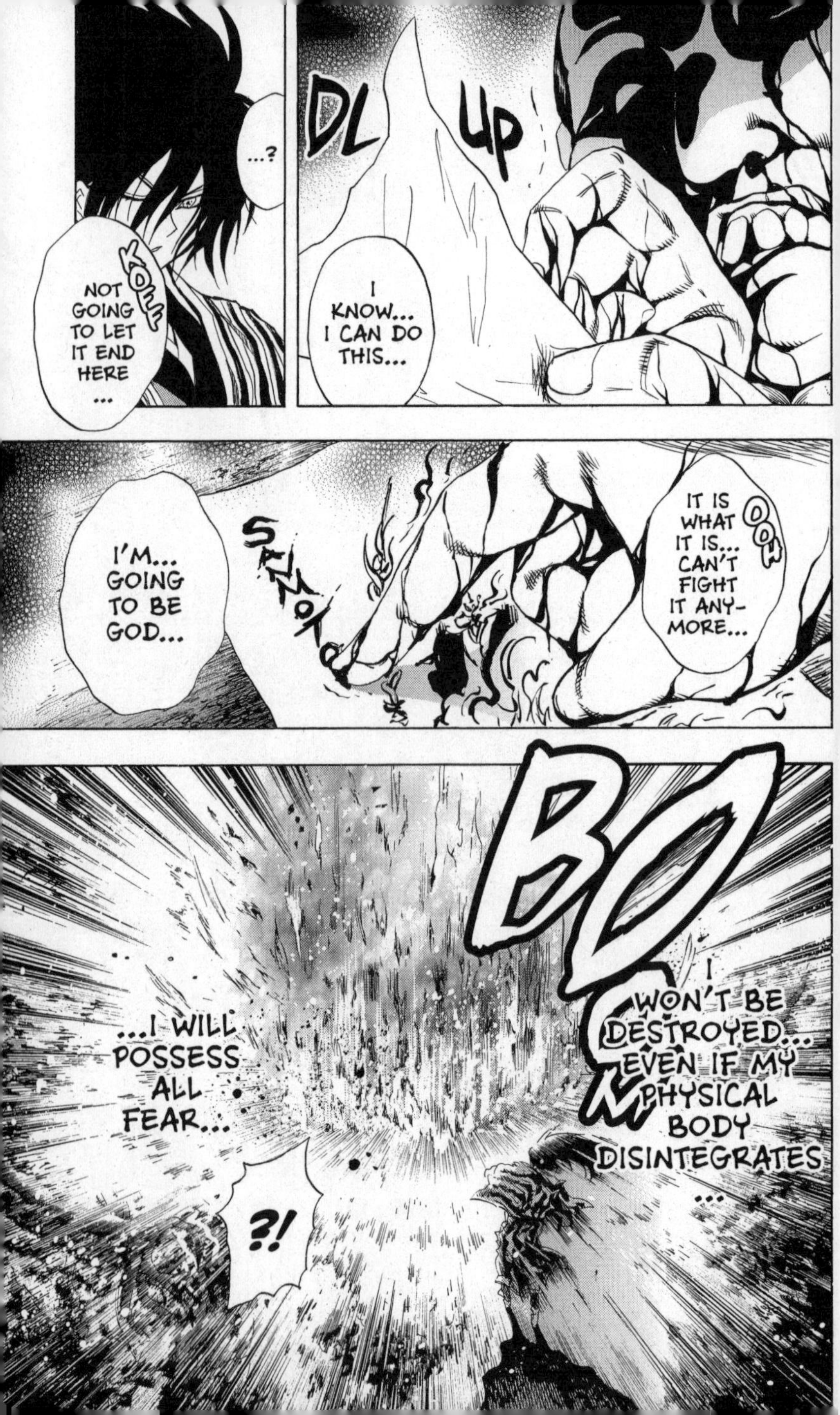
DL UP
I KNOW... I CAN DO THIS...
...?
KOH
NOT GOING TO LET IT END HERE ...
IT IS WHAT IT IS... CAN'T FIGHT IT ANY-MORE...
OOH
I'M... GOING TO BE GOD...
BOON
I WON'T BE DESTROYED... EVEN IF MY PHYSICAL BODY DISINTEGRATES ...
...I WILL POSSESS ALL FEAR...
?!

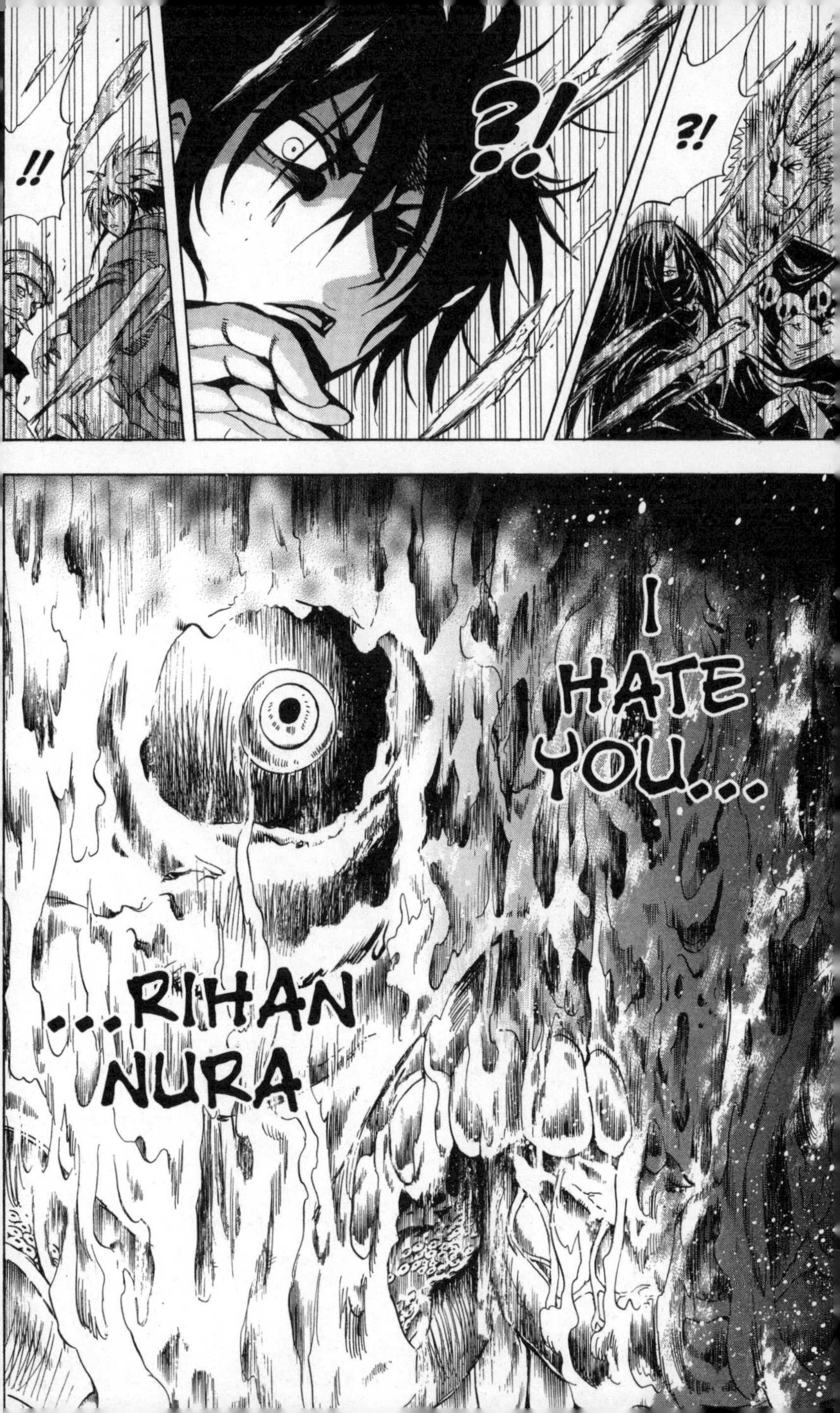
?!
?!
!!
I HATE YOU...
...RIHAN NURA

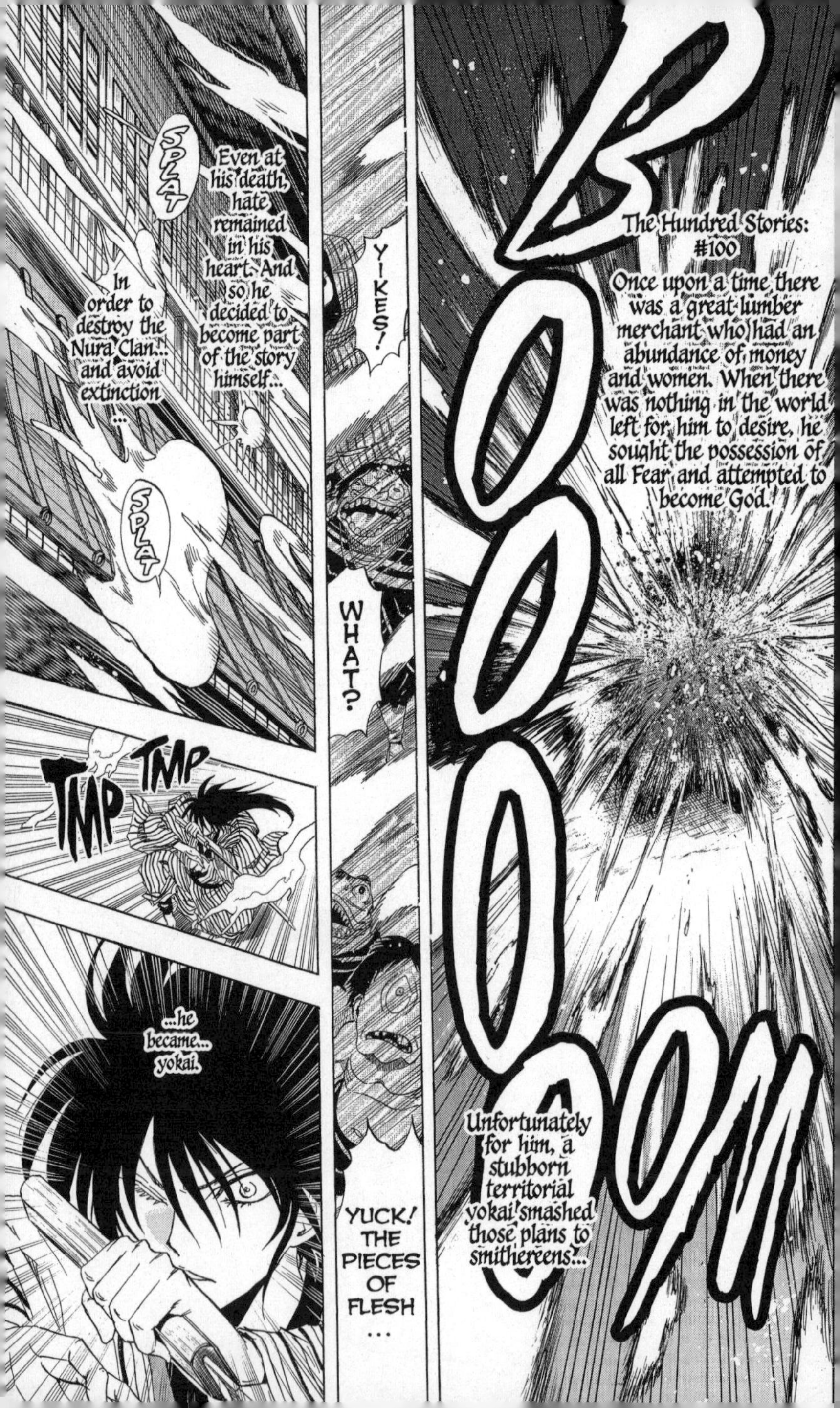

The Hundred Stories: #100
Once upon a time there was a great lumber merchant who had an abundance of money and women. When there was nothing in the world left for him to desire, he sought the possession of all Fear and attempted to become God.
BOOOM
Unfortunately for him, a stubborn territorial yokai smashed those plans to smithereens...
YIKES!
WHAT?
YUCK! THE PIECES OF FLESH...
Even at his death, hate remained in his heart. And so he decided to become part of the story himself...
SPLAT
In order to destroy the Nura Clan... and avoid extinction...
SPLAT
TMP TMP
...he became... yokai.

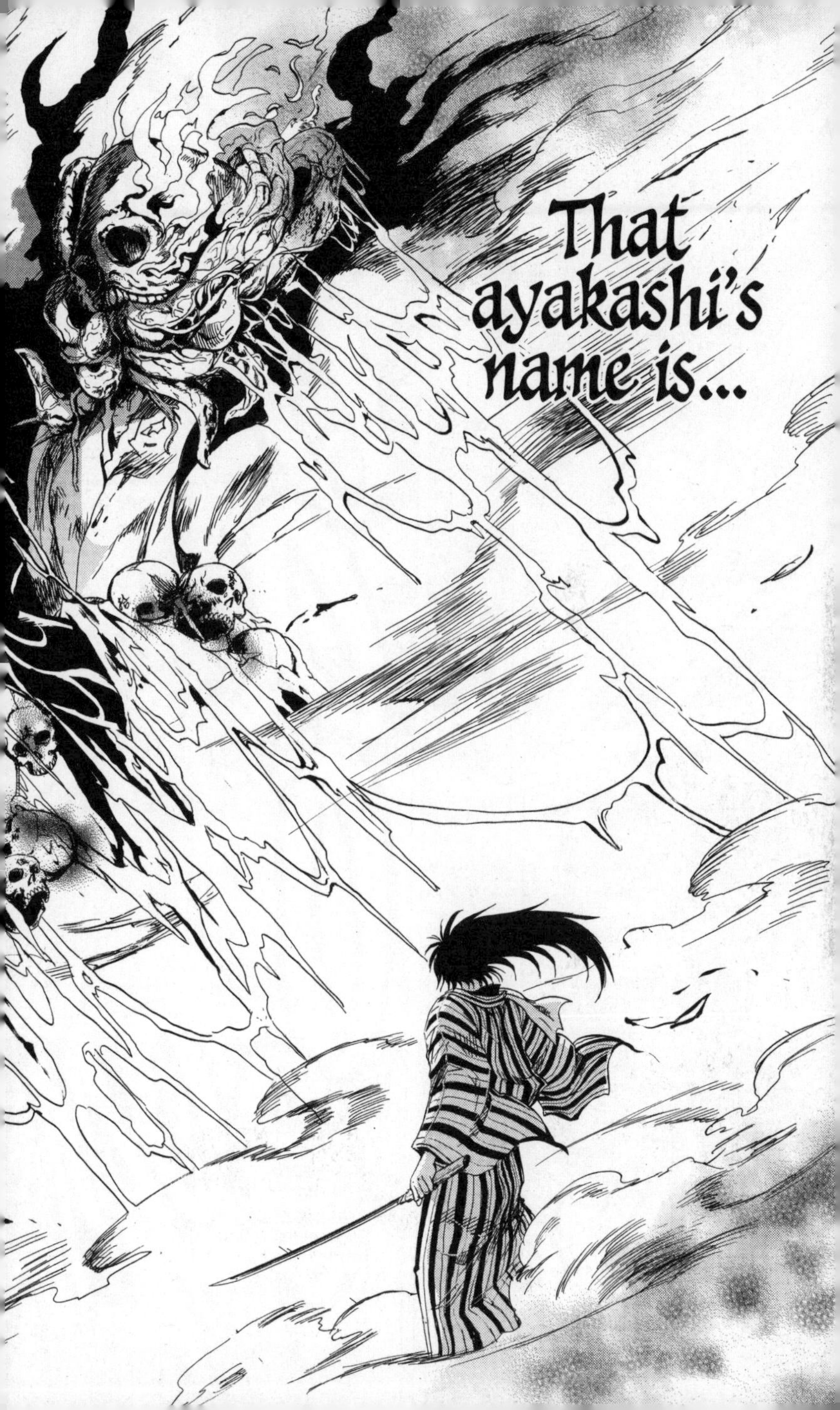
That ayakashi's name is...

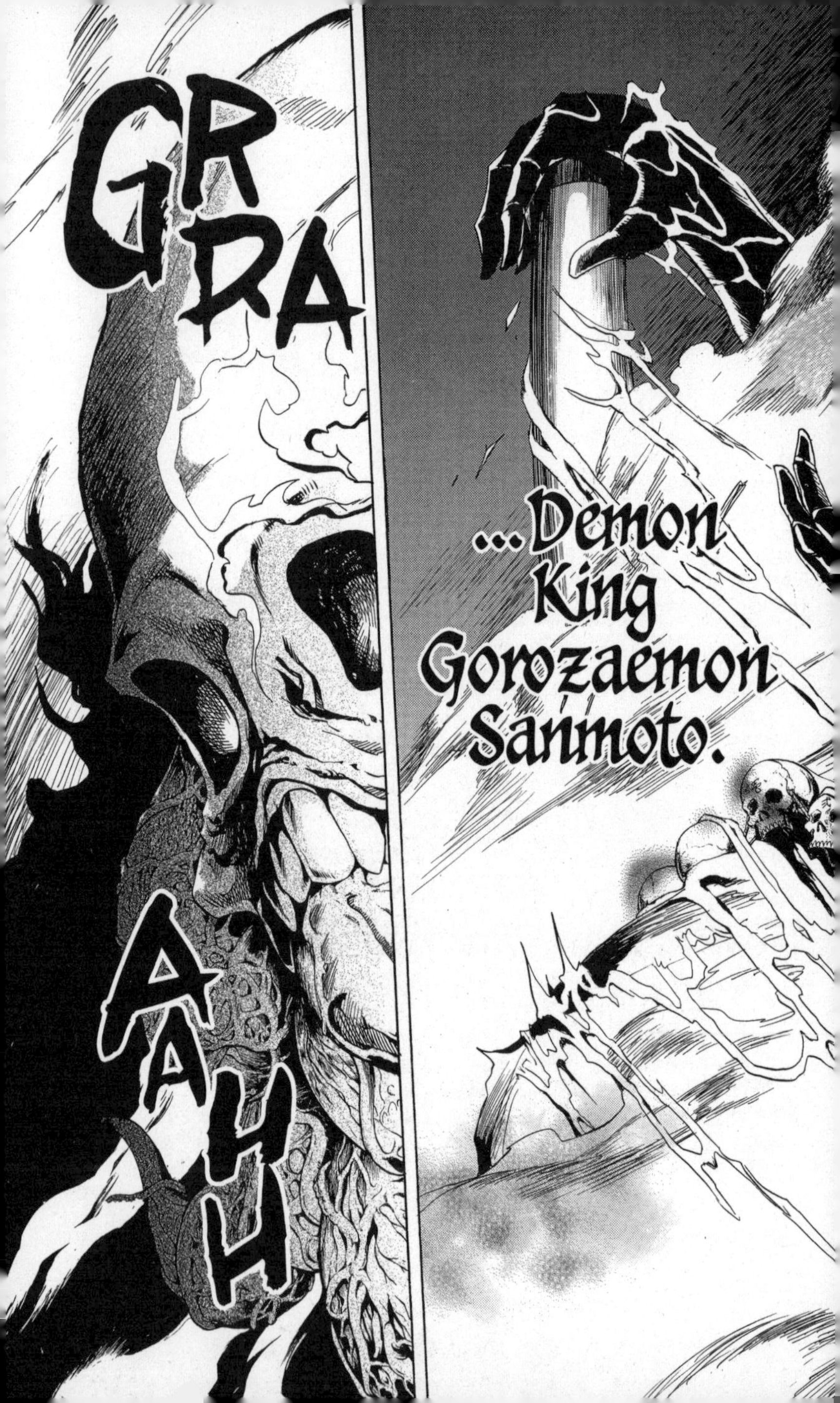
...Demon King Gorozaemon Sanmoto.
GRRAAAAH

Sanmoto's Love ♡

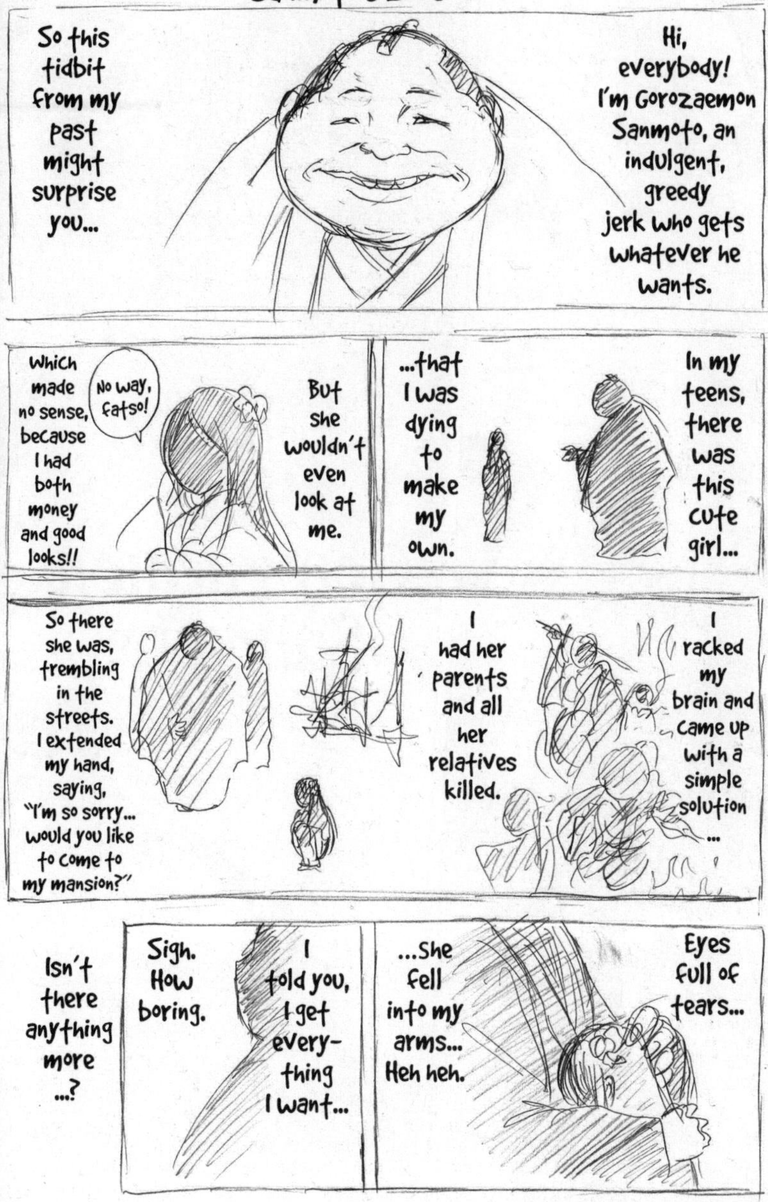
Hi, everybody! I'm Gorozaemon Sanmoto, an indulgent, greedy jerk who gets whatever he wants.
So this tidbit from my past might surprise you...
In my teens, there was this cute girl...
...that I was dying to make my own.
But she wouldn't even look at me.
No way, fatso!
Which made no sense, because I had both money and good looks!!
I racked my brain and came up with a simple solution...
I had her parents and all her relatives killed.
So there she was, trembling in the streets. I extended my hand, saying, "I'm so sorry... would you like to come to my mansion?"
Eyes full of tears...
...She fell into my arms... Heh heh.
I told you, I get everything I want...
Sigh. How boring.
Isn't there anything more ...?

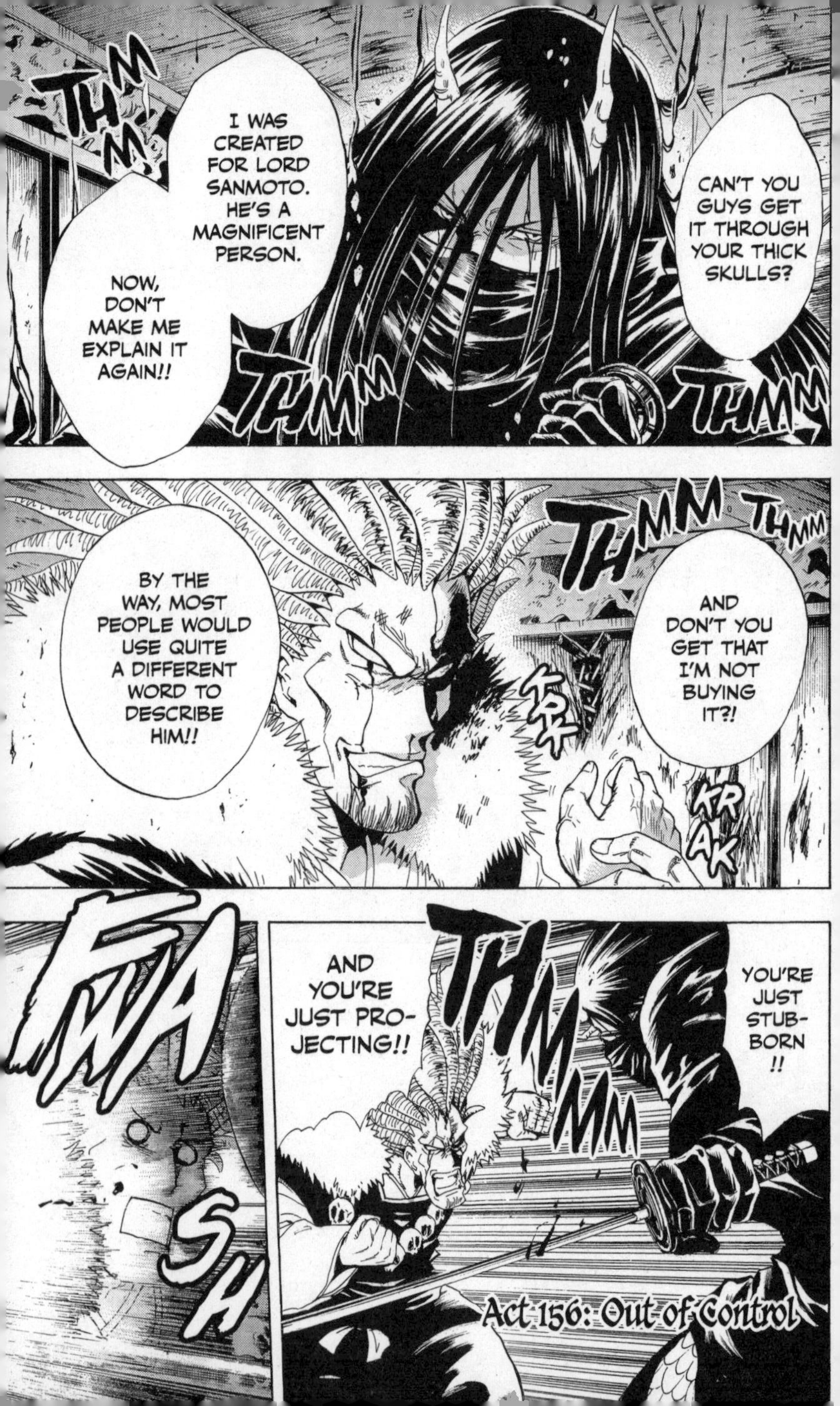
THMM
CAN'T YOU GUYS GET IT THROUGH YOUR THICK SKULLS?
I WAS CREATED FOR LORD SANMOTO. HE'S A MAGNIFICENT PERSON.
NOW, DON'T MAKE ME EXPLAIN IT AGAIN!!
THMM
THMM
THMM THMM
AND DON'T YOU GET THAT I'M NOT BUYING IT?!
KRAK
KRK
BY THE WAY, MOST PEOPLE WOULD USE QUITE A DIFFERENT WORD TO DESCRIBE HIM!!
YOU'RE JUST STUB-BORN !!
THMMM
AND YOU'RE JUST PRO-JECTING!!
Act 156: Out of Control
FWA
SH

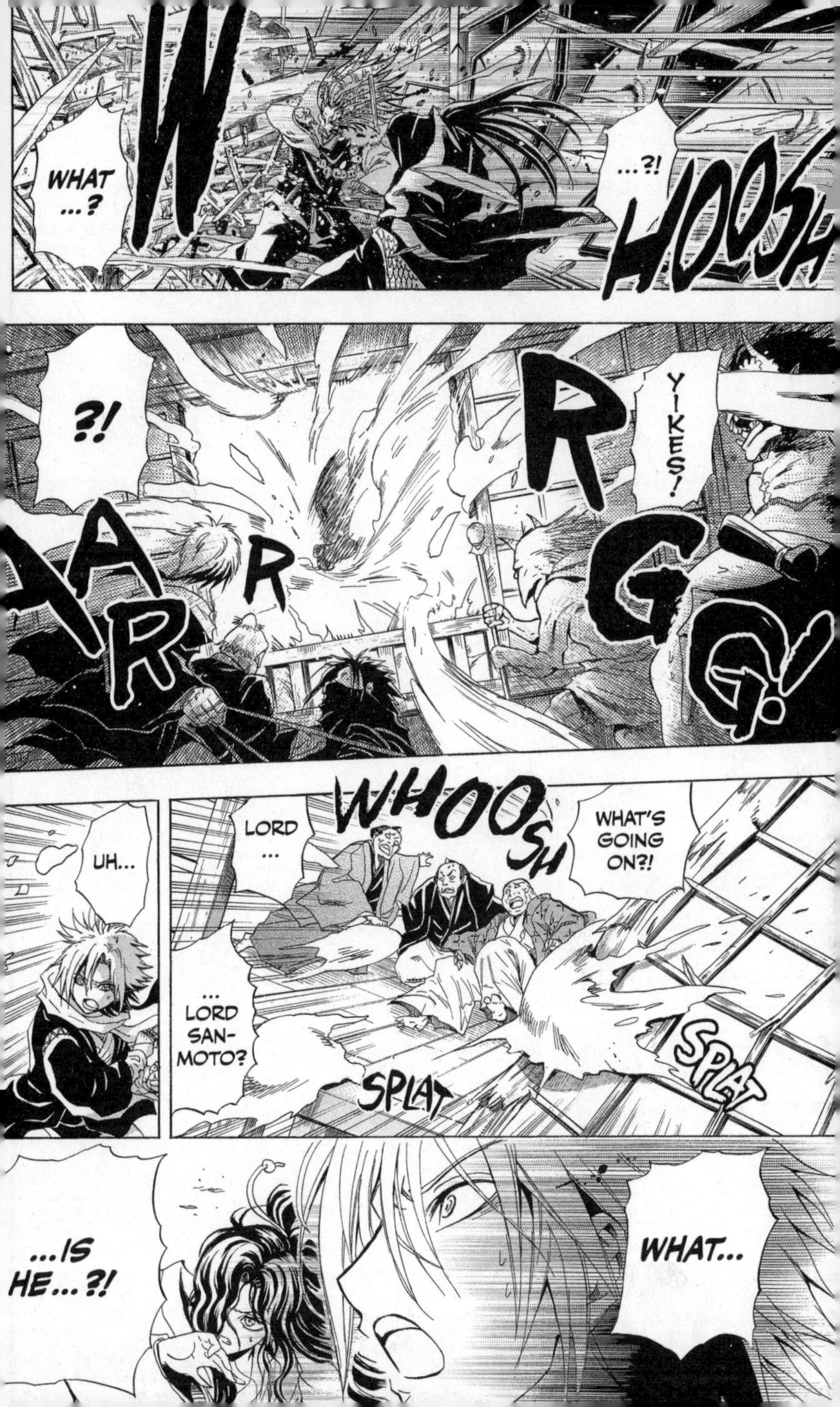
...?!
WHOOSH
WHAT ...?
YIKES!
RRGG!
ARR
?!
WHAT'S GOING ON?!
WHOOSH
LORD ...
... LORD SAN-MOTO?
SPLAT
SPLAT
UH...
WHAT...
...IS HE...?!

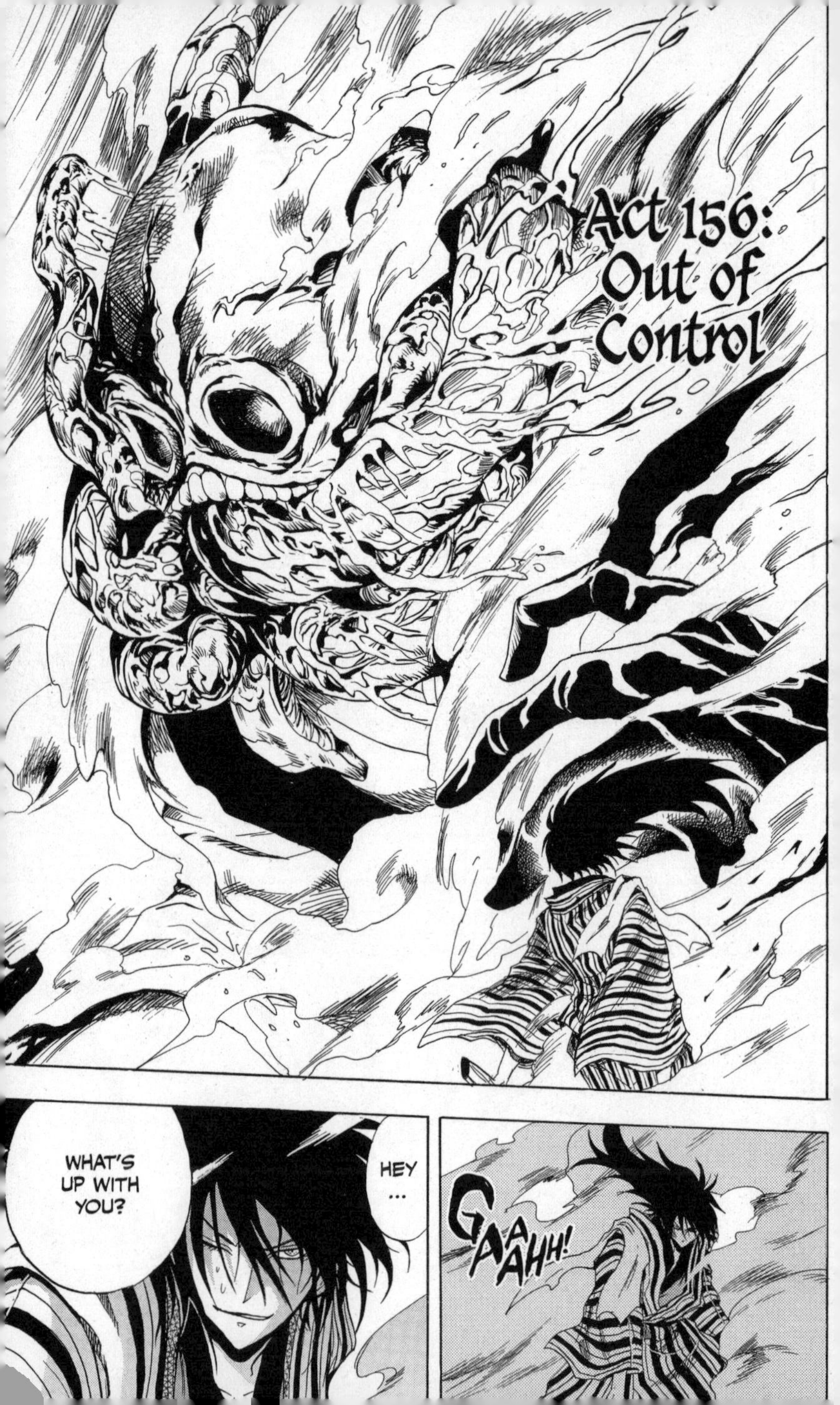

Act 156:
Out of Control
GAAHH!
HEY ...
WHAT'S UP WITH YOU?

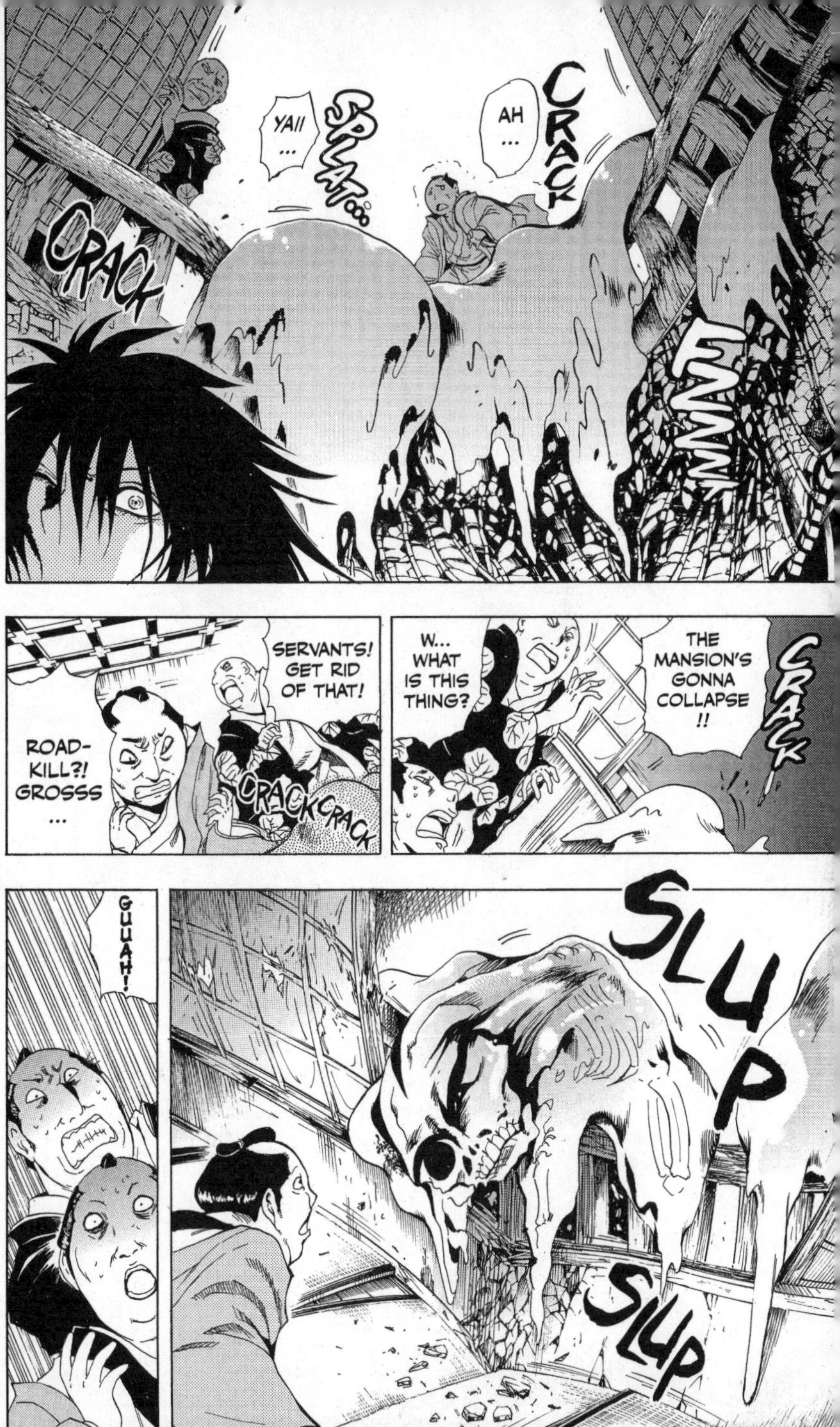
CRACK
AH ...
SPLAT
YAII ...
CRACK
CRACK
THE MANSION'S GONNA COLLAPSE !!
W... WHAT IS THIS THING?
SERVANTS! GET RID OF THAT!
ROAD-KILL?! GROSSS ...
CRACK CRACK
SLUP
SLUP
GUUAH!

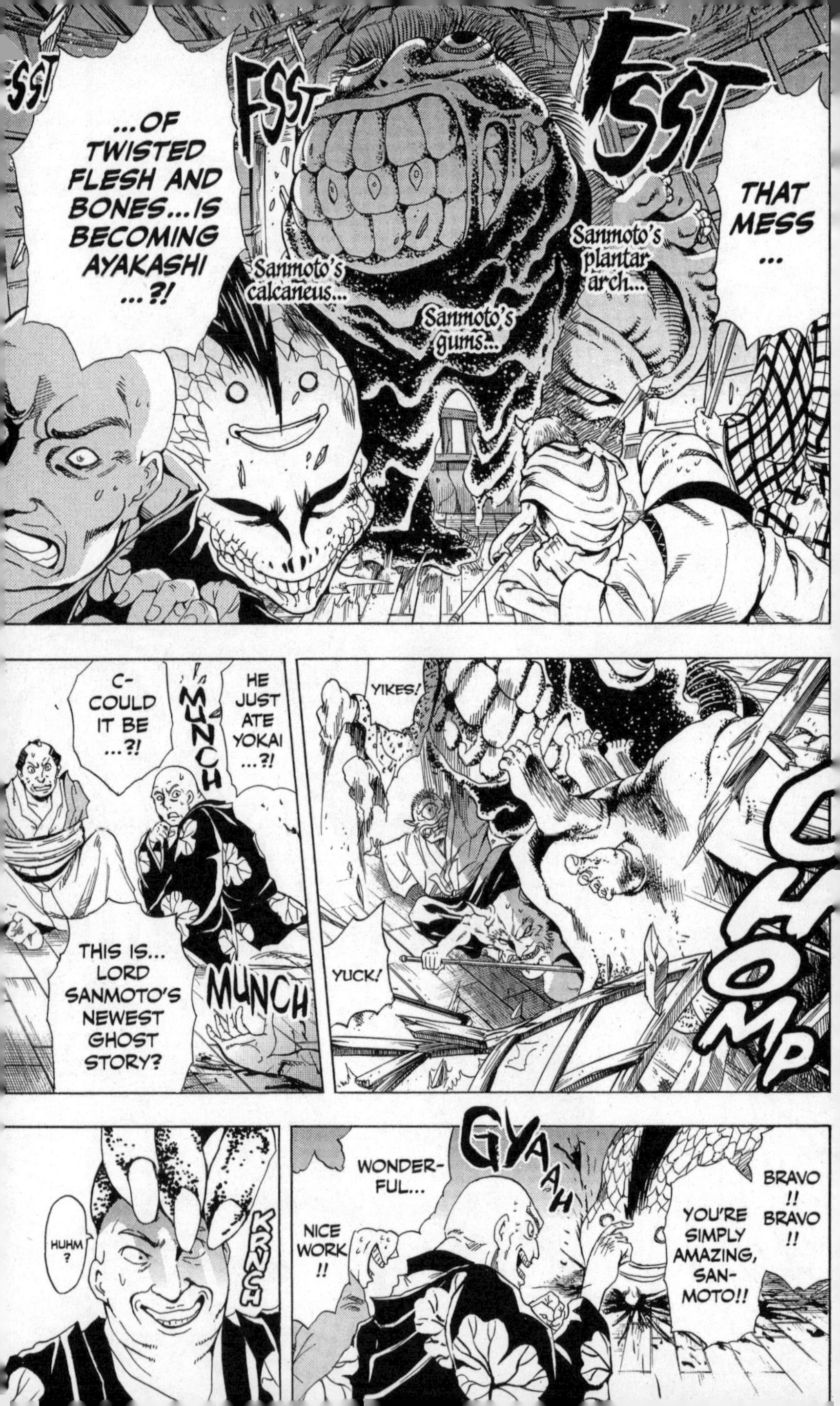
FSST
THAT MESS ...
Sanmoto's plantar arch...
Sanmoto's gums...
FSST
Sanmoto's calcaneus...
...OF TWISTED FLESH AND BONES...IS BECOMING AYAKASHI ...?!
SST
CHOMP
YIKES!
YUCK!
HE JUST ATE YOKAI ...?!
MUNCH
C-COULD IT BE ...?!
THIS IS... LORD SANMOTO'S NEWEST GHOST STORY?
MUNCH
BRAVO!! BRAVO!!
YOU'RE SIMPLY AMAZING, SAN-MOTO!!
GYAAAH
WONDER-FUL...
NICE WORK!!
KRNCH
HUHM?

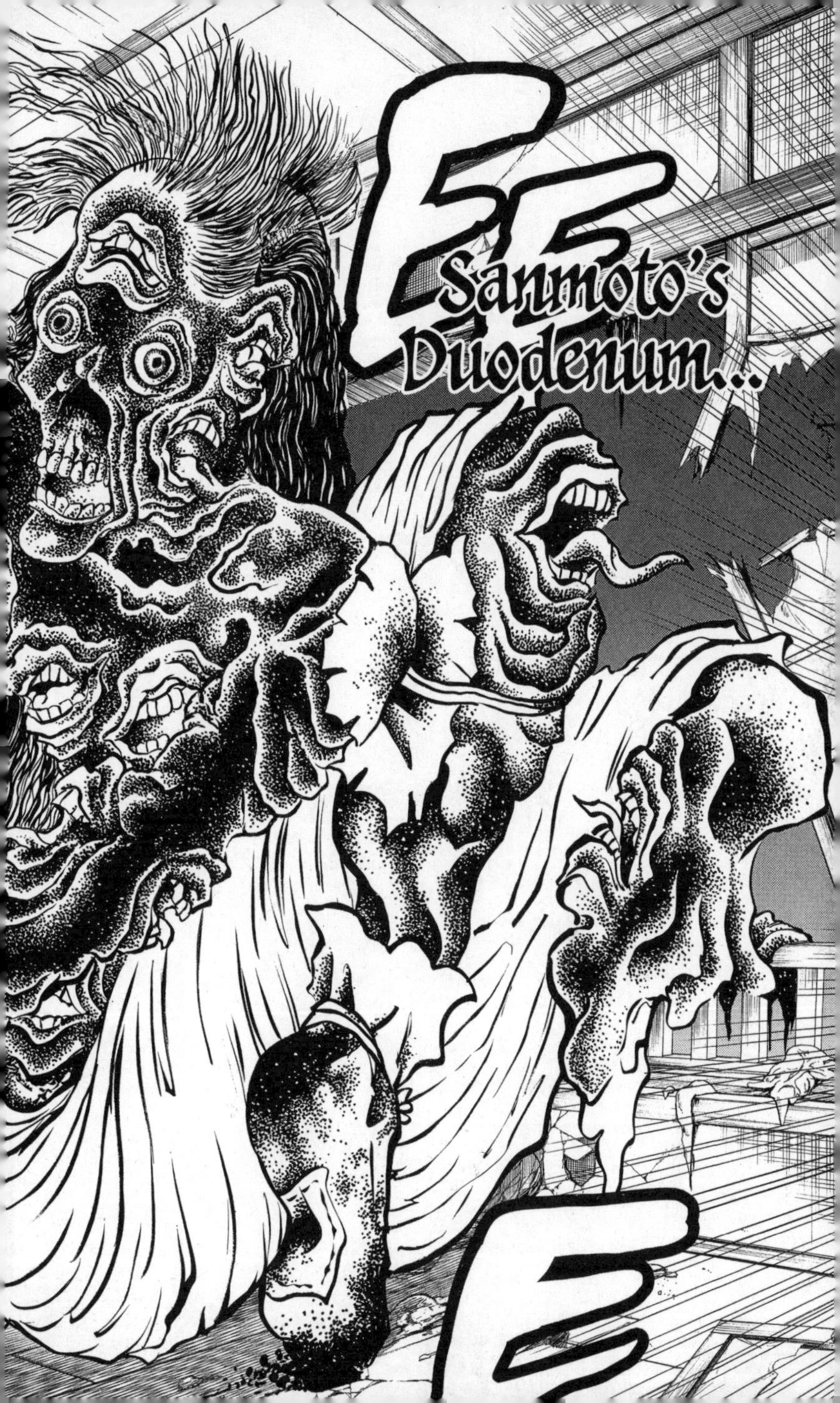
Sanmoto's
Duodenum...

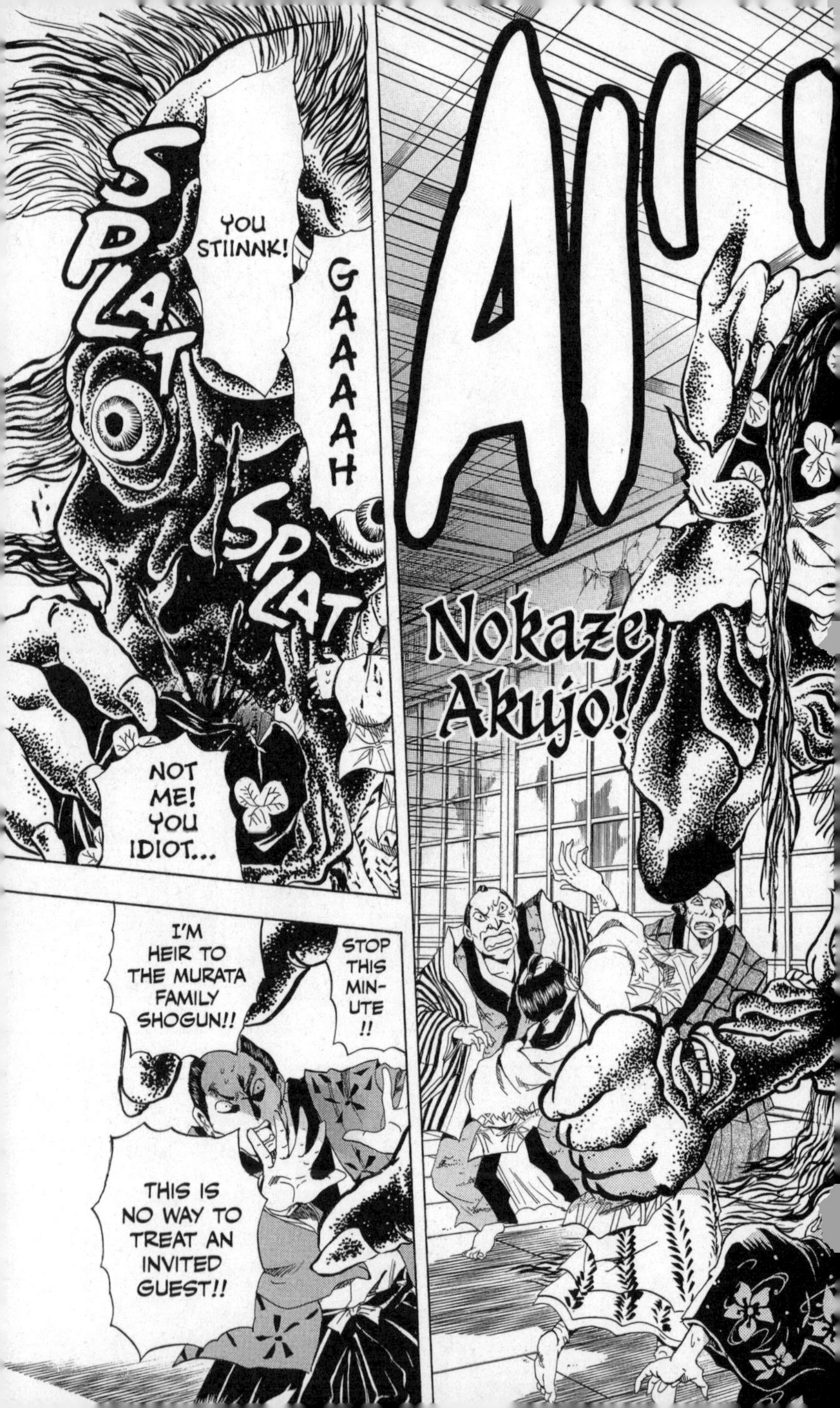
Nokaze Akujo!
GAAAAAH
YOU STIINNK!
SPLAT
SPLAT
NOT ME! YOU IDIOT...
STOP THIS MIN-UTE!!
I'M HEIR TO THE MURATA FAMILY SHOGUN!!
THIS IS NO WAY TO TREAT AN INVITED GUEST!!

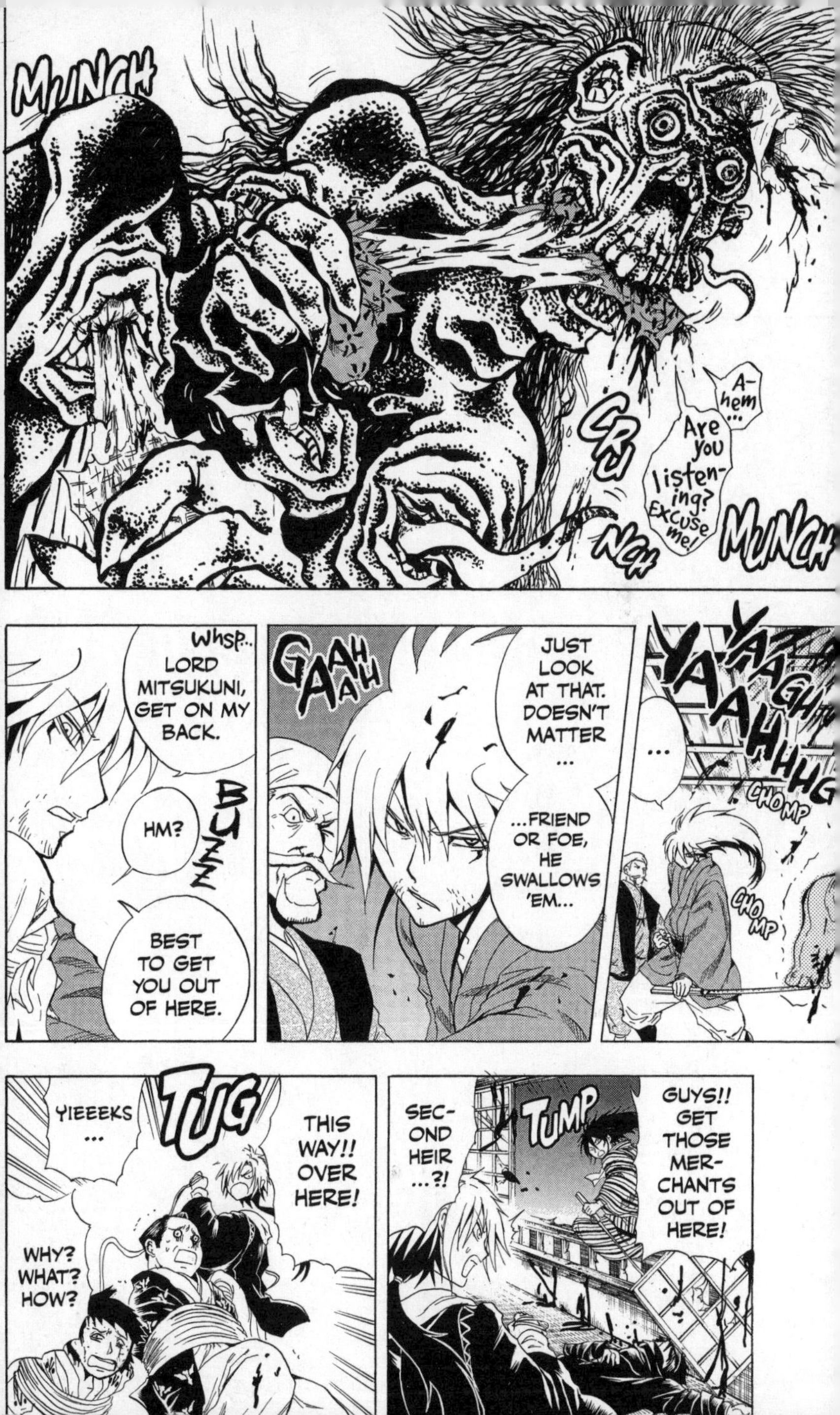
A-hem... Are you listening? Excuse me!
MUNCH
CRUNCH
MUNCH
YAAGH
YAAAHHHG
...
CHOMP
CHOMP
JUST LOOK AT THAT. DOESN'T MATTER ...
GAAAAH
...FRIEND OR FOE, HE SWALLOWS 'EM...
Whsp.. LORD MITSUKUNI, GET ON MY BACK.
BUZZ
HM?
BEST TO GET YOU OUT OF HERE.
GUYS!! GET THOSE MER-CHANTS OUT OF HERE!
TUMP
SEC-OND HEIR ...?!
THIS WAY!! OVER HERE!
TUG
YIEEEKS ...
WHY? WHAT? HOW?

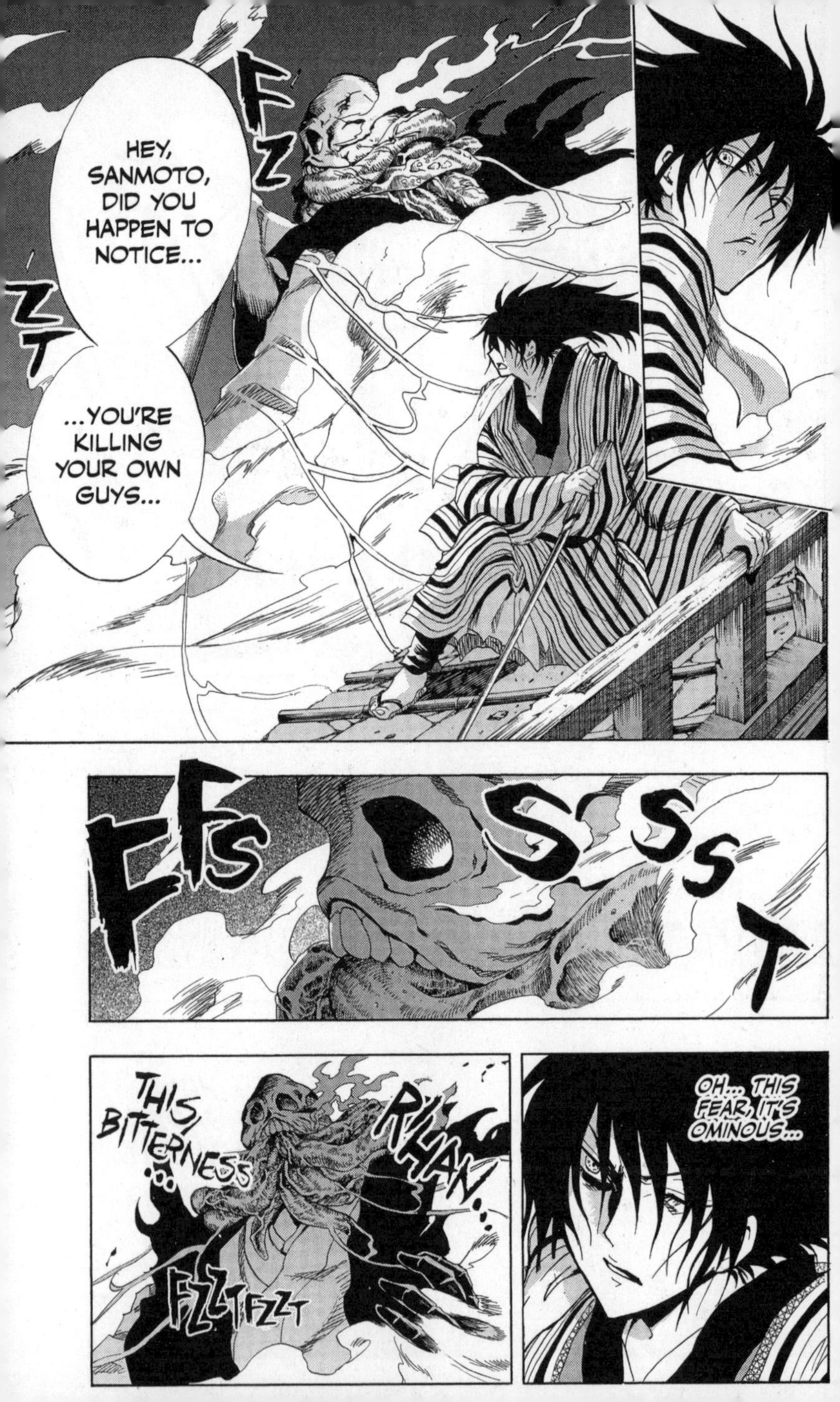

FZ
ZT
HEY, SANMOTO, DID YOU HAPPEN TO NOTICE...
...YOU'RE KILLING YOUR OWN GUYS...
FSSSST
OH... THIS FEAR, IT'S OMINOUS...
THIS BITTERNESS...
RIHAN...
FZZT FZZT

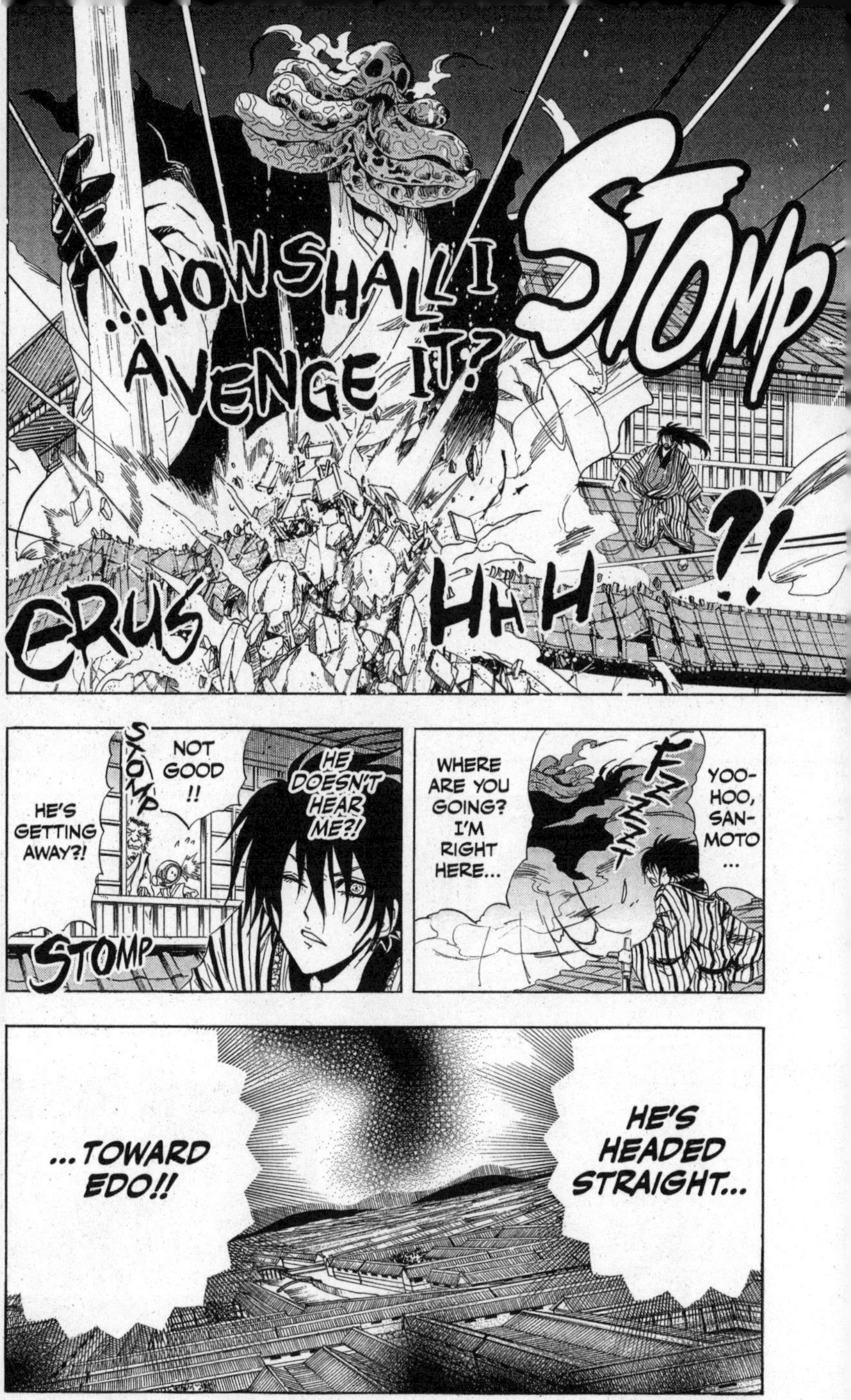
STOMP
...HOW SHALL I AVENGE IT?
CRUSHHH
?!
YOO-HOO, SAN-MOTO...
FZZZZT
WHERE ARE YOU GOING? I'M RIGHT HERE...
HE DOESN'T HEAR ME?!
NOT GOOD!!
STOMP
HE'S GETTING AWAY?!
STOMP
HE'S HEADED STRAIGHT...
...TOWARD EDO!!

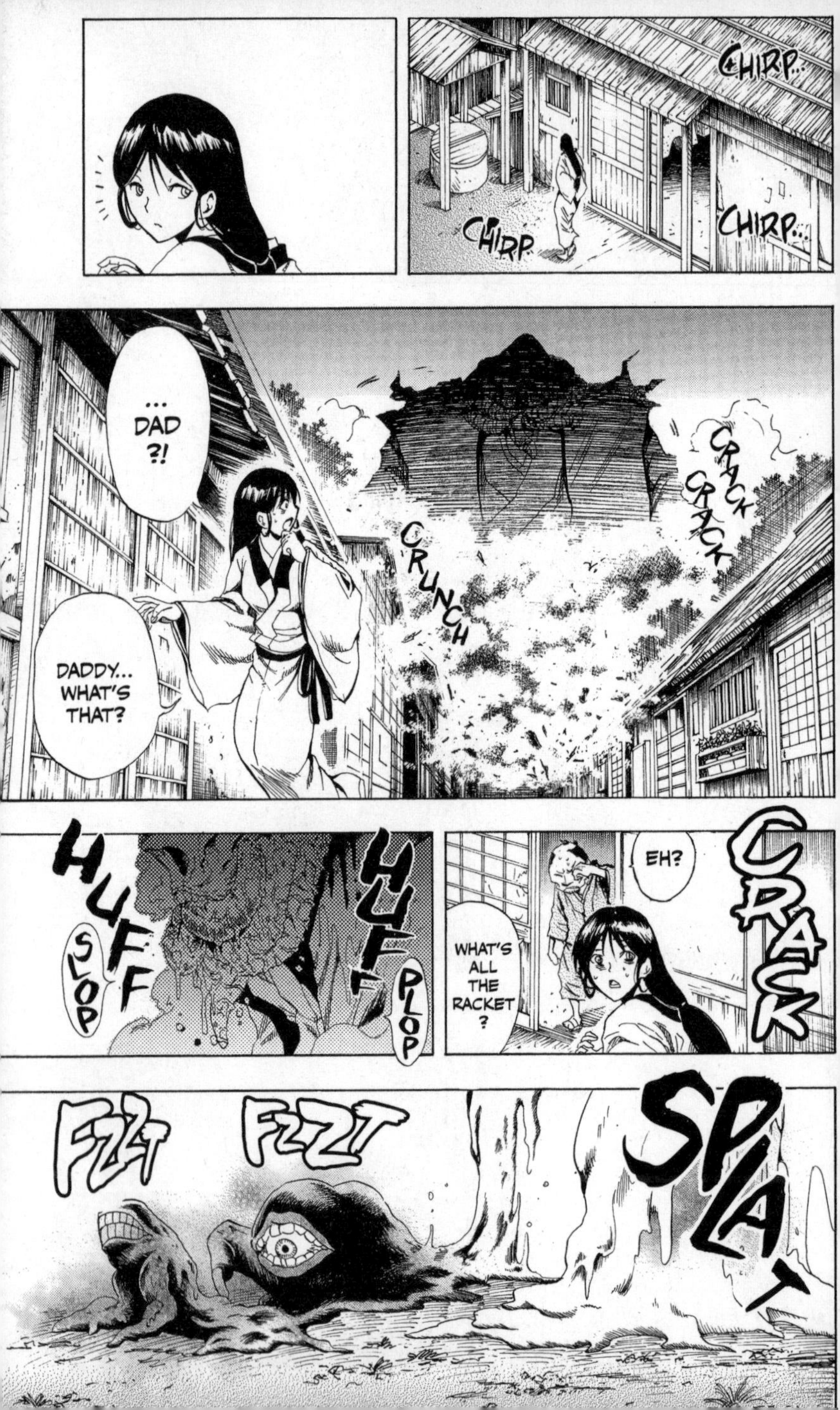
CHIRP...
CHIRP...
CHIRP
CRACK CRACK
CRUNCH
... DAD ?!
DADDY... WHAT'S THAT?
CRACK
EH?
WHAT'S ALL THE RACKET ?
HUFF
PLOP
HUFF
SLOP
SPLAT
FZZZT
FZZT

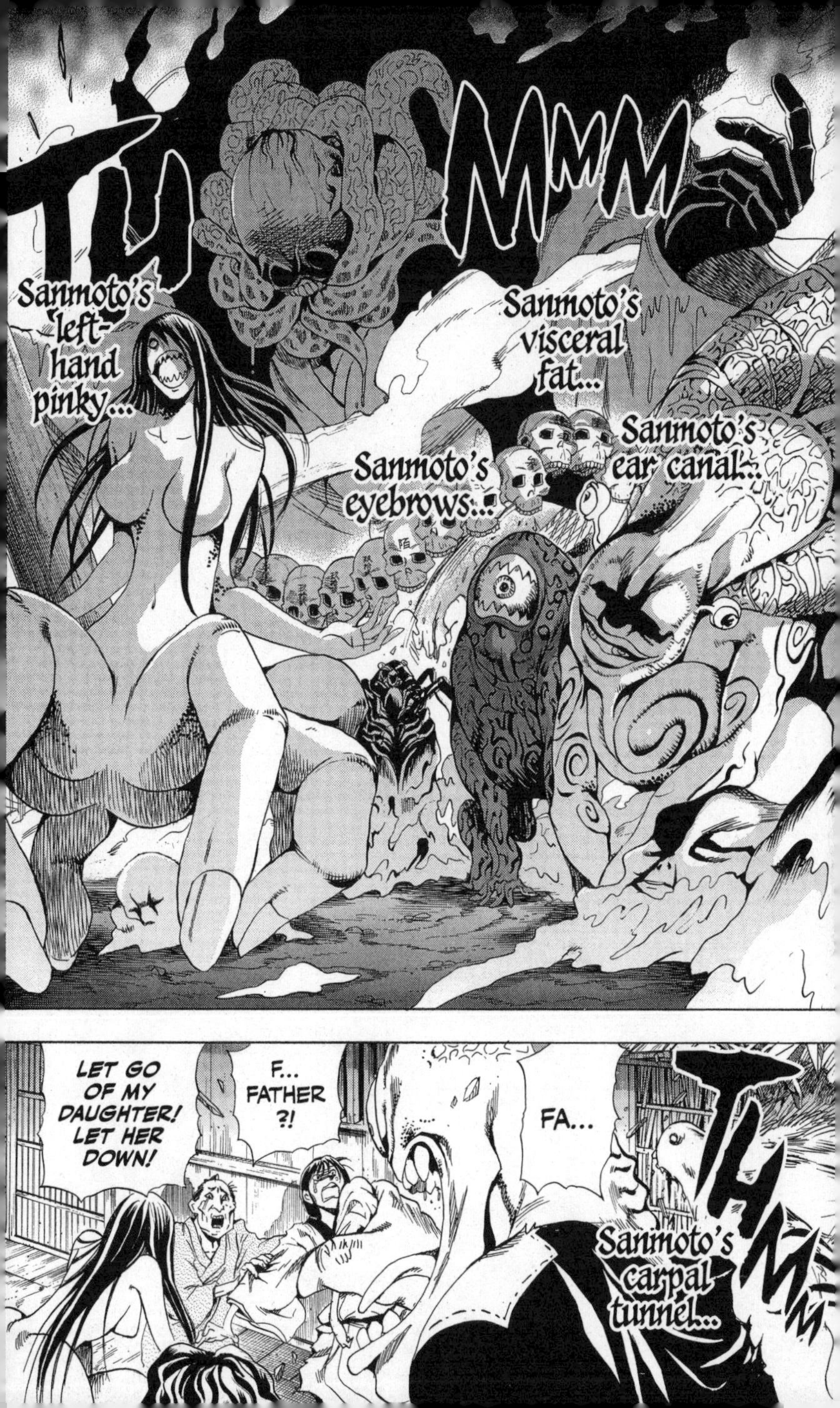
TUMMMM
Sanmoto's visceral fat...
Sanmoto's ear canal...
Sanmoto's eyebrows...
Sanmoto's left-hand pinky...
TAMM
Sanmoto's carpal tunnel...
FA...
...
F... FATHER?!
LET GO OF MY DAUGHTER! LET HER DOWN!

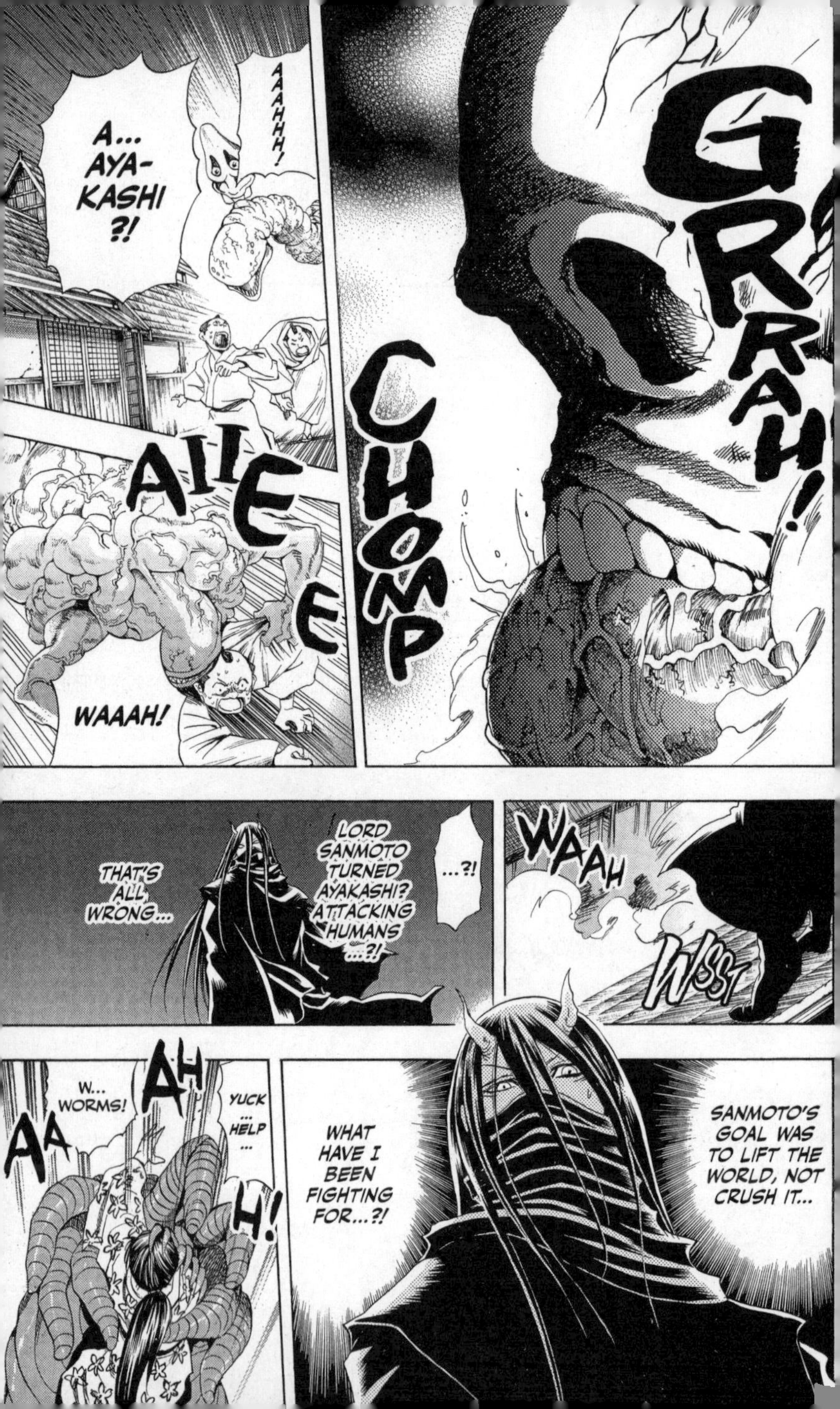
GRRAH!
CHOMP
AAAHHH!
A... AYA-KASHI ?!
AIIEEE
WAAAH!
WAAAH
WSST
...?!
LORD SANMOTO TURNED AYAKASHI? ATTACKING HUMANS ...?!
THAT'S ALL WRONG...
SANMOTO'S GOAL WAS TO LIFT THE WORLD, NOT CRUSH IT...
WHAT HAVE I BEEN FIGHTING FOR...?!
YUCK ... HELP ...
AAAAH!
W... WORMS!

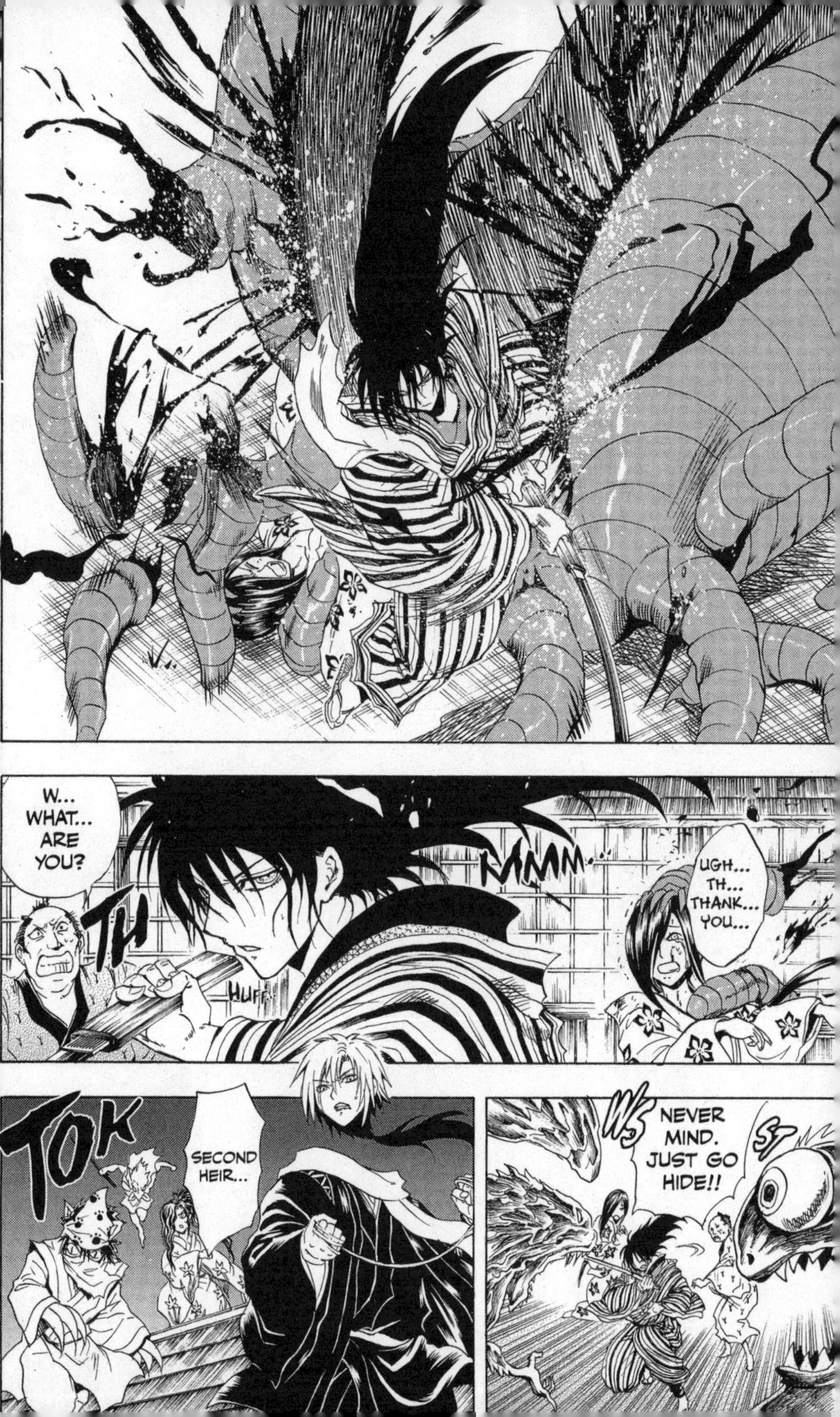
UGH... TH... THANK... YOU...
MMM
W... WHAT... ARE YOU?
TH
HUFF
ST
NEVER MIND. JUST GO HIDE!!
WS
SECOND HEIR...
TOK

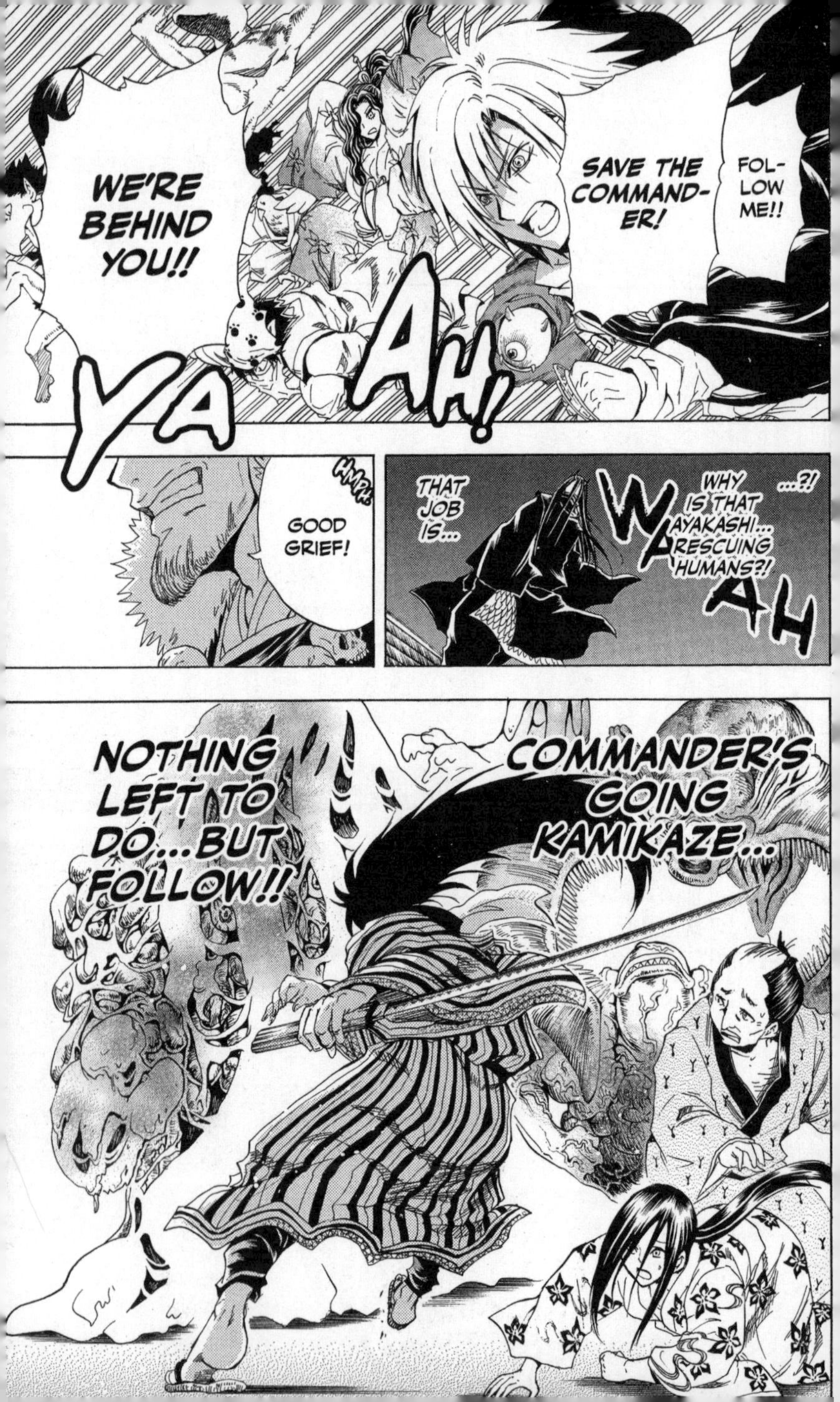
FOL-
LOW
ME!!
SAVE THE
COMMAND-
ER!
WE'RE
BEHIND
YOU!!
YAAH!
...?!
WHY
IS THAT
AYAKASHI...
RESCUING
HUMANS?!
WAAH
THAT
JOB
IS...
HMPH
GOOD
GRIEF!
COMMANDER'S
GOING
KAMIKAZE...
NOTHING
LEFT TO
DO...BUT
FOLLOW!!

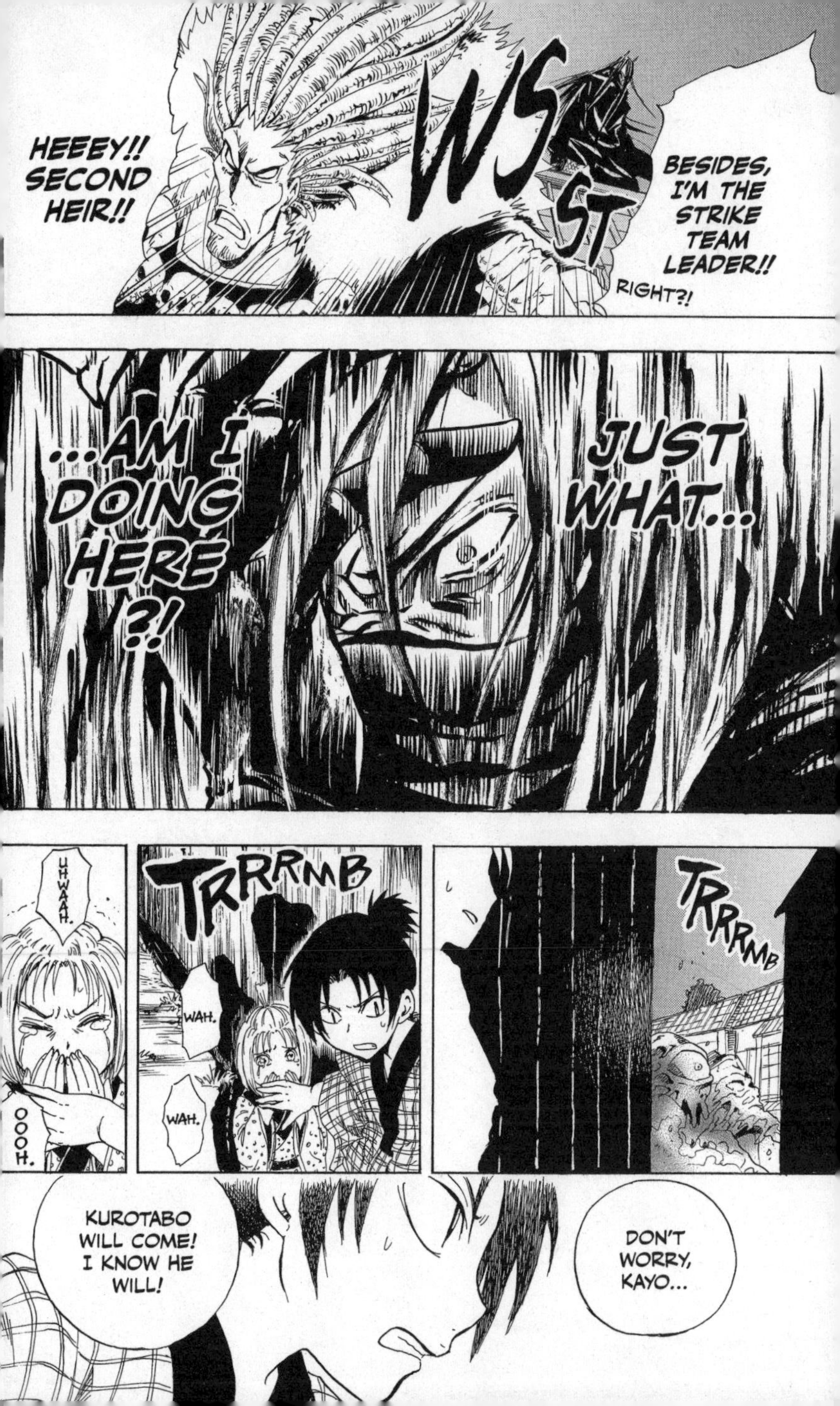
WSST
BESIDES, I'M THE STRIKE TEAM LEADER!!
RIGHT?!
HEEEY!! SECOND HEIR!!
JUST WHAT...
...AM I DOING HERE?!
TRRRMB
TRRRMB
WAH.
WAH.
UHWAAH.
OOOH.
DON'T WORRY, KAYO...
KUROTABO WILL COME! I KNOW HE WILL!

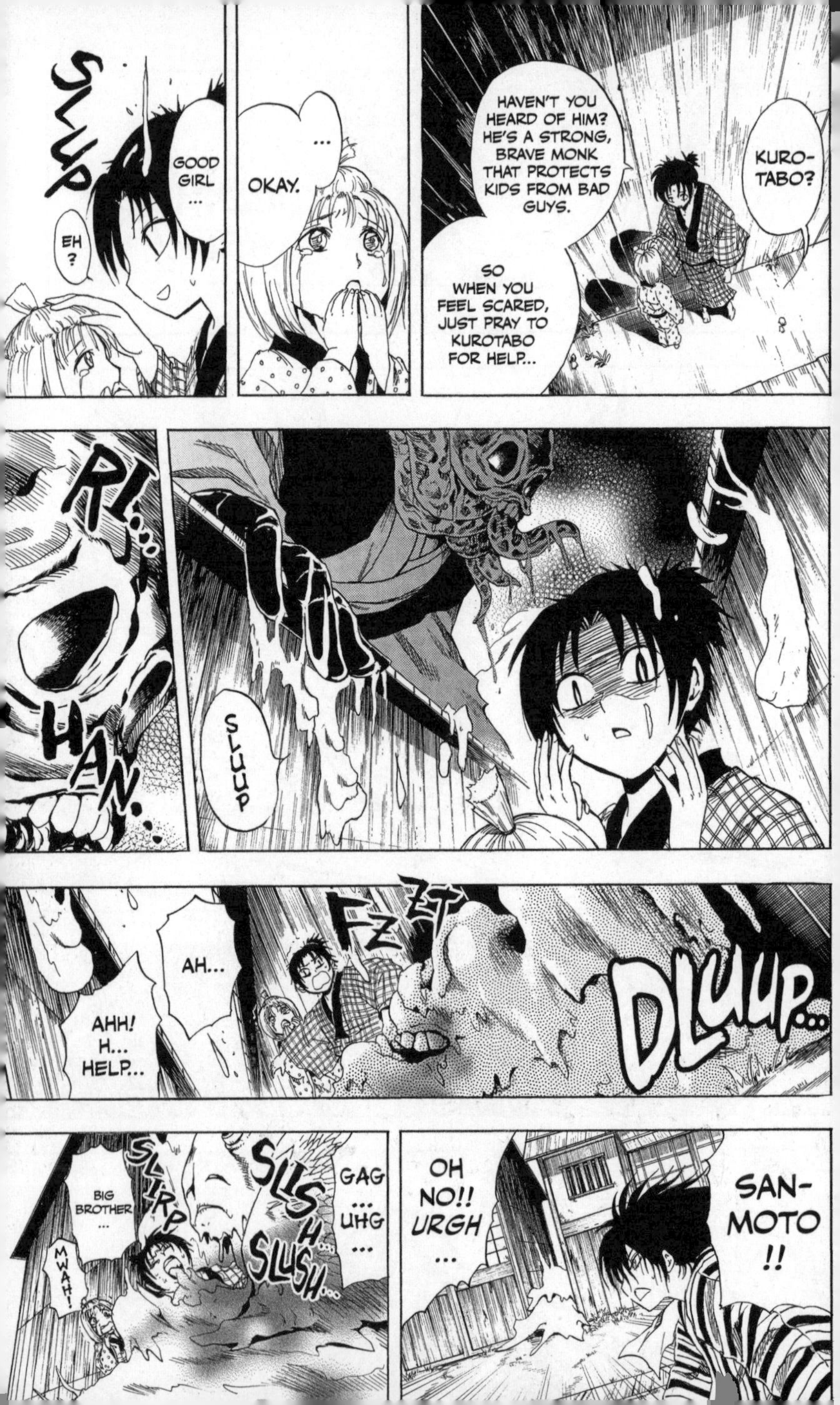
KURO-TABO?
HAVEN'T YOU HEARD OF HIM? HE'S A STRONG, BRAVE MONK THAT PROTECTS KIDS FROM BAD GUYS.
SO WHEN YOU FEEL SCARED, JUST PRAY TO KUROTABO FOR HELP...
...
OKAY.
GOOD GIRL ...
SLUP
EH ?
SLUUP
RI...
HAN...
DLUUP...
FZZT
AH...
AHH! H... HELP...
SAN-MOTO !!
OH NO!! URGH ...
GAG ... UHG ...
SLUSH... SLUSH...
SLIRP
BIG BROTHER ...
MWAH!

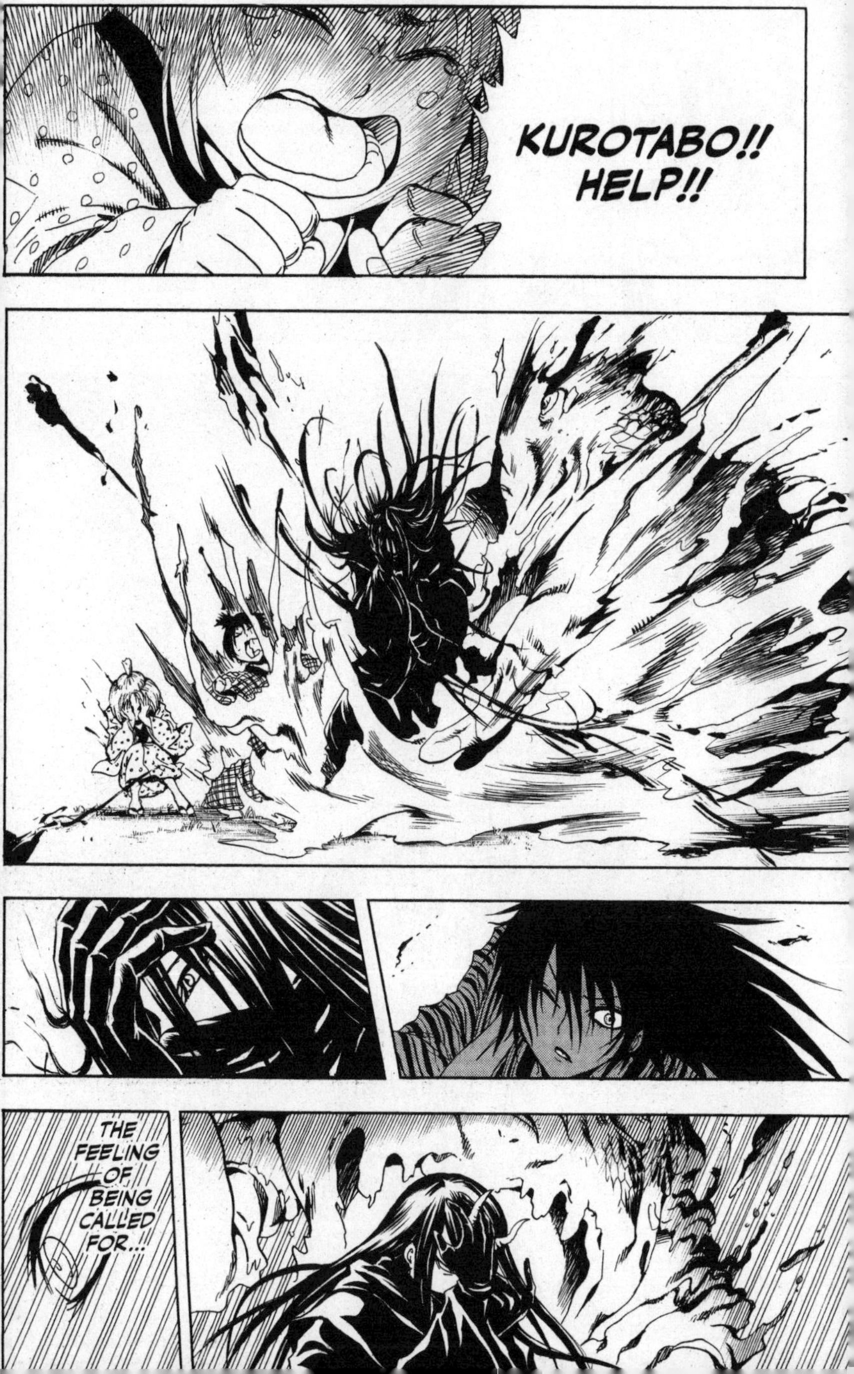
KUROTABO!! HELP!!
THE FEELING OF BEING CALLED FOR...

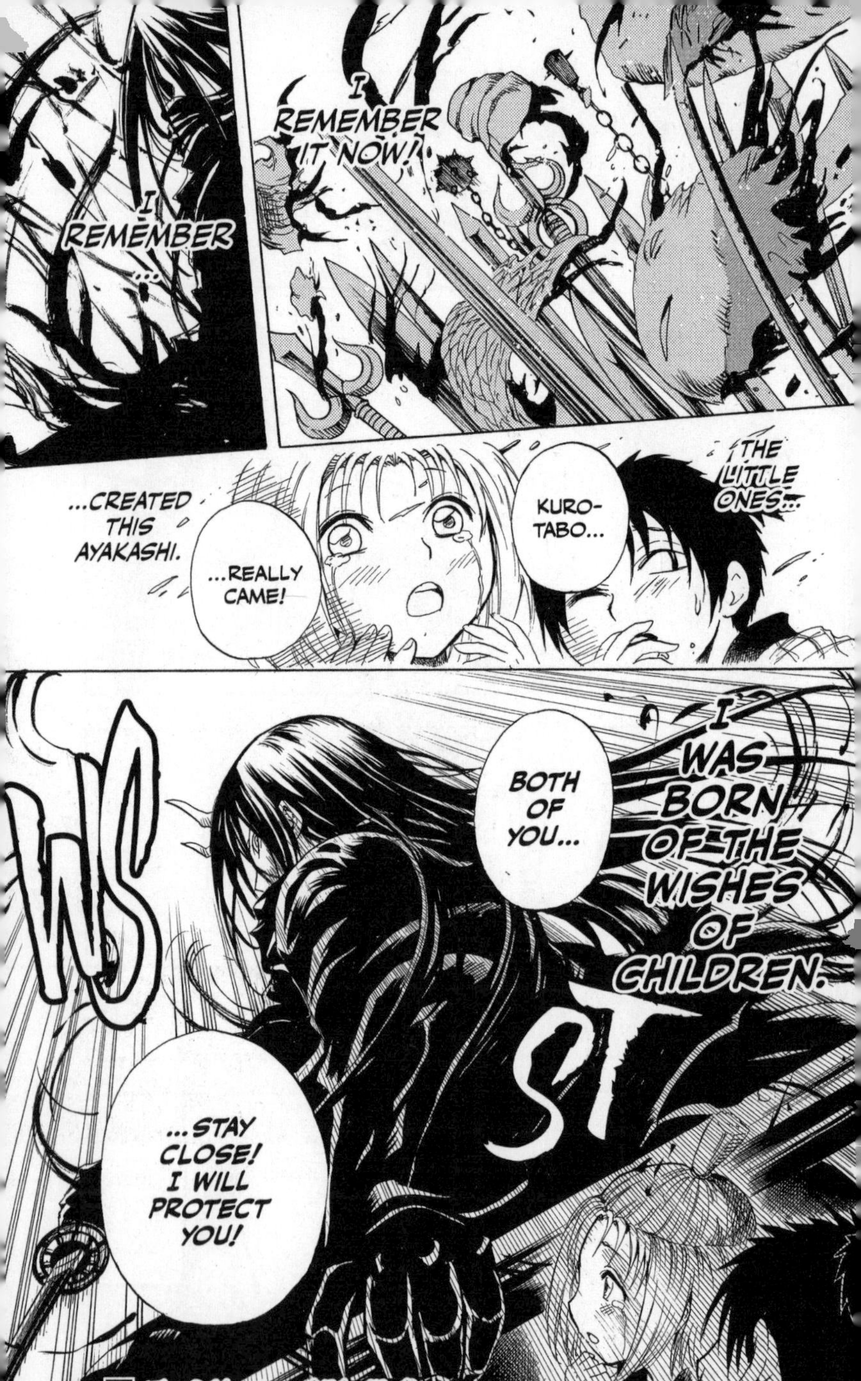
I REMEMBER IT NOW!
I REMEMBER ...
THE LITTLE ONES...
KURO-TABO...
...REALLY CAME!
...CREATED THIS AYAKASHI.
I WAS BORN OF THE WISHES OF CHILDREN.
BOTH OF YOU...
WS
ST
...STAY CLOSE! I WILL PROTECT YOU!

BONUS STORY

RIHAN NURA'S BRIDE

HIROSHI SHIIBASHI

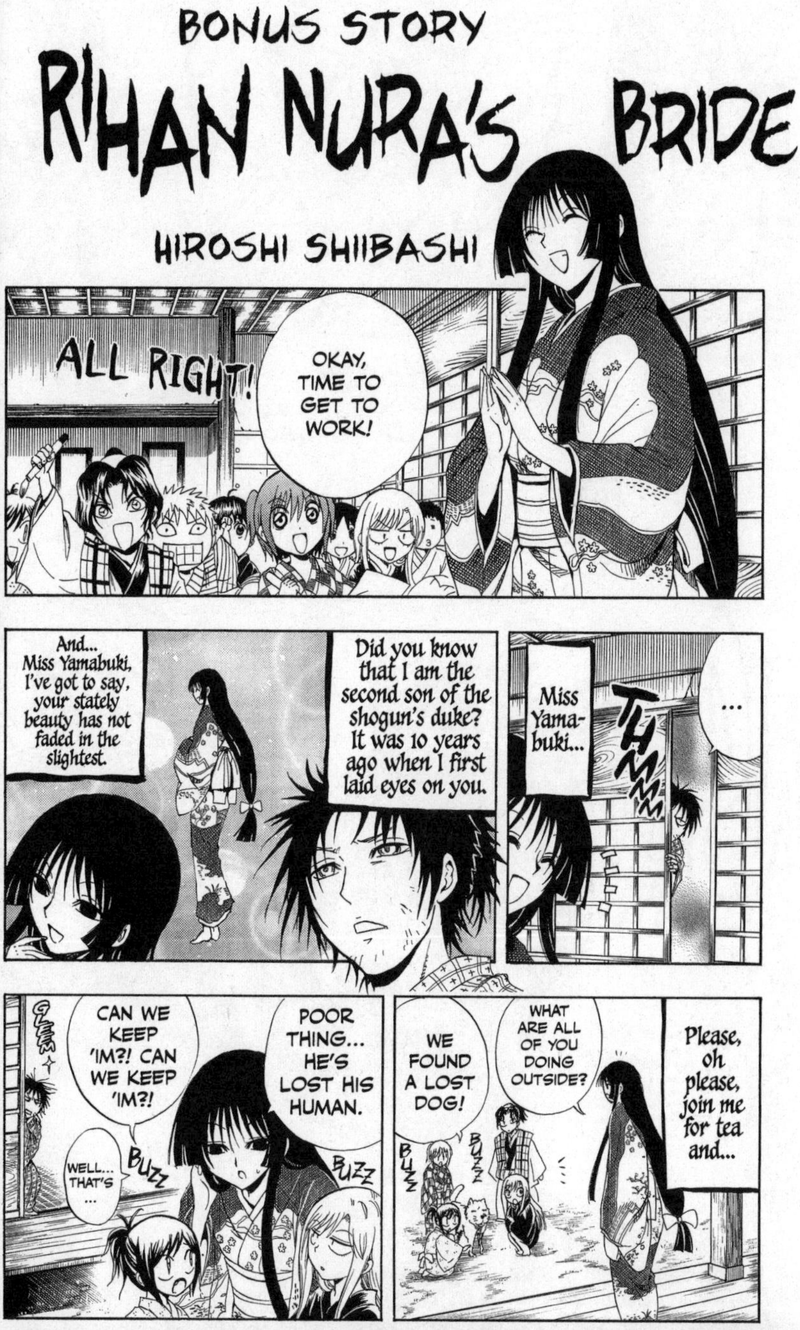
OKAY, TIME TO GET TO WORK!
ALL RIGHT!
...
Miss Yamabuki...
THMMM
Did you know that I am the second son of the shogun's duke? It was 10 years ago when I first laid eyes on you.
And... Miss Yamabuki, I've got to say, your stately beauty has not faded in the slightest.
Please, oh please, join me for tea and...
WHAT ARE ALL OF YOU DOING OUTSIDE?
WE FOUND A LOST DOG!
BUZZ
BUZZ
POOR THING... HE'S LOST HIS HUMAN.
BUZZ
CAN WE KEEP 'IM?! CAN WE KEEP 'IM?!
GLEEM
BUZZ
WELL... THAT'S ...

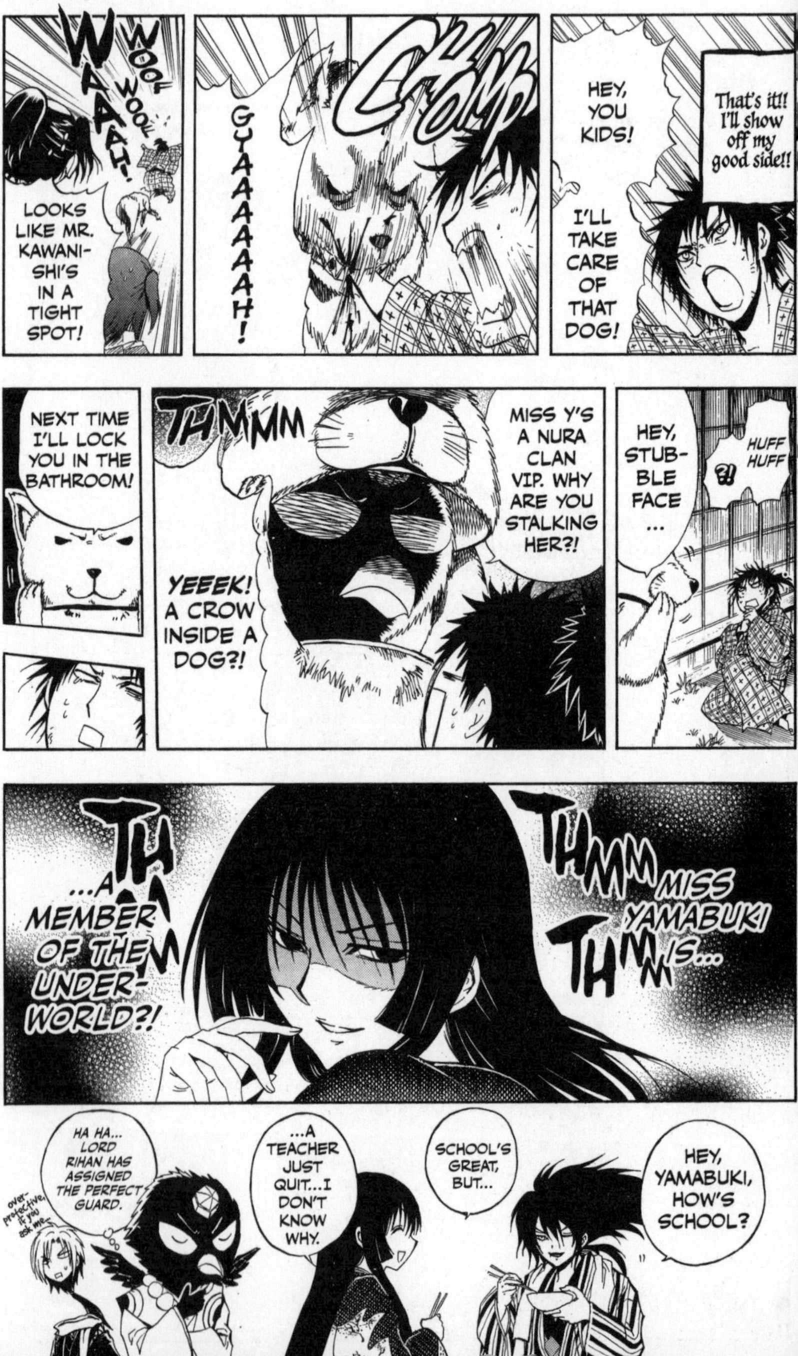
That's it!! I'll show off my good side!!
HEY, YOU KIDS!
I'LL TAKE CARE OF THAT DOG!
CHOMP
GYAAAAAAAAH!
WOOF WOOF
WAAAAH!
LOOKS LIKE MR. KAWANI-SHI'S IN A TIGHT SPOT!
HEY, STUB-BLE FACE ...
HUFF HUFF
?!
MISS Y'S A NURA CLAN VIP. WHY ARE YOU STALKING HER?!
THMMM
YEEEK! A CROW INSIDE A DOG?!
NEXT TIME I'LL LOCK YOU IN THE BATHROOM!
THMMM
MISS YAMABUKI
THMMM
IS...
THMMM
...A MEMBER OF THE UNDER-WORLD?!
HEY, YAMABUKI, HOW'S SCHOOL?
SCHOOL'S GREAT, BUT...
...A TEACHER JUST QUIT...I DON'T KNOW WHY.
HA HA... LORD RIHAN HAS ASSIGNED THE PERFECT GUARD.
over-protective, if you ask me.

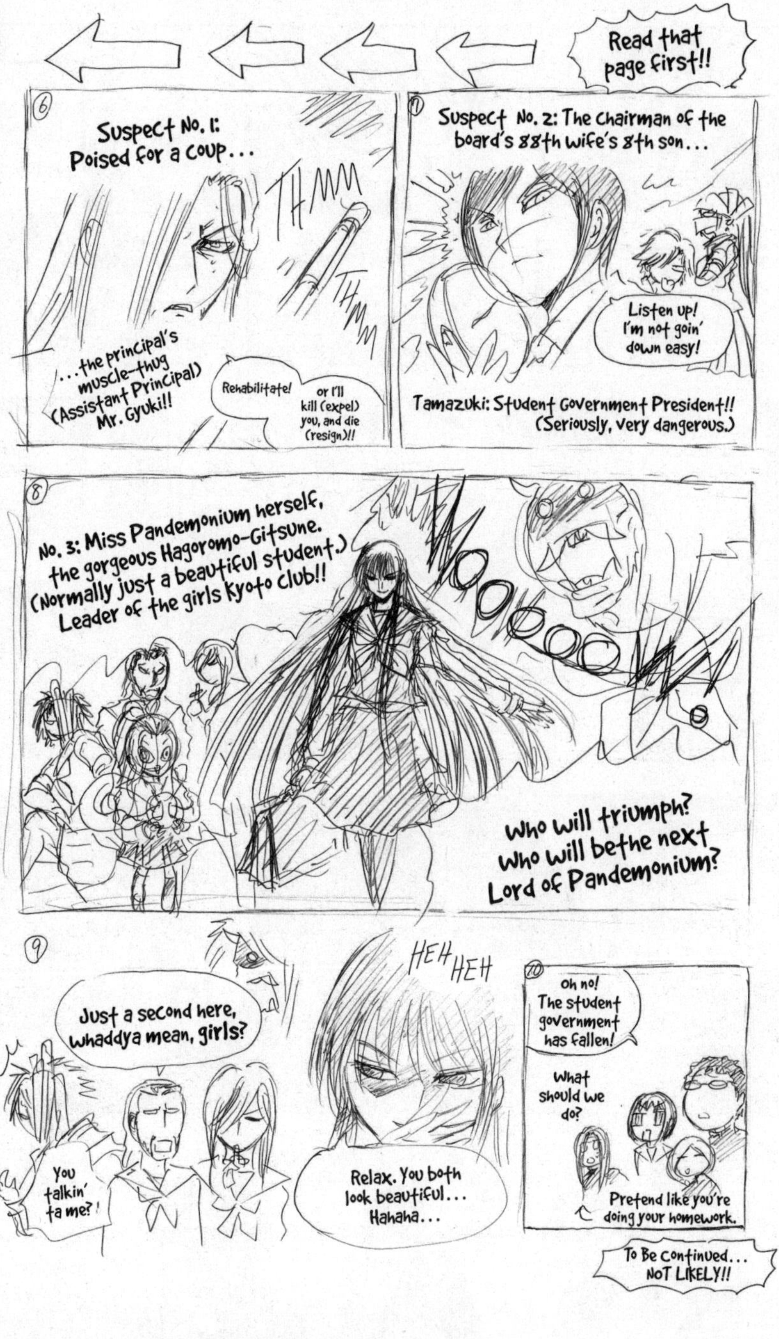
Read that page first!!
Suspect No. 1: Poised for a coup...
THMM
THMM
...the principal's muscle-thug (Assistant Principal) Mr. Gyuki!!
or I'll kill (expel) you, and die (resign)!!
Rehabilitate!
Suspect No. 2: The chairman of the board's 88th wife's 8th son...
Listen up! I'm not goin' down easy!
Tamazuki: Student Government President!! (Seriously, very dangerous.)
WOOOOOOW
No. 3: Miss Pandemonium herself, the gorgeous Hagoromo-Gitsune. (Normally just a beautiful student.) Leader of the girls kyoto club!!
Who will triumph? Who will bethe next Lord of Pandemonium?
HEH HEH
Relax. You both look beautiful... Hahaha...
Just a second here, whaddya mean, girls?
You talkin' ta me?
Oh no! The student government has fallen!
What should we do?
Pretend like you're doing your homework.
To Be Continued... NOT LIKELY!!

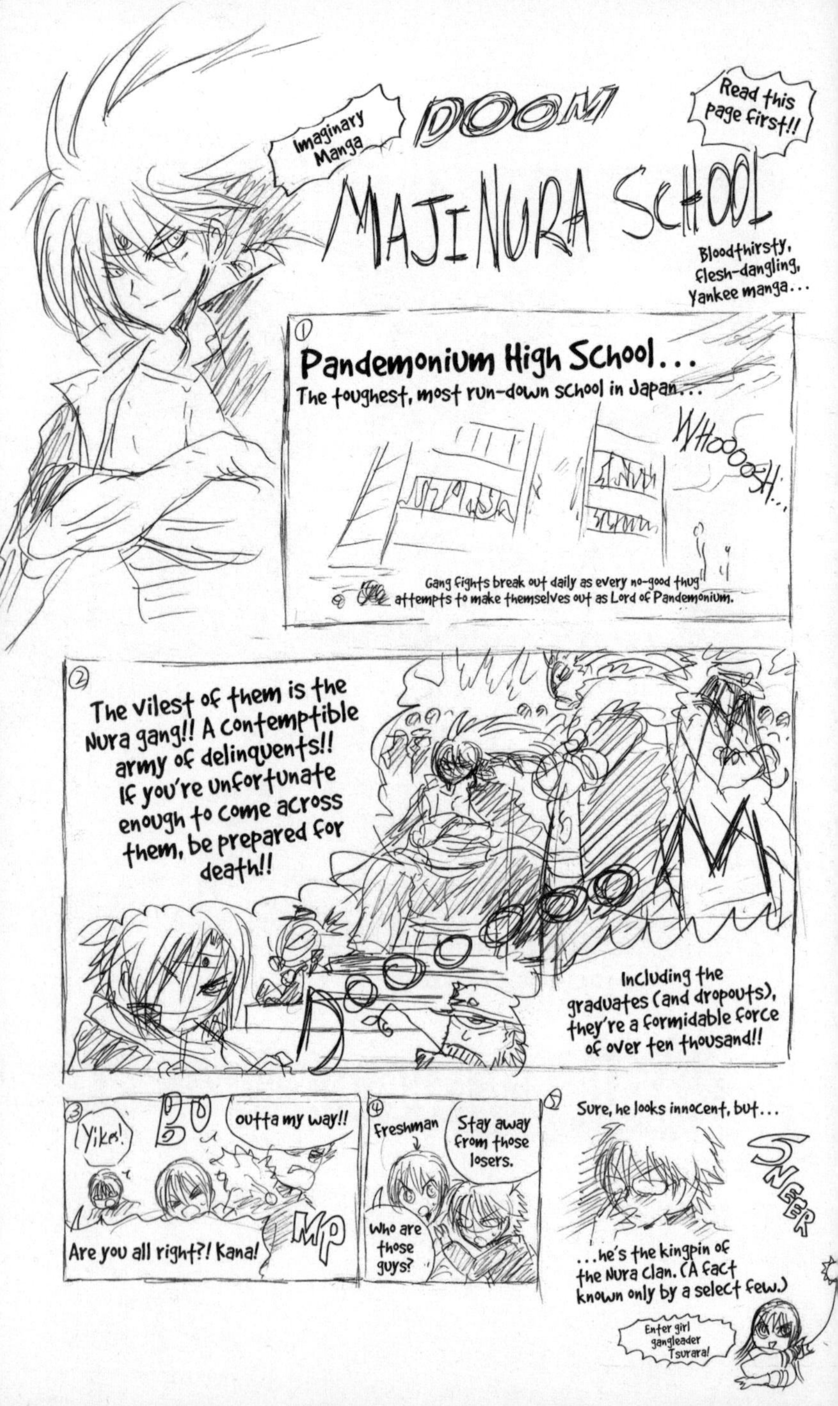
Read this page first!!
DOOM
Imaginary Manga
MAJINURA SCHOOL
Bloodthirsty, flesh-dangling, Yankee manga...
①
Pandemonium High School...
The toughest, most run-down school in Japan...
WHOOOOSH...
Gang fights break out daily as every no-good thug attempts to make themselves out as Lord of Pandemonium.
②
The vilest of them is the Nura gang!! A contemptible army of delinquents!! If you're unfortunate enough to come across them, be prepared for death!!
DOOOOOOOOM
Including the graduates (and dropouts), they're a formidable force of over ten thousand!!
③
Yikes!
BO
outta my way!!
MP
Are you all right?! Kana!
④
Freshman
Stay away from those losers.
Who are those guys?
⑤
Sure, he looks innocent, but...
SNEER
...he's the kingpin of the Nura Clan. (A fact known only by a select few.)
Enter girl gangleader Tsurara!

IN THE NEXT VOLUME...

GHOST STORY: KUDAN

Rihan and Kurotabo join forces in decadent Edo Period Japan, forming an otherworldly bond in order to vanquish their enemy. Little do they know that the Hundred Stories clan and its leader—the dreadful, dismembered Sanmoto—are far from defeated! Back in the present, a yokai named Kudan is spreading rumors that Rikuo is bent on world destruction and must be stopped by any means...

AVAILABLE FEBRUARY 2014!